The Return of the Native

Rebecca Earle

The Return of the Native

Indians and Myth-Making

in Spanish America,

1810–1930

Duke University Press

Durham and London

2007

© 2007 Duke University Press
All rights reserved
Printed in the United States of America on acid-free paper ∞
Designed by C. H. Westmoreland
Typeset in Warnock Pro by Achorn International
Library of Congress Cataloging-in-Publication Data appear
on the last printed page of this book.

 *Contents*

 *Acknowledgments*

I would like to thank the Leverhulme Trust, the British Academy, and the British Arts and Humanities Research Council for their financial support, and the University of Warwick for granting me several terms of study leave, without which this work would never have been completed.

I would also like to thank the many colleagues who in one way or another assisted my research. I owe particular thanks to Ariadna Acevedo Rodrigo for thought-provoking comments about patriotism and nationalism; Jens Andermann for probing questions into the role of museums in nineteenth-century nationalism; Tonya Blowers for late-night discussions of postcolonial theory; Theodore Buttery for invaluable help on understanding Mexican coinage; David Cahill and Peter Marshall for enthusiasm and support while this project was still in its infancy; Patricia D'Allemand for material on José María Vergara y Vergara; Dario Euraque for details on Honduran historiography; Will Fowler for information about Mexican politicians; Rodrigo Gutiérrez Viñuales for articles and images; Efraín Kristal for sterling advice on nineteenth-century literature; Anthony McFarlane for reading prototype chapters; Sergio Mejía for references to José Manuel Groot; Iris Montero for guidance on José María Alzate and his *Gaceta*; Tristan Platt for dredging his notes on Chayanta; Shirin Rai for the perspective of a political scientist; Steiner Saether for long-distance discussions of the meaning of "Indianness"; Patience Schell for articles and insights into Chilean museums; John Schwaller for guidance about the collection of preconquest codices; Douglass Sullivan-González for drawing my attention to the richness of Guatemalan independence day speeches; Guy Thomson for many books and much encouragement; and Mark Thurner for his thoughts about Peruvian *historia patria*. I am also very grateful to the anonymous Duke University Press readers for their comments and advice.

Finally, I thank David Mond for his confidence and enthusiasm about this project. This book is dedicated to him.

 *Introduction*

On "Indians"

"Indians," as everyone knows, were invented by Europeans. As European settlers and explorers roamed the Caribbean and then the American mainland in the years after 1492, they began to classify the inhabitants of this new world as "Indians." In so doing they created a cultural and ethnic category that had not previously been imagined by the continent's original residents. The varied groups that had settled the Americas prior to the arrival of Europeans did not consider themselves members of a single community. On the contrary, some indigenous groups were not aware of the existence of the other societies with whom they were to be linked as fellow "Indians." Others denied any connection between themselves and those peoples that they considered less developed; the Mexica of Central Mexico traded and warred with many of their neighbors, but they did not always regard them as their equals. They viewed the lowland Huastecas, for example, as uncivilized and wild, and therefore quite different from themselves. Thus, prior to the arrival of Europeans the category of "Indian" did not exist. During the three-hundred-year period of Spanish colonialism some did embrace the new category, thereby becoming "Indian," while others clung persistently to older identities.[1] The problematic nature of the very concept of the "Indian" has led many scholars to substitute terms such as "Native American" or other less obviously European labels. This book, however, is concerned with Indians. It studies precisely the European concept encoded in the word "Indian." Like Robert Berkhofer, who has analyzed representations of North American native peoples, I use the word "Indian" to refer specifically to the "white image of these persons."[2] The fact that this term imposed a new and essentially artificial unity on disparate societies should not impede studying the meanings it had for its many users.

As the historian Blanca Muratorio has noted, in Spanish America the "Indians [who were] evoked, internalized, or rejected . . . took diverse forms in different historical periods."[3] The historical period I explore in this book—the years between 1780 and 1930—is sometimes described as Latin America's "long nineteenth century."[4] The end points of this chronology are the vast Túpac Amaru Rebellion, which swept the Andes in the years between 1780 and 1782, and the collapse of democratic governments in the wake of the 1929 Wall Street crash. The attraction of this long time frame, however, is not that these boundary events are of paramount importance to my study, but rather that this period covers the broad era from the breakup of the colonial state to the consolidation of the new nations born out of the ashes of Spanish colonialism. I focus most explicitly on the hundred-odd years from the start of the wars of independence in the 1810s to the centenaries of independence in the 1910s and 1920s, although I will look backward to the events of the 1780s and forward to the 1930s.

My aim in this study is to understand the ways in which "Indians" were incorporated into the elite idea of the nation in Spanish America. Beginning with the wars of independence, the figure of the Indian was variously employed in the construction of Mexico, Colombia, Peru, and the other states created after the end of Spanish rule. For some countries, the processes through which this happened have already received considerable attention. In particular, historians such as David Brading have shown convincingly that the Aztec past came to form a central part of Mexican nationalism.[5] Building on what Brading called the "creole patriotism" of Mexican savants and chroniclers in the eighteenth century, Mexican insurgents in the 1810s celebrated independence from Spain as a revindication of the Aztecs: although Spanish conquistadors had overthrown the legitimate Aztec empire in the sixteenth century, Spain's defeat three hundred years later at the hands of anticolonial revolutionaries was declared to avenge this injustice.[6] Subsequent generations of Mexican patriots held varied opinions about the view that the Republic of Mexico was a continuation of the Aztec empire, but with the Mexican Revolution of 1910, the apotheosis of the Aztecs appeared complete. Today metro stops in Mexico City are named after Aztec emperors.

This process has often been described as a uniquely Mexican approach to national history. Elsewhere in Spanish America, scholars such as Benedict Anderson insist, revolutionaries looked forward to a new, utopian future, not back to the ancient past.[7] Yet while Buenos Aires may not have metro stations with indigenous names, Argentina's very national anthem describes it as a continuation of the Inca empire:

The Inca is roused in his tomb
And fire is rekindled in his bones,
On seeing his sons renewing
His *patria's* former splendour.[8]

Argentines, according to the anthem, are the sons of the Inca. Guatemala's capital city does not have a metro, let alone stations named after Maya kings, but the Guatemalan state issued a postage stamp showing a feather-crowned "Indian princess" in 1878, nearly a decade before it placed a president on a national stamp, "that most universal form of public imagery other than money"[9] (see figure 1). In this book I tell a coherent story about the place of "the Indian" within Spanish American elite nationalism in the first century after independence that accounts not only for the subsequent construction of Mexico City metro stops named after Aztecs but also for the Argentine national anthem, Guatemalan postage stamps, and a wealth of other details from a variety of countries that complicate stories of Mexican exceptionalism.

The central feature uniting the Mexican metro stop, the Argentine national anthem, and the Guatemalan stamp is their focus on the distant pre-Columbian past rather than on the indigenous present. (We can tell that the Guatemalan stamp depicts a preconquest Indian because no one in 1878 Guatemala believed that contemporary indigenous people wore feather crowns, whereas this was precisely how pre-Columbian Indians were represented.) One of this book's arguments is that when indigenous elements were incorporated into official visions of the nation during the first century of independence they were as representatives of ancient, long-vanished cultures located in the preconquest past. Recognizing this distinction between the pre-Columbian past and the indigenous present is key to understanding the functioning of elite nationalism in nineteenth-century Spanish America. Starting with the wars of independence from Spain in the 1810s, I show how advocates of independence across Spanish America began to describe the new nations they sought to create as continuations of the pre-Columbian civilizations destroyed by the conquistadors in the sixteenth century. Independence from Spain was thus said to

Figure 1. Pencil drawing for the 1878 Guatemalan "Indian Woman" stamp. The figure, probably designed by a French artist, shows a fanciful Indian princess with a feather tiara, framed by two quetzals. This was one of the earliest Spanish American stamps to employ a (pseudo) indigenous theme. *Source*: Afinsa Auctions sale catalogue. Courtesy of Afinsa, Spain.

avenge the injured ghosts of the indigenous leaders who died resisting the conquest. These heroic figures were the true fathers of Spanish America. Through the distinctive logic of independence-era rhetoric, the newly independent Spanish American nations traced their ancestry back to preconquest days. The pre-Columbian past thus formed an essential part of national history, much more glorious than the "three hundred years of tyranny" of which the colonial era was said to consist. It was in this heady period that Argentina acquired its national anthem.

In the decades after independence from Spain, that interpretation of history lost favor. Far from viewing their nations as originating in the distant pre-Columbian past, scholars, politicians and poets began to reconsider the merits of the colonial period, and asked themselves whether the moment of conception had not instead occurred in 1492, when Columbus first brought Christianity and European civilization to the hemisphere. The historian (and future president of Argentina) Domingo Faustino Sarmiento denounced independence-era celebrations of indigenous resistance to the conquest as a "deceitful claim to supposed fraternity with the Indians, intended to create a rift between ourselves and our fathers."[10] "Our fathers," according to Sarmiento, were the conquistadors, not the Indians. Others maintained that while the distant seeds might have been planted by Columbus, birth itself occurred not in 1492 but in the 1810s with the outbreak of independence from Spain. "We come from the village of Dolores; we descend from Hidalgo," was how the Mexican liberal Ignacio Ramírez put it, thereby dating the existence of "Mexico" from the independence leader Miguel Hidalgo's 1810 proclamation against Spanish rule in the hamlet of Dolores.[11] The view that either Mexico or Argentina was heir to the Aztec or Inca past came in for prolonged ridicule in many parts of Spanish America.

Yet at the same time, this legacy of independence continued to exert a subtle, if often unacknowledged, influence. Historical studies invariably paid at least some attention to the pre-Columbian era, as the development of "national" history during the nineteenth century reveals. Museums and collectors manifested an increasing interest in preconquest archaeological remains, and writers and poets continued to celebrate the ancient past in their prose and verse. By the end of the century many Spanish American states were willing to embrace pre-Columbian history as a part of their national heritage. When the Ecuadorian government was asked to build a pavilion to represent the country at the 1889 Paris Universal Exposition, it chose to erect an "Inca palace"[12] (see figure 2). At roughly the same time the Guatemalan government placed the fanciful Maya princess on one of its stamps. Nonetheless, although preconquest history might be welcomed into the national past, contemporary indigenous peoples were rarely accepted as part of the national present. Far from benefiting from positive appraisals of the pre-Columbian era, they were on the contrary perceived largely as a problem for the republican

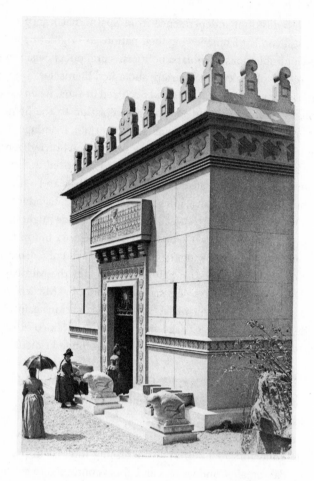

Figure 2. Ecuadorean Pavilion, Paris Universal Exposition, 1889. The pavilion, an "Inca palace" intended to be reminiscent of an Andean solar temple, proclaimed Ecuador's pride in its preconquest heritage. *Source*: Picard, *Rapport Général*, 2: plate facing 219. Courtesy of the Bodleian Library.

state, and were often declared incapable of participating in the political life of the nation. Moreover, they were said to have lost contact with their own preconquest history, the ownership of which was instead claimed by the creole elites who in 1870s Mexico erected statues to Cuauhtémoc, the last Aztec prince, and in 1920s Peru performed "Inca" dramas delivered in an archaic version of Quechua that was inaccessible to most native speakers (see figures 3 and 4).[13]

This book thus constitutes an exploration of national memories. The idea that national memories might be preserved in museums, statues, and the iconography of the state (such as postage stamps) derives in part from the work of Pierre Nora and his associates on *lieux de mémoire* ("sites of memory") in France.[14] But the nineteenth-century Spanish American republics differed from France, where virtually all postrevolutionary governments have defined themselves in relation to the French Revolution. In Spanish America there were competing points of origin ranging from the distant pre-Columbian past to events postdating the break from Spain, the meaning of each itself the subject of controversy and reinterpretation. If in nineteenth-century France the French Revolution was the "time of *history*," in Spanish America there was less consensus on when history began.[15] This concern with origins, which are as much mythic as historic, underlies nineteenth-century elite nationalism. I study these conflicting national genealogies through a diverse set of sources. In subsequent chapters I examine patriotic poetry, postage stamps, place names, independence day celebrations, museum holdings, and romantic dramas, as well as constitutions, decrees, and the multivolume national histories written in the decades after independence and today often unread except as sources of factual data. Drawing on this vast archive I illustrate the development of elite national memory in Spanish America in the first hundred years after independence. In so doing, I illuminate the complex legacy with which Spanish America entered the twentieth century.

NATIONALISM (AND PATRIOTISM)

This book explores the sense of national identity developed by members of the political and intellectual elite in Spanish America in the first century after independence from Spain. As nineteenth-century Spanish America is often cited as a region that *failed* to develop an effective nationalism,

Figure 3. Miguel Noreña, statue of Cuauhtémoc, 1887. This Mexico City monument to the Aztec prince Cuauhtémoc was unveiled in 1887 amid great pomp. The impressive pedestal contains further scenes from the hero's life. *Source*: Courtesy of the Biblioteca Francisco Xavier Clavigero, Universidad Iberoamericana.

Figure 4. Martín Chambi, *Theatre Group with Director Luis Ochoa*, Cuzco, 1930. Chambi's photograph shows Cuzco theater director Luis Ochoa surrounded by his troupe. The actors are dressed for the performance of an Incaic drama, complete with sun medallions and elaborate headgear. *Source*: Ranney and Mondéjar, eds., *Martín Chambi*, 102.

I need to justify my claim that some sort of national identity can be discerned in the region during that century.[16] I would like first to clarify what I am *not* claiming. I do not believe that nineteenth-century Spanish American elites articulated nationalisms that embraced the whole of their states' populations. Insofar as any sector of society harbored even semi-inclusive images of what the nation might be, such imaginings were more likely to be found in subordinate groups than among the elite; some of the richest and most interesting historical work on the nineteenth century of the last decade has concerned precisely the nationalisms of subaltern groups such as indigenous communities and peasant villagers.[17] Eric Hobsbawm's observation that "the nationalism of élite minorities" differs from a "nationalism which possesses or develops a mass basis among the people" is surely correct. Nonetheless, I disagree with Hobsbawm's assertion that such elite nationalism does not qualify as nationalism at all. Limited though it was (and in subsequent chapters I will probe its limitations), the national sense articulated by nineteenth-century elites in Spanish America did not differ quite as much as Hobsbawm implies from the nationalism based on "national consciousness or an attachment to the symbols and institutions of nationhood" that he views as true nationalism.[18] The latter symbol-based nationalism, which Hobsbawm describes as typical only of the period after 1880 in those states that developed any sort of nationalism whatsoever, was, I argue, characteristic of the nationalist sense articulated by nineteenth-century Spanish American elites from its birth in the early nineteenth century.[19] Part of my thesis in this book is that the nationalism characteristic of nineteenth-century elite mentalities was largely cultural, residing in symbols, iconographies, and imaginings.

How then might we describe this nineteenth-century elite nationalism? The nationalist sentiment articulated by these men and, less frequently, women rarely accepted the majority of their states' populations as fellow nationals. Nor did it necessarily maintain very close ties to any particular geographical region. Elite nationalists were interested in geography; they composed geographical studies of their republics, agonized over the intrusion of foreign troops into its heart, and participated in international commissions seeking to determine the boundaries of each state. Nonetheless, elite nationalism was not founded on a territorial vision. "The *patria* is not the soil," proclaimed the Argentine liberal Juan Bautista Alberdi.[20] It was rather a set of ideals, a way of thinking. It was possible for men such as Alberdi to venerate the *patria* even if its precise limits were vague or in dispute. The nation was a commitment and a project whose membership consisted essentially of the small group of patriots sensitive enough to appreciate the idea of the patria, a term meaning simultaneously "motherland" and "fatherland." Their number might perhaps increase with time to include a larger section of the population, but the failure of these elites to imagine an inclusive nation does not mean that they had no concept of a nation whatsoever. As the anthropologist Martha Bechis has noted, "at times, the words 'nation,' 'constitution,' 'State' had no direct reference for the creoles, but they uttered them with the hope of furthering a reality which they knew was under construction."[21] Because of this focus on the patria, some scholars have preferred to label these sentiments patriotism rather than nationalism.[22] Patriotism, in the view of political scientists such as Maurizio Viroli, is a devotion to liberty and republican government, whereas nationalism is a commitment to the "spiritual and cultural unity of the people."[23] Patriotism resides in the realm of reason, while nationalism is nourished on a diet of sentiment. In my view the concern with the patria typical of nineteenth-century Spanish American elites was essentially nationalistic in its focus on feelings and emotions rather than the specifics of governmental structure. In the words of a Chilean orator in 1843, "The patria is not simply a part of that land inhabited by millions of men, it is the preferential point in which we hope for happiness . . . in short it is a part of the heart."[24] "The patriotic emotion," explained the Peruvian scholar Eugenio Larrabure y Unanue three decades later, is like "an electric current," which stirred the "mysterious depths of the human soul."[25] In essence this nationalism was a sentiment, a love of the patria, which existed primarily in the realm of philosophy and feeling.

This concept of the nation as an idealized space for patriotic sentiment accords very well with the interpretation of nationalism articulated by Benedict Anderson in his celebrated *Imagined Communities.* Anderson's analysis of Spanish American history has been criticized on a number of fronts, in particular for its assertion that creole nationalism was the consequence of individual circulation through the colonial bureaucracy, as well as for its equation of elite, creole nationalism with a broad-based nationalist sentiment.[26] Nonetheless, Anderson's work has played a crucial role in reorienting scholarly understandings of the nationalist process toward directions that can fruitfully be employed when considering

Spanish America, despite his own difficulties in applying his theories to that region. Anderson argued that a nation resides not so much in political, ethnic, or geographic features, as in the ways in which people think. Nations are made by people deciding that they form part of some common enterprise, which we may call the enterprise of nationalism. Exactly which people decide this is a matter that Anderson at times ignored, but his attention to the role of imagining has transformed the analysis of nationalism, in particular because as an imagined entity the nation has to be represented to acquire meaning. Ernest Gellner expressed this pithily when he noted that "it is nationalism which engenders nations, and not the other way round. Admittedly, nationalism uses the pre-existing, historically inherited proliferation of cultures or cultural wealth, though it uses them very selectively, and it most often transforms them radically."[27] The ways in which these borrowings and transformations occur is in itself an important part of the study of nationalism. Hobsbawm, Nora, and others have shown that nationalism is often constructed on a base of (borrowed and transformed) symbols, ceremonies, and practices. Their studies of the places where memories, particularly national memories, are crystallized, and of the "invented" nature of many traditions, national or otherwise, help us understand the importance of the symbolic to the enterprise of nationalism.[28] Ceremonies and symbols help make nationalism imaginable.

Central to this process is the creation of a national past, which endows the perhaps very new nation with a sense of antiquity. When Homi Bhabha observed that "nations lose their origins in the myths of time" he drew attention to this process of invention as well as to the subsequent obscuring of those foundational inventions.[29] Even Anthony Smith, who regards nationalism as a far more organic and ancient sentiment than do many other scholars, has noted the importance of "common myths and historical memories" to the formation of a sense of national identity.[30] In this book I am therefore concerned centrally with the role of the past in the construction of elite national identities.

Analysis by certain postcolonial critics has drawn attention to the particular challenges that history poses to nations formed out of former colonies, where interpretations of the past are often deeply embedded in the political struggle for independence, and where the attempts at locating the "authentic" past so central to nationalism are particularly problematic. Seeking authenticity in the precolonial era, which appears to provide an alternative to colonial culture, may instead create "a calcified society whose developmental momentum has been checked by colonization," as Abdul JanMohamed noted with reference to African nationalism. In other words, celebrating the precolonial era as the true national past raises the fear that national culture is essentially obsolete or trapped in bygone times and therefore backward. On the other hand, any attempt to incorporate aspects of the colonial era raises the specter of what JanMohamed calls historical catalepsy, which condemns postcolonial society as a "vacant imitator" of colonial culture and thus devoid of any genuinely authentic past of its own.[31] Both options appear problematic, although Bhabha has suggested that the colonial, and, potentially, post-colonial experience is located precisely in that moment of imitation.[32] Imitation and mimicry, rather than authenticity, perhaps mark the postcolonial, just as the search for history and origins signifies the national. An *authentic* past, in other words, is perhaps both a necessary component of nationalism and difficult to obtain in postcolonial situations. Whether or not nineteenth-century Spanish America fits comfortably within concepts of "postcoloniality," the observations of postcolonial criticism about the conflictive nature of the past hold some relevance for the region, where elite efforts at imagining the nation were rent by internal anxieties about the weight of history.

Scholars have also taught us that nationalism usually employs notions of gender to shape its image of the nation. For example, the republican nationalisms articulated first with the American Revolution in 1776, and subsequently in France and Spanish America, constructed citizenship around an essentially masculine subject. "No one can be a good citizen who is not a good *father,* good *son,* good *brother,* good friend, and good *husband,*" stated virtually all of the revolutionary constitutions composed in Colombia between 1810 and 1819, echoing the French Constitution of 1795.[33] The quintessential citizen was thus conceived as male (although some women contested the association of citizenship with masculinity). The sociologist Carlos Lissón expressed this view clearly when he noted in 1867 that Peru achieved independence "because its sons became men."[34] On the other hand, the nation itself was often represented as female, as were its attributes such as liberty, progress, or constitutionality. The Mexican artist Petronilo Monroy's *Allegory of the Constitution of 1857* illustrates well this use of gender to symbolize the state's more abstract qualities (see figure 5). The work, exhibited in 1869, shows a young woman

Figure 5. Petronilo Monroy, Allegory of the Constitution of 1857, c.1869. Monroy's painting employs a young woman to embody the principles of the 1857 Mexican Constitution, although the constitution excluded women from being citizens. Source: Widdifield, Embodiment of the National, plate 3. Courtesy of the Museo Nacional de Arte, Mexico City.

who both represents and displays the Mexican Constitution of 1857. As Stacie Widdifield has shown in her discussion of this painting, although the decision to depict the constitution as a young woman, rather than a mature one, provoked criticism, the choice of a female figure did not. Widdifield notes that "the plentiful presence of the woman in this painting, as well as in numerous other sculptural and painted monuments of the Mexican national period, is an index to her absence or exclusion from the sites of power and nationhood that the Constitution of 1857 aimed to create."[35] We shall have occasion to observe not only the use of gendered iconography to construct the nineteenth-century Spanish American state, but also the place of indigenous imagery within these constructions. The 1878 Guatemalan stamp depicting the Indian princess is but one example of the framing of acceptable indigenousness within a gendered structure that linked an abstracted nation to concepts of femininity.

RACE AND NATION

As I have noted above, the very concept of the "Indian" is a historical construct whose precise meaning in colonial and independent Spanish America continues to be debated by scholars. Some have stressed the importance of juridical and fiscal categories to being "Indian": in this formulation, indigenousness consisted particularly of paying the head tax known as the Indian tribute and possessing entitlement to the use of communal land.[36] These factors undoubtedly influenced the functional meaning of being an Indian, although not all scholars view them as its central or fundamental designators. A number have argued that being Indian was determined more by social and cultural criteria. This view has been set forth with particular clarity by Douglas Cope in a study on plebeian culture in colonial Mexico City. Cope's work stresses that racial identities were essentially social. They were certainly not based solely on physical appearance: as Cope noted, when individuals "wished to convince the authorities of someone's racial status, they went beyond physical characterization" by adding information about dress, speech, occupation, and name.[37] Ancestry might also be discussed, but this did not necessarily provide definitive answers; the parish records in which racial classifications were supposed to be recorded sometimes either omitted information on race or contained ambiguous or contradictory classifications. Family members themselves might disagree about the race of other relatives. As Cope notes, for plebeians "defining race was functional rather than logical, pragmatic rather than theoretically sound."[38] Until the nineteenth century scholarly thinking in both Europe and Spanish America generally regarded race as similarly mutable. Scientific writings stressed the importance of climate, diet, and other factors in determining race.[39] Such attitudes remained typical of nineteenth-century Spanish America; indigenousness continued to be defined largely in social, cultural, and perhaps juridical terms by most sectors of society, including the elite groupings with whom this book is concerned. Even after the rise of "scientific" racism in the second half of the nineteenth century, elite Spanish Americans clung to a non-Darwinian vision of race. As Nancy Stepan has shown, neo-Lamarckian views, which stressed the influence of the environment on evolution, rather than Darwinism, proved fundamental in the region.[40] For every savant who proclaimed that the Indian's cranium was the wrong shape to admit progress there was another who suggested that such physical defects might be corrected by convincing indigenous people to wear Western clothes or to eat more meat. Indeed, Peter Wade has suggested that scholars of race in Spanish America would do well to question any division between "biological" and "cultural" concepts of race. At the height of "biological" racial thinking, he notes, elements of "what today would be called cultural influences" were included within the "very conception of biology."[41] Environment and other external factors, in other words, were often acknowledged to be important influences even by scientists who believed in immutable racial types.

Whether "the Indian" was a cultural, social, or even biological being, scholars today are in broad agreement that the indigenous population, and race more generally, were "fundamental to and even constitutive of the very process of nation-making."[42] The importance of race to the imagining of nationality in postindependence Spanish America is an area of innovative ongoing research. This literature has been central to shaping my own focus on the preconquest past as an important element of nineteenth-century elite nationalism. A number of recent works have explored the interface between elite and plebeian concepts of the nation and have analyzed the challenges that Spanish America's racial diversity posed to elite nation-builders; both Mónica Quijada and Nicholas Shumway have made important contributions to this area in the case of Argentina, for example.[43] In addition, a series of studies by scholars such as Mauricio Tenorio Trillo,

Blanca Muratorio, and Deborah Poole have shed light on the centrality of iconographies—visual and discursive—to the articulation of elite (and other) nationalisms during the nineteenth century, and more specifically on the place of preconquest imagery within those iconographies.[44] These analyses themselves build on foundations laid by a previous generation of scholars who explored the development of creole patriotism and its interactions with the preconquest past.[45] Such works, together with many others that I cite later, helped form my own vision of the place of the preconquest past within elite national identity in nineteenth-century Spanish America, although in becoming my own this vision at times (inevitably) departed in significant ways from the approaches and interpretations of the works that inspired it. My book differs from these other studies most strikingly not so much in the many details of interpretation (although I will highlight particular differences), as in my emphasis on the pre-Columbian era as a fundamental challenge to nineteenth-century elite nation-building, and in my focus on more than one country. In telling a coherent story about the role of the preconquest past in the construction of elite national identities in a number of different states my work puts more emphasis on continuities within the continent's history than has been common in recent studies of the nineteenth century, where the single nation has played a prominent role in organizing analysis. As this book makes clear, I believe that nationalism is a phenomenon best studied in a broad regional and chronological context. Cross-national comparisons also throw light on distinctive regional particularities. At the same time that I chart the principal themes shaping elite responses to the past I also record some significant variations. The place of the preconquest era within elite thinking in Guatemala and in Argentina, for example, is comparable but by no means identical. These modulations, alongside the dominant motifs, together reveal the distinctive features of nineteenth-century elite nationalism.

My study focuses on Argentina, Chile, Peru, Colombia, Guatemala, and Mexico, although I have included examples and material from other states as well. My purpose in selecting these regions was twofold. First, they were home to a variety of preconquest cultures ranging from the large settled empires of the Aztecs and Incas and the smaller principalities of the Muiscas, as well as of the Quichés, Cakchiquels, and other Maya peoples, to the nomadic societies of the Argentine and Chilean plains. As I will show, elite interpretations of these peoples varied substantially during the nineteenth century; the pampas-dwelling Araucanians, for example, were sometimes described as hardy republicans and sometimes as barbarous savages.[46] By referring to a range of pre-Columbian cultures I highlight the flexibility and variability of elite responses to the preconquest past. Second, the set of core countries contains states whose nineteenth-century histories differed greatly in many regards. The economic successes of Argentina and Colombia scarcely compare; Chile succeeded in attracting many European immigrants, while Guatemala did not. Nonetheless, the process of elite nation-building reveals substantial continuities—as well as some illuminating differences—across the region. The common origins of these states in the independence movements of the early nineteenth century, and the uniformity of creole culture across Spanish America—itself continually strengthened by transnational contact between individual writers and politicians—helped form a language of elite nationalism that became the lingua franca of the entire continent, and which makes feasible a comparative study. This book does not—cannot—tell the definitive story of how elite groups understood "the Indian" during the nineteenth century, but by exploring this question comparatively it helps map the contours of the elite imagination and provides a framework for interpreting other elite encounters with the indigenous world.

My argument is structured around seven chapters. In the first two ("Montezuma's Revenge" and "Representing the Nation") I explain the role of the mythologized "Indian" within the nationalist discourse elaborated during the independence era. In chapter 1, I trace the efforts by insurgent ideologues to construct "national" pasts for an independent Spanish America that accorded a pivotal role to the preconquest period—an effort that placed particular emphasis on the bonds of metaphorical ancestry believed to link creole revolutionaries with the indigenous heroes of the conquest and preconquest eras. In the second chapter I examine the use of pre-Columbian imagery within the state iconographies—flags, coins, coats of arms—created in the independence years. I conclude by tracing the progressive elimination of much of this imagery from state symbols in the decades after independence. Replacing these discarded indigenous emblems were the leaders of the independence movements themselves: it was the insurgent hero Simón Bolívar, rather than an Araucanian warrior, who now represented the nation. Yet while indigenous figures were often removed from state iconography after 1830, the attitudes toward pre-Columbian civilizations expressed during independence formed a current—a way of thinking about the past—that flowed into nineteenth-century elite nationalist thought. The rest of the book traces the influence of this current.

In chapter 3 ("'Padres de la Patria': Nations and Ancestors") I probe the genealogical metaphors that shaped elite nationalism during the nineteenth century. While metaphors of genealogy dominated the articulation of elite nationalism throughout the nineteenth century, after independence these nationalist genealogies largely abandoned the tentative identification with the preconquest past enunciated during the independence era in favor of a revindicated Spanish identity. The region's elites thus ceased to claim pre-Columbian history as part of their personal ancestry. Such abandonment, however, implied neither a loss of interest in the preconquest epoch nor its exclusion from the "national" histories composed, often with state sponsorship, in the decades after independence. Chapter 4 ("Patriotic History and the Pre-Columbian Past") studies the development of national history. In it I chart the incorporation of the indigenous past into *historia patria* ("patriotic history")—for at the same time that most elite nationalists were beginning to view their own heritage as essentially Iberian, scholarly studies were concluding that the era preceding the arrival of Columbus had been a time of culture, albeit a culture inferior to the one subsequently introduced by the Spanish. With some exceptions, preconquest indigenes were proclaimed to have been civilized, indeed romantic. In chapter 4, in addition to examining historical writings I also consider literary depictions of the pre-Columbian era by looking at the writings of both well-known figures such as Rubén Darío and largely forgotten individuals such as the Colombian poet José Joaquín Ortíz. Their works interpreted the precolonial era as a mythical time replete with adventure and romantic intrigue. The civilized and attractive nature of precolonial peoples presented in both scholarly and literary texts helped establish the preconquest era as a suitable element of the national past, even if it did not constitute part of the personal heritage of their authors.

In chapter 5 ("Archaeology, Museums, and Heritage") I focus on the material remains of the pre-Columbian era. I construct the history of preconquest monuments and artifacts during the nineteenth century by tracing first the development of legislation designed to protect pre-Columbian relics, which evolved under the dual pressures of nation-building and the new academic discipline of archaeology. I then explore the importance of museums to the nationalist enterprise. That museums display interpretations of the past has been recognized by both recent scholarship and the individuals who established Spanish America's national museums in the nineteenth century. Thus the mayor of Santiago, Benjamín Vicuña Mackenna (himself the founder of an important Chilean museum), could describe the British Museum as "the most authentic and succinct *book of universal history* that we have read."[47] Museums of national history were thus texts of historia patria. In chapter 5 I also explore the display of pre-Columbian materials in Spanish American exhibits at world's fairs, which were held with increasing frequency in the second half of the nineteenth century.

In chapter 6 ("Citizenship and Civilization: The 'Indian Problem'") I move from the nineteenth-century status of the preconquest era to that of the indigenous present. Through a reading of congressional debates, legal codes, political essays, and poems I examine the wedge driven between the indigenous past and the indigenous present via the so-called Indian problem: that is, the view that indigenous people, incapable as they were of participating in civic life, prevented the nation from progressing. While the pre-Columbian past began slowly to be incorporated into the national heritage alongside the colonial period, contemporary indigenous peoples were declared to have lost their connection to that past. The preconquest past was thus "de-Indianized." I end this book with a discussion of this legacy for twentieth-century Spanish America. Chapter 7 ("Indigenismo: The Return of the Native?") examines the success of the cultural and political movement known as *indigenismo* in bridging the gulf that elite nationalism had constructed between the preconquest past and the indigenous present. The complex genealogies claimed by Spanish American elites, which tried to accommodate differing, and potentially conflicting, heritages—indigenous, Hispanic, creole—were only partially resolved in the early twentieth century by the celebration of racial mixing (*mestizaje*), which was popularized across the hemisphere alongside indigenismo. In the epilogue I sketch briefly the continuing resonance of these debates in contemporary Spanish America.

 *Chapter 1*

Montezuma's Revenge

On 19 May 1822, ten months after Lima's declaration of independence from Spain, the city's principal theater inaugurated its new stage curtain. The Teatro de Lima, established in the eighteenth century, had recently reopened after substantial improvements, including, in addition to the new curtain, a café for the theater's patrons. The reopening was hailed as an auspicious event that augured well for the city's future. After the first performance in the refurbished building one newspaper noted proudly that "the production has improved so much that cultured visitors no longer have reason to yearn for the Europe of which they speak so highly."[1] New Legislation stipulating a two-month prison sentence for smoking inside the theater was also expected to raise Lima's standing "in the eyes of foreigners," although in practice travelers were to complain for many decades that Limeños and Limeñas alike smoked ceaselessly during intermissions.[2] The new curtain, specially painted to commemorate the defeat of royalist forces, depicted the "father of the Incas" emerging from behind a hill. At his side an allegorical "daughter of the wind" announced America's freedom to the indigenous Araucanian chief Lautaro, who listened appreciatively. The sun, rising above the Andes mountains, shone benevolently over the happy scene. The allegories of "peace" and "justice" completed the design.

The refurbished Teatro de Lima addressed several concerns of Lima's new republican elite. The improved facilities and production reassured them that their city possessed the civilized infrastructure characteristic of a true (European) nation.[3] At the same time, it reminded them that Peru, although a newcomer—or a mere aspirant—to the ranks of nation, nonetheless enjoyed a long and distinguished history, to which the curtain alluded through the figures of the Inca and the Araucanian. An independent Lima was therefore both up to date and steeped in history. Nonetheless, the particular history commemorated on the curtain may seem peculiar. Lautaro, the indigenous hero of a sixteenth-century epic recounting Spain's conquest of central Chile, possessed no specific links to Lima, or indeed to Peru, and his place within a Peruvian nationalist iconography is not immediately apparent. The Incas, although indisputably Peruvian, have often been described as the patrimony not of Lima or of Peru as a whole but rather of Cuzco, the seat of the former Inca empire.[4] Nonetheless, Lautaro and a paternal Inca featured prominently on the new curtain, which was praised alongside the improved theatrical performances and the smoking ban as evidence for Lima's bright future. In this chapter and in the one following I explain both the peculiar contours of Lima's Inca romance and, more broadly, the role of the preconquest past within the insurgent ideology that constituted independent Spanish America's first model of elite nationalist discourse.

MONTEZUMA'S REVENGE

The significance of the pre-Columbian past to independence-era rhetoric has long been recognized in the case of Mexico, where what David Brading has called "creole patriotism" enjoyed an early development.[5] There, an autochthonous patriotism, an affirmation of a distinct Mexican-creole identity, had begun to develop in the seventeenth century. By the late eighteenth century it was in full flower, encouraged by the hostility with which the Spanish crown generally viewed the political and social ambitions of creoles, who responded with a vociferous articulation of their own merits. Savants and poets elaborated a rich discourse that emphasized the wealth of Mexico's distinctive heritage and the special providence that God had designed for Mexico, as revealed in the Virgin of Guadalupe's apparition on the hill of Tepeyac in 1531. The preconquest, and more specifically Aztec, past played an important role within creole patriotism, alongside the celebration of Mexico's unique Catholic destiny. From the first decades of the seventeenth century, creole writers were praising the glories of the Aztec capital Tenochtitlán and lamenting indigenous mistreatment at the hands of the Spanish. As early as 1615 Juan de Torquemada's *Monarquía indiana* had compared the Aztecs with the ancient Greeks and Romans, clearly implying, as John Leddy Phelan observed, "that Aztec society was the 'classical antiquity' of Mexico."[6] Other works, such as Mariano Veytia's *Historia antigua de México* and the varied writings of Carlos de Sigüenza y Góngora, developed the correlation between the Aztecs and the cultures of European classical antiquity.[7] Francisco Xavier Clavijero, the greatest eighteenth-century exponent of creole patriotism, further elaborated this thesis in his *Historia antigua de México* (1780–81), in which he also challenged the assertions of certain European scholars that America's pre-conquest peoples, from the Aztecs to the Incas, had been mere savages devoid of culture.[8] Such rhetoric further stressed that the true heirs of the Aztecs were the scholarly creoles themselves, rather than contemporary indigenous people. As Anthony Pagden notes, creole patriotism sought to "appropriate the past of the ancient Indian empires . . . for the glorification of a white American-born élite."[9] This appropriation of preconquest history was accompanied by increasing calls for greater political rights to be accorded to the viceroyalty's creole population. Their authority, forged in the conquest and developed over generations, was, creoles claimed, unjustly thwarted by second-rate Spaniards who monopolized all official posts and discriminated against more worthy creoles.

By sketching the contours of an alternative history distinct from that of the Peninsula, creole patriotism provided a language for nationalists seeking independence from Spain. Many scholars have noted how creole patriotism governed the rhetoric of the Mexican independence movement that developed after 1810.[10] The rebellion led not only to substantial popular mobilization but also to the articulation of an explicitly anti-Spanish ideology that justified independence and excoriated colonial rule within a framework laid down by the tenets of creole patriotism. The view that Mexican history predated the Spanish conquest was expressed in insurgent speeches, poems, festivals, proclamations, and legislation. Because it was based on the unjust overthrow of the legitimate Aztec empire, Spanish rule was declared to be wholly illegitimate, "three hundred years of tyranny," during which the Indians, "our fathers," had been miserably oppressed by the Spanish.[11] This interpretation of the past is implied in the very titles of such pro-independence works as Fray Servando Teresa de Mier's *History of the Revolution in New Spain Anciently Known as Anáhuac,* for Anáhuac was the supposed name of the former Aztec empire. As Mier's title suggests (and as Brading has observed), the new state envisioned by Mexican insurgents traced its ancestry back to preconquest times.[12] It had suffered under three centuries of Spanish oppression, but now it would free itself. In thus seeking to end Spanish rule, republican leaders explained, they were but asserting the natural rights of the sovereign state of Mexico. They were not innovators but renovators; not revolutionaries but liberators; not traitors but patriots.

By endowing Mexico with an ancient history, creole patriotism also provided a pantheon of "national" heroes in the form of the Aztec emperors who had resisted the Spanish conquest. These men made regular appearances in insurgent discourse, where they endorsed independence and execrated the Spanish. "In the silence of the night Moctezuma's shade ceaselessly demands that you exact vengeance for his gods and for those innocent victims whom [the conquistador Pedro de] Alvarado sacrificed in the temple of Huitzilopochtli," insisted Carlos María de Bustamante, a tireless advocate of Mexican independence and later the publisher of many historical works.[13] When Bustamante composed the address to be delivered at the opening of the 1813 insurgent Congress of Chilpancingo, he invoked the spirits of the great Aztec leaders to bless the assembly: "Spirits of Moctehuzoma, Cacamatzín, Cuauhtimotzín, Xicotencatl and Cantzonzi . . . celebrate this happy moment in which your sons have united to avenge the crimes and outrages committed against you, and to free yourselves from the claws of tyranny and fanaticism that were going to grasp them for ever. To 12 August 1521 [the date of Hernán Cortés's capture of the Aztec capital] there succeeds 14 September 1813. In that day the chains of our serfdom were fastened in Mexico-Tenochtitlán, in this day in the happy village of Chilpancingo they are broken forever."[14] In this speech, as Brading has noted, "we encounter a clear affirmation of a Mexican nation, already in existence before the conquest, now about to recover its Independence."[15] Through such affirmations, revolutionary Mexicans sought to endow an independent Mexico with what Benedict Anderson called the "image of antiquity so central to the subjective idea of the nation."[16]

In the case of Mexico, we can see clearly how the well-developed creole sense of separateness helped shape the distinctive nationalism (which I call indianesque nationalism) of the movement for independence.[17] Yet the emergence of creole patriotism, incontrovertible for Mexico, did not occur everywhere in Spanish America. Peru, it has been argued, experienced a somewhat analogous development, but the existence of a fully developed sense of creole identity, or indeed of a partially developed sense of creole identity, is less clear for areas such as Río de la Plata or

Colombia. In these regions there were far less coherent creole traditions of separate identity, as well as less obvious examples of prevenient indigenous empires crushed by the conquistadors on which to draw. Typically, the exuberant invocation of the Indian past is seen as a uniquely Mexican phenomenon. Thus the historian Anthony McFarlane has asserted that, with the exception of Mexico, "when creoles sought to define their new condition in proclamations and written constitutions, they were rarely intent on locating an historic 'nation' to legitimate projects for independent states. Indeed, in many regions, creoles had no myths of a glorious Indian past to which to turn."[18] Nonetheless, even in those areas that might appear to offer little scope for celebrating the indigenous past, creole insurgents adopted indianesque rhetoric because it provided a versatile and robust justification of independence. In regions as diverse as Río de la Plata, Colombia, Chile, and Peru, creole revolutionaries exalted preconquest America by proclaiming it, rather than the colonial era, the true point of national origin. This was the sentiment that animated the design on the Teatro de Lima's stage curtain. This rhetoric had everything in common with the language used by Mexican revolutionaries. As in Mexico, the existence of sovereign preconquest empires was affirmed. Insurgents in Colombia thus hailed the capital's 1810 revolt against colonial rule as a resumption of the independence lost with the conquest, when the indigenous Muiscas had been overthrown by the Spanish and their ruler, the Zipa, replaced by foreign tyrants.[19] As in Mexico, the Edenic nature of pre-Columbian civilizations was celebrated in poems, speeches, and drama. Before the conquest, the insurgent priest Pedro Ignacio de Castro Barros told his listeners in 1815 Tucumán, "the Americans tranquilly enjoyed the great benefits of their patria and swam contentedly in a broad ocean of happiness."[20] Preconquest America, such remarks made clear, was a terrestrial paradise peopled by prelapsarian patriots. Crushed by three centuries of Spanish tyranny, their nations had languished. Now, under the leadership of the revolutionaries, who presented themselves as the legitimate heirs to these ancient indigenous kingdoms, they would free themselves from Spanish oppression. In language highly reminiscent of Bustamante's speech for the Congress of Chilpancingo, the Chilean official Mariano Egaña celebrated the insurgent general José de San Martín's entry into Lima by invoking the conquest-era Araucanian chiefs Caupolicán, Colocolo, and Lautaro, the hero of Lima's theater curtain:

"Caupolicán, Lautaro and Colocolo seem to revive to congratulate their sons for the happy fate of our continent. Realized today the hopes that they held at the time of their death, they see not only their *patria* independent and the wrongs they suffered avenged, but their *patria's* freedom sustained by the independence of neighboring countries. The successors of Manco [Capac, the first Inca], sent forth from their tombs, seem to accompany the triumph of General San Martín and introduce him into the capital of the empire that Spanish tyranny established on the ruins of that of the Incas, and from the plains of Cajamarca the shade of [the Inca] Atahualpa arises to conduct the hero to place the banner of independence over the throne of the viceroys."[21] In this dense passage Egaña simultaneously described insurgents as the sons of conquest-era indigenous heroes, labeled a postcolonial Peru the continuation of an Araucanian state, and saluted independence for avenging the unjust overthrow of the Inca monarchy. Indianesque rhetoric was nothing if not versatile.

The legitimacy of independence thus derived in part from the legitimacy of the preconquest civilizations that had governed America before the arrival of the Spanish. Spanish rule, in contrast, was nothing more than an unjustified "usurpation," and Spain a "vile usurper."[22] The colonial period itself was dismissed as a time of darkness and three centuries of barbarism. As the historian Hans-Joachim König has shown, the phrase "three hundred years of slavery" became a slogan of the independence movement in many parts of Spanish America.[23] For example, the Peruvian national anthem, composed in 1821, condemned the colonial era's "three centuries of horror." In his opening address to the Buenos Aires Patriotic Society in 1812, the insurgent lawyer Bernardo de Monteagudo lamented that "for the space of more than three hundred years humanity in this part of the world has groaned with no comfort other than suffering, and no consolation other than waiting for death, and seeking in the ashes of the tomb asylum from oppression."[24] The phrase's importance as a slogan is demonstrated indirectly by the efforts that royalist propagandists took to debunk it. The Colombian royalist José Antonio Torres y Peña satirized the insurgents' constant repetition of the expression, complaining that it was used even by men whose own fathers held lucrative colonial posts, and who therefore could scarcely claim to be victims of Spanish oppression.[25] (I will return to the ambiguities of insurgent rhetoric later in this chapter.) As in Mexico, evidence that colonial rule had truly been three hundred years of slavery was found particularly in the mistreatment of the indigenous population. The abuse had begun with the conquest, as the 1819 constitution of the United Provinces of South America insisted: "Since the Spanish seized these countries, their preferred system of domination was extermination, destruction and humiliation. The plans for this devastation were put into action and have continued without intermission for the space of three hundred years. They began by assassinating the monarchs of Peru and then did the same with the other princes and primates they encountered."[26] (Preconquest America thus consisted of legitimate monarchies governed by princes, rather than savage tribes ruled by chieftains, as many royalists claimed.)

For revolutionaries in South America as in Mexico, independence was therefore a resumption of ancient rights lost in the conquest. A "national song" published in a Lima newspaper in 1822, a year after the city's conversion to the insurgent cause, expressed that view clearly:

> Now revives the beloved patria
> of the Incas, the sons of the sun,
> the empire of the great Moctezuma,
> [and] the ancient nation of the Zipas.
> Indian heroes, all America
> salutes you with hymns of love,
> and offers you, in just homage,
> the broken sceptre of the cruel Spaniard.[27]

An independent Peru was therefore a revival of the Inca empire, independent Mexico the same as the Aztec empire, and independent Colombia a resuscitated version of the preconquest Muisca "empire," whose rulers, the Zipas, enjoyed a sudden elevation in status, becoming the equals of the Inca and Aztec monarchs in insurgent discourse. Moreover, just as Mexican revolutionaries described independence as avenging Montezuma, so insurgent writers farther south label Spain's defeat the revenge of Lautaro and of the Inca Atahualpa. "And now it is known across the land / That the cold ashes of the Incas / Revive in the tomb and, roused, / Proclaim San Martín their avenger," wrote the insurgent Colombian poet José Joaquín de Olmedo, thus hailing the insurgent general José de San Martín as an avenger of the Incas.[28] At last the unquiet ghosts of the Incas and Aztecs could be laid to rest. 'Sated now with Iberian blood sleep / The shades of Atahualpa and Montezuma," was how the Venezuelan scholar Andrés Bello put it in 1826.[29]

In their celebration of preconquest cultures insurgents responded not only to the exigencies of the nationalist urge but also to the many European voices that condemned preconquest America—and by extension the creoles themselves—as barbarous. As Antonello Gerbi has shown in a magisterial work, eighteenth-century Europe experienced a vigorous debate about the nature of the Americas and its inhabitants.[30] European writers and philosophers such as the Comte de Buffon, Cornelius de Pauw, William Robertson, and G. T. F. Raynal loudly condemned the climate of the Americas as unwholesome and its inhabitants as weak, impotent, and effeminate. In their view Indians past and present were mere savages, while Europeans long resident in America's noxious climes invariably degenerated. The flora and fauna were described as similarly flawed. The Americas were thus doomed, climatically and racially, to inferiority. These views, widely known and debated in Spanish America, helped shape the discourse of independence by augmenting the precepts of creole patriotism and prompting outraged responses across the region. Fiercely rejecting European charges of American inferiority, creole insurgents revindicated the achievements of the ancient American empires as part of a larger defense of the Americas, for they perceived a clear link between the climatic determinists and the Spanish colonizers: namely, both wrongly insisted that creoles were degenerate, lazy, and constitutionally unfit to govern themselves.[31] In defending the Aztecs and the Incas, creoles were implicitly defending themselves from European claims of degeneracy and inferiority.

The insurgent celebration of the pre-Columbian world also challenged the claims of increasingly vociferous royalist rhetoric, itself a response both to the "Dispute of the New World," as Gerbi labeled the European debate about the Americas, and to the revolutionary movement in Spanish America, which had arisen after Napoleon's invasion of the Iberian Peninsula. Deeply pained by the gross ingratitude that America showed its motherland in her hour of need, royalists not only condemned creoles for their disloyalty but also defended the conquest as an irruption of civilization over a continent hitherto submerged in darkness. Preconquest Indians, royalists insisted, had not been the wise sages of insurgent rhetoric. They were vicious and degraded heathens, living without laws or the knowledge of God. In an 1811 letter to the insurgent government in Bogotá, the royalist council of the coastal town of Santa Marta taunted their opponents with a bleak description of the continent's state prior to the arrival of Europeans. Before the conquest, the council reminded the insurgents, there had been no colleges, no monasteries, no palaces, indeed no buildings at all. The Indians had not been natural philosophers. "What sort of science did they teach in the University of the Jungle?" mocked the council.[32] Rare was the royalist who saw any virtue in preconquest America.[33] The insurgent celebration of the preconquest past, in other words, formed part of a dense polemic about the nature of the Americas, ancient and modern, in which the status of preconquest peoples reflected directly on the legitimacy of creole claims to authority.

AZTECS, INCAS, AND ARAUCANIANS

The preconquest era thus played an important role in insurgent rhetoric not only in Mexico but across Spanish America. This rhetoric stressed the beneficent nature of preconquest societies, denounced the colonial era as three hundred years of tyranny, and presented independence as Montezuma's and Atahualpa's revenge. In this section I examine the development of a pan-American pantheon composed of patriotic Aztecs, Incas, and Araucanians. These numinous figures were evoked in countless works of propaganda that stressed not only their heroic qualities but also their commitment to the insurgent cause.

The urtext of independence-era celebration of the Araucanians was Alonso de Ercilla's sixteenth-century epic poem the *Araucana*, "perhaps the most widely-read book in Chile" at the time of independence.[34] The poem, which describes Spanish efforts to establish control over central Chile (Arauco) is prolix in its praise of the valor and bravery of the local indigenous warriors who resisted the conquistadors. Caupolicán, Colocolo, Lautaro, Tucapel, Galvarino, and the other Araucanian leaders emerge as appealing figures, at times more admirable than the Spaniards themselves. The *Araucana's* importance for the development of nationalist sentiment in Chile was eloquently described by Francisco Antonio Pinto, vice president of Chile between 1827 and 1829, who recalled the impact of reading the *Araucana* as a youth: "Around [1805] I read for the first time the *Araucana* by Ercilla, and we used to gather in a little group to enjoy reading it. It wasn't because we enjoyed the beauty of its poetry, which we were not in a condition to know how to appreciate, but because of the heroic deeds of the Araucanians and the Spaniards, which we considered to be our own, as we were compatriots of the former and descendants of the latter. This work was what began to awake in our hearts love of our fatherland, warlike sentiments, thirst for glory, and a vague yearning for independence."[35]

For Chilean insurgents the deeds of Lautaro and his companions provided an inexhaustible source of heroic imagery, as the historian Simon Collier has demonstrated.[36] Insurgent leaders were likened not only to the heroes of ancient Rome but also to those of the *Araucana;* San Martín, announced the *Gazeta Ministerial Extraordinaria de Chile,* was "able to wage war with the skill of Fabius and the spirit of Lautaro."[37] Journals, speeches, and poetic sketches praised the valor, virtue, and democratic zeal of the Araucanians, while patriotic newspapers—*Araucanian Monitor, Araucanian Enlightenment, The Araucanian, Post of Arauco, Araucanian Decade, Araucanian Alert, Araucanian Insurgent*—broadcast their ideology in their titles.[38] Later Chilean scholars even claimed that patriotic parents named their children after the characters of the *Araucana* in preference to Catholic saints.[39]

The Araucanians offered Chilean insurgents a past that was not only heroic but also national. Juan Egaña's 1819 *Pehuenchean Letters,* a reworking of Montesquieu's *Lettres persanes,* illustrates well the view that anti-Spanish revolutionaries were continuing the struggle begun by the Araucanians in the sixteenth century. (Egaña, a Chilean insurgent with conservative leanings, regarded both the Araucanians and the Incas as models for the future republic of Chile.)[40] The book consists of a series of letters exchanged between two Pehuenches—Egaña described the Pehuenches as a branch of the Araucanians—in which they comment on life and politics in independence-era Chile. Egaña's indigenous correspondents were vastly erudite; their letters discussed the Prussian legal system, the writings of Aristotle and Cato, and Napoleon's advances across Europe. Readers learned that not only had the Araucanians exceeded all other nations in eloquence and in their grasp of astronomy and hydraulics, but also, perhaps most importantly, in their "federative political system."[41] These accomplishments lent importance to the support that the two Pehuenches gave to Chile's independence movement. The learned protagonists state clearly that the cause of Chilean independence "is the same as that for which our nation sustained more than two hundred years of wars."[42] Altogether, Egaña made clear that the Araucanians were admirable, modern patriots whose heritage Chileans could embrace with pride. They were simultaneously autochthonous and enlightened, American and civilized, historic and modern: the perfect nationalist symbol.

Despite their very specific geographical links to central Chile, the Araucanians were celebrated across South America in revolutionary poetry and verse. The leader of Lima's revolutionary masonic lodge went under the pseudonym of "Caupolicán," while Lautaro, as we have seen, adorned Peruvian theater curtains.[43] Republicans in Buenos Aires, whose familiarity with these indigenous heroes was due in part to the widespread fame of the *Araucana,* and in part to the movement of individual insurgents, made constant use of Araucanian imagery in their own propaganda.[44] The poet José Manuel Sánchez y Alonso, for example, composed various works honoring the warlike heroes, including *Arauco Liberated,* which was written to celebrate San Martín's victory at Maipú, and *The New Caupolicán, or The Brave Patriot of Caracas,* an 1815 theatrical monologue whose title alone demonstrates both the attempt to identify the ongoing antiroyalist insurgency with indigenous resistance to the conquest, and also the extremely vague nature of patriotic national geographies.[45] The Lautaro Lodge, General San Martín's secret revolutionary society, likewise commemorated Ercilla's heroes.[46] Across South America "Arauco" became a poetic synonym for "Chile," that "fertile Patria of the great *Caupolican.*"[47]

The Araucanians thus formed part of the heroic heritage of all South American insurgents. The other great source of patriotic mythology was the Inca empire. In his 1826 *Repertorio Americano* the Venezuelan savant and grammarian Andrés Bello described an English painting depicting the 1532 meeting of the Inca Atahualpa and the conquistador Francisco Pizarro. (Bello was at the time resident in London.) The painting pleased him, as it portrayed the "innocence, sweetness and confidence" of the Peruvians and the "wickedness, senseless ferocity and perfidy" of the Spaniards.[48] Bello had no doubt that the consequences of this encounter would be familiar to his insurgent audience. As "*all our readers know,*" he wrote, it had been followed by "a horrid slaughter of the innocent and unsuspecting Peruvians." Patriotic creoles could be expected to know the details of the Incas' defeat. Bello's readers would have gained their knowledge from several sources. First, European writers had for some decades been exploring the Incas' dramatic potential. From the mid-eighteenth century the Inca empire had been celebrated in the operas and writings of literati such as Jean-Philippe Rameau, Jean-François Marmontel, and Mme. de Grafigny, who saw ancient Peru as both a source of romantic drama and a mirror to the corruption of the Old World. The Incas, Voltaire had proclaimed in 1736, lacked "only our vices to be equal in every respect to the Europeans."[49] European familiarity with the Incas derived primarily from Garcilaso de la Vega's *Comentarios reales de los Incas*, a highly idealized history of the Inca empire composed in the early seventeenth century by the son of an Inca princess and a conquistador. Garcilaso's image of Inca benevolence, familiar in Spanish America both in its own right and reflected back via the works of Marmontel and others, played as important a role in shaping insurgent elite discourse as did the *Araucana*. In addition, as Alberto Flores Galindo has shown, creoles—at least in Peru—were subtly influenced by colonial Andean legends of an Inca utopia, even if they sought to strip those memories of their more alarming transformative potential (a matter to which I return in chapter 2).[50] Drawing on these sources, revolutionary poets and politicians from Buenos Aires to Bogotá rhapsodized about "the sweet Incas," whose achievements they celebrated and whose benign government they praised.[51] "Plato's Republic, the utopia of Thomas More, seem actually to have existed on this continent . . . The Inca emperors appeared fathers rather than lords: alive they were loved, and dead, lamented," announced the speaker at an 1812 memorial service for patriot soldiers held in Tucumán.[52] "The government of our Peruvian Incas was so wise that it scarcely appears possible, but it is indubitable that it existed," insisted a Porteño newspaper in 1816.[53] The Incas were admirable, and they were "ours." Even more than the Araucanians, the Incas were viewed as the patrimony of revolutionaries throughout South America. Although in republican discourse "the land of the Incas" invariably meant Peru, insurgents in many parts of South America described their projected nations as continuations of the Inca empire. Continuity is expressed clearly in Bernardo de Monteagudo's 1809 work "Dialogue between Atahualpa and Ferdinand VII in the Elysian Fields," in which Monteagudo, a creole lawyer from Tucumán, imagined an otherworldly encounter between "the shade of Atahualpa" and the reigning Spanish monarch Ferdinand VII (who was, of course, alive in 1809). When Ferdinand laments that Napoleon has unjustly seized his throne, Atahualpa sympathizes with him, observing that he suffered a similar fate when the Spanish conquered his patria.[54] Although Ferdinand at first argues that the two cases are not comparable, he ultimately concedes that Atahualpa's overthrow was no less unjust than his own. Won round by Atahualpa's arguments, the Spanish monarch himself blesses American independence: "Convinced by your reasoning, I agree with what you say, and therefore, if I yet lived, I myself would urge [Americans] to liberty and independence, rather than live subject to a foreign nation."[55] Here the political import of patriotic history is laid bare: those who accept that the conquest was unjust must support independence. Monteagudo's dialogue was joined by similar poems with titles such as "Proclamation of the Imprisoned Inca Huáscar" and "The Prediction of Viracocha: Message from This Prince to the Inca His Father," in which other members of the Inca dynasty denounced Spanish tyranny and urged modern Americans to support independence.[56]

While insurgents in Chile, Peru, and Río de la Plata embraced the Araucanians and the Incas, in Mexico nationalist propaganda concentrated on the Aztecs in preference to the many other indigenous groups that had also inhabited the region at the time of the conquest.[57] The Aztecs, like the Araucanians and the Incas, also enjoyed a following outside their ostensible homeland. Non-Mexican insurgents named the occasional warship after Montezuma, but for most the true hero of the Mexican conquest was Cuauhtémoc, the last Aztec prince. The death of Cuauhtémoc at Cortés's hands in 1525—the monarch was first tortured and then hanged—provided a rich opportunity to condemn Spain and to present an independent Mexico as a restoration of Cuauhtémoc's usurped empire.[58] Thus the Colombian José Fernández Madrid, who in 1816 had served briefly as president of the insurgent Santafé Congress, in 1827 composed a five-act tragedy titled *Guatimoc* (an alternate spelling of the emperor's name), which presented Cuauhtémoc as a Mexican patriot. "Mexico yet lives / As long as you and I still live . . . Yes, free, or dead; slaves, never!" vows the ill-fated hero. In Fernández Madrid's work Cuauhtémoc and his companions (labeled the "fathers of the nation") strive nobly but unsuccessfully to save their "unhappy patria" from the conquistadors. The play ends as the dying Cuauhtémoc exclaims, "Oh Gods! Will you tolerate these evildoers / and will their crimes remain unpunished?"[59] Contemporary theatergoers could supply the unspoken "No," for in 1827 Mexico was no longer a

Spanish colony. Fernández Madrid thus invited his audience to view Mexican independence as a vindication of Cuauhtémoc's death.[60] The iconic figures of the Araucanians, Incas, and Aztecs, who appeared in insurgent propaganda across Spanish America, were joined by lesser luminaries such as the Muiscas, who had inhabited central New Granada at the time of the conquest and who also featured regularly in insurgent rhetoric from the former viceroyalty.[61]

These preconquest figures occupied a distinctive place within insurgent discourse. Their role was, in part, to represent through their sufferings the injustice of the conquest, thereby demonstrating the justice of independence. In addition they performed a more complex task. As I argued in the introduction, a nation requires a national past. The preconquest figures discussed here were evoked not only to legitimate independence but also to form part of the history of the nations that insurgent leaders hoped to create, even as the vagueness about who "owned" the Incas and the Araucanians revealed the fragility of those nationalist dreams. When Mariano Egaña insisted that an independent Chile was the patria of Caupolicán, Colocolo, and Lautaro, he was helping to forge a national past. It was partly for this reason that insurgent ideologues so often compared Lautaro and Manco Capac to the warriors and sages of Greece and Rome. Such comparisons signaled the formation of an American tradition equal to those of the ancient European world. Although a number of scholars have argued that, outside Mexico, Spanish American insurgents sought not to endow the Americas with an ancient history but rather to abolish the past altogether, attempts at constructing a national past are discernible within these strange and, to later eyes, implausible evocations of Incas and Araucanians.[62] As the Peruvian minister of state put it in 1822, "All nations in turn have at some time been free." To be a nation, in other words, it was necessary to have a past history of freedom.[63] This was precisely what the preconquest era provided for revolutionaries. The nationalist pretensions of the indianesque are revealed particularly clearly in the civic festivals established across Spanish America after 1810.

FESTIVALS OF INDEPENDENCE

Scholars have for some time been interested in how the festivals held in colonial and independent Spanish America reflected the identities of festival organizers, participants, and spectators. For example, colonial festivals provided an opportunity for displays of both imperial grandeur and creole pride. As Linda Curcio-Nagy has shown in her analysis of festivals in colonial Mexico City, these public spectacles celebrated colonial rule through elaborate comparisons of government officials with the heroes of classical Greece and Rome.[64] At the same time, colonial festivals might also display signs of incipient creole patriotism through the eulogizing of the conquistadors. Civic Festivals in early-eighteenth-century Lima, for instance, praised "great Cortés and Pizarro, who exceeded the Romans in service to their kings."[65] The indigenous elites who at times participated in such events also sought to present their own visions of the past.[66] Histories of one sort or another thus played an important role in colonial festivals. From independence, civic festivals presented specific images of the nation's history both in the particularities of the celebrations and, more broadly, through the very establishment of an annual cycle of commemorative events. A civic festival—a "day of memories," in the words of a later Chilean scholar—implied that the new nation had something to remember.[67] The insurgent festivals held during the wars of independence thus laid claim to the past at the same time that they marked the creation of an entirely new festive calendar.

Newness is perhaps the most obvious feature of many of the festivals organized by revolutionary governments. Within a year the 1810 May Revolution in Buenos Aires was being memorialized in a civic festival that became an annual Porteño event.[68] By 1812 Mexican insurgents had declared 16 September, the date of the 1810 Grito de Dolores that launched the war against Spain, to be a national holiday, although actual celebrations do not appear to have occurred until 1825.[69] The entry of insurgent troops into important cities, as well as significant revolutionary victories, were also honored with parades, speeches, and other celebrations. Nonetheless, despite the recent nature of the events celebrated (or, more accurately, precisely because of their newness), these festivals not only adapted many features of the colonial festival but also incorporated verbal and visual displays of preconquest history intended to endow the festival, and thereby the emergent nation, with a past.

Throughout independence-era Spanish America, Indians, or more often allegorical figures representing Indians, played a prominent role in these festivals. Indigenous figures had often participated in colonial festivals, where their principal function had been to illustrate the grandeur of Spain's achievement in christianizing the Americas. A 1748 "native festival" in Lima, for example, included indigenous figures clothed in feathers who "celebrated with flutes and whistles their happy subjugation" to Catholicism.[70] In insurgent festivals, however, the indigenous figure played a quite different role. Instead of commemorating Spain's triumphant victory over paganism, the insurgent Indian both emblemized the legitimacy of American independence and manifested the long history to which the nation laid claim. The 1821 Mexico City celebrations of the Oath of Independence included tableaux vivants of indigenous figures armed with bows, arrows, and the Aztec war axe, or *macana*. In the celebrations in Ayapango, "seven little Indian girls with swords in hand headed the parade." In San Miguel el Grande (now San Miguel de Allende), the celebratory procession included not only allegorical figures representing fame, but also two hundred marchers dressed as Chichimecs, with bows, arrows, and feather headdresses, and carrying flags incongruously adorned with Aztec-style hieroglyphs.[71] In Buenos Aires, the 1811 commemoration of the May Revolution featured dancers dressed as "Spaniards" and "Americans," with the Spaniards wrapped in togas and the Americans "with coloured feathers at their waist and head like Indians." (The indigenous inhabitants of 1811 Río de la Plata no more wore feather skirts than nineteenth-century Spaniards wore togas; the festival's organizers had in mind an archaic Indian familiar to the creole imagination as a personification of the American continent, whose features I will discuss in chapter 2.) One of the "Indian" dancers was led away in chains, only to be released later amid general rejoicing.[72] A year later, the celebration of the failure of a counterrevolutionary conspiracy included four children dressed as Indians who "sang from time to time various songs in harmony."[73] In Lima, "the spirit of Peru, represented by the Inca Viracocha garbed in the attributes of the [Inca] empire," accompanied by women dressed as sun virgins, marked Bolívar's entry into the city in 1825.[74] That the spirit of independent Peru could be represented by an Inca illustrates clearly the link drawn between the preconquest past and the revolutionary present.

The speeches and commemorative poetry read at such festivals likewise confirmed the importance of the precolonial past to constructions of the emergent nation. These festivals made clear that the continent's history began prior to the conquest, when its inhabitants had enjoyed the wise and paternal government of the Aztecs, Incas, and Araucanians. Until the conquest, explained one Estéban Soto in his 1816 speech marking the May Revolution in Buenos Aires, America under the rule of "the great Motezuma and the celebrated Atahualpa" had been governed by "its own laws, as wise, politic and orderly as those of Crete, Sparta, Rome and Greece."[75] For Soto, as for colonial creole patriots, the preconquest world was the American equivalent of European classical antiquity. Porteño independence had, moreover, been described during festivities the previous year as the recovery of America's "ancient rights," "taken from our fathers [by the] tyrannical Spanish invasion."[76] The losses suffered by "our fathers" the Indians, such speeches implied, were avenged through independence. A bond of metaphorical ancestry united independence-era Spanish America with the continent's preconquest civilizations. In the next section I explore this insurgent genealogy.

"OUR FATHERS THE INDIANS"

In 1849 the Chilean historian Miguel Luis Amunátegui commented on a feature of independence-era rhetoric that struck virtually all of his contemporaries as ironic, or at best odd: namely, the passionate self-identification of creole insurgents with the indigenous leaders overthrown by the Spanish conquest. "Creoles in whose veins Spanish blood circulated declared themselves the heirs and avengers of the Aztecs, the Incas and the Araucanians who had been massacred centuries earlier by their fathers," he wrote. "*Montezuma, Atahualpa* and *Caupolicán* were the war cries with which they steeled themselves for combat."[77]

Both creoles and peninsular Spaniards often described the colonial relationship in terms of familial metaphors. Spain was a parent sometimes described as kind and loving, and sometimes as tyrannical, and in extreme cases not a parent at all but a hateful stepmother. The American colonies were children who either sheltered under the protecting care of their Spanish parent or, having reached maturity, perhaps prepared to leave the family home. This image, by no means unique to the Spanish world, shaped the rhetoric of independence and provided a powerful metaphor for royalists and revolutionaries alike. Royalists lamented the ingratitude of creoles who callously ignored their stricken mother[land] and abandoned her to Napoleon's advance. Republicans countered that stepmother

Spain had never deserved the title of parent at all.[78] If Spain was not a parent but an evil stepmother, who then were their true fathers?

An alternate, American, genealogy consisted of Atahualpa, Montezuma, and Caupolicán. In poetry and proclamations, creole revolutionaries stressed their familial links to the Incas, Aztecs, and Araucanians, and described themselves as the metaphorical sons and grandsons of these heroic men. In Mexico, Bustamante referred to the Aztecs as "our fathers," although he himself was of entirely Spanish descent.[79] In Chile, creole revolutionaries described themselves as the heirs of the Araucanians: the republican general Francisco Calderón praised Chilean patriots as the "sons of Caupolicán, Colocolo and Lautaro," while the supreme director Ramón Freire invoked "our fathers, the Araucanians."[80] If Chileans did not support independence, insisted the insurgent *Monitor Araucano* in 1813, then future generations would say, "What idlers, what dandies, what egoists were the *famous descendents of the immortal Colocolo!*"[81] San Martín's troops were variously described as "the valiant sons of Tucapel and Lautaro" and the "grandsons of the Inca Atabaliva [Atahualpa]," while Peruvian soldiers were urged to fight "in the name of their father the Inca."[82] Nor was it the Incas, Aztecs, and Araucanians alone who were claimed as metaphorical ancestors; the Chilean journalist Camilo Henríquez, for example, composed a play set in independence-era Quito in which the patriotic heroine not only praises the masculine valor of the indigenous Omaguas in resisting the Spanish conquest but also proudly proclaims, "The blood of the original inhabitants of this country runs through our veins."[83] Guatemalan insurgents, in turn, were the "sons of Kachiquel"—descendants of the conquest-era Quiché warrior.[84]

Because they were heirs to these preconquest empires, insurgents were sometimes described as being Indians themselves. "I too am an Indian," San Martín insisted in 1816.[85] Patriotic poetry regularly referred to revolutionaries as "Indians." The identification between "patriots" and "Indians" can be seen clearly in the Peruvian independence-era song "La chicha":

Patriots, with chicha [maize beer]
fill the gourd
and happily toast to liberty . . .
Every Indian insists
with cup in hand

that he must abhor
every tyrant.[86]

Similarly, the Argentine poet Bartolomé Hidalgo's *cielitos* described republican troops as Indians: "Sky, little sky / keep your chocolate. / Here we are pure Indians / and drink only yierba mate."[87] His 1818 *Cielito of the Triumph of Maipú*, which celebrated San Martín's defeat of royalist forces in Chile, likewise runs:

But well done the Indians!
They didn't let up even for the devil.
"Death to all Galicians [Spaniards],
Long live the Patria," they shouted.[88]

In all three poems "Indians" refers to the insurgent soldiery, whose status as Indians signifies not their ethnicity but rather their patriotism. Although Nicholas Shumway argues that Hidalgo's poetry was directed at gaucho troops and therefore does not represent the views of the revolutionary elite in Buenos Aires, I believe that it reflects if not the views of the revolutionary elite then the widespread dissemination of an elite ideology that saw insurgents as the descendents of the Aztecs and Incas.[89]

Through this genealogy, creole ideologues became the victims of the conquest alongside the indigenous population. "But who would have believed / That the Spanish monarch / Would usurp *our* kingdom / And consider it a great deed?" marveled a Peruvian poet.[90] "Where is the inhabitant of America who can say: 'I have been exempted from the general law that condemned my fellow citizens to the rigours of tyranny?'" asked Mexican delegates at the 1813 Congress of Chilpancingo.[91] Porteño writers lamented the time when "the Spaniards usurped the crown of our legitimate kings, fathers and predecessors."[92] This rhetoric was not simply a response to the ethnic composition of particular insurgent armies: both Miguel Hidalgo, leading an army composed largely of indigenous people and *castas* (as persons of mixed ethnicity were known), and Agustín de Iturbide, addressing the creole elite, described Mexico's colonial period as three hundred years of slavery.[93]

Since creoles were the metaphorical sons of the Incas and the Aztecs, they were also the brothers of contemporary indigenous people, as the

Lima Congress explained in 1822 when it addressed provincial indigenes as "beloved brothers." "Do not be surprised that we call you brothers," it proclaimed. "We truly are; we descend from the same fathers, we form a single family."[94] The Chilean newspaper *Aurora de Chile* expressed these sentiments clearly when it suggested that "henceforth let us call ourselves 'Indians,' so that our brothers should know the worthy esteem in which we hold them; or if for some reason that I can't understand this is in any way inappropriate, on those occasions when it is necessary to refer to them let them be called "our brothers the Indians."[95] The Junta Provisional Gubernativa of the United Provinces of Río de la Plata likewise described the viceroyalty's indigenous population as "our brothers . . . America's first-born sons."[96] The indigenous past thus revealed the "magnificence of *our* ancestors," as the creole Juan José Castelli told a group of indigenous soldiers assembled at the pre-Inca ruins of Tiahuanaco in 1811.[97] Creoles, as much as the indigenous population, were heirs to the grandeur of the preconquest past. Indeed, once creole revolutionaries had laid claim to that past, contemporary indigenous people became irrelevant to nationalist poetics—aside from their ability to display the stigmata of colonialism. Thus in a number of regions the very term "Indian" was abolished in the vain hope that the human signified would follow the demise of the signifier (see the appendix).

THE AMBIGUITY OF RHETORIC

These evocations of the preconquest era served both to justify political independence from Spain and also to endow the emergent nations of Spanish America with "national" pasts. To assert this, however, is not to claim that these creole revolutionaries envisioned unified nations. On the contrary, the limitations of these invocations of the indigenous past are one of their most notable features. As a number of historians have observed, creole patriots rarely included contemporary indigenous people in their rhetorical celebrations of the indigenous past, despite their occasional reference to contemporary indigenes as "brothers."[98] Their language did not offer an inclusive image of the nation. Instead, this rhetorical celebration of the preconquest past rested on a paradox. On the one hand, the deliberate cultivation of a national identity based partially on an appeal to the former glories of preconquest empires meant that the indigenous past had to be valorized. Thus revolutionary leaders lauded the achievements of the Aztec and Inca empires and encouraged the cultivation of indian-esque ceremony. The noble figure of the preconquest Indian was claimed as the original ancestral figure of all Mexicans, all Chileans, all Americans. On the other hand, to the great distress of republican leaders, contemporary indigenous populations seemed to display few of the virtues ascribed to their illustrious predecessors. In republican eyes they were dirty, degraded, and, infinitely worse, just as likely to support the royalists as their metaphorical cousins, the insurgents. Republicans therefore evolved a double discourse on "Indians." Prior to the conquest, they proclaimed, Indians had been noble creatures, and it was from them that modern America had sprung. After the conquest, Indians had sadly degraded to such an extent that they now bore scant resemblance to their glorious ancestors. The insurgent journalist Vicente Panzos Silva thus simultaneously praised the benign government of the Incas and denounced contemporary (royalist) Indians as "weak minded men . . . the most degraded portion of the population of South America."[99] This fall was generally held to be the fault of the three hundred years of sufferings inflicted by the Spanish. "The degradation of the Indian to the point at which we see him is the fault of the oppressor government that has brutalized us for three consecutive centuries," insisted the Colombian revolutionary and scientist José Francisco de Caldas.[100] "Only three hundred years of shameful domination were necessary to desolate the most populous continent, and, worse, to reduce to the level of beasts the descendants of the wise legislators of Peru," denounced an Argentine newspaper.[101] San Martín likewise lamented that Peru's indigenous population was "submerged in the moral degradation to which the Spanish government reduced them."[102] "Three hundred years of slavery" became the explanation for the unimpressive appearance of contemporary indigenous peoples. The true descendants of Atahualpa, of Montezuma, were thus the creole revolutionaries themselves.

Yet the authors of these self-identifications with the Indians elsewhere described themselves as true descendants of the first conquerors and explorers. "Inhabitants of the new Continent, generous sons of Columbus," was how one republican newspaper addressed its readers.[103] "Americans: who among you can say that he does not descend from a Spaniard?" asked the 1821 Plan de Iguala.[104] Creole revolutionaries, moreover, emphasized their familial and cultural links with Spain and insisted that the discrimination that they suffered at the hands of the Spanish was particularly odious because it was based on a false distinction between creoles and peninsulars. Rather than artificially divide the Spanish race into these two groups, they insisted, the Spanish should recognize the profound links that bound *españoles europeos* (European Spaniards) to *españoles americanos* (American Spaniards). Even Mier, author of *History of the Revolution in New Spain Anciently Known as Anáhuac,* insisted on his Hispanic origins: "I am a nobleman and a gentleman, not only because of my degree of doctor . . . nor solely because of my well-known links to the most distinguished Spanish nobility, since the Dukes of Granada and Altamira are related to me . . . but also because in America I am the descendent of the first conquerors of the New Kingdom of Leon."[105] Thus creole revolutionaries maintained that they were as Spanish as the Peninsulars and as Iberian in their outlook and worldview as the first conquerors, from whom they descended and whose glorious deeds brought them honor.

This rhetoric of sameness, it will immediately be apparent, is not wholly compatible with the rhetoric of indianesque nationalism. Consequently, as Pagden has noted, creole nationalism "was poised forever on the edge of absurdity."[106] The discomfort caused by this situation is reflected in the poetry of the Colombian insurgent José Fernández Madrid (author of the 1827 *Guatimoc* discussed above). In his 1825 poem "The Death of Atahualpa" he observed:

Not without violence will my muse cover
with execration the name of Spain,
remembering its crimes and frauds:
my hand trembles and refuses to record
so much greed, fanaticism and cruelty:
Spanish blood runs through my veins.[107]

This conflictive situation is similarly manifest in the uncomfortable language of another revolutionary text, which attempts the difficult balancing act of combining a defense of the ancestral rights of descendants of the conquistadors with a condemnation of the conquest: "Americans: unhappy sons of the patria: your fathers and grandfathers conquered these vast regions of the new world at their own expense, slitting the throats of 15,000 of its innocent inhabitants . . . and what has been the recompense of their great and distinguished crimes? Americans: weep over your condition and recognize the barbarous and unjust hand that has degraded and vilified you . . . The lands conquered with the money, arms and blood of your ancestors were formed into colonies in the broadest sense of the word."[108] The rights of the creoles, this author suggests, derived from the atrocities committed by their fathers and grandfathers. In his 1814 memoir the creole royalist José Antonio Torres y Peña mocked such conflicting rhetorics by commenting that "the same men who pride themselves on being the descendants of the conquistadors heap crimes on the heads of their fathers."[109] This discursive impasse was only partially resolved by avoiding altogether the use of either "Indian" or "Spaniard." Thus creoles began to label themselves not as *españoles americanos* but simply as "Americans."[110] This portmanteau term allowed its user to refer indiscriminately to indigenous peoples, creoles and anyone else, with a single all-embracing epithet. Thus Simón Bolívar in his "Jamaica Letter," an eloquent denunciation of anticreole discrimination, described the victims of the conquistadors as "we Americans."[111] By metonymy, the suffering Indians came to stand for the disgruntled creoles.

Yet such syntactical solutions could not resolve the fundamental division that creole revolutionaries drew between the glorious preconquest past and the debased indigenous present. While the indigenous heroes of the pre-Columbian and conquest eras helped shape insurgent nationalism by providing independent Spanish America with its own past, the contemporary indigenous population at best illustrated the evils wrought by the conquest, and at worst revealed a fundamentally debased nature that in itself made problematic any identification between the preconquest past and the indigenous present. As a limited nationalist mythology, indianesque nationalism functioned best when no attempts were made to connect the preconquest past with the indigenous present. The inability of indianesque nationalism to imagine any sort of civic space within the nation for the contemporary indigenous population is illustrated by the discussions that followed an 1816 proposal to place an Inca on the throne of an independent Río de la Plata, with which this chapter ends.

THE "INCA PLAN"

On 6 July 1816, in a secret session of the insurgent Congress of Tucumán, delegates discussed a proposal to convert an independent Río de la Plata into a monarchy headed by an "Inca." The military commander Manuel Belgrano was one of the more outspoken supporters of the idea. He felt that a "moderated monarchy," such as the restored Inca dynasty would offer, could attract great support among the inhabitants of the interior provinces. He also drew delegates' attention to the injustice of the Inca dynasty's original overthrow by Spain. By returning the noble house to the throne, the congress would be righting an ancient wrong. From Jujuy the insurgent caudillo Martín Güemes also backed the proposal, and for several weeks delegates at the congress appeared to favor reestablishing the Inca empire.[112]

Here then was a concrete proposal to restore the Incas to power. Other revolutionaries from Francisco de Miranda to Bolívar toyed with the idea of naming the highest-ranking official in a putative insurgent government the "Inca," but none had imagined that this post would be occupied by an actual descendent of the Incas.[113] The Congress of Tucumán's proposal, the so-called Inca Plan, went far beyond mere rhetoric, aiming as it did to place political power in the hands of contemporary indigenous people, or at least one such person. How was this plan received by the inhabitants of Río de la Plata? We know the response of one man, the editor of the *Crónica Argentina,* one of the unofficial insurgent papers published in Buenos Aires in 1816–17. The editor himself described his reaction to the proposals, which he had read in a rival newspaper: "When we saw the two proclamations inserted recently into [issue 55 of the *Censor*], one from Colonel Don Martín Güemes to the towns of the interior, and the other from General Don Manuel Belgrano to the army, announcing the restoration of the Inca throne, we at first imagined that they were making use of a political metaphor to designate our empire."[114]

This is as clear a piece of evidence as one could wish for the prevalence of indianesque nationalism in independence-era Buenos Aires: on hearing proposals to restore the Inca empire, the editor of the *Crónica* immediately assumed that it was some sort of political metaphor, rather than a concrete suggestion. The editor indeed went on to remind his readers of how common this imagery had become. For some time, he noted, people had been saying that *"It would be unjust not to remember the Incas;* to them, and consequently to the Indians who were their family, *belongs this land on which we stand."*[115] He himself employed indianesque images in his own newspaper, whose emblem was variously an Incaic solar face or an Andean landscape with a llama and a rising sun. Never, however, did the editor expect these nationalist metaphors to be taken literally.

The reaction of the *Crónica's* editor, Vicente Panzos Silva, to the "Inca Plan" reveals both the prevalence of indianesque nationalism in Buenos Aires and its inability to express proposals for concrete social reform. As a "political metaphor" the "Inca Plan" was so familiar as to be tiresome. As a concrete proposal it amounted, in the editor's view, to poorly thought-out royalism. How, he asked, could Belgrano and Güemes "proclaim as re-established and ready to rule a dynasty that exists only in Garcilaso's *History* and the poems of Marmontel?"[116] By citing the originary text of elite fascination with the Incas—the 1609–17 *Comentarios Reales* by Garcilaso de la Vega—alongside Marmontel's 1777 *Les Incas, ou, La destruction de l'empire du Pérou,* the *Crónica's* editor further revealed his familiarity with the rhetoric of indianesque nationalism while at the same time la-beling as illusory any attempt to restore political rights to the indigenous population that was based on it. The Inca empire, he insisted bluntly, was irretrievably dead: "If in truth after only three days the corpse of Lazarus was in such a revolting condition that it cost the Omnipotent great effort to restore it to life, the skeleton of the Inca dynasty must be completely unbearable."[117] A talented satirist, Panzos reported in a further issue that some individuals in Portugal apparently believed that the sixteenth-century King Sebastian would miraculously return to the Portuguese throne. He continued: "Tender readers! Are you moved to laughter and compassion by the sad preoccupation of those who await the return of an individual who died in 1578? Know then that there are among you those who with no less fanaticism proclaim the return of a monarchy that ended in 1533, by announcing the restoration of the Incas whose rule concluded in that year. In vain did the barbarous Pizarro, assisted by Father Valverde, have Atahualpa smothered: this emperor is again at your gates."[118]

The editor of the *Crónica's* belief that indianesque nationalism should not be taken literally seems to have been shared by other Porteño journal-ists. The ensuing newspaper debate over whether monarchy was compat-ible with democracy contained few further references to the Incas. Panzos accused the advocates of the Inca Plan of being crypto-monarchists: "Bel-grano is a royalist; he wants a monarchy."[119] Advocates of the plan in turn labeled its opponents closet royalists. "You are sons of the Spanish, you bear in your blood the virus of ambition, which all the mercury in the world cannot purge," insisted the editor of the *Censor,* thereby suggesting that being Spanish was akin to having a venereal disease, likewise cured with mercury.[120] No one in the capital paid much more attention to the idea of restoring the Incas, once it became clear that the original proposal was not a metaphor.

The debate about the Inca Plan indicates both the power and the limitation of indianesque nationalism during this formative period. As the editor of the *Crónica* indicated, this language was pervasive in political discourse in the years after 1810. In proclamations, speeches, poetry, and festivals, revolutionary leaders traced the ancestry of independent Spanish America back to preconquest days, thereby endowing with a grand historic tradition the nations they sought to create. The Tucumán delegates' brief flirtation with a restored Inca empire was the result of this long marination. They differed from other creole ideologues only in their temporary conviction that indianesque nationalism could provide a model not only for the past but also for the future.

In the next chapter I examine the history of national symbols—coins, flags, state shields—which allow us first to probe further the use of preconquest and indigenous emblems to symbolize the state during the independence era, and then to trace their increasing marginalization in subsequent decades, as the Spanish American elites began imagining new pasts for their nations.

 *Chapter 2*

Representing the Nation

In 1813, as part of its celebrations of the 1810 May Revolution in Buenos Aires, the city of Salta decided to modify its coat of arms. The city's arms had hitherto shown a "lofty hill cloaked in beautifying trees," "two powerful rivers which bathe it," and a Spaniard successfully resisting attack by a hostile Indian. The coat of arms paraded through the streets at the 1813 festivities, however, revealed a new design. The tree-covered hill and the two rivers remained, but now the Spaniard appeared "defeated in the presence of the Indian."[1] The motives and meanings behind this alteration reflect clearly the indianesque nationalism that I discussed in chapter 1. Whereas the colonial shield had depicted the triumph of the Spanish conquest, the new coat of arms showed colonialism vanquished by an independent, insurgent America, symbolized by the victorious Indian. The transformation—indeed radical reversal—of the message encoded in Salta's coat of arms is representative of the broader nation-building process underway in independence-era Spanish America, both in its substitution of an anticolonial iconography for proconquest imagery and in its recognition of the importance of iconography in constructing the patria. In this chapter I examine the nineteenth-century creation of a symbolic language to represent the new Spanish America. I explore the visions of the national past expressed in such unobtrusive but ubiquitous sites of official memory as place-names, coins, and state shields, looking first at the iconography created during the independence period, which was simultaneously revolutionary and unstable, and then at the transformations wrought on these symbols over subsequent decades by the development of new nationalist iconographies based on the heroes of independence themselves. These surprisingly eloquent venues chart the rise and fall of indianesque nationalism, at the same time underscoring the fundamental importance of iconography to the nationalist imagination from the very start of the independence process. Some scholars have argued that "cultural" nationalism dependent on emblems and ceremonies was a phenomenon of the late nineteenth century, when states were most able to employ widespread literacy and their own easy access to print to reach large audiences.[2] The nationalism of creole revolutionaries certainly did not depend for support on Spanish America's extremely limited infrastructure of print technology, but it did make ample use of symbols and emblems to embody their projected nations.

ANÁHUAC, BOGOTÁ, CAUPOLICÁN

A brief perusal of any atlas of Spanish America shows a striking variety of place-names. Mexico, for example, possesses towns and villages with captivating hybrid names (San Andrés Tuxtla, Santiago Ixcuintla), names that hint at an ancient origin (Iztlán, Tlaxcala), and names clearly of more recent invention (Ciudad Madero, Allende). Place-names, as one nineteenth-century Mexican scholar put it, are "mute witnesses of history," recording the region's multiple transformations.[3] But when did Mexico become Mexico? Prior to the Spanish conquest, there had been no single term for the varied geographies currently united in the Republic of Mexico, and during the colonial era, although "México" (or "Méjico") had often been used to refer to the Spanish colony, its official title was the Viceroyalty of New Spain. It was only with independence that the country's leaders christened their country "México." They did this in order to stress the new state's connection to the preconquest past, as the name recalled the Mexica, or Aztecs. (The spelling "México" was regarded as preferable to "Méjico," since the former was believed to reflect more authentically the indigenous Náhuatl pronunciation.) Some enthusiasts even fought to make the "Republic of Anáhuac" the country's official title; the insurgent priest Servando Teresa de Mier thus preferred to speak of "Anahuacans," rather than "Mexicans."[4] Its new name not only emphasized Mexico's preconquest heritage but also eliminated references to a quite different heritage, for the colonial title of "New Spain" had underscored the colony's reliance on the Iberian Peninsula for its identity. By replacing "The Viceroyalty of New Spain" with "Mexico" insurgent leaders deliberately discarded the semantic link to the former metropolis. Mexico became the country's official name at the same time that the province of Nuevo Santander (New Santander) became Tamaulipas, and Nueva Galicia (New Galicia) became

Xalisco—changes that similarly rejected colonial interpretations of the region as a transplanted Spain.

Mexican insurgents were not alone in using nomenclature to proclaim their new vision of history. Across Spanish America revolutionaries rechristened places whose names had commemorated Spain with indigenous names. In Peru patriotic renaming celebrated the Incas. After his capture of Lima, José de San Martín rebaptized the city's fortifications so that the "King's Bastion" became the "Bastion of Manco-Capac" in an assertion of Peru's Incan, rather than colonial, heritage.[5] Manco Capac, the first Inca, literally replaced the defeated Spanish monarch. In Chile the new names recalled the Araucanians; by 1826 Chile had replaced the colonial Province of Concepción with the departments of Caupolicán and Lautaro. Two of the four vessels of Chile's first "national" naval squadron were likewise named the *Lautaro* and the *Araucano*. Other independence-era Chilean ships included the *Galvarino* (previously the HMS *Hecate*), the *Tucapel,* and, for good measure, the *Moctezuma.*[6] This iconographic appreciation of the Araucanians contrasts sharply with colonial attitudes. In 1796 the city of Talca had requested that its coat of arms show the defeat of "the terrible Indian chief" Lautaro.[7] In Colombia, the former Viceroyalty of New Granada, the new names recalled the indigenous Muiscas, with the exception of the new title for the country itself, which commemorated Columbus, in a further illustration of the partial and ambiguous nature of elite identifications with the preconquest past. The viceregal capital previously known as "Santa fé" or "Santa Fe de Bogotá" became simply "Bogotá," while the region around Bogotá renamed itself "Cundinamarca," which, according to its 1811 constitution, was its "first and original name," given to it by the Muiscas.[8] The renaming processes underway in independence-era Spanish America, in other words, illustrate what Daniel Milo has called the "nationalization of the right to name."[9] The framers of the incipient states created out of the former Spanish colonies consciously selected new place-names that evoked the pre-Columbian empires whose overthrow they claimed to avenge. The insurgent view of Spanish America's history was thus embedded in the continent's very geography. For Eric Hobsbawm, the invented nature of these postindependence Spanish American place-names provides good evidence of the minor role that nationalism played in the independence process.[10] In my view, it illustrates instead precisely the sort of invented past that scholars such as Benedict Anderson, and indeed Hobsbawm himself, have taught us to expect the nationalist process to produce.

Insurgents were conscious of the significance of these renamings, for they recognized the importance of symbols to the national project. The new flag created by Manuel Belgrano for the United Provinces of Río de la Plata was, he insisted in 1812, "the sign that now distinguishes us from the other nations."[11] For this reason it was important to replace Spanish emblems with a new American iconography. When San Martín designed a new Peruvian flag sporting an Incaic sun he justified the innovation by noting that "the conservation of symbols that recall its long period of oppression is incompatible with Peru's independence."[12] The Chilean leader Bernardo O'Higgins likewise defended the minting of new coinage to replace colonial coins depicting the Spanish monarch Ferdinand VII by explaining that "in an epoch in which the august emblems of liberty are everywhere substituted for the execrable image of the former despots, it would be extraordinarily absurd for our coins to conserve that infamous bust of usurpation personified," Ferdinand VII being "usurpation personified" because colonial rule was a usurpation of the ancient rights of the Araucanians.[13] O'Higgins's call to eliminate the iconography of "usurpation personified" was echoed by Mexican writers. "Neither in the cathedral nor on the pillory, nor even less on our coins, [let there be] nothing that reeks of Spain's old tyrannical domination over America," proclaimed "Anita la Respondona" in an 1821 Mexican pamphlet. She appealed for purely "Mexican" emblems such as eagles, cactuses, arrows and the Aztec war axe, or *macana*, "in place of fleurs de lys, lions, castles, fleeces."[14] In keeping with such requests, the image of lions and castles (the emblem of Castilla y Leon) were in the independence years removed from state symbols across Spanish America and replaced by a new iconography drawn from the indigenous past.

INDIAN PRINCESSES

A central figure in this insurgent iconography was the Indian princess. Dressed in a simple shift and adorned with a feather crown, the Indian princess appeared on coins, medals, flags, and state shields from Mexico to Chile. Paintings showed Indian princesses protected by Simón Bolívar, the hero of American independence. Ladies garbed as Indian princesses participated in insurgent festivals, crowning republican heroes with laurel wreaths, parading in celebration of a recent victory, planting liberty trees, and generally representing the patria (see figures 6–8).[15] In creating the Indian princess, revolutionary iconographers drew on European representations of the "Four Continents." In Europe an allegorical tradition, dating back to the sixteenth century, of depicting the continents as female figures assigned a distinctive iconography to America. America was usually represented as an Indian queen, naked except for her crown of feathers and surrounded by the attributes of a Caribbean culture: bows, arrows, parrots, crocodiles, and perhaps a human limb or two (see figure 9). Although with the establishment of the thirteen colonies the Indian queen's associations broadened to include British North America and, later, the United States, the use of a regal Indian to represent Spain's American colonies was well established by 1810.[16] When used by Spanish artists the allegory was usually clothed, rather than naked, so as to distance Spain's colonies from the barbarism conveyed by nudity. This iconography was often used on colonial medals and coins. The birth of the future King Charles IV, for example, was commemorated in Mexico by a medal showing a classically dressed female figure, representing Spain, handing the infant prince to Mexico, depicted as an indigenous woman crowned with feathers.[17] Similarly, an 1809 loyalist allegory presented Mexico as an Indian woman with a feather crown and quiver, who joined with Spain in swearing to avenge the imprisoned Ferdinand VII (see figure 10).[18] Sometimes, less frequently, royalist iconography depicted America as an Indian man. This was the case, for example, in an 1814 Mexican medal in which metropolis and colony were represented as two warriors, Spain as a classical figure, and America as an indigenous man armed with a bow and arrow.[19] The distinctive feature of such royalist iconography was that it represented both Spain and its colonies in a unified allegory. The imagery showed an empire united by loyalty to the monarch and the Catholic faith.

Republicans transformed this familiar iconography. The break with Spain does not seem to have prompted anything equivalent to the "crisis of representation" that Lynn Hunt located in revolutionary France; Spanish American insurgents did not come to question "the very act of representation itself," but they did refashion the emblems of empire.[20] In republican hands, the Indian princess came to represent American autonomy rather than imperial unity and indigenous submission. The emblems

CONSTITUCION

DEL ESTADO DE

CARTAGENA DE INDIAS

SANCIONADA

*En 14. de Junio del año de 1812.
Segundo de su Independencia.*

CARTAGENA DE INDIAS: EN LA IMPRENTA
DEL CIUDADANO DIEGO ESPINOSA

Figure 6. Title page of the Constitution of the State of Cartagena, 1812. An Indian represented the ephemeral State of Cartagena on its official coat of arms. The shield shows an indigenous woman, recognizable by her quiver of arrows and feather headdress, seated under a palm tree. The broken shackles at her feet symbolize Cartagena's newfound liberty. Source: *Constitución del Estado de Cartagena*.

Figure 7. *The Political Resurrection of America*, 1821. In this Mexican print, America, helped to her feet by Agustín de Iturbide, is an Indian princess so weakened by Spanish tyranny that, as the patriotic octave explains, she had neither "bow, nor arrows, nor quiver": she has been stripped of her rightful attributes by an oppressive Spain. *Source*: Courtesy of the Biblioteca Nacional de México.

Figure 8. Pedro José Figueroa, *Bolívar and the Indian "America,"* 1819. In Figueroa's painting Simón Bolívar protects an allegorical figure representing America. Her feather crown, bow, and arrows make clear that she is an Indian princess. *Source*: Courtesy of the Casa Museo Quinta de Bolívar, Bogotá.

Figure 9. Maarten de Vos, *America*, 1594. European depictions of the Four Continents showed America as an Indian princess. She typically wore a feather crown and carried a bow and quiver of arrows, as she does in this pen and wash drawing by a Flemish artist. *Source*: Courtesy of the Stedelijk Prentenkabinet, Musea Antwerpen, Antwerp.

La antigua y Nueva España, Juran en
manos de la Religion vengar à Fernando VII

Figure 10. María Francisca de Nan, *Allegorical Dream*, 1809. This print from a royalist pamphlet shows "Old and New Spain" swearing, in the presence of Religion, to avenge the imprisoned Spanish monarch Ferdinand VII. Old Spain is a classical figure armed with a sword, while New Spain (Mexico) is an indigenous woman clad in a *huipil*, or tunic, and equipped with a feather headdress and a quiver of arrows. *Source*: Courtesy of the Nettie Lee Benson Library, University of Texas at Austin.

of the state—the coats of arms, coinage, flags, and medals created to symbolize the new Spanish American nations—employed this revolutionary
Indian to represent American liberty. Insurgent Colombian coins of the
1810s were embossed with crowned Indian maidens and indigenous warriors. One series, for example, showed an Indian princess and, on the reverse, a pomegranate (or *granada*, referring to New Granada) in place of
the bust of the king and the pillars of Hercules that had adorned colonial
coinage (see figure 11).[21] The significance of replacing the Spanish monarch with an indigenous woman is made clear by the hostility with which
royalists greeted these new iconographies. The Quito-based loyalist writer
Pedro Pérez Múñoz derided the coin for revealing, in his view, that republicans "would rather be heathen Indians than Spanish Catholics."[22] The
Indian emblems of creole nationalism were for this royalist an eloquent
sign of revolutionary savagery. State shields and flags likewise adopted the
indigenous imagery employed on coinage. After its break from Gran Colombia, the state emblem of Venezuela featured an indigenous woman, and
the 1812 shield of the Chilean Patria Vieja included two Indians.[23] Commemorative items too used the figure of an Indian princess to represent
independent America. An 1821 medal honoring Agustín de Iturbide depicted Mexico as a *huipil*-clad Indian princess adorned with a feather
crown, and the ceremonial sword presented in 1825 to Simón Bolívar by the
municipality of Lima was likewise decorated with crowned Indian figures
(see figure 12).[24] This imagery also graced the buildings in which the newly
established republican governments met. In 1825 the Bolivian Constitutional Assembly decreed that its chambers be decorated with a hammered
golden sheet showing "a beautiful Indian girl, symbolizing America, . . .
embracing the liberator [Bolívar] with her right arm and the grand marshal
of Ayacucho [Antonio José de Sucre] with her left"; insurgents perceived
no difficulty in allowing "a beautiful Indian girl" to symbolize America.[25]

The use of an indigenous woman to represent the nation contrasts sharply
with the virtual exclusion of all women from civic life that was envisioned
in both legal codes and patriotic discourse. Nowhere in independence-
era Spanish America were women permitted to be citizens: citizenship
was expressly constructed around a premise of masculinity. Women were
intended to relate to the nation via their role within the household rather
than through active engagement with the rights and duties of citizenship.

Figure 11. Obverse and reverse images on an eight real coin, United Provinces of New Granada, 1821. This silver coin shows an Indian princess adorned with a feather crown on the obverse, and a pomegranate, or *granada*, on the reverse. The design was first used in 1813. *Source*: Courtesy of Michael Shaw.

This expectation is displayed in the Chilean journalist Camilo Henríquez's 1817 play *Camila, or The Patriot of South America*, in which the eponymous heroine earns her title of "patriot" in part by delivering proindependence monologues but primarily by displaying unswerving loyalty to her husband. It is this latter virtue, rather than any active undertakings, that makes her "a fine model for the female patriots of South America."[26] The use of the archaic Indian princess within the iconography of the new Spanish American states illustrates particularly clearly the preference that insurgent leaders felt for displays of feminine patriotism that did not leave the arena of the symbolic.[27]

Once established as an emblem of liberty and America, the Indian princess could be replaced by bows and arrows or other indigenous paraphernalia; to allude to the principles of Spanish American independence it was necessary only to allude to Indians. Thus the 1815 coat of arms of the United Provinces of New Granada depicted bows and arrows alongside the traditional pomegranate, while that of Funza showed a bow and arrows, a lance and "other distinctive Indian weapons." These emblems were intended, according to their designers, to "remind us that in this place the ancient Indian sovereigns held court."[28] The Aztec war axe, or *macana*,

Figure 12. Sword presented to Simón Bolívar, 1825. The magnificent ceremonial sword given to Bolívar by the Municipality of Lima after the Battle of Ayacucho was decorated with indianesque motifs. The golden hilt features the bust of a crowned Indian princess, as well as a jewel-studded bas-relief of an indigenous couple holding aloft a Phrygian hat. *Source: Mundial*, Lima 1924 (special edition for centennial of Battle of Ayacucho).

was incorporated into designs for Mexican coins and medals alongside the Aztec eagle and cactus, itself transformed from a sign of Mexico City into an emblem of the country as a whole, which also featured on many of Mexico's independence-era banners.[29]

The use of this imagery placed indigenousness firmly in the past; the designers of these symbols did not believe that contemporary indigenous peoples wore feather crowns or carried macanas. These emblems were instead the markers of the preconquest Indian, familiar to Spanish American elites from both the Four Continents imagery and from the eighteenth-century European illustrations of Inca princesses made popular by such works as Mme. de Grafigny's *Lettres d'une péruvienne*.[30] Other insurgent emblems likewise stressed the location of patriotic indigenousness in the distant past. This is particularly clear in the solar imagery common across South America in the independence years.

INCA SUNS

Oh Sun! Sacred father of the Incas.

—JOSÉ MARÍA SALAZAR (1820)

For Spanish American insurgents such as the Colombian poet José María Salazar, the sun was the "sacred father of the Incas," and therefore a symbol of independence.[31] Endowed with a human face and sporting wavy solar rays, Incaic suns appeared across revolutionary South America, yet as emblems they were complex and ambiguous. Their heritage was partly European: in eighteenth-century Europe the sun was a popular symbol of kingship; it also played an important role in Christian iconography, where it represented either Christ or Christianity as the true light.[32] This European tradition was transplanted to Spain's American colonies, endowing the sun with a certain Catholic, imperial resonance. The most significant factor shaping the meaning of the sun in Andean countries, however, was the Inca sun cult. Spanish authorities in Peru had long been aware that the sun had a particular significance in Incaic religion. Chroniclers from Cieza de León onward described how the Incas had viewed the sun as a creator deity and traced royal descent from the sun.[33] Notwithstanding its links to European iconography, by the seventeenth century the solar face was recognized as a distinctive mark of the Inca state, and the Inca monarchs were often portrayed with such a sun adorning their chests (see figure 13).[34] Because of the sun's perceived links to the Inca monarchy, the colonial state periodically forbade Peruvian indigenes from painting or otherwise depicting solar images.[35] In particular, officials recommended that sun imagery be banned in the wake of the 1780 Túpac Amaru Rebellion, which had sought to overthrow Spanish rule and replace it with a re-created Inca empire.[36] By 1810, the sun was thus widely recognized as an Incaic symbol in Andean countries and was, moreover, considered to have anti-Spanish connotations. For this reason it was an obvious symbol for revolutionaries. Because of the association of the sun with the Inca state it suggested resistance to Spanish rule and could therefore be employed to evoke independence. On the other hand, its use indicates very clearly the problematic nature of indianesque nationalism, for the sun evoked not only autonomous rule but also, potentially, indigenous rebellion. In Peru in particular the sun was a powerful and somewhat dangerous symbol. It is therefore both almost inevitable and very surprising that creole revolutionaries made use of the sun as an emblem of revolt.

Insurgent sun imagery was first used in Buenos Aires, far from the epicenter of the old Inca empire. There the earliest republican coinage, minted in April 1813, had an Incaic solar face on one side and the coat of arms of the *cabildo* (town council) on the other. The sun motif was designed by the Cuzqueño Juan de Dios Rivera, and this link to Cuzco strengthens the view that the sun was intended to be an Incaic symbol.[37] This design is still in use, and adorns the current one peso Argentine coin (see figure 14). In 1815, when Porteño republicans produced a second series of these coins (following their recapture of the silver mint at Potosí), the smaller denominations were termed *soles* (suns) rather than *reales* (royals) as they had been in the colonial era.[38] Once again, indigenous nomenclature replaced names that evoked Spain's rule. Three years later the sun was added to the Argentine flag, where it has remained to the present day.[39]

It was Peru, of course, that had the greatest claim on sun imagery as the former seat of the Inca empire. Revolutionaries across South America referred to Peru as the "empire of the sun," and Peruvians as the "sons of the sun."[40] An Incaic sun was employed in Peru on official seals, documents, flags, and commemorative medals; indeed, the Orden del Sol (Order of the Sun) created by San Martín in 1821 to award exceptional military service explicitly traced its use of sun imagery back to the Incaic sun cult. As the

Figure 13. Felipe Guaman Poma de Ayala, "The first coat of arms of the Inka," 1616. The use of a solar face to represent the Inca empire was well established by the early seventeenth century. This image, from the Andean writer Guaman Poma de Ayala's *Primer nueva corónica y buen gobierno*, depicts the "coat of arms" of the Incas, which includes a radiant solar face, demonstrating the monarch's descent from the sun. *Source*: Courtesy of Det Kongelige Bibliotek, Copenhagen.

Figure 14. A 1996 Argentine peso. Argentine coinage still displays the Incaic solar face first used on coins in 1813. *Source*: Author's collection.

decree establishing the order explained: "The star that in former times was the second deity adored by the Peruvians, after their invisible Pachacamac, is today for us a sign of alliance, an emblem of honor, a recompense of merit, and in short, the historical expression of the land of the Incas, recalling the celebrated times that preceded its enslavement, as well as the happy days in which it recovered its independence."[41]

Sun imagery, in other words, was a symbol of America's former independence, "the celebrated times that preceded its enslavement." Those receiving the medal were told that "if there was a time when the star that precedes the day was adored by the fathers of our ancestors as the visible God of nature . . . today the epoch has returned in which that same star, reminding Peruvians of what they were, forms the standard that unites them and restores to their naturally ardent and brave breasts the energy always lost by those who live long under the shadow of slavery."[42] Soldiers awarded the Orden del Sol were thereafter entitled to place an image of the sun over their front door in lieu of the colonial coats of arms abolished as incompatible with the republican ethos.[43] The Peruvian flag created by San Martín in 1820 likewise sported a sun, as did the uniforms designed by Bernardo de Monteagudo for high-ranking government officials.[44]

Creoles had thus moved from prohibiting the use of Incaic emblems, as they had done in the wake of the Túpac Amaru Rebellion, to using them themselves.[45] They even began to encourage indigenous peoples to do the same. In an 1822 proclamation to the "Indians of the interior provinces" the Lima Congress scripted an indianesque fantasy for the celebration of independence: "Brothers! The day on which you receive this letter you will see your father the Sun dawn more happily over the peaks of your volcanoes in Arequipa, Chachamí, Pichupichu, Corupuna, Sulimana, Sarasara, Vilcanota, Ilimani. Therefore embrace your children, congratulate your wives, scatter flowers over the tombs of your fathers, and sound sweet *yaraviés* on your drums and flutes and dance happy *cachuas*, shouting out: now we are ourselves, now we are free, now we are happy."[46] This was one of the few occasions on which elite insurgent rhetoric specifically included indigenous people in the category of "sons of the sun," and the Lima Congress was at pains to clarify that this inclusion was not at the expense of creole claims to that status. The Lima Congress thus addressed the "Indians of the interior provinces" as "noble sons of the Sun, beloved *brothers*," so as to emphasize that Peru's indigenous population enjoyed no special or exclusive claim on the Inca heritage. As siblings, creoles and indigenes alike inherited the mantel of Tawantinsuyo. The Congress's anxiety to underline their inheritance of the Inca past was sensible, for events during both the colonial era and the independence years themselves revealed quite different stories about who might own the Incas.

INCA NATIONALISM, CREOLE NATIONALISM

It is striking that sun imagery and the Incas more generally were embraced even by Peruvian elite revolutionaries, whose receptiveness to their appeal one might expect to have been limited by the Túpac Amaru Rebellion of 1780. The vast rural uprising had resulted in the deaths of thousands of creoles and Spaniards, and tens of thousands of indigenous people, including the rebellion's leader, José Gabriel Condorcanqui. The movement had been accompanied by a serious effort to revindicate persistent Andean memories of the preconquest state governed by the Incas. Not by chance had Condorcanqui taken as his nom de guerre the name of the last Inca, Túpac Amaru. The idea of an Andean utopia, a fusion of preconquest customs with elements of Christianity, fueled the rebels, as Alberto Flores Galindo had shown in his evocative study *Buscando un Inca*.[47] The Túpac Amaru Rebellion illustrates the power of so-called Inca nationalism as a counterhegemonic discourse in Peru, a fact that Spanish officials realized at the time. In a 1781 discussion of the causes of the uprising, Cuzco's Bishop Juan Manuel Moscoso explicitly connected the memory of the Inca empire with an indigenous propensity to revolt, commenting that "Indians everywhere present to us living portraits of that age which they wish to see restored to the total prescription of the laws of the gospel."[48] Cuzco's intendant similarly felt that the indigenous nobility's memory of "their antiquities and freedom" led only to "hatred of the dominant nation."[49] Invocations of the Incas and commemoration of their empire, such men argued, helped power resistance to the colonial state. It underpinned indigenous opposition to domination by peninsular Spaniards and creoles alike.

After the rebellion's defeat the Spanish state responded with a deliberate assault on the symbols of Inca nationalism. Even prior to the capture of Túpac Amaru, Cuzco's bishop had called for the destruction of all portraits of the Inca nobility and Incaic coats of arms, and for the prohibition of Inca-style garments.[50] The indigenous population was likewise discouraged from wearing black "as a sign of mourning for the death of their last emperor." Certain dances were prohibited, and Garcilaso de la Vega's *Comentarios Reales* was censored.[51] In 1782 rebel *cacicazgos* (the area under the authority of a *cacique*, or local indigenous leader) were suppressed, and the crown further abolished Inca titles of nobility, the use of which "makes a profound impression on those of their class."[52] This period thus saw the end of seventeenth- and early-eighteenth-century customs that had presented the Spanish viceroys as the continuation of the Incas, and which had allowed the indigenous nobility to parade in Inca garb through the streets of Cuzco and Lima.[53] This assault on the emblems of Inca prestige continued until the last years of the colony. After the 1805 conspiracy by Gabriel Aguilar and Manuel Ubalde, which had aimed (in a rather unlikely fashion) at installing an Inca on a Peruvian throne, the fiscal of the Council of the Indies (and former intendent of Cuzco) Benito de Mata Linares urged the crown to implement measures aimed at eradicating any remaining influence of the Inca nobility. Citing his "thirty year's experience" in Peru, and blaming the Aguilar and Ubalde plot on the "superstitious obedience and blind love which all the Indians profess for those who claim to descend from the old Incas their sovereigns," he called for the expulsion of Inca nobles from Cuzco, the prohibition of any festivals or cofraternities "which remind the Indians of their former domination," and the installation of troops on the Inca ruins of Sacsahuaman.[54]

The Túpac Amaru Rebellion, with its attempted revival of an Inca state, formed a persistent memory that loomed over subsequent attempts at revolution in Peru. For creoles, the recollection of the generalized attack on whites was a source of deep anxiety. As Flores Galindo has noted, creole intellectuals came to see themselves as a threatened minority. "Uncertainty, doubt, insecurity defined this intellectual elite . . . Only at the eleventh hour would they join the patriot ranks."[55] Thus the creole elite, the motor for revolution in many other regions, remained quiescent in Peru well into the 1810s. For Peru's indigenous majority, on the other hand, the idea that the Inca would return to avenge his people (the myth of Inkarrí) served to mobilize further opposition to white domination. During the wars of independence rumors of the advent of "the Inca king" prompted several indigenous revolts directed equally against all whites. In Tarma in 1812, for example, residents claimed that they had been told that "a gentleman was coming, a son or relative of the Inca King, to cut off the heads of all the whites, take away their things and estates, so that the Indians would again be masters of their lands."[56] For the Andean population, the Inca empire could become an emblem of indigenous unity against creoles and Peninsulars alike.

The legacy of the Túpac Amaru Rebellion meant that the viceroyalty of Peru entered the era of independence with a very different relationship to the indigenous past from regions such as Mexico, where no comparable indigenous uprising had occurred prior to Hidalgo's 1810 revolt. In Peru, the celebration of the preconquest state was inextricably linked to a broad attempt at social and political revolution which had aimed to overturn not only Spanish colonialism but also the racial hierarchies of Peruvian society. In Peru the rhetoric of indianesque nationalism carried a charge, a significance, that it lacked elsewhere. Peruvian royalists indeed stressed that it could lead only to the extermination of all whites; the royalist commander Pío de Tristán thus warned that the insurgents were on track to "eliminate from this hemisphere all castes that are not the one that would re-establish the empire of the pagan Incas."[57] Under these circumstances, the adoption of the indianesque by Peruvian insurgents is particularly meaningful, as scholars have claimed that this legacy of Inca nationalism impeded the development of creole nationalism in Peru. David Brading in particular has asserted that "unlike their Mexican counterparts, patriots in Peru had failed to create and propagate images and myths through which their *patria* could be celebrated."[58] In this and the previous chapter I have tried to show that, on the contrary, indian-esque nationalism was typical of many parts of Spanish America during the independence era, including Peru. Even Peruvian elites, traumatized though they were by the indigenous uprisings of the 1780s, employed this rhetoric once they had established their commitment to independence. The experiences of the late colonial era surely restrained the development of the independence movement in Peru, but after the Limeño elite con-verted to the insurgent cause (with San Martín's encouragement) they dis-played the same enthusiasm shown elsewhere for lauding the preconquest past and inventing indianesque iconographies. In so doing they, like other Peruvians before them, drew from the deep wells of Andean messianism. At the same time, as a number of scholars have shown, the creoles who popularized the use of the sun as an emblem of the republic had little intention of transforming the social or economic position of Peru's in-digenous peoples.[59] Instead, they sought an Andean, Incaic past stripped of its profoundly transformative potential. As Flores Galindo noted, they strove to convert the Incas into "beings from the remote past, comparable to Greek divinities: beautiful and distant."[60] The popularity that indian-esque nationalism enjoyed even in Peru underlines how far removed this ideology was from a serious critique of the status of the contemporary indigenous population. It was sufficiently disconnected from questions of genuine indigenous empowerment as to allow Peru's creole insurgents to invoke the rights of the sixteenth-century Inca Túpac Amaru without at the same time summoning the menacing shade of the eighteenth-century revolutionary Túpac Amaru.[61]

SYMBOLIZING THE POSTINDEPENDENCE STATE

Indian princesses and Incaic suns were small elements of the nation-building process initiated at independence, which sought to endow Span-ish America with its own usable past. Representations of this past were displayed on the emblems of the new Spanish American states in order to proclaim their dignity and historic autonomy. After independence these states (and their successors) would continue to represent themselves with official iconographies, but they were under no ideological compulsion to continue using the same emblems and symbols to do so. Moreover, after independence patriotic myth making no longer necessitated trawling the distant past for heroism, as an entirely new pantheon lay at hand in the persons of the *próceres*—or heroes—of independence.

The decades after 1840 saw the development of the state cult of the heroes of independence, whose importance was proclaimed not only in history texts and patriotic speeches but also via statues, postage stamps, coinage, and the geography of Spanish America itself.[62] The roots of this cult lay in the independence era, which saw the first efforts at official commemoration. From 1818, for example, the Porteño newspaper *El Abogado Nacional* began publishing biographies of San Martín and other military leaders.[63] In 1825 the colonial Audiencia of Charcas was renamed first "Bolívar" and then "Bolivia" in honor of Simón Bolívar. In Peru a series of men including Mateo Pumacahua and Vicente Angulo were declared national heroes in 1823. In the same year Miguel Hidalgo's remains were ceremonially interred in the Mexico City cathedral, and some patriots recommended renaming the town of Dolores (where Hidalgo had begun the insurgency in 1810) "Villa de Hidalgo."[64] Moreover, patriotic orators began to invoke not the shades of Atahualpa, Lautaro, and Montezuma but rather those of the revolutionary heroes themselves: "Respectable shades of the many patriots who have watered the tree of liberty with your own blood and who rest in the grave, if my voice can reach you, come forth for a moment from the depths of your tombs and contemplate the crimes that are committed in the land that you wished to make happy," intoned one young writer in 1820 Río de la Plata.[65] "Venerable spirits of the fearless Hidalgos, Allendes, Morelos, Matamoros, Galianos, Guerreros and Abosolas," declaimed the speaker at Puebla's 1833 independence day celebrations, "accept this sacrifice from my convulsed lips and rest tranquilly in the silence of your tombs."[66] An 1827 civic festival held in Toluca to celebrate Mexican independence similarly included "fourteen boys richly garbed" not as Aztecs but as Hidalgo and Allende.[67] States, moreover, began trying to "nationalize" the heroes of independence, whose achievements might be admired by the entire world but who belonged to the individual countries that claimed them as their own. "The glories of the Great Bolívar are Venezuela's," insisted officials in 1840s Caracas.[68] Here, in the independence era, national elites believed to have found a pristine historical moment ideally suited to represent the nation, far more satisfactory than the independence-era celebration of Aztecs and Incas. To demonstrate its importance writers began to compare the period of independence with the achievements of European antiquity, much as indianesque nationalism had stressed the similarities between the classical world and the Aztec and Inca empires. As always, European history provided the touchstone for elite nationalists in Spanish America. Referring to republican Río de la Plata's 1811 campaign against royalist forces in Montevideo, the liberal Argentine historian Vicente Fidel López declared: "This part of our history is unique. With the exception of the Peloponnesian War, when Athens, amid glories and disasters, lost its fatal dominance over the other Greek hegemonies, the history of the world presents no event as worthy of study and as interesting as that offered by the peoples of Río de la Plata in this emergency."[69] "One day this Iliad will find its Homer!" exclaimed a Mexican orator in 1868, alluding to independence.[70]

The official celebration of these heroes manifested itself most flamboyantly during eras of economic growth and political stability, often, but not always, under the auspices of liberal governments; it was in such periods that states were most able to disseminate their visions of the nation through public acts of commemoration. Liberals were also attracted to the possibility of constructing a secular alternative to the panoply of saints celebrated by the Catholic Church, whose authority they generally opposed.[71] Peru dedicated its first statue to Bolívar in 1858 in the midst of the guano boom; the same decade saw the publication of the first works of official history, which were devoted in large part to the independence era.[72] In Venezuela the celebration of Bolívar grew markedly under the auspices of the liberal caudillo Antonio Guzmán Blanco, who between 1870 and 1887 presided over the establishment of a strong, not to say dictatorial, central government. Those years witnessed the creation of a growing number of civic festivals dedicated to Bolívar's memory; a national exhibition in honor of the centenary of his birth; and the systematic erection of commemorative monuments. In addition, in 1879 the currency of Venezuela was renamed the bolívar.[73] Even in areas where stability proved elusive, the development of a cult of the próceres usually reflected an attempt at elite nation-building. In Río de la Plata, the 1852 defeat of Juan Manuel de Rosas was followed by both a series of civil conflicts aimed at establishing a united Argentina and a concerted effort at creating a pantheon of "national" heroes. Independence-era figures such as San Martín and Belgrano were honored not only in the lengthy biographies of Bartolomé Mitre but also on bank notes, postage stamps, and commemorative statuary.[74] By the 1880s so thoroughly were the leaders of independence enthroned as national icons in Colombia that the conservative writer Soledad Acosta de Samper could announce, somewhat regretfully: "We have no popular heroes other than those of the war of independence."[75]

Progress in establishing this heroic pantheon can be traced through nineteenth-century maps, which record the ever-increasing accumulation of commemorative place-names recalling the leaders of the wars of independence. In Mexico, Vicente Guerrero was the first insurgent to have a region named in his honor; in 1849 the nation acquired the state of Guerrero. With the mid-century liberal reform era came the states of Hidalgo and Morelos, and Iturbide became a territory under the emperor Maximilian. The colonial city of Valladolid was likewise rebaptized "Morelia," also in honor of José María Morelos.[76] Simón Bolívar was commemorated in cities and provinces in Argentina, Bolivia, Colombia, Ecuador, Peru, and Venezuela. Venezuela, for example, renamed the colonial city of Santo Tomás de Angostura "Ciudad Bolívar" in 1846, and by 1874 an entire province was created bearing Bolívar's name.[77] Colombia established not only the department of Bolívar but also the departments of Santander, Nariño, and Sucre.[78] Chile created the Provincia de O'Higgins in 1883, named after the insurgent leader Bernardo O'Higgins.[79] By 1891 there were seventy-eight places in Argentina named "San Martín," and some twenty named "Veinticinco de Mayo" after the date on which Buenos Aires made its first moves toward independence. The scale of this process of substitution is evident in the Venezuelan Constitution of 1901, which lists the nation's provinces as follows: "Apure, Aragua, Bolívar (formerly Guayana), Barcelona, Carabobo, Cojedes, Falcón (formerly Coro), Guárico, Lara (formerly Barquisimeto), Mérida, Miranda (formerly Caracas), Maturin, Sucre (formerly Cumaná), Nueva Esparta (formerly Margarita), Portuguesa, Táchira, Trujillo, Yaracury, Zamora (formerly Barinas), and Zulia (formerly Maracaibo)."[80] "One does not invent geography," insisted a Colombian scholar in 1884, but states did invent geographical names.[81]

With the development of the cult of the próceres came the abandonment of indianesque iconography on state emblems. Several forces explain this development. First, the fierce repudiation of colonial heritage inherent in indianesque nationalism never sat comfortably with the region's creoles; as I noted in the previous chapter, elite revolutionaries had oscillated between the wholehearted endorsement of the preconquest past as the wellspring of nationality and the insistence that their own status and importance derived precisely from their Spanish heritage. Even while suggesting in 1812 that patriots should refer to themselves as "Indians," the *Aurora de Chile* had acknowledged that this might result in "some inconvenience," which, the author of the proposal noted disingenuously, "I am unable to understand."[82] The tensions inherent in indianesque representations of the state mitigated against its survival as an articulation of elite nationalism in the decades after independence. This discomfort caused by the unstable independence-era alliance of preconquest Indians and creole revolutionaries is evident in the pains that later generations of scholars took to dismiss indianesque nationalism as mere whimsy or inexplicable insurgent nonsense. From the 1840s the oddities of insurgent rhetoric became a topic of regular comment by writers of all political persuasions. The conservative Peruvian priest Bartolomé Herrera in 1846 described the independence-era view that "Peruvian independence and the reconquest of the Inca empire . . . [were] one and the same thing" as "one of the *truly crazy ideas* of which there was no shortage during the period of emancipation."[83] The liberal Argentine writers of the Generation of 1837 commented on the peculiar taste of the insurgents, whose bizarre fascination with the preconquest era had led to such rhetorical excesses. Vicente Fidel López, for instance, observed that:

> In those days, wishing to ennoble itself with grandiose and poetic traditions, in imitation of European nations, the *peculiar* patriotism of the sons of the European conquistadors turned its back on the heroic traditions of their race, because of local grievances, and showed itself enamoured of, enthusiastic for, the opulent legends and memories left in American lands by the majestic and opulent Inca Empire. All the rancour that the indigenous race might have invoked against the sixteenth-century conquest (if they had revived and recovered their lands) had by some *curious* process transferred itself to the hearts and patriotism of the sons of those very conquistadors, who had made their own the complaints that would have been just in the

mouths of the original Indians, but which in the mouths of the heirs of the conquest were simply *absurd*.[84]

The idea of placing a descendant of the Incas to an Argentine throne—the "Inca Plan" so popular with Manuel Belgrano in 1816—López described as "absurd," "burlesque," a "senseless pretension," "theatrical nonsense."[85] Indianesque nationalism, such men insisted, was an embarrassing aberration because it denied their essentially Spanish heritage.

Equally important in understanding the abandonment of indianesque symbolism was the pervasive fear of disorder that haunted the creole imagination throughout the century. The indigenous imagery used during independence began to evoke not historic autonomy but rather latent anxieties about Spanish America's capacity for progress. Perhaps, as hostile royalists had hinted during the wars of independence, indigenous symbols simply made manifest the region's essential barbarism. Fears that the continent was descending into uncivilized chaos were expressed with particular clarity by the Argentine liberal and future president Domingo Faustino Sarmiento. In Chile, where he had been exiled for his opposition to Rosas, Sarmiento composed a pithy denunciation of caudillo rule that contrasted the small pockets of civilization observable in cities with the vast, barbarous wasteland that constituted the majority of Argentine territory. It was from the countryside that uncivilized caudillo rulers like Facundo Quiroga (the book's ostensible target) and Rosas himself emerged, buttressed by the support of the rural population. *Civilization and Barbarism*, published first in 1845, again in 1851, in French in 1853, and subsequently in other languages, achieved such circulation largely because it articulated widespread creole fears about the inherent backwardness of the mass of the population and their tendency to support dubious caudillo rulers such as the Argentine Rosas or the Guatemalan Rafael Carrera. For Sarmiento it was the Indians, together with the mixed-race peoples who inhabited rural areas, who were responsible for the continent's lack of progress. During the colonial period he wrote: "Two distinct, rival and incompatible forms of society, two differing kinds of civilization existed . . . : one being wholly Spanish, European and cultivated, the other barbarous, American and almost wholly of native growth."[86] The indigenous, the native, the American, had become a sign of barbarism, not a source of pride.

Indigenous iconography thus began to disappear from state emblems in the decades after independence. In 1836 the Venezuelan government decided to replace the bow and arrow on its state shield, "which today are exclusively the weapons of savage peoples," with a European sword and lance intended to denote "the triumph of civilized and cultured peoples."[87] Indigenous imagery now represented the barbarous indigenous present rather than historic autonomy and the glorious indigenous past. In Colombia, the revolutionary Indian who had symbolized liberty and the republican state was replaced with more classical images. After 1821 a feminine bust garbed in a toga was employed on coinage in preference to the Indian princess embossed on previous coins, as Hans-Joachim König has noted. The classical bust was described in later decades as a "bust of the republic," whereas the Indian princess was said to have been simply an "Indian woman crowned with feathers"; an indigenous woman, it seems, now represented only herself, not the republic.[88] In Peru, the solar face on the first national shield was replaced in 1825 by a new design showing a vicuña, a quinine tree, and a cornucopia, items that (aside from the classical cornucopia) were local but not specifically indigenous. In addition, the Orden del Sol was abolished altogether on the grounds that it "conformed poorly" to the republican ethos.[89] In a wholly emblematic fashion the official newspaper published in Cuzco in 1829 changed its name from the indianesque *Cuzco Sun* to the *Cuzco Minerva*.[90] The Roman goddess of wisdom replaced the Incaic sun. New place-names likewise ceased honoring the Araucanians and the Aztecs, and when indigenous imagery was preserved it was often reinterpreted.[91] The radiant sun used to this day on Argentine flags and coinage continued to be extolled as an emblem of the state, but its specifically Incaic associations were replaced with a more generalized link to freedom and the May Revolution.[92]

Elite dissatisfaction with the use of indigenous imagery within the symbols of nationality is illustrated clearly by the rewriting of independence-era national anthems that took place in several countries in the last decades of the nineteenth century. For example, Peru's national anthem, composed in 1821, lamented the nation's three centuries of subjugation at the hands of the Spanish and presented independence as a vindication of Peru's "Inca and Lord."[93] In the early republican period an additional stanza, derived from another independence-era song, was incorporated into the national anthem as the first verse. The lyrics described the cruel oppression that Peruvians had suffered under Spanish rule:

Long years the oppressed Peruvian
Dragged the ominous chain:
Condemned to a cruel servitude
Long years he groaned in silence.[94]

Independence-era Peruvians would have recognized this metaphor, which presented all Americans as the heirs to the defeated Incas, subjected to three hundred years of slavery at the hands of the usurping Spanish. By the end of the nineteenth century, however, the suggestion that Peru was a (metaphorical) reincarnation of the Inca empire held little appeal for the Peruvian state, equipped as it now was with heroes of a more recent vintage. Peruvian officials began to look closely at these lyrics, and they were not pleased with what they saw. In particular, the references to Peru's oppression at the hands of the Spanish were deemed insufficiently glorious for a national anthem, and in 1901 the government ordered the lyrics to be changed. Determined to replace these "humiliating" and "antiquated" verses with something more elevating, the government of Eduardo López de Romaña—flush from a decade of sustained economic growth—commissioned four new stanzas from the modernist poet José Santos Chocano. These new verses contained no references to subjugation, slavery, chains, or Incas. They instead celebrated the achievements of San Martín and the importance of industry.[95]

The mere presence of allegorical indigenous figures in sites of official commemoration became problematic, notwithstanding their previous ubiquity in independence-era iconography. In Quito the unveiling in 1892 of a statue to the insurgent hero Antonio José de Sucre provoked outrage because it depicted the prócer "in the attitude of liberating and protecting a young Indian woman [intended to symbolize] the motherland." Commentators objected that Sucre, far from liberating an allegorical motherland, appeared to be embracing a "bashful and intimidated Indian woman." Instead of representing the patria, the indigenous figure merely provoked embarrassing suspicions of an improper relationship between the independence hero and an indigenous woman.[96] In her analysis of this incident Blanca Muratorio has stressed the concerns about mestizaje that underlay the objections to the statue; here I would like to highlight what it reveals about the transformation in the iconographic potential of the figure of the Indian over the nineteenth century. In 1825 the intimate mingling of próceres and indigenous women in the commemorative plaque designed for the chambers of the Bolivian Constitutional Assembly—with its "beautiful Indian girl, symbolizing America, . . . embracing . . . the Grand Marshal of Ayacucho [Sucre]"—had aroused no protest because the use of indigenous figures to represent the state served a necessary nationalist function. By the end of the century, however, a statue of an indigenous woman was merely an indigenous woman and not an emblem of liberty or a symbol of Ecuador, much as the *india coronada* (crowned Indian woman) embossed on Colombian independence-era coins began to be viewed simply as a depiction of an indigenous woman. Indigenous figures no longer possessed the allegorical power to represent the state that they had enjoyed during the independence era.

THE PERSISTENCE OF MEMORY

Yet while indigenous imagery lost much of its earlier ability to represent the state, indianesque nationalism nonetheless exerted a subtle lure on elite discourse, for it had framed the expression of patriotism during the independence era and provided Spanish American nations with a coherent nationalist language complete with its own symbols and emblems. Thus the rejection of indigenous imagery was nowhere complete, and the symbols of indianesque nationalism—Incas, Aztecs, Indian princesses— continued to appear even in some state emblems. At roughly the same time that Peru revised its national anthem to eliminate references to the indigenous past, it issued a stamp depicting the Inca Atahualpa.[97] In 1878 the Guatemalan state placed an Indian princess on a stamp (see figure 1). In Mexico the government of Porfirio Díaz erected several statues to preconquest figures, including a monument to the Aztec prince Cuauhtémoc that was unveiled in Mexico City amid considerable public ceremony in 1887 (see figure 3).[98] The Mexican state likewise never abandoned its Aztec-inspired coat of arms.

In the right setting indianesque nationalism retained considerable vitality as a patriotic, anticolonial discourse. In Cuba, which remained a colony of Spain until 1898, proindependence sentiments did not gain momentum until the 1850s. With the advent of a coherent nationalist movement, however, came the articulation of an indianesque version of Cuban history stressing the importance of the island's precolonial heritage. Various works of patriotic poetry and prose celebrated Cuba's conquest-era population, emphasizing both its historic liberty and its enslavement at the hands of the Spanish. José Fornaris's 1855 *Cantos de Siboney*, for example, eulogized the island peoples massacred by the Spanish in the early sixteenth century. Fornaris, like the creole insurgents of the 1810s, presented these conquest-era peoples as ancestors to the current generation of revolutionaries.[99] Other works such as Pedro Santacilia's *Lecciones orales sobre la historia de Cuba*, published in New Orleans in 1859, not only condemned the Spanish conquest but also lauded the heroic behavior of the indigenous cacique Hatuey, who renounced his conversion to Catholicism on learning that he might encounter Spaniards in Heaven. Like the creole patriots of the 1810s, Santacilia compared Cuba's indigenous population to the ancient Romans. He described Hatuey as "that Indian with the heart of a Roman, worthy of figuring among the heroes of antiquity."[100] Others stressed Hatuey's patriotism. In Juan Cristóbal Nápoles Fajardo's poem "Hatuey and Guarina" patriotism compels the chief to leave his beloved Guarina and fight the Spaniards: "I must—oh sorrow! / be deaf to the voice of love / because the patria calls me," he explains.[101] As Christopher Schmidt-Nowara has noted, "The construction of Antillean prehistory was a patriotic endeavour, an attempt to craft a national history and to create national symbols . . . Prehistory became a space of national authenticity and autonomy from Spain."[102] The development in midcentury Cuba of indianesque rhetoric hints at its powerful ability to articulate anticolonial sentiment within a nationalist framework.

Elsewhere in Spanish America, even while postindependence governments removed indigenous iconography from their state symbols, unhappy with the idea that their modern nations might be represented by archaic Indians, poets and writers demonstrated the continuing vitality of indianesque nationalism as a patriotic language for discussing the independence era itself. Its association with the wars of independence gave it a certain authenticity and power to evoke the period's glories. It was, as the Peruvian writer Manuel Fuentes noted sarcastically in 1866, "the phraseology invented about half a century ago and repeated by *patriots* ever since."[103] For many decades after the events they honored, the civic festivals held to commemorate independence from Spain, particularly those held under the auspices of liberal governments, were the preserve of indianesque nationalism. An independence-day speech delivered in Arequipa in 1864 illustrates precisely the tendencies deplored by Fuentes: the speaker denounced the colonial "three centuries of horror" during which "the descendants of the great Manco Capac and the inhabitants of all America wept with the tears of a slave."[104] Such rhetoric characterized civic festivals in many parts of Spanish America. "The laments of Moctezuma, the pitiful signs of Atahualpa reached the heavens. Spaniards: do you not recall how the ill-starred Cuauhtémoc expired amid pain and torments? Do you not recall Xicotencal of Tlaxcala [a warrior and statesman executed by the Spanish in 1521], who . . . floundering in his own blood, bequeathed you a thousand curses for your cruelty?" asked Manuel Zacarías Velázquez in his 1844 independence day speech delivered in Guatemala City, far from the Inca and Aztec heartlands.[105]

In Mexico patriotic writers in particular continued for many decades to draw from the deep wells of indianesque nationalism when discussing independence, which surely reflects the firm roots that creole patriotism had established in colonial Mexico. The writings produced by both liberals and moderates in celebration of independence lauded precolonial Mexico as a terrestrial paradise inhabited by wise ancestral figures. One 1851 speech, for example, evoked preconquest Mexico in the following excess of rhetoric: "Hernán Cortés plies the waves in the ship of his ambition, propelled by the winds of his pride, and sights a new world, whose innocent inhabitants until that moment lived peacefully in their dwellings enjoying the finest fruits of the soil. The trees were inhabited by a thousand colourful birds which happily sang out their freedom. The fields were sown with exquisite flowers, which tinted the emerald green with which nature garbed them; their fragrance and odour perfumed the air. The waters that ran in the brooks were crystalline; the lamb enjoyed them without thinking of the Wolf that wished to devour it. Over the roofs of our ancestors' simple dwellings the beautiful sun shone its brilliant rays . . . And all was happiness!"[106]

The passing of these great civilizations was presented in independence day poetry as a tragedy of epic proportions. Orators lamented the defeat by the conquistadors of "our ancestors the Indians" and continued to decry Spain's "usurpation" of the Aztec empire and the imposition of three centuries of slavery, just as they had done during the independence years.[107] Independence therefore avenged the Aztecs; its leaders were "Moctezuma's worthy offspring," "the sons of Anáhuac."[108] Missing from most non-Mexican independence day writings, however, was this insistence on a genealogical link, albeit metaphorical, with the indigenous past. With rare exceptions (such as the Cuban case discussed above), writers outside of Mexico ceased to present themselves as the sons of the preconquest heroes whose overthrow independence avenged.[109] This most characteristic and distinctive aspect of independence-era patriotism was abandoned in most other parts of Spanish America in the first decades after independence, despite the retention of other aspects of the indianesque. If Spanish Americans were not the sons of the Incas and the Araucanians, then whose children were they? The search for the fathers is the subject of the next chapter.

 *Chapter 3*

"Padres de la Patria": Nations and Ancestors

In 1894 a debate took place among Mexico City's leading newspapers, prompted by an article written by Francisco Cosmes for the independence day celebrations of that year. Cosmes, an influential journalist and politician, had titled his piece "To Whom Do We Owe the Fatherland?" and it was his answer that proved provocative. Mexico's true father, Cosmes proclaimed proudly, was none other than the conquistador Hernán Cortés: "The Patria was born, not in 1810, not in 1821, but on the day that Cortés, its true father, established the foundations of Mexican nationality."[1] To this assault on Miguel Hidalgo's (and Agustín de Iturbide's) status as "founding fathers," Cosmes appended an extended attack on those misguided individuals who believed "that the Mexico of today—that is, a society that speaks Spanish, is civilized along European lines, and keeps the Indian firmly under foot—was conquered by Cortés and dominated by the viceroys, and that independence was a vindication of the rights of that nation defeated by the Spanish. Even today there are persons of good faith who, like modern-day Calypsos, are inconsolable because Cuauhtémoc's feet were burned."[2]

The version of national history ridiculed here by Cosmes is precisely the one that I outlined in the first chapter of this book. Cosmes, however, had little time for indianesque nationalism. Mexico's civilization, he announced, was Spanish, "owing nothing to the Aztecs, not even descending from them." In the previous chapter I began to sketch the erasure of indigenous imagery from the emblems of the state; Cosmes's polemical essay, however, advocated far more than the mere removal of indigenous figures from coins and coats of arms. Instead, he proposed to uproot the indigenous past from the nation's very history. In his article Cosmes offered a defense of Mexico's Spanish heritage that excluded any indigenous legacy whatsoever.

Had elite Mexican patriotism traveled so far from the independence era that by 1894 every vestige of the preconquest past was rejected with the thoroughness recommended by Cosmes? In fact, Cosmes did not enunciate a majority view even among the Porfirian elite. Reactions to his article ranged from approval to horror, and the responses fell along political lines. Conservative newspapers were delighted. This was the first time, proclaimed the conservative *Voz de México*, that a liberal writer "had given voice to his race, to the glory of his race, to the history of his race"—Mexico's "race" being in their eyes Hispanic. They were particularly pleased with Cosmes's attack on those who saw independence as a revindication of the Aztec empire; patriotism, they felt, had at last "abandon[ed] the enchilada stall in favor of the church."[3] It was high time, in their view, that Mexico stopped pretending to be Indian and accepted its Christian identity. Liberal newspapers, on the other hand, were scandalized. *El Siglo XIX*, the most influential liberal paper, likened Cosmes's article to the scribblings of the Spanish journalist Adolfo Llanos de Alcaraz, who in past decades had used the occasion of 16 September [Mexico's independence day] to publish "some article praising the conquistadors, denigrating our heroes, and insulting Mexicans." Llanos de Alcaraz had been obliged to leave the country, the paper observed suggestively.[4] The liberal *Monitor Republicano* agreed with Cosmes that Mexican independence was not a revindication of the Aztecs, but it was unwilling to endorse his claim that Cortés was the nation's founding father. That opinion, it felt, was "foolish and unpatriotic"; the correct view was that the arrival of Cortés was part of the slow movement of progress, of which the conquistador himself was unaware.[5] *El Diario del Hogar* in turn maintained that Cortés, far from being Mexico's father, was "at most our step-father." In order to support this claim it asked several notable academics to comment on Cosmes's article, but their remarks clarified nothing. The historian Ezequiel Chávez maintained that the true founders of Mexican nationality were the Catholic missionaries who followed in Cortés's wake, and also the insurgents of 1810. The liberal writer and politician Justo Sierra offered a convoluted definition of the difference between "nationality" and "nation," asserting that Cortés was the "founder of [Mexican] nationality," while leaving to Hidalgo the honor of being the "padre de la patria," or "father of the nation."[6]

Cosmes responded to these criticisms by opining that his views were clearly too advanced for the time.[7] Everyone, however, agreed with his assertion that in previous decades the celebrations of national independence held on 16 September had been highly deficient. The "invectives against Spain" and the "typical slogan of 'three centuries of odious servitude'" (referring to the colonial period) that had characterized earlier celebrations were universally rejected as "savage" and unworthy.[8] Everyone, moreover, accepted without comment Cosmes's framing of the question of Mexico's history within the language of paternity. "Who," they all asked, "was Mexico's true father?" These events reveal both continuities and discontinuities in the rhetoric of Mexican elite nationalism in the eighty-odd years since the war of independence from Spain. During the wars of independence, as I argued in the previous chapters, the patriotic rhetoric of indianesque nationalism prescribed a distinctive genealogy for the emergent Mexican nation, which was declared to be a continuation of the Aztec empire. Even more strikingly, the leaders of independence had presented themselves as the heirs of the great Aztec heroes, the sons of Anáhuac. The 1894 debate between Cosmes and his interlocutors suggests that this vision of nationality retained some adherents in late-nineteenth-century Mexico (those "persons of good faith who are inconsolable because Cuauhtémoc's feet were burned"), but that it no longer enjoyed hegemonic sway over Mexican elite nationalists. Other versions of Mexico's ancestry also clamored for attention. If Mexicans were not the sons of Cuauhtémoc, perhaps they were instead the sons of the conquistador Hernán Cortés, as Cosmes suggested, or perhaps of heroes of a more recent vintage, such as the independence leader Miguel Hidalgo whose paternity Justo Sierra championed. Unchanging, however, was the tendency to approach the idea of the nation via the language of genealogy. In this chapter I examine the use of genealogical metaphors to articulate images of the nation's history. I focus particularly on the relative importance of the preconquest, colonial, and independence eras to elite understandings of the nation. In so doing I highlight the intertwining of personal and national heritage that took place within elite nationalism. When politicians and thinkers asked who "our" fathers were, they were inquiring simultaneously about their personal genealogies and the origins of the state, in ways that illustrate particularly clearly the tendency for these men (and the occasional woman) to view the nation as essentially their own.

By the 1840s the different political and economic tendencies arising from independence had solidified into political parties in most parts of Spanish America. Historians have often attempted to map political affiliation onto social, regional, or economic categories; less attention has been paid to how political affiliation correlated with attitudes toward national history. In fact, conservatives across Spanish America held nearly identical views on their nations' origins. Rejecting the independence-era idea that their patrias dated back to preconquest days, conservative writers suggested that birth, or at least conception, occurred not in the distant pre-Columbian era but rather in 1492 with Columbus's arrival in the Americas (or possibly a few years later, depending on the speed with which Spain's civilizing influence was thought to spread). This was the opinion of the conservative Peruvian priest Bartolomé Herrera, who in his 1846 sermon on Peruvian independence explained that, following Peru's birth at the time of the conquest, it had enjoyed a happy childhood under Spain's maternal care: "For three centuries the motherland carried us in her arms." The Republic of Peru was thus "not conquered but created by the conquest."[9] Similar views were expressed roughly two decades later in Guatemala by another priest, who, on the occasion of Guatemala's independence day, asserted that during the colonial period the infant America had sat contentedly in the "Motherland's lap." Like Herrera, he regarded Columbus's arrival in the Americas as the beginning of history: "Here, gentlemen, is the first day of our appearance in the life of nations."[10] This was essentially the same view advanced by the *Voz de México* in 1894.

Particularly characteristic of such conservative rhetoric was an extended complaint about the anti-Spanish, indianesque version of history inherited from the independence era. "It is absurd and ridiculous to continue vociferating against the Spanish, we who are their sons, from whom we have received everything: civilization, language, habits, customs, and the greatest of all gifts: the Christian religion," insisted the Colombian officer Joaquín Posada Gutiérrez in his memoirs.[11] Conservatives thus condemned as irrelevant all denunciations of the conquest. "What good would it do us today to speak of the cruelties of Pizarro and Cortés? To declaim pointlessly, to perorate vainly and needlessly?" asked the Guatemalan José Milla in 1846.[12] In the same year the Mexican conservative Antonio G. del Palacio explained in his 16 September independence-day oration: "Gone are the days in which celebrating independence meant arousing your ire against your fathers, because . . . why confuse ourselves? Our ancestors are the descendants of the conquistadors."[13]

Conservatives thus offered an alternative ancestry; rather than being the sons of Montezuma or Atahualpa, they were the scions of Spain. In a speech for 16 September 1850 that drew particular praise from conservative newspapers the Mexican poet José Ignacio Esteva hailed the conquest for having brought Christianity to Mexico and thus ending Aztec cannibalism and human sacrifice. Refusing to condemn the conquistadores, he proudly proclaimed that "we are all sons or grandsons of the conquistadors, and our patria is likewise the daughter of [Spain]."[14] The conquistadors, rather than preconquest indigenes, were thus "our ancestors." Similar views were expressed in 1853 by a conservative orator in San Salvador, who explained that in his independence-day speech he would not insult the Spanish because they were "our fathers" and "our brothers."[15] Since Spanish Americans were Iberia's children, to view Spain with anything other than gratitude and veneration would be to "spit in the face of our fathers."[16] The Indians, far from being our fathers, were merely "our predecessors in the use of this land," in the words of one Colombian conservative.[17] Conservatives thus rejected explicitly the idea that they were the descendants of preconquest cultures, and they offered instead an alternative, Iberian genealogy.

Accompanying such ringing declarations of Spanish ancestry was a defense of the conquest as the origin of contemporary Spanish American society. The spokesman of Mexican conservatism, Lucas Alamán—heir to a wealthy Guanajuato mining family who held various government posts in the decades after independence—generated a voluminous body of writings on Mexican history and politics. As David Brading has noted, Alamán "dismissed [Bustamante's] attempt to constitute the Aztec empire as the historical foundation of contemporary Mexico," insisting that "we are not the nation despoiled by the Spaniards but one in which everything originated with the conquest."[18] Alamán expatiated on this theme time and time again, setting the tone for all future conservative histories of Mexico. The conquest, he wrote, "created a new nation in which there remained no trace of that which had gone before: religion, language, customs, laws, inhabitants: all are the result of the conquest."[19] Conservatives elsewhere shared

Alamán's insistence that the continent's culture was essentially Spanish. Central American conservatives noted that during the colonial period the Spanish "transmitted to us their religion, their language, their habits and their customs: they shared with us their knowledge and their industry, their legislation was our legislation, with the modifications required by our circumstances . . . we must confess that our social order owes everything to Spain."[20] "'Atrocious or not, [the conquest] is the origin of our rights and our existence,'" wrote the conservative Venezuelan savant Andrés Bello.[21]

More dramatically, some conservatives presented the relationship between the conquest and independence as consummation rather than retribution. The conquest and independence "are brothers in one cause: the cause of humanity. Humanity therefore blesses these two events, and I too, who here bless independence, must be just, as I am in my heart: I also bless the conquest," editorialized the conservative Mexican paper *El Universal* in 1851.[22] The heroes of independence were thus essentially Spanish in nature. "The genius of Simón Bolívar, his fiery eloquence, his indomitable constancy, his magnificent generosity: are these the qualities of indigenous tribes? Are they not rather characteristics that the Spanish nation should claim as its own?" asked the Colombian politician and grammarian Miguel Antonio Caro in 1881.[23] Not all conservatives went so far as to describe independence as perfecting processes begun with the conquest, but all agreed that independence was compatible with their Spanish, Catholic heritage. In the Guatemala of Rafael Carrera, for example, conservative priests developed an intricate theological justification for independence that presented Central America's 1821 Act of Independence as a special covenant between God and Guatemala in which Guatemala promised to preserve its Catholic heritage. As Douglass Sullivan-González has shown, this view was expressed par excellence in the patriotic orations delivered by the Guatemalan cleric Juan José de Aycinena, who interpreted independence as a method of preserving the faith "which we inherited from our fathers."[24] In short, whether or not independence was seen as a completion of the conquest, conservatives agreed that it was in no way a revival of preconquest empires.

Such conservative views evolved fundamentally out of the rhetoric developed by royalists during the wars of independence. In the 1810s royalist propagandists not only rejected the insurgent celebration of the preconquest era but also defended the conquest for introducing civilization and Christianity to a barbarous continent.[25] "Oh unhappy Indians! . . . Turn your eyes to the horrible, fearful chaos of slavery, idolatry and barbarism from which you were rescued by the power and religiosity of Spain," intoned one independence-era royalist tract.[26] For royalists the conquest was a triumph over evil, and the colonial period was an uplifting, if ultimately unsuccessful, act of Spanish altruism. It was, in the words of another loyalist pamphleteer, "the inspiration of God working through the Spaniards and . . . [it] was to the benefit of the Indians."[27] In addition, royalists ridiculed both the attempts by insurgents to claim metaphorical indigenous ancestry and the indianesque celebrations of indigenous achievement.[28] Later generations of conservatives drew on these discursive strands in their own defense of the conquest and rejection of indianesque nationalism, although, as I argue in the next chapter, most postindependence conservatives abandoned royalist claims that the preconquest period had been a time of utter barbarism.

Like royalists, conservatives considered Christianity to be central to the continent's identity. A particular respect for the authority of the Catholic Church, which has often been described as a key feature of nineteenth-century conservatism, thus shaped conservative responses to the past and helped valorize the conquest and colonial era as the origin of their own Christian identity. While insurgents had dismissed as mere hypocrisy Spanish claims to have introduced Christianity to the continent (and in some cases had constructed elaborate theologies that provided the hemisphere with independent access to the Gospel), conservatives embraced the conquest as the origin of their faith and, thereby, their culture. Conservative views of the past at times also reflected disenchantment with the nineteenth-century present. Alamán's five-volume *History of Mexico*, which defended his nation's colonial heritage, was published shortly after the 1847 start of the devastating indigenous uprising known as the Caste War, which threatened creole control of the Yucatan Peninsula. As David Bushnell and Neil Macaulay note, Alamán's readers could reflect on the fact that "there had been no caste wars when Hapsburg or Bourbon kings ruled Mexico."[29] To conservative eyes, such disorder, which reflected so poorly on republican governments, further highlighted the achievements of Spanish colonialism.

In 1888 a discussion took place in Buenos Aires among several of the capital's leading intellectuals about whether to replace the historic Pirámide de Mayo with a new statue. The pyramid, a marble structure erected in what is now the Plaza de Mayo in honor of the 1810 May Revolution, had undergone several face-lifts in the preceding decades, and in 1888 some thought it was due for another. The liberal historian Vicente Fidel López maintained that the existing pyramid was a tasteless mishmash unworthy of the heroic event it purported to commemorate. He called for the structure to be replaced by something more elevating. On the other hand, Andrés Lamas, another liberal writer and politician, defended the pyramid as a historic monument that ought to be preserved intact. Discussion of the pyramid led inevitably to a consideration of the meaning of the May Revolution itself. Despite disagreeing about the appropriate fate of the pyramid that commemorated it, López and Lamas agreed that independence (or more particularly, the May Revolution in Buenos Aires) marked Argentina's "point of departure, . . . the first day of its own life, of the national life of the former colony: on this day begins its history, its own exclusive history."[30]

The idea that 1810 marked their moment of birth had by the late nineteenth century become standard among the Porteño intelligentsia. The May Revolution was the "epoch in which we were born into the life of nations," as the historian and sociologist Ernesto Quesada put it in 1895.[31] This view had begun to emerge during the war of independence itself, but it was developed with particular clarity by the liberal Generation of 1837.[32] This rough grouping of individuals opposed to the rule of Juan Manuel de Rosas created the language of Argentine liberalism that became the dominant force in Argentine elite politics after the fall of Rosas in 1852. Their ideas provided the liberal program for the remainder of the century. Although most scholarly attention has focused on their infatuation with France as a model for Argentina's future, the Generation of 1837 also analyzed Argentina's past. Its members advanced their interpretation of the May Revolution in many works stressing that independence was a creative act that brought into existence something entirely new—"an American idea," as the anti-Rosas journalist José Rivera Indarte put it: the birth of the patria.[33] The poet Esteban Echeverría expressed this position clearly in his writings. "Our life and that of the Patria begin in May," he insisted.[34]

If the May Revolution marked the birth of the patria, who were its parents? Echeverría provided a poetic answer: the founding father was not one of the heroes of independence such as José de San Martín, but rather Spain itself. America, he explained, was a "virgin beloved by the creator." Spain, "with lascivious eyes gazed on her beauty . . . and for three centuries she was his slave." Echeverría thus converted the conquest into an amorous episode.[35] The fruit of this relationship was the patria. Spain, in the person of the conquistadors, was the father; America, the beautiful slave, the mother. Indians played no role whatsoever; the procreating force was Spanish. The same idea was expressed even more clearly in another poem composed for the 1844 independence day celebrations in Montevideo (where exiled members of the Generation of 1837 had gathered). For extra emphasis its author made the conquistadors and Spain both father and mother: "Our valiant but unjust *fathers* / Enslaved the Indians . . . / America in her breast will engender / A hundred Spains who will emulate the deeds / Of their common *mother*."[36] The conquistadors were the fathers of the Generation of 1837, and Spain was the mother of Argentina. The Generation of 1837 thus rejected the view that independence was a revindication of the Inca empire: "The dispute between the Indians and the conquistadors is quite different from that that arose in 1810 between Spaniards and creoles [*españoles europeos y españoles americanos*]," explained Rivera Indarte.[37] Indianesque celebrations of Indian resistance to the conquest, complained the sometime-member of the Generation of 1837 Domingo Faustino Sarmiento, feigned "a supposed fraternity with the Indians, in order to create a rift between ourselves and our fathers."[38] Spain, these writers insisted, was their parent. This did not imply that Argentine liberals admired all aspects of Spain; rather, they believed themselves to be heirs to both Spain's virtues and its vices. As Sarmiento, often described as an Hispanophobe, noted: "Spain thus reproduced itself in America: to blame it for having caused intentionally the ills it has bequeathed us would be the same as if a young black man should blame his equally black mother for conceiving the infamous and sinister plan of making him black from birth."[39] Sarmiento employed his disdain for people of color in a critique of Spain; being Spanish was in his view as undesirable as being black, but Argentina was nonetheless

Spanish. Most liberals of the Generation of 1837 shared Sarmiento's view that Argentine culture, for better or for worse, came from Spain; Juan Bautista Alberdi, whose writings provided the basis for the 1853 national constitution, made clear that Argentine civilization had European roots, while the country's persistent barbarism was an indigenous legacy. "We, who call ourselves Americans, are nothing other than Europeans born in America. Bones, blood, color, everything is from abroad," he wrote in 1852.[40]

These attitudes changed remarkably little after the influx of European immigrants in the last decades of the nineteenth century. While the nearly six million immigrants who arrived in Argentina between 1871 and 1914 had a dramatic impact on the nation's economy, they did not alter the belief of most elite intellectuals that Argentina either was or ought to be essentially Spanish in character. Although some public figures praised the cultural diversity introduced by Italian, Jewish, and Turkish immigrants, the most vociferous group of elite nationalists instead decried the increasingly "cosmopolitan" nature of Argentine, and particularly Porteño, life. Their concerns prompted the development of a *criollista* sentiment that further emphasized Argentina's Spanish roots and celebrated its colonial heritage.[41] Although this creole heritage was set in opposition to "European" culture, advocates of criollismo made clear that their mistrust of European culture did not include a rejection of Argentina's Spanish heritage. "We Argentines have not ceased to be Spanish," insisted the criollista writer Manuel Gálvez via his fictional alter ego Gabriel Quiroga.[42] For criollistas Spain was Argentina's loving mother, its "ancestral home."[43] They agreed with the Generation of 1837 that Argentina's character was essentially Spanish; they differed only in the degree of enthusiasm they felt for this Iberian heritage.

Like the conservatives who viewed independence as a completion of processes begun in the conquest, Argentine liberals argued that the roots of independence lay in the early sixteenth century. "The Argentine Republic," insisted the historian Vicente Fidel López, "is a spontaneous evolution of Spanish nationality and the Spanish race."[44] In his *Historia de San Martín* the writer and president Bartolomé Mitre located the origins of independence in the rebellious character of the conquistadores themselves, whose "spirit of individualism . . . they bequeathed to their descendents through their blood along with their instincts for independence."[45] The leaders of independence were thus the sons of the conquistadors: Argentines were thus simultaneously the sons of San Martín and the grandsons of Iberia.[46] The criollista poet Leopoldo Lugones expressed this idea clearly in his 1927 *Ancestral Poems*, which he dedicated to his forefathers: "Bartolomé Sandoval, / conquistador of Peru . . . / maestre de campo Francisco de Lugones, / . . . Don Juan de Lugones the encomendero, / . . . their son and grandson, . . . / [and] Colonel Don Lorenzo Lugones, / who marched with the first patriot army."[47] Leopoldo Lugones was the descendent of a prócer of independence who was himself the scion of a conquistador. An unbroken chain passing through the independence and colonial eras linked Lugones with his conquistador ancestor, but there the chain stopped. The Generation of 1837 and their spiritual descendants the cultural nationalists of the early twentieth century thus advanced an interpretation of the past that differed strikingly from the indianesque views propagated in Buenos Aires during the war of independence. Unlike the patriots of 1810, they did not view the May Revolution as the continuation of any prevenient indigenous empire. May, to them, represented the birth of a democratic idea, nourished by its Iberian heritage.

Chilean liberals, whose familiarity with Argentine liberalism was greatly enhanced by the presence in Chile of many exiled Argentines during the period of the Rosas dictatorship, shared with the Generation of 1837 a simultaneous belief that independence was the moment of birth of a new nation, and that the nation's ancestry was fundamentally European. Independence had engendered the Chilean nation: "It is twenty four years since . . . our beautiful Chile was born to civilization," explained one Chilean newspaper in 1834, on the anniversary of Chilean independence.[48] Thus in one sense insurgent leaders such as Bernardo O'Higgins were the "fathers of Chile."[49] At the same time, elite Chileans began to trace their ancestry back to Europe rather than to the Araucanians whom the insurgents had described as their own spiritual fathers. During the conquest, explained the historian Diego Barros Arana during the Chilean state's midcentury assault on autonomous Mapuche communities, "*our fathers* did not fight to destroy an organized nationality [or] a previously established civilization. In Chile they fought against semi-savage tribes, against peoples who were barbarous, albeit brave and steadfast."[50] Fellow historian Luis Miguel Amunátegui similarly admired the achievements of "our fathers the conquerors of America."[51] For these writers, "our fathers" were the conquistadors as much as the heroes of independence. As in Argentina, in Chile the degree of enthusiasm that elite writers felt for their Iberian heritage increased steadily as the century progressed. The socialist writer Francisco Bilbao's 1844 *Sociabilidad chilena* was an extended critique of Chile's Spanish heritage, to which Bilbao ascribed most of his nation's contemporary problems.[52] For Bilbao Chile's tragedy was precisely its Hispanic past. Fifteen years later the editor of the influential newspaper *El Mercurio* instead described Spain as "the beloved mother who caresses us," the "noble and ancient patria of our ancestors."[53] By the end of the century Chilean elites had wholly embraced their Spanish identity. "In Chile as in Peru, no one wants to be Indian, mestizo, or Araucanian, and everyone boasts of having illustrious, purely Spanish origins," observed the Peruvian ex-president Francisco García Calderón, who was exiled to Chile following his country's defeat in the War of the Pacific.[54]

Liberals elsewhere shared the view that, like it or not, their origins were Spanish. Spain, explained the Colombian liberal José María Samper, was his "patria of the past."[55] For Colombian liberals preconquest Indians might be "our ancient Indians," much as conservatives had labeled them, but the Spanish were "our fathers."[56] As was the case in Chile, this attitude was not incompatible with the oft-expressed view that the leaders of independence were the "fathers of the nation," who had signed "the Republic's birth certificate."[57] These men were the fathers of the nation, but their own heritage was Spanish. Even those who, like Sarmiento, were critical of Spain's legacy, agreed that their nation's cultures were essentially Iberian. From Peru, the writer and political radical Manuel González Prada lamented that "in our blood ferment the vices and virtues of our grandfathers," who, he made clear, were Spanish.[58] Like Sarmiento, González Prada blamed his nation's difficulties in part on this Spanish heritage. Peru, he felt, should not seek to import any further aspects of Spanish culture. To do so, he claimed, would be like transfusing the blood of a "decrepit and wasted grandfather" into a sick patient.[59] Spain, then, was Peru's aged grandfather. For these men the Spanish heritage was a poor thing but their own.

Such negative assessments of America's Hispanic heritage became increasingly uncommon as the century wore on. By the 1870s liberals in most parts of Spanish America had begun to praise the positive legacies of their Iberian parent. As the modernist Peruvian poet Luis Benjamín Cisneros asked in 1886:

What does it matter that the young nations,
in whose veins seethes
Spanish blood beneath the American sun,
brandish their various flags
on land and soil in the spherical extension,
if there is one banner that the scions
and the mother share in common . . .
. . . that of Spain?[60]

In Central America liberal writers likewise began to celebrate Spain as their historic mother. Addressing Spain, the 1897 independence-day orator in Guatemala City announced: "Today, with the passage of time, which has extinguished ancient hatreds and healed old wounds, we do not hesitate to recognize you as our mother and we Latin Americans can say how much and how truly we love you." Celebrating independence, he asserted, should not require him to "hurl a thousand hurtful accusations against the motherland."[61] Spain, explained a Honduran writer, was the beloved "mother of our fathers."[62]

In Mexico, appreciation of the colonial era was expressed particularly strongly in the years after 1871, which saw an intense dissemination of nationalist rhetoric under the auspices of the dominant liberal party.[63] Previously, liberals and moderates had persisted in denouncing the suffering inflicted during the colonial period, sometimes with an eroticism similar to that employed by the Argentine poet Echeverría. "To [Columbus's] eyes the virgin America reclining on a carpet of flowers appeared as beautiful as a dream of love," enthused Benigno Arriaga in his 1869 independence day speech.[64] The war over Texas in the 1840s and the French intervention of the 1860s had both been met with rhetorical outpourings of anguish over the desecration of Moctezuma's throne.[65] Denunciations of Spanish rule began, however, to be accompanied not only by calls for the vindication of the Aztecs but also by assertions of several entirely different heritages. Reflecting the deep roots that creole nationalism had sunk in Mexico, preconquest warriors continued to be "our fathers" and the insurgents of 1810 remained the "descendants of Cuauhtémoc," but to this family tree were joined other, newer branches.[66] As elsewhere, in Mexico the heroes of independence themselves began to be claimed as "padres de la patria." Mexicans, the elite liberals discovered, were also Hidalgo's sons. Sometimes they were the "sons of Cuauhtémoc and Xicotencal, of Hidalgo and Morelos," and sometimes, in a more stream-lined genealogy, simply of Hidalgo.[67] "We come from the village of Dolores; we descend from Hidalgo," insisted the liberal journalist and politician Ignacio Ramírez (himself of indigenous parentage).[68] Independence, wrote Justo Sierra, was the "baptismal certificate of our nationality."[69] Thus 1810 was a date of birth as well as rebirth.

This insurgent genealogy was melded with the older indianesque gene-alogy through the medium of progress; writers and politicians began to describe Mexican history as a process of gradual development from the preconquest days to the pinnacle of modernity achieved under Porfirio Díaz. Together these various stages "form parts of our grandiose whole," as General Riva Palacio explained in 1871.[70] The reigning positivism of the Díaz regime helped shape a coherent vision of national history as an ever-improving upward progression. Nonetheless, the heritage of modern, nineteenth-century Mexico began to be described as essentially Spanish, even if its history included the preconquest era. The historian José María Vigil, from 1880 the director of Mexico's National Library, thus asserted that although it was necessary to study the pre-Columbian period, it was in the colonial period that one found the origin of "our customs and our habits."[71] The Spanish too were thus "our fathers," joining the Aztecs and the insurgents in a vast patriotic genealogy. "Oh Mother Spain, your great shadow is present in all our history; to you we owe civilization," intoned Sierra in an 1883 independence day speech.[72] While in previous decades Mexicans had been told in such speeches that they possessed real or met-aphorical indigenous blood, now they were declared the sons of Spain. Mexico's "religion, language, customs, and indeed the blood that circu-lates in its veins are unimpeachable witnesses" of Spain's maternal influ-ence, explained another patriotic orator.[73]

Historians have offered various explanations for Spanish America's im-proved relations with its colonial past, most often stressing growing hos-tility to the United States as a driving force. Certainly by midcentury the United States had replaced Spain as the primary enemy for regions such as Mexico. When the Mexican national anthem—written in 1854—condemned the profanation of national soil by foreigners it alluded to the recent U.S. invasion rather than the Spanish conquest. Efforts by Spain itself to foment *hispanismo* (a celebration of "Hispanic" values and culture) are also considered to have born fruit in the development of a pan-Hispanic sentiment that contrasted the spiritual values of Hispanic culture with the crass materialism of the United States.[74] These factors surely contributed to the more favorable assessment of the colonial past that developed in most parts of Spanish America by the 1870s (and in some places earlier). At the same time, I believe that other forces were also at work. As I have noted, nationalism requires the invention of a national past. During the independence era elite nationalists toyed with the idea that the national past might be located in the preconquest era. After independence, the unstable nature of a past that required creole elites to profess indigenous heritage led to its rejection; indeed, it was precisely this aspect of indianesque nationalism that attracted most negative commentary in later decades of the nineteenth century. The independence era, moreover, offered a plethora of heroes whose deeds could be commemorated on coins, stamps, and other state emblems and whose images could be used to represent the new nations in place of the indigenous icons popular during the period of independence itself, as I argued in chapter 2. Yet while independence came to constitute the nation's moment of supreme glory, it scarcely constituted a past. The inability of the recent events of independence to form by themselves a national past is manifest in the many works of nineteenth-century scholarship dedicated precisely to determining the origins of the *independence movement*.[75] Independence, like the nation itself, needed its own past, its own history. It is for this reason that nineteenth-century discussions of independence so often led to discussions of the movement's origins; it is not a coincidence that many of the comments about the continent's history cited in this chapter are extracted from the *discursos cívicos,* or civic speeches, delivered at independence day celebrations.

The national past thus lay precisely in the place from which the formative independence movements had originated. During the independence period, as we saw, this point of origin was believed to lie in the distant preconquest empires. With the rejection of indianesque nationalism, the origins of the independence movement began to be located instead in the colonial era, which moved to occupy the position of national past. This view was expressed clearly by the liberal orator at the 1885 independence day celebrations in Guatemala City, who, like earlier conservatives, argued that independence completed the creative process begun with the conquest: "Independence matched the conquest. For this reason the poem of American liberty is the only one worthy to continue the poem of the discovery and colonization . . . Columbus, were he alive, would say to Cortés, Pizarro and Balboa, 'I discovered this world so that you could conquer it,' and the latter would speak thus to Bolívar: 'We battled with the Indian in order that from his blood and ours would be born sons such as you, to proclaim from the heights of Chimborazo the liberty of America.'"[76] Spanish American history ran from Columbus to Cortés to Bolívar, much as the Argentine poet Lugones had described his own ancestry in the quotation discussed above. Note also that for this speaker the fruit of the encounter between indigenous warriors and conquistadors was a creole—Simón Bolívar—and not a mestizo. The logic of nation-building itself, combined with the fundamentally creole identity shared by Spanish America's political and economic elites, led to the positive reevaluation of the colonial era as the cradle of independence.

The effect of the pan-American liberal rapprochement with Spain was that by the end of the nineteenth century liberal and conservative national genealogies came to resemble each other. Each accepted Spain as a historic mother. In 1892 both conservative Colombia and liberal Guatemala celebrated the quatrocentenary of Columbus's arrival in the Americas, an event that marked the start of what in the 1820s had been described in both regions as three centuries of tyranny. To be sure, there were some differences between the celebrations in these two countries: the Guatemalan festivities, unlike their Colombian analogue, included a large contingent of indigenous Maya who participated "on the official order of the national government."[77] Guatemala's liberal regime had not entirely shed its attachment to indianesque nationalism, which stipulated some sort of indigenous dimension to civic festivals, although the effect of obliging the Maya to celebrate the arrival of Columbus was that the Guatemalan commemoration bore closer resemblance than its organizers perhaps appreciated to colonial festivals in which catechized Indians celebrated "with flutes and whistles their happy subjugation" to Spanish rule.[78] Republican history had come full circle.

The centenaries of independence held in 1910 provide a useful perspective from which to assess changing elite perceptions of the continent's heritage. Naturally, the celebration of the heroes of the wars of independence occupied a central position in all commemorations, and many governments sponsored the publication of eulogizing biographies and document collections. Argentina's Pro-Centenary Commission even considered renaming Tierra del Fuego "Territorio de Mayo" ("May Territory"), in honor of the 1810 May Revolution.[79] At the same time, states across Spanish America saw the centenary as an opportunity to commemorate Spain. From Mexico to Argentina official celebrations hailed Spain as a historic mother, and included substantial Peninsular participation. Alfonso XIII's aunt, the Infanta Isabella, headed a delegation to Argentina, the Marqués de Polavieja led the delegation to Mexico (where he awarded Porfirio Díaz the Order of Charles III), and the grandson of the royalist general Pablo Morillo led the Spanish delegation to Venezuela.[80] The inclusion of the grandson of this arch-enemy of Spanish-American independence in the independence day celebrations suggests the extent to which patriotic versions of history had altered over the past century. The Colombian festivities likewise made sure to include no tactless references to royalist wartime atrocities; a commemorative stamp showing six patriots executed by the Spanish in 1816 was withdrawn so as not to offend Spain, and speakers were at pains to ascribe independence to Colombia's "Iberian element."[81] Across the continent governments erected statues to Spain, installed commemorative plaques on colonial buildings, and renamed streets in honor of Isabel la Católica.[82] These acts were intended to commemorate "the origins of the close cordiality that today exists between noble Spain" and the people of the Americas.[83] The colonial period, no longer a time of darkness, was instead hailed as the "indestructible foundation of our collective existence," the source of civilization.[84] These intimate ties were evoked in a 1910 Colombian centenary volume, which contrasted the pale shadows cast by preconquest peoples with the deep impressions left in the minds of creoles by the colonial era:

How can we compare the conquering race with the unfortunate indigenous tribes? Ah—it is right that we should render tribute to those prehistoric

"Padres de la Patria" 95

antecedents, the homage that every people owes to the past; it is right that we admire the heroism with which those great bronze-skinned leaders accepted their adverse fate and confronted death. We cannot be ungrateful towards people who inhabited our soil, started a civilization and transmitted to us some of their ethnic condition and more than a drop of their blood. But nonetheless—how distant from us are those Muiscas, Panches and Pijaos; how removed from every aspect of our spiritual life! Their great leaders pass before our imagination like vague shadows, some tragic, the majority blurred and pale, like those whom Aeneas saw thronging the banks of the Acheron, demanding to be admitted to the fearful Stygian region. In contrast, how much the colonial epoch offers our eyes and our spirit. And how natural this is, since part of it persists and continues: since there are areas in the heart of Bogotá where the shades of the *oidores* [viceregal officials], and colonial gentlemen appear to pass by, [alongside] the carriages of the viceroys; since even our speech preserves colonial expressions.[85]

Indians were "prehistoric antecedents" who played no real role in the creation of modern Colombia and who in any event had long since vanished. Indigenousness, in other words, was part of the deep past, whereas the colonial period formed a vital element of the present. "Our American glories," insisted another Colombian centenary orator, "are the glories of Spain; our heroes are the sons of Spanish gentlemen."[86]

The uniform acceptance of Spain accompanied varied attitudes toward the indigenous past. In 1910 Mexico, the historic parade that formed part of the capital's celebration marked the three most important eras of Mexican history: conquest, colonial, and independence, excluding the pre-Columbian. The conquest itself was depicted not as a bloody slaughter but as a friendly meeting between Moctezuma and Cortés, with a cast of nearly one thousand Indian warriors, priests, and virgins. The festivities also saw the inauguration of several displays at what is now the Museo Nacional de Antropología, which gave pride of place to the Piedra del Sol—the so-called Aztec calendar stone—and other monumental pre-Columbian remains.[87] In Argentina, mention of the indigenous past was more muted, in keeping with the tendencies established by the Generation of 1837. The sumptuous centenary volumes produced by Manuel Chueco made virtually no mention of the indigenous population, past or present, although Argentina itself was described as a nation formed by the union of Spanish conquistadors and Indian women.[88] Argentina, the offspring of this encounter, was a *criolla*, a beautiful creole woman; as in 1885 Guatemala, the outcome of racial mixing was the creole not the mestizo. The special centenary edition of *La Nación* agreed that the indigenous past had contributed "a tiny drop of Quechua blood" to Argentine creole culture, which gave it a special je ne sais quoi and heightened its beauty. However, the paper noted, if Indian culture has not been completely destroyed by the conquest, as some mistakenly believed, it was nonetheless destined to be superseded, as the Indians themselves recognized: "The innocent and ignorant Indians could admit that the conquistadors belonged to a superior race created to dominate them."[89] Contemporary indigenous people figured in Bogotá's centenary celebrations only long enough for a speaker to declare that "the indigenous race was annihilated in America," although the indigenous past was symbolically present in the form of two enormous statues from the pre-Hispanic site of San Agustín, transported to the city especially for the festivities.[90]

FATHERS AND HEROES

Who then were the Fathers? Independence-era insurgent writers had stressed the links that bound them to the preconquest past, and also, somewhat contradictorily, to the conquistadors. "Our fathers" were Atahualpa and Lautaro and also the conquerors and encomenderos who had colonized the continent. By the centenary of independence patriotic prose emphasized instead the ties between Spain and the independent Spanish American republics. "The fathers of the nation" were perhaps the heroes of independence, the próceres who were commemorated on coinage and stamps, in monuments, place-names, and poetry, but their mother was none other than Spain herself. The view that the region's heritage was essentially Spanish was completely compatible with the image of the próceres as fathers of the country, and even of independence as the time when the nation was born, since the próceres themselves were understood to be the offspring of that Spanish heritage. Francisco Cosmes's assertion that the conquistador Cortes was Mexico's true father was offensive not because his critics denied the importance of the colonial era to Mexico's history but because Cosmes sought to usurp for Cortes the position of

"Padres de la Patria" 97

"padre de la patria," a title by then inextricably linked with Miguel Hidalgo and the other leaders of the independence movement.

By the centenary of independence most intellectuals agreed that those independence leaders had been primarily of creole descent. As the Mexican archaeologist Manuel Gamio was to put it a few years later, "It should be said once and for all without hypocritical reservations that [independence] was accomplished by those of European tendencies and origin."[91] This was a widely held view of independence outside Mexico as well; the Ecuadorian scholar Pío Jaramillo stated pithily in 1925 that "the war of independence was the work of the Spanish or the sons of Spaniards born in America."[92] There was, moreover, broad agreement that the indigenous population had played no positive role in the entire process. Indians were instead represented either as indifferent to this apogee of national self-expression or as supporters of the Spanish crown. As one Chilean writer put it in 1911, independence-era Araucanians were royalist because "they did not have the aptitude to understand the supreme importance of the revolutionary movement."[93] Independence was instead an intergenerational struggle between Spain and her New World offspring. In the words of the Guatemalan historian Antonio Batres Jáuregui:

> The independence of the former Spanish overseas provinces was in no sense the fruit of a reaction by the conquered against the conquerors. It was rather the inescapable and logical conclusion to the awesome struggle between two portions of the conquering race, one creole and the other peninsular. The original masters of these beautiful regions did not rise up in arms, demanding liberty from the king of Spain. The glorious standard of rebellion was brandished neither by Aztecs, nor by Muiscas, nor by Araucanians, nor by Quichés and Cakchiquels. The aborigines were spectators, or at times the instruments of the Spaniards born on American soil, who from Chile to Mexico fought heroically for the freedom of the colonies under the orders of Bolívar, Miranda, San Martín, Sucre, Páez, Hidalgo and Morelos, who could not invoke the shades of Atahualpa, Lautaro, Cuauhtémoc, Tecum-Umán or Lempira, since in the end through the veins of those próceres ran the blood that gave life to Hernán Cortés, Pizarro, Valdivia and Alvarado. It was not the autochthonous races revindicating their empire but rather the Colony that fought for liberty. The transatlantic legions of *Old Iberia* were defeated by the leaders and improvised armies of an-

other *Young Iberia,* which, abjuring the name and system of its forbearer, preserved its indomitable spirit and its characteristic pride.[94]

Thus at the centenary of independence political and intellectual elites, like their independence-era predecessors, viewed their nations through the lens of metaphorical ancestry, but that ancestry no longer linked the creole present to the preconquest past. Rather it united colonial and national history under a single umbrella of Hispanism. The increasing emphasis on the independence movement itself as a uniquely heroic moment in the continent's history, in other words, was entirely compatible with the positive reevaluation of the colonial era.

Where did this leave the indigenous past, excised from the symbols of the state, removed from the personal ancestry of the elite, and excluded from the nation's own moment of national glory? A number of scholars have implied that during the nineteenth century the elite disregard for contemporary indigenous people (a matter I will discuss further in chapter 6) extended to the preconquest era as well. By 1850, Mónica Quijada has claimed, "the heroic Indian, the myth of the independence era, had been converted into a wild beast lacking any capacity for civilization."[95] This interpretation, although largely correct as a description of elite attitudes toward the contemporary indigenous population, does not describe the complex place of the preconquest past within postindependence elite nationalism. After abandoning indianesque models of the past, nineteenth-century elites began to reposition the preconquest era within national history. In the next two chapters I examine the new roles that elite nationalism assigned to the pre-Columbian era, beginning with its place in the patriotic historical texts composed across postindependence Spanish America.

 *Chapter 4*

Patriotic History and the Pre-Columbian Past

The close connection between history and patriotism is so obvious as
to constitute a commonplace . . . The patria is a historical creation.
—JOSÉ DE LA RIVA-AGÜERO, *La historia en el Perú*

In 1876 the Peruvian naval lieutenant José Manzanares contacted the
government of Manuel Pardo to request support for a patriotic enterprise. Manzanares had written a historical study whose completion and
publication costs he hoped the government would underwrite. The two-
volume work, which Manzanares considered of "true national interest,"
consisted of a study of navigation that culminated in a volume devoted
to the history of the Peruvian navy. Manzanares argued that *The History
of the National Navy* would be particularly useful for teaching students at
the Escuela Naval, where he worked. This claim seems to have convinced
the government, for in April 1876 it approved his request.[1] Such support
was not unusual; during the nineteenth century governments across Spanish America sponsored the publication of works of national history, and
even books published without direct government funding might receive
subsequent endorsement as "official" history. The Ecuadorian government, for example, adopted Juan León Mera's 1875 *Catechism of the Geography of the Republic of Ecuador* as an official school text soon after
its publication.[2] These often multivolume works are known collectively
as *historia patria*, which we may loosely translate as "patriotic history"
although its more precise meaning is "history of the patria." Works of
patriotic history occupied an important place in the elite national project
for several reasons. First, their authors were generally themselves members of the political and economic elite. As E. Bradford Burns noted, in
nineteenth-century Latin America most historians were "connected at
one time or another, in one way or another with the governments."[3] Most

also shared a common background of economic privilege, including, in many cases, extended sojourns in Europe. They bathed collectively in the streams of romanticism, positivism, and other intellectual currents, and they often saw themselves as partners in a joint enterprise. Together they formed a transnational scholarly community maintained through regular correspondence, the exchange of books and ideas, and constant citation of each others' works.[4]

The views expressed in their writings were thus the views of a compact and powerful elite. The importance of historical writings to the articulation of elite ideology has been shown very clearly by Edward Said in his seminal work *Orientalism*. Said's study of how Western intellectuals helped create "the Orient" laid bare the connections that link scholarship with political and economic ambitions, and his analysis encouraged attention to the political role of historical writings in other parts of the world. In this chapter I consider the contribution of patriotic history to elite efforts at nation-building in nineteenth-century Spanish America, looking in particular at its role in creating and expressing particular images of the precolonial past, for at the same time that the pre-Columbian period was being expunged from the personal genealogies of national elites, it was contributing to the formation of "national" pasts through its incorporation into the region's literary and historical heritage.

These nineteenth-century historical writings are examples of what Pierre Nora has called *lieux de mémoire*, or "sites of memory"—that is, places where the past is symbolically and deliberately preserved. Lieux de mémoire need not be physical sites such as an archive or a monument; scholars have used the concept to describe many things, including songs and celebrations. Clearly books, particularly historical studies, may also constitute sites of memory. Nora has claimed that only certain works of history—"those that reshape memory in some fundamental way or that epitomise a revision of memory for pedagogical purposes"—may be considered true lieux de mémoire.[5] The works of national history produced during the nineteenth century in Spanish America function as sites of memory in that they sought to create new *national* memories for the states and regions whose pasts they chronicled. Historia patria aimed, often explicitly, at developing a sense of national history that it was the patriotic duty of the state to propagate. As one Venezuelan newspaper put it, in a crescendo of resonant words, "it is incompatible with *civilization* and *patriotism* for a *citizen* to be ignorant of his Patria's history."[6] Altogether, the images of the past presented in such historical studies are not the ideas of a group of obscure scholars. Instead, they are the carefully worked-over result of an explicitly nationalizing process, carried out by individuals close to their nation's governing heart. The scholar-politicians who composed the works of nineteenth-century history studied in this chapter used these texts to construct the nation's past at the same time as they hinted at its future. I begin this chapter by noting the importance that nineteenth-century elites ascribed to historical writings, and then I examine the place accorded to the preconquest era within these patriotic histories. I conclude by comparing the treatment of the precolonial period in nineteenth-century historia patria with its place in nineteenth-century fiction, which itself served as a site of nation-building. Together these genres helped convert the preconquest era into an evocative, folkloric preamble to true national history.

"A PEOPLE WITHOUT HISTORY CANNOT HAVE A CHARACTER THAT SETS THEM APART"

The importance of historical writing to the nationalist enterprise was recognized across Spanish America in the decades after independence. History was understood to assist in both creating a distinct national identity and fomenting patriotic sentiment. In Chile, the government, fresh from its victory over the Peruvian-Bolivian Confederation, set about sponsoring its first history text (Claude Gay, *Physical and Political History of Chile*) in 1839, the same year in which the Chilean History Society was founded.[7] In subsequent decades the state funded the publication of a series of other works, including José Javier de Guzmán, *The Chilean Instructed in the Topographical, Civil and Political History of his Country* (1843), and Vicente Fidel López, *Manual of Chilean History for Use in Primary Schools* (1845).[8] There was, Chilean newspapers proclaimed, "nothing . . . so useful and fundamental for the man destined to serve his *patria* with intelligence as a knowledge of history. The man well versed in history can be an expert patriot."[9] State sponsorship was in part responsible for the emergence in Chile of the vibrant historical community that was later to produce such works as Miguel Luis Amunátegui's *Discovery and Conquest of Chile* (1862) and his *Precursors of Chilean Independence* (1870–72), as well as Diego Barros Arana's multivolume *General History of Chile* (1884–1902).[10] The growth in the system of public education in the second half of the nineteenth century further heightened the elites' sense of the importance of history in general, and historical textbooks in particular, in shaping good citizens.[11]

The first substantial history of independent Colombia (the ten-volume *History of the Revolution of the Colombian Republic, 1824–27*) was composed by José Manuel Restrepo while he served as minister of the interior. Although the Colombian historical community did not benefit from the same degree of governmental support as did Chilean historians, historical writings in Colombia were similarly acknowledged to play a vital role in fomenting patriotism and "civilization." A review of José Antonio de Plaza's 1850 *Memoirs for the History of New Granada from Its Discovery to 20 July 1810* thus noted that "a profound knowledge of the history of the *patria* is an absolute necessity for any individual who has ambitions of feeling reasonably civilized."[12] The liberal writer Manuel Ancízar agreed that understanding "his own history" would help "arouse the feeling of patriotism in the American spectator."[13] The Venezuelan scholar Juan Esté expressed clearly the civilizing, patriotic power ascribed to history in his 1858 *Introduction to the History of Venezuela,* in which he stated that "republicans should instruct themselves in history, because only by being enlightened and virtuous will they be able to be true patriots, working to attain the prestige and sovereignty of the democratic institutions intended to achieve the beautiful ideal of liberty, that most noble aspiration of our distinguished liberators."[14] For this reason Venezuelan governments had from the 1840s commissioned the publication of national histories, such as Rafael María Baralt and Ramón Díaz's *Concise History of Venezuela.*[15]

Peruvian governments, as Mark Thurner has shown, also began commissioning historical writings in the 1840s. The distribution to "scientific establishments" of Mariano de Rivero and Jacob von Tschudi's *Peruvian Antiquities* (1851) was underwritten by the Peruvian Congress, and the liberal regime of Ramón Castilla subsequently hired Sebastian Lorente to compose a series of historical studies.[16] As elsewhere, in Peru historical texts were believed to play an important role in the formation of patriotic sentiment; even its critics described General Manuel de Mendiburu's multivolume *Historical-Biographical Dictionary of Peru during the Period of Spanish Domination* as a "*patriotic* and honorable" effort.[17] "In the

State's labor to stimulate national culture the study of historia patria must hold pride of place," insisted the Peruvian president José Pardo in 1906.[18]

In Argentina, the creation of an official, national history is usually dated from the appearance in 1857 of the *Gallery of Argentine Celebrities* by Bartolomé Mitre, himself the first president of a united Argentina. Mitre and his fellow members of the Generation of 1837 believed that historical studies should help guide political decisions.[19] At the same time successive governments put ever-greater emphasis on pubic schooling, which accorded an important place to the teaching of history. These activities occurred in the years after the 1852 defeat of the conservative caudillo Rosas by a coalition of provincial governors, which led to the formation of the Argentine Republic out of the diverse provinces of the Río de la Plata. The writing of explicitly national histories thus coincided with a period of explicit nation-building. The vast increase in immigration into Argentina in the years after 1880, itself a response to government stimulus, further heightened the focus on history as a method for integrating the new arrivals. Writing in 1899, the influential physician José Ramos Mejía observed with approval that in state primary schools immigrant children were "systematically and insistently told about the patria, the flag, moments of national glory and heroic historical episodes." Other writers such as Ricardo Rojas, the future rector of the University of Buenos Aires, agreed that through appropriate state-sponsored history curricula immigrants could learn about Argentina's true creole heritage.[20]

Even in regions such as Central America, where political elites vacillated throughout the century between a commitment to Central American union and more fragmented visions of the state, the importance of history to shaping the nation was acknowledged, even if the precise geography of the "nation" was not. "The history of a nation is one of its most important books . . . All nations should have their particular history," insisted the Honduran politician and scholar José Cecilio del Valle shortly after Central American independence from Mexico.[21] "The history of its own country will endow Central America with a more refined patriotism and a character that is truly its own," agreed a Guatemalan official in 1834, at roughly the same time that Mariano Gálvez, the Guatemalan head of state, commissioned a history of Central America from the liberal scholar Alejandro Marure, the holder of the first chair in universal history at the Guatemalan Academy of Studies.[22] The overthrow of Gálvez's government in 1838 temporarily derailed Marure's project, for the conservatives who replaced Gálvez preferred to sponsor their own historians, such as Manuel Montúfar y Coronado, the author of *Memoirs for the History of the Central American Revolution* (1832).[23] When the liberal party returned to power in Guatemala in the 1870s, it again commissioned national histories, or just as often, histories of Central America. Works such as José Milla's 1879 *History of Central America from Its Discovery by the Spanish (1502) to Its Independence from Spain (1821)* and Lorenzo Montúfar's seven-volume *Historical Review of Central America* (1878) were the outcome of this liberal sponsorship. These texts were intended both to replace the version of history presented in earlier conservative studies and to endow Central American nations with an important attribute of civilization and national identity: a historicized past. "A people without archives, without history, without traditions, cannot have a character that sets them apart, that makes them play an honorable role in the magnificent evolutions of progress," explained the orator at the inauguration of the Honduran national archive in 1888.[24]

In Mexico the composition of true national histories is often alleged not to have occurred until the 1880s, after the imposition of a centralized program of state-sponsored education under the rule of Porfirio Díaz.[25] It was then that works such as Guillermo Prieto's *Lessons in Historia Patria Written for the Students at the Military Academy* (c.1886) and Justo Sierra's *Catechism of Historia Patria* (1894) appeared. The best-known example of these works of Porfirian history is doubtless the 1884–89 *Mexico through the Centuries,* a five-volume compendium written on government commission by a team of writers including Vicente Riva Palacio, Alfredo Chavero, and Julio Zárate.[26] These works were certainly intended to "awaken the feeling of patriotism," but whether the start of a national historical tradition should be dated so late is debatable.[27] From the 1830s there had been calls for the teaching of modern Mexican history, and under the presidency of Antonio López de Santa Anna Mexican history was added to the curriculum of secondary schools.[28] Moreover, it was during the Santa Anna years that such influential conservative histories as Lucas Alamán's *History of Mexico* (1848–52) appeared. Prior to this, governments during the 1820s had funded an ambitious program of historical publications under the supervision of Alamán and Carlos María de Bustamante. The patriotic potential of history was thus recognized long before the apogee of post-reform liberalism under Porfirio Díaz, even if his predecessors did not fund historical writings to the same degree that he was able to do. While the works produced in the 1830s differed in many ways from those composed during the Porfiriato—Guy Rozat, among others, has offered a nuanced analysis of these differences—all acknowledged the importance of historical writings to the nationalist enterprise.[29]

Scholars debated throughout the century the most appropriate contours of historical practice, and they often criticized the type of historical work produced by others. Bustamante's indianesque invocations of Aztec shades in his 1820s *Historic Portrait of the Mexican Revolution* evoked nothing but scorn in later scholars. "What can one think of a man who in his writings seriously says that devils appeared to Moctezuma?" asked the liberal writer Lorenzo de Zavala in 1832.[30] In 1840s Chile the conservative scholar Andrés Bello engaged in a lengthy dispute with his former student José Victorino Lastarria over the relative importance of factual data and philosophical interpretation in the writing of history. The Argentine historian and president Bartolomé Mitre disdained the historical studies of his compatriot Vicente Fidel López as excessively vague and lyrical, and insufficiently grounded in firm documentation. As the century progressed, moreover, scholars increasingly sought "scientific" laws that might explain historical events, and they sneered at earlier generations who had ignored such truths.[31] The practice of history thus varied from individual to individual and over time. There was nonetheless broad agreement that "History"—however conducted—consisted of a truthful examination of past events. It was this emphasis on truth that distinguished history from other genres of writing; as the Mexican scholar Manuel Larrainzar noted in 1865, historians who ignored this requirement would find that instead of composing history "they had written only a novel."[32] There was, moreover, agreement that history played an important role in the nationalist process. In short, for most Spanish American governments and elite intellectuals, the study of the past was a tool with which to foment patriotic nationalism. Its patriotic power was widely acknowledged from the 1840s if not earlier, and by the turn of the new century it had been elevated to a position of unassailable patriotic importance. The link between history and patriotism was "so obvious as to constitute a commonplace," noted the Peruvian historian José de la Riva Agüero, before observing that the patria itself was "a historical creation."[33] Historical writing was thus believed to be an important if not central reflection of patriotic sentiment. "The intensity of national feeling correlates with the abundance of historical writing," insisted Francisco García Calderón, the son of a Peruvian president, in 1912.[34]

A CIVILIZED PAST?

What place did the pre-Columbian era occupy in these patriotic histories? Most histories of Spanish America written during the nineteenth century dedicated at least a few pages to the preconquest period, and some devoted considerably more: over a quarter of the Ecuadorian scholar (and archbishop) Federico González Suárez's three-thousand-page *General History of the Republic of Ecuador* (1890–1903) examines the preconquest era. Whether this period qualified as part of true "national" history, or merely as a sort of preface to it, was another matter. As I argued in the previous chapter, by the 1870s most elite intellectuals came to believe that their own heritage lay, for better or for worse, with Spain and the colonial era and not in the distant pre-Columbian past. On the other hand, the significance of possessing an ancient history was not lost on nineteenth-century nationalists. Most often historians settled on the version of national history articulated by the Mexican educator Justo Sierra, who explained in 1910 that "all that pre-Cortesian world . . . is ours, is our past; we have incorporated it as a *preamble that lays the foundations for and explains our true national history*."[35] Preconquest history, in other words, was a prelude to "real" history. Given its role as preface, scholars seldom implied that the preconquest period formed the most significant part of their region's history. That honor was reserved for the independence era to which most nineteenth-century history texts gave pride of place.[36] Nonetheless, while the pre-Columbian era was rarely presented as either elite intellectuals' personal point of origin or their nations' most important historical moment, by midcentury a familiarity with the pre-Columbian era was widely described as part of the essential knowledge of civically minded people because of its role in the construction of the continent's past. In most parts of Spanish America the preconquest period formed a latent element of nationalist history, underpinning the colonial and independence eras to give Spanish America a deep history comparable to that of the Old World. In keeping with its role as an ancient preamble to true national history the preconquest era was generally presented in scholarly writing as a time of culture and civilization, albeit of a civilization inferior to that subsequently introduced by the Spanish. (Precisely what the term "civilization" was understood to mean will be considered in greater detail in chapters 5 and 6. Here I note merely its unquestionably positive connotations.)

Nineteenth-century scholarly treatment of the preconquest past has been best studied for Mexico, where historians from the first decades after independence praised the Aztecs (in particular) in their studies and textbooks. As early as the 1820s the Mexican Congress had established a publishing program, run by Bustamante and Alamán, charged with printing illustrated works that emphasized the achievements of the Aztecs. (This program was conceived within a fundamentally indianesque framework; Fernando de Alva Ixtlilxóchitl's colonial chronicle, for example, was published [in French] under the title *Horrible Cruelties of the Conquerors of Mexico*).[37] These volumes stressed the high level of civilization reached by the inhabitants of Anáhuac.[38] Bustamante in particular arranged the republication of many works about the Aztecs, including Bernardino de Sahagún's sixteenth-century *Historia de las cosas mexicanas*. In addition, he personally penned an account of preconquest history aimed at Mexican girls with the intention of convincing them that "they can look upon our ancient nations as politic and cultured peoples."[39] Throughout his life Bustamante defended the Aztecs against charges of barbarism, for example, explaining that their religion, however bloody, was based on the same principles as those underlying Catholicism.[40]

During the years before the midcentury liberal Reform, although only a small number of "history books" were published, elite versions of national history were nonetheless disseminated via the many patriotic speeches declaimed at civic festivals and subsequently printed in newspapers and pamphlets.[41] Those delivered by liberals and moderate Santanistas presented an essentially indianesque account of Mexican history that stressed the achievements of the Aztecs and other preconquest peoples.[42] The ancient Greek and Roman sages, announced the prominent Santa Anna supporter José María Tornel, "did not resolve civic dissentions and discord more successfully than did the legislators of the Aztecs, the Zipas and the Incas."[43] America's preconquest history yet again fulfilled a role comparable to that of the Greeks and Romans within the history of Western

Europe. Liberals in turn described preconquest Mexico as a majestic land of heroes. "The Rome of the New World was called Tenochtitlán," insisted one patriotic writer in 1849.[44] The views articulated in such speeches differ from those expressed in some of the better-known writings by pre-reform liberals such as Lorenzo de Zavala and José María Luis Mora, and suggest that the anti-indigenous sentiments held by these men were not typical of all elite Mexican liberals. David Brading is thus not wholly correct to say that "most early nineteenth-century Mexican liberals dismissed the Aztecs as mere barbarians."[45]

Writings by early-nineteenth-century Mexican conservatives and those who supported Maximilian during the French intervention were also sympathetic to preconquest cultures. The dean of Mexican conservatism, Lucas Alamán, encouraged the study of preconquest peoples, even as he insisted that true Mexican history had begun with the conquest. The emperor Maximilian himself commissioned official explorations at the pyramids of Teotihuacán. Scholars serving in his government, such as Francisco Pimentel, composed lengthy studies of Mexico's pre-Columbian peoples, who, they stressed, had been highly cultured despite their unfortunate habit of human sacrifice. The Aztecs, Pimentel argued, displayed "exquisite urbanity."[46] Manuel Orozco y Berra, who was later to publish his *Mexico's Ancient and Conquest History* (1880) at the expense of the government during the Porfiriato, also served in the imperial regime of the emperor Maximilian. Like Pimentel, Orozco y Berra admired the achievements of Aztec culture, which, like Tornel, he compared favorably to those of the ancient Greeks and Romans.[47] After the liberal Reform, as larger numbers of historical studies began to be published the consensus remained that the Aztec empire (as usual, the primary focus of scholarly attention) had been a great civilization, whose only weak point was its religion. Writers and essayists agreed that the preconquest population had been civilized, and that Mexicans could justly view its achievements with pride.[48] Other "precursor" cultures, such as the Toltecs, also drew praise.[49]

Mexican historians were not alone in elevating preconquest peoples to the status of "civilizations." Most works of nineteenth-century historia patria described at least the Aztecs and the Incas as civilized. Those empires, noted the Colombian historian José María Samper, had been "powerful and very advanced in civilization."[50] Comparisons with the great

Patriotic History and the Pre-Columbian Past 109

civilizations of the Old World of course signaled particularly clearly the efforts by nineteenth-century intellectuals to forge Spanish America's preconquest cultures into a homegrown equivalent of ancient Greece and Rome. "Babylon, Egypt, Greece and Rome are not the only empires worthy of nourishing a generous imagination," insisted Mariano de Rivero and Jacob von Tschudi in their 1851 *Peruvian Antiquities*, for the achievements of the Incas were equally impressive.[51] Peruvian, Ecuadorian, and Bolivian scholars, whose nations could all claim some fragment of Tawantinsuyo's former glory, joined to praise the "paternal government of the Incas," as did writers from Colombia, at a greater geographical remove.[52] Even during the later decades of the century, when, under the influence of William Prescott's 1847 *History of the Conquest of Peru*, Peruvian historians began depicting the Incas as despotic tyrants, they did not doubt the empire's status as a great civilization, as Mark Thurner has shown.[53] Peru, proclaimed the president of the Instituto Histórico in 1906, was the proud owner of the "history and remains of one of the most ancient and greatest civilizations of ancient times, . . . the grandiose Inca civilization."[54] The appeal of the Inca empire was made manifest in the peculiar proposal to create a unified Peruvian-Bolivian state that was put forward in 1880 (in the midst of the War of the Pacific) by the Colombian writer Simón Martínez Izquierdo together with the Peruvian Justiniano Cavero Egúsquiza. They explained that the citizens of the new state would be called Incas, "so that when any citizen is asked his nationality he can reply 'I am an Inca.' What more could one want!" Of course, as Cecilia Méndez has noted, being an Inca is quite different from being an Indian.[55] In subsequent chapters I will explore in greater detail the differences between Incas and Indians.

In Argentina, Inca civilization was praised particularly by those scholars who believed that there had been a significant Inca presence in their country. The liberal historian Vicente Fidel López, who not coincidentally insisted that the Inca empire had included parts of northwestern Argentina, presented a very attractive image of the Incas in his writings. Cuzco, he wrote, was an "American Rome."[56] Once again links to the ancient civilizations of the Old World served to elevate those of the New World. The view that Inca culture was part of a distinctive American past wholly comparable, and compatible, with classical European antiquity was shared by Francisco Moreno, the Argentine savant and director of the influential

Museo de la Plata. The exterior of the museum (constructed in the 1880s) was thus decorated with friezes based on designs taken from the temples of Palenque and Tiahuanaco, the latter of which was believed to be an Inca site. "I have tried," Moreno explained in 1891, "to endow the decoration with an ancient American character, which nevertheless would match with the Greek lines."[57] The Incas, in other words, "matched" the Greeks. Not all of López's and Moreno's contemporaries agreed with their positive account of the Inca state. The historian-president Bartolomé Mitre, for example, scribbled onto the margins of his personal copy of López's 1871 *The Aryan Races of Peru* his objections to López's claim that the Incas were Aryans. Contradicting López's views on the subject, Mitre insisted that the Incas had possessed only a very inferior civilization at the time of the Spanish conquest.[58]

Other preconquest peoples besides the Aztecs, their "precursor" cultures, and the Incas were accorded the status of civilizations in nineteenth-century historia patria. From Colombia, the conservative writer José Antonio de Plaza praised that region's preconquest population, singling out the Muiscas as "the most civilized in the New World," after the Aztecs and the Incas.[59] Many Colombian scholars agreed with Plaza that the Muiscas had enjoyed an "advanced" civilization.[60] That the Muiscas were believed to have possessed a calendrical system perhaps comparable to that of the Aztecs further enhanced their civilized status.[61] Geographically proximate cultures such as the Quimbaya were also characterized as civilized by at least some Colombian writers, while the Ecuadorian scholar-priest Federico González Suárez detailed the achievements of various of the cultures residing in (what would become) Ecuador at the time of the Inca conquest in the fifteenth century.[62] In Central America and Mexico writers from the midcentury generally insisted that the preconquest Maya also counted among the "continent's civilized nations," although in their view the same could not be said of the modern Maya, who in 1847 had unleashed in the Yucatan a devastating attack on creole society known as the Caste War.[63] Notwithstanding these recent events, the ancient Maya were declared to possess what one scholar called "an advanced civilization," fully comparable to that of the Incas.[64] Indeed, the historian Darío Euraque has argued, the high level of civilization attributed to the Maya led nineteenth-century scholars in Honduras to "Mayanise" that region's preconquest peoples.[65]

This is not to imply that every preconquest population was labeled as civilized and therefore admirable. It was widely agreed that pre-Columbian America had possessed its share of savages. Thus although Colombian scholars might agree that the Muisca had possessed a great civilization, Colombia was nonetheless acknowledged to have been full of other "uncultured tribes" at the time of the conquest.[66] Similarly, the achievements of the Aztecs did not endow every group within preconquest Mexico with the attributes of civilization. Guillermo Prieto's 1891 *Lessons in Historia Patria* thus divided Mexico's preconquest population into three groups: "civilized," "semicivilized," and "barbarous."[67] Likewise the Maya might have been civilized, but scholars maintained that Central America had also been home to many "barbarous tribes." Antonio Batres Jaúregui singled out as particularly barbarous those who "walk about totally naked."[68] Yet even those writers who doubted that particular preconquest cultures were entirely civilized might be prepared to see some virtues in them. Preconquest peoples were often praised as valiant, hardy, and "patriotic." In early-twentieth-century Colombia, for example, conservative Antioqueño writers praised preconquest indigenes as untutored patriots, filled with a "noble notion of love for the patria."[69] In 1840s Chile, writers combined dismay at the backward customs of the conquest-era Araucanians with a certain admiration for the heroic qualities of Lautaro and Caupolicán. Historians such as Lastarria acknowledged the Araucanians to have been "men of bronze," "a spirited and valiant people," even if they were barbarians.[70] Later scholars tended to follow this approach, stressing that the Araucanians had been barbarous yet still heroic. Miguel Luis Amunátegui thus described the Araucanians as brave warriors while insisting that the conquest was nonetheless a struggle "of barbarism against civilization."[71]

In Chile the scholarly assessment of the conquest-era Araucanians hardened during the years of the Chilean state's annexation of Mapuche territory, which began in the 1850s. The increasing southerly movement of European settlers and internal migrants put pressure on indigenous lands south of the Bío-Bío River, which offered both agricultural zones and coal mines. The Chilean state responded to this situation with a military program aimed at "pacifying" the region and incorporating it into national territory. The "pacification of Araucanía" was accompanied by increasingly negative assessments of the capacities of the precolonial Araucanians. At times during the "pacification," a mere reference to the civilized nature of the conquest-era Araucanians was criticized as antipatriotic. When in 1859 a Catholic journal described Araucanía as the "classical land of heroes," it was roundly condemned by other newspapers for its naive romanticism.[72] The scholar and liberal politician Diego Barros Arana, writing in the last decades of the century, was stark in his assessment of Chile's preconquest population. He asserted flatly that preconquest Araucanian society lacked "the slightest trace of organization."[73] In his view the conquest-era Mapuche were, moreover, incapable of experiencing any "tender and delicate sentiments, which are found only in persons of a much more advanced civilization."[74] The other indigenous cultures dwelling in preconquest Chile he classified as even more barbarous. The inhabitants of Tierra del Fuego, in particular, enjoyed the "sad honor of occupying the lowest rung on the ladder of civilization," in Barros Arana's opinion.[75] The impact of the Araucanian war on scholarly assessment of the preconquest Mapuche can be seen particularly clearly in the writings of Benjamín Vicuña Mackenna. In his parliamentary speeches in favor of war Vicuña Mackenna described conquest-era Araucanians as the ancestors of the deceitful nineteenth-century savages who without qualm murdered innocent Christians and each other.[76] A decade later, after the successful imposition of Chilean control of Araucanian territory, Vicuña Mackenna composed a biography of the conquest-era Araucanian hero Lautaro in which he argued that Lautaro was simultaneously "Indian, barbarian, vicious, brave, heroic, warrior with great natural gifts, sublime patriot, all at the same time."[77] As long as the contemporary Mapuche were not considered as a particular threat to the Chilean state, historians felt able to ascribe at least some positive qualities to pre-Columbian and conquest-era Araucanians.

In Argentina, scholars were criticizing nomadic preconquest peoples some decades before the 1879 "conquest of the desert" that aimed at eradicating indigenous autonomy in southern Argentina; indeed, the historian Nicholas Shumway has argued that elite scorn for the indigenous population past and present paved the way for the 1879 war.[78] The Argentine liberals of the Generation of 1837 such as Domingo Faustino Sarmiento, Juan Bautista Alberdi, and Bartolomé Mitre presented a uniformly somber picture of the preconquest era in their homeland, which, they insisted, had been a time of unredeemed barbarism, aside perhaps from the small incursions of Inca civilization in the northwest. Sarmiento, whose widely read *Civilization and Barbarism* contrasted the civilized European life of Argentina's cities with the backwardness of the countryside, was scathing in his assessment of the Pampas dwellers who inhabited the region at the time of the conquest. The Araucanian heroes after whom Argentine and Chilean insurgents had named ships, newspapers, and secret societies were for him merely a horde of "filthy Indians": "For us Colocolo, Lautaro and Caupolicán, notwithstanding the noble and civilized garb in which [Alonso de Ercilla] draped them, are nothing more than some filthy Indians, whom we would nowadays have had hanged were they to reappear in an Araucanian war against Chile."[79] The conquest had been both inevitable and beneficial, not because it had replaced one civilization with a superior one, but because it had introduced civilization to a continent wholly lacking therein. "By exterminating a savage people whose territory they were going to occupy [the Spanish] simply did what all civilized peoples do with savages," Sarmiento explained. "It may be very unjust to exterminate savages, to suffocate nascent civilizations, to conquer people in possession of privileged terrain, but thanks to this injustice, America, instead of remaining abandoned to savages, incapable of progress, is today occupied by the Caucasian race, the most perfect, the most intelligent, the most beautiful and the most progressive of those that people the earth. . . . Thus, in this way, the population of the world is subject to revolutions that recognize immutable laws: the strong races exterminate the weak; civilized peoples supplant savages in possession of the earth."[80]

Likewise, Alberdi, another influential figure in the liberal Generation of 1837, presented preconquest peoples as the antithesis of civilization. In the chapter "Civilizing Action of Europe in the South American Republics," in his 1852 *Bases y puntos de partida para la organización política de la República Argentina*, Alberdi asserted that "all the civilization in our land is European . . . In America everything that is not European is barbarous: this is the only distinction that matters."[81] Like Sarmiento, with whom he disagreed on many other matters, Alberdi disdained the independence-era celebration of the Araucanians: "When we say *comfortable*, proper, *good, comme il faut*," he asked, "do we allude to the Araucanians? . . . Who would not prefer a thousand times over to marry his sister or daughter to an English shoemaker in preference to an Araucanian princeling?"[82] (Alberdi's use of French marked his own distance from the uncivilized

Araucanians.) For his part, López, despite his admiration for the Incas, insisted that all other preconquest indigenes inhabiting Río de la Plata had been insuperably savage.[83]

The unwillingness of the Argentine liberal elite to admire these preconquest societies was surely the consequence of the all-too-evident continuities linking conquest- and colonial-era Pampean cultures with those of the nineteenth century. Until the "conquest of the desert" by the Argentine military in the 1870s, the Pehuenche, Mapuche, and other indigenous Pampean peoples resisted efforts to forcibly incorporate them into the Argentine Republic, thereby maintaining the same nomadic lifestyle that had foiled all earlier efforts at incorporation. The determination of the Generation of 1837 to populate the zones south of Buenos Aires with European immigrants placed particular pressure on relations between indigenes and the Argentine state. It was thus difficult for Argentine elites to maintain that preconquest and contemporary indigenous peoples were unconnected, with the one an important part of national heritage and the other a challenge to the modern state—a separation that formed a key part of elite celebration of the preconquest past in other regions, as I argue in the following chapters. The persistence of indigenous Pampean groups as a political challenge to the Argentine state therefore rendered difficult the sorts of celebrations of the Araucanians characteristic of the independence era, when the anticolonial potency of indianesque nationalism overshadowed its problematic nature and the indigenous horsemen had posed less threat to the revolution in Buenos Aires. Such factors, as much as any objective assessment of the level of culture achieved by preconquest Pampas dwellers, shaped the response of Argentine elites to the region's pre-Columbian past.

With the suppression of these indigenous groups, however, Argentine elites began to view the preconquest past with more equanimity. First, the theories of evolution developed in the second half of the century accorded a particular importance to very ancient human remains that might shed light on the origins of the human species. Argentina was rich in fossils of all sorts. The Argentine scholar Francisco Moreno was thus able to use the fossilized human remains he found in the Pampas to argue for the Argentine origin of all humankind. In this sense preconquest Patagonians became "our fossil grandfathers."[84] Argentina's preconquest population might not have been civilized but it was perhaps the source of all civilization. The preconquest past thus merited study not because it revealed ancient splendors, but because of its scientific importance. In addition, the ever-increasing number of immigrants arriving in Argentina encouraged a section of the nation's intelligentsia to view the preimmigrant past with a certain nostalgia that embraced even the "primitive" indigenes with whom their conquistador fathers had so valiantly battled. Thus the criollista academic Ricardo Rojas argued that although Argentina was essentially Spanish, schoolchildren should also study "the indigenous races that inhabited it—their character and the remains of their civilization."[85] By 1927, when immigration had created a capital city in which nearly three-quarters of the adult population was foreign-born, these ancient Indians had become "the autochthonous heroes who defended the national soil from the intrusive invaders of a different race."[86]

While the interpretations of the preconquest past by Chilean and Argentine liberals were shaped in part by the desire to justify the replacement of contemporary Amerindians with European settlers, other forces determined the attitudes of ultramontane conservatives such as supporters of the Colombian Regeneration, a political movement associated with President Rafael Núñez during the 1880s. Drawing on the traditions established by royalist commentators during the wars of independence, these thinkers maintained that the non-Christian state of preconquest America impeded the development of anything resembling civilization. All preconquest indigenous people had therefore been savages whose development had begun only after the arrival of Europeans—who brought Christianity to a continent previously submerged in darkness. The conservative Colombian scientist and scholar Vicente Restrepo thus insisted that all of Colombia's preconquest Indians had either been outright savages or at best had suffered from the spiritual degradation inevitable in societies lacking "the foundation of Truth."[87]

The non-Christian state of preconquest America posed a challenge to those who believed that civilization consisted fundamentally in being Christian, yet for all but a minority of elite intellectuals this did not prove an insuperable hurdle to appreciating at least some aspects of the preconquest era. In this regard the ancient cultures of the Old World provided a useful model, for neither the much-admired Greek city-states nor the Roman republic had been Christian, yet both had been incorporated into the elite heritage of many of the countries of Western Europe. This offered a template for the incorporation into national histories of eras and cultures linked only incompletely to the contemporary nations that claimed them as their own. Nineteenth-century historia patria thus hovered uncomfortably between visions of the nation as a personification of an elite history born in the colonial era and those that stressed the nation's ancient roots. Interpreting the preconquest era as even a preamble to national history began the process of separating the nation from its elite backers. It implied that there was more to the continent's history than its development after the arrival of Spanish settlers. National history, in other words, was perhaps not wholly identical to the personal histories of Spanish America's creole elites. On the other hand, approving accounts of preconquest history also served an elite nationalizing agenda, for they endowed the region with an ancient past whose glories might be appropriated by the elite state for its own nation-building purposes. In the next section I explore the role of fiction in this process.

FOUNDATIONAL FICTIONS AND NATIONAL FOLKLORE

Doris Sommer, in her study of nineteenth-century Spanish America's "foundational fictions," argued that national consolidation, patriotic history, and the romantic novel go hand in hand. The romantic novels composed in the first century after independence "fueled a desire for domestic happiness that runs over into dreams of national prosperity; and nation-building projects invested private passions with public purpose."[88] History and the novel together formed part of the larger process of nation-building. Sommer's work shows the importance of literature to the nationalist process in nineteenth-century Spanish America. Here I follow Sommer in considering literature's contribution to nation-building, but I focus not on the use of marriage as a metaphor for social consolidation—this was Sommer's primary concern—but rather on the ways in which nineteenth-century novels and poetry worked within a larger framework of nation-building to convert the preconquest past into a species of folklore. Although different in many ways, the romantic poetry and prose produced at mid-century and fin-de-siècle modernist writings presented very similar interpretations of the pre-Columbian past, which, for writers of both groups, served as a folkloric prelude to true national history. As with the historical writings discussed above, fictional works set in the precolonial era were composed almost exclusively by members of the elite. Indeed, political, historical, and literary works often flowed from the same pen. The Ecuadorian Juan León Mera composed political polemics, historical catechisms, and romantic poetry. Vicente Fidel López was not only a noted historian but also an acclaimed author of historical novels. Literary works that represented earlier eras formed part of the larger elite effort at nation-building, for, like works of history, they sought to endow Spanish America with a past.

A concern with the "nationalist" potential of the pre-Columbian past is evident in the very earliest literary works produced in independent Spanish America, as I argued in chapter 1. Drawing on late-eighteenth-century Europe's fascination with indigenous motifs, together with the nationalist rhetoric of the independence era, insurgent writers employed indigenous topics to give their works a "national" flavor, while at the same time beginning the process of converting indigenous history into a sort of mythologized folklore. The insurgent writer José Fernández Madrid, for example, titled his 1825 collection of preconquest-themed poetry *Peruvian National Elegies*.[89] Subsequent works conceived under the star of romanticism, the dominant literary mode in midcentury Spanish America, continued to use indigenous settings as an attractive framework for often-invented folklore. The poem "Caicobé," written by the liberal Argentine scholar José María Gutiérrez while in exile in Montevideo, for example, recasts the Apollo and Daphne myth as a Guaraní legend of an indigenous woman turned into a mimosa tree in order to save her (and the sacred amulet she wore) from defilement.[90] The preconquest era was here converted into an American version of a Greek legend by implicitly removing pre-Columbian peoples from the realm of history into the world of myth. In contrast to history, myths and legends were meaningful not because they were true but because they were beautiful and symbolic; it was precisely in the nineteenth century that "mito," or "myth," entered the Spanish vocabulary as a term for a legend or an orally transmitted traditional tale.[91] Poetic fictions such as those of Gutiérrez thus created literary, rather than literal, stories about the past. Spanish American romantics, although inspired by European writers such as Walter Scott, Mariano José de Larra, and François-René de Châteaubriand, deliberately sought out "original," local themes—including indigenous ones—in order to create new, national legends.[92] Indeed, throughout the century poems and novels employing indigenous motifs were likely to be described as "national," and the title "National Legends" (or some variant thereof) was given to a number of preconquest-themed literary collections in several countries.[93]

Romantic poems dedicated to the physical geography of Spanish America—its rivers, mountains, and other natural features—similarly evoked preconquest peoples as a method of conveying the passage of time. In such works the invocation of pre-Columbian cultures served to emphasize the immense antiquity of the Americas, while at the same time locating these cultures firmly in the distant past. In a poem from the 1850s, the Colombian poet José Joaquín Ortíz asks the Tequendama waterfall:

Where, O River, are those peoples
who once dwelled in this region?
What has become of the conquering Zipas
who sat upon the throne of gold?[94]

The cascade, whose waters had flowed since the distant era of the Zipas, bore witness not only to Colombia's antiquity but also to the disappearance of its indigenous population. The Cuban poet José María Heredia posed similar questions to the pyramid at Cholula.[95] Spanish America's natural environment was linked even more explicitly to the vanished preconquest population in works that recounted supposed indigenous legends explaining the formation of particular caves, hills, or other natural features. The Cuban poet Juan Cristóbal Nápoles Fajardo's poem "The Sage of Yarigua" tells the story of the hill from which the famous preconquest sage Guanaley once prognosticated. It concludes:

A century passed and then another,
and Guanaley perished;
his poor dwelling collapsed
never to rise again.
Lost was the sweet peace
of Guáimaro and Sibanicú,
In Cuba the sabicú tree trembled,
the grass burned in the fields,

but by the same name is known
the hill of Caisimú.[96]

The hill remained, but the Indians did not. The geography of Cuba was thus endowed with poetic richness without the requirement of a continuing indigenous presence. Like historical writings, such poetry helped furnish the region with a deep past. Like the national romances described by Sommer, they were attempts at creating foundational fictions. As the Dominican scholar Pedro Henríquez Ureña observed in 1905, such works were part of an effort to convert "the *history* of the New World Indians" into a Spanish American "*epic.*"[97] An epic, unlike history, need not be strictly true to be meaningful.

Continuing the trend established by these romantic writers, the fin-de-siècle modernists also depicted the precolonial era as a mythologized, poetic time, a true American antiquity. The poetry produced by Rubén Darío, the most influential modernista, celebrated the Aztecs and Incas alongside ancient Rome, imperial China, and the mysterious world of the Arabs, for like them, the Incas seemed to Darío to possess a poetic beauty quite absent from the modern world in which he was obliged to live. "If there is poetry in our America," he announced, "it is in old things: in Palenque and Utatlán, in the legendary Indian and the sensuous and delicate Inca, and in great Moctezuma upon his chair of gold."[98] Preconquest history, which for the Nicaraguan Darío meant Aztec and Inca monarchs, was the location of a truly American poetics. In his view the only thing in Spanish America worthy of comparison to the glories of the Parthenon were the ruins of Palenque; as for the historians cited above, for Darío pre-Columbian civilization constituted Spanish America's classical antiquity. This equivalence was made explicit in his poem "To Bolivia," in which he ascribed to the Incas an importance equal to that of ancient Greece in shaping his youthful imagination:

In the blue days of my golden youth
I often dreamt of Greece and of Bolivia:
in Greece I found the nectar that alleviates nostalgia
and in Bolivia I found an archaic fragrance.[99]

The long-vanished Incas (represented by the archaic fragrance of the high Andes) offered a Spanish American version of the classical heritage symbolized for Darío by the divine nectar on which the Olympians supped. Just as romantic poets such as Gutiérrez had transformed Greek myths so as to construct national legends, so modernistas saw the preconquest epoch as the time of Spanish American mythology.

The Peruvian modernist José Santos Chocano likewise celebrated the incaic past, which, unlike Darío, he claimed as part of his own ancestry, alongside the similarly poetic colonial period. As the opening of a volume of verses dedicated to the Spanish monarch Alfonso XIII explained:

> Sire, I have another muse who is not the Spanish muse,
> although in her blood there flows the blood of Spanish ancestors.
> She feels at times Indian and at times Castilian:
> she is the daughter of a Catholic Queen and the Sun.[100]

Colonial and preconquest: both were magical, and equally important, noble. Just as his Hispanic heritage was symbolized for Santos Chocano by the image of a queen, the Incaic state was emblematic of a divine nobility, for the Sun from which Santos Chocano's poetry descended was none other than the Inca himself, the *hijo del sol,* or son of the sun. As Antonio Cornejo Polar has noted, such modernist imaginings of the preconquest past displayed an undisguised adulation of aristocracy.[101] Altogether, the preconquest era was considered a magnificent source of poetic inspiration, suffused as it was with romantic yearning. Its primary feature, aside from its nobility, was a chivalric sensuality best expressed in the imagined courtly romances that fascinated such writers. "I would exchange half of my slight prowess in the Spanish language for an equal ability in the one which Moctezuma spoke on the Mexican throne, and the sweet and gracious tongue with which the princes of Huaina-Cápac captivated the daughters of the sun," sighed the Ecuadorian essayist Juan Montalvo in 1888.[102] Nostalgia dominated the modernist ethos.

For both romantic and modernist writers, the precolonial period was a fairy-tale time in which delicate Indian princesses wept for love of brave indigenous warriors. The elaborate plot of Juan León Mera's 1861 novel-length poem *The Sun Virgin* illustrates well the typical treatment of the era. Mera set his Inca romance—loosely based on Marmontel's *Les Incas*—in the conquest era. Cisa, a young, beautiful, indigenous woman, is prevented from marrying her beloved Titu by a jealous rival. The rival arranges for Cisa to be appointed an Inca sun virgin on the very day of the wedding. Before the marriage can be solemnized the distraught Cisa is removed to the *acllahuasi*, the convent housing the virgins dedicated to Inti, the sun god. The novel ends with the two lovers united in Christian marriage following the very opportune arrival of Spanish conquistadors.[103] Other works employed similarly romantic plots. Próspero Pereira's 1858 play *Akímen Zaque, or The Conquest of Tunja* intertwined an account of the Spanish conquest of central Colombia with a romance involving the indigenous leader, or Zaque, and a beautiful indigenous girl.[104] In Ignacio Rodríguez Galván's 1842 poem "Moctezuma's Vision" the mighty Aztec emperor falls in love with a poor Indian maiden.[105] The precolonial era, in other words, offered a setting for romantic narratives of national folklore. Preconquest ruins were singled out as particularly poetic. The Colombian poet José Joaquín Ortíz thus cited the "ruins of a temple in which the Muiscas worshipped Bochica [the Muisca creator god]" as a suitable object of poetic inspiration.[106] Sometimes these romances ended happily; more often, as in the Uruguayan poet Adolfo Berro's "Yandubayá and Liropeya" (1840) or the Mexican Eligio Ancona's *The Martyrs of Anáhuac* (1870), the narrative concluded with the tragic deaths of the protagonists.[107] In Ancona's novel the Aztec heroine expires following the sacrifice to Huitzilopochtli of her infant son, who is mistakenly believed to be the offspring of a liaison with a newly arrived conquistador.

Or perhaps the Indian princess might suffer torments of guilt because the object of her affections was a recently arrived Spaniard rather than the worthy indigenous prince to whom she was betrothed. In the Colombian writer Felipe Pérez's play *Gonzalo Pizarro* an Inca princess discovers that the brave conquistador whom she loves is in fact her own father. This revelation occurs minutes before the wedding that would have joined them in incestuous union. (The extended time frame of the Spanish conquest of Peru worked to the advantage of the narrative; the princess had been conceived during a furtive encounter between the conquistador and a *ñusta*, or Inca princess, in the earliest days of the conquest.)[108] Similar themes are explored in the Chilean writer Salvador Sanfuentes's 1885 verse novella *Inámi*, in which Antonio, a Spanish youth, happens upon the island inhabited by the beautiful but ill-fated Inámi. The story follows their doomed love affair, which ends with Inámi's death and Antonio's departure from the island.[109] In contrast, the Inca princess in Santos Chocano's

1906 play *The Conquistadors* kills both herself and the lustful Spaniard who desires her by kissing him with poisoned lips.[110] Such works set in the conquest era offered generally pessimistic opinions on the possibility of incorporating the indigenous population into the nation. Rarely did these mixed-race romances end with the successful marriage of Indian princess and Spaniard. Instead, a tragic death usually awaited any indigenous maiden romantically entangled with a European. If Sommer is correct in reading the happy endings of some nineteenth-century "national romances" as reflecting an optimistic longing for social cohesion, then the writers of the works discussed here did not envision the incorporation of the indigenous population into the national body. Within these romances the indigenous protagonists were confined to the past, prevented by death itself from becoming active participants in either the colonial period or the national era that succeeded it. The stories of these doomed lovers might thus form part of the nation's heritage—Sanfuentes's novella described itself as both an "indigenous legend" and a "national legend"—but their indigenous protagonists could not.

When not engaging in romantic intrigues these literary Indians announced their obsolescence even more explicitly. "My century has passed," explains the Aztec ruler to the poet in Rodríguez Galván's "Prophecy of Cuauhtémoc."[111] The "last Inca" in the Colombian José Eusebio Caro's 1835 poem invoked his "father Sun" before killing himself; "To die free!" he exclaims.[112] For the conservative Caro the Inca was a poignant emblem of a doomed race whose glories were linked solely with the past. Other poets ventriloquized through indigenous princes when musing on the ephemeral nature of all human life.[113] "Distance" (through antiquity or exoticism) marked the Indian in these works. Their era was a bygone time and their place was far away from the life of the modern nation.[114] Overall, the treatment of indigenous themes in such literary works helped establish the preconquest period as part of the national past, even as that past was presented as distant and mythologized.

Alongside works depicting colonial and independence-era history, paintings on precolonial themes were likewise celebrated for their "national" qualities. At Mexico's national art academy (the Academy of San Carlos, established in 1781), the production of paintings based on indigenous themes was encouraged after the establishment of a liberal government in the decades after 1860, as Stacie Widdifield has shown. Students, notes

Widdifield, "were as likely to be assigned pre-Hispanic Mexican themes as biblical and European historical ones."[115] National art exhibitions began to include such works as Rodrigo Gutiérrez's 1875 *Deliberation of the Senate of Tlaxcala,* which depicted, in Widdifield's words, "a nativized Roman senate" (see figure 15).[116] The painting—purchased by the Mexican government for display at world's fairs—illustrates the indigenous Tlaxcalan leadership in the act of deciding whether to ally themselves with either the recently arrived Spanish conquistadors or with the Aztecs, their former enemies. The Tlaxcalan leaders adopt noble poses, gesturing rhetorically in heroic fashion, while their fellow senators listen intently to the learned discussion. Tlaxcala is thus presented in Gutiérrez's painting as a civilized polity whose leaders comported themselves like those of that other Senate located in ancient Rome. The classical world again provided a model for the interpretation of the Spanish American past. The orientalizing tendencies of the modernist movement provided another model. The symbolist painter Saturnino Herrán's *Our Ancient Gods,* begun in 1914 and unfinished at the time of his death in 1918, was intended to form part of Mexico City's new Teatro Nacional (today's Palacio de Bellas Artes) (see figure 16). Just as earlier Mexican artists had refracted their vision of the preconquest past through the lens of European academic traditions, so Herrán employed the tenants of symbolism to depict the pre-Columbian era. For Herrán the period was typified by languid youths, clothed in gorgeous golden headdresses and elaborately knotted loincloths. The influence of Japanese prints—so significant in late-nineteenth-century French painting—is discernable in Herrán's stylized posings. Pictorial interpretations of the ancient indigenous world thus combined an appreciation of international artistic developments with the more local forces of elite nationalism. The outcome was a distinctive image of the preconquest world as at times classical, at times orientalized and exotic, but always distant.

Other countries that lacked Mexico's long history of official artistic instruction also witnessed the production of works of art based on precolonial themes, although with a lesser degree of state-level organization. In nineteenth-century Peru, the small Academy of Drawing encouraged promising artists to study in Europe, where they were exposed to European traditions of academic art, including its reverence for history painting. On their return to Peru a number began producing works based on themes from Peruvian history. For example, after studying at the Academy

Figure 15. Rodrigo Gutiérrez, *Deliberation of the Senate of Tlaxcala*, c.1875. Gutiérrez's painting, showing conquest-era Tlaxcalans deciding whether to ally with the Spanish or the Aztecs, creates a Mexican equivalent of the Roman senate. It is a visual depiction of the creole ambition to convert the indigenous past into an American version of classical antiquity. *Source*: Widdifield, *The Embodiment of the National*, 103. Courtesy of the Museo Nacional de Arte, Mexico City.

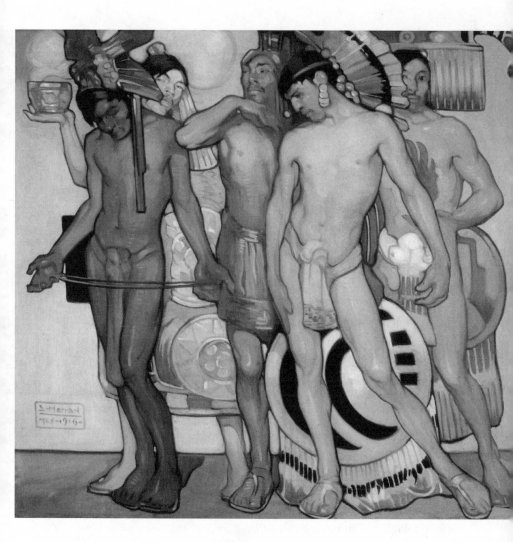

Figure 16. Saturnino Herrán, *Our Ancient Gods*, 1914–18. Herrán's drawing depicts Mexico's ancient deities as languorous youths equipped with fabulous headgear. The work is a study for a never-completed mural intended for the National Theater in Mexico City. *Source*: Courtesy of Museo Andrés Blaisten, www.museoblaisten.com.

of Fine Arts in Florence Luis Montero painted his 1865–67 *Atahualpa's Funeral* (see figure 17). The painting depicts the unfortunate Inca on his bier, shackles still hanging from his wrists, surrounded by Spaniards. On the left a group of Inca women bewail his death, in a swirl of bodies that contrasts sharply with the still, upright figures of the Spaniards. In 1868 the painting was exhibited in Lima to great public acclaim, and the Peruvian congress later purchased it for a considerable sum.[117] *Atahualpa's Funeral* was the first of a series of paintings by European-trained Peruvian artists dedicated to Peruvian themes; in subsequent decades, following Peru's defeat at the hands of Chile in the War of the Pacific, the Peruvian state itself began sponsoring paintings that depicted events from Peruvian history, as the art historian Natalia Majluf has noted.[118] These works included paintings illustrating both scenes from colonial and republican history—such as the painting owned by the National Library of Núñez de Balboa discovering the Pacific—and also more ancient subjects.[119] In 1896, for example, Carlos Baca-Flor produced a shimmering depiction of the ransom of Atahualpa, and in 1901 José Effio painted a (rather wooden) *Cahuide at the Defense of Sacsahuaman,* based on a print included in the 1853 Madrid edition of Prescott's *History of the Conquest of Peru.* (Cahuide, or Titu Cusi Huallpa, was an Inca general who led a heroic but unsuccessful resistance to the Spanish siege of Cuzco in 1536.) These paintings were often of monumental size, as befitted works of "national" art; Montero's painting measures nearly 4m x 6m, for example.[120]

The position of the precolonial era in paintings and works of literature complimented its role in historical writings. Patriotic history assigned the pre-Columbian period a position as prologue to the nation's real history, while in literature and art that distant epoch, largely stripped of any proximity to contemporary nineteenth-century culture through its very antiquity or exoticism, was freed to form a fund of images helpful in establishing the past so necessary for the enterprise of nationalism. Poetry and indigenous history thus merged into one fecund ur genre: "There is no sadder and more beautiful *poem* than American *history,*" insisted José Martí with reference to the preconquest past.[121] Conversely, as Guy Rozat notes, historical works devoted to the pre-Columbian era might take on the qualities of a romantic novel.[122] The conversion of indigenous history into national folklore explains why elites in 1870s Peru might listen happily to "the cantata of Manco-Capac," a composition named after

Figure 17. Luis Montero, *Atahualpa's Funeral*, 1865–67. Montero's monumental painting attracted more than 15,000 viewers when it was displayed in Lima in the 1860s. This is one of the many prints made of the image. Montero's work helped establish Peruvian history—including precolonial history—as a respectable genre for Peruvian artists. *Source: Perú en el primer centenario.* Courtesy of the Bodleian Library.

the first Inca, and why their homes might display "specimens of Peruvian bric-à-brac, consisting of statuettes of Incas and Coyas [Inca queens]."[123] It similarly explains why cookbooks in mid-nineteenth-century Mexico included recipes for "Moctezuma's dessert" alongside those for "insurgent soup."[124] While nibbling Moctezuma's dessert, members of the Porfirian elite might even enjoy tunes played on the "Zapotec"-style piano allegedly spotted by one turn-of-the-century Mexican journalist.[125] By converting preconquest history into something long, long ago, both historia patria and nineteenth-century artistic works eased its incorporation into the "national" heritages imagined by Spanish American elites.

"THE SUPERIOR CULTURE OF CHRISTIANITY"

While many nineteenth-century writers were prepared to defend precon-quest peoples as civilized, and perhaps even eat Moctezuma's pudding, by the 1840s virtually none claimed that pre-Columbian cultures had been more advanced than those of Europe. During the first years after independence, some intellectuals, notably in Mexico, continued to rail against the colonial period as a time of darkness, a step backward from the achievements of the pre-Columbian era.[126] Within a few decades, however, claims that preconquest America had exceeded Europe in culture and civilization died out with the abandonment of the indianesque as the dominant form of historical rhetoric. After midcentury the superiority of European civilization was taken for granted by elite writers of every political persuasion. European, and indeed Spanish, civilization, however flawed, was acknowledged as having been superior to all Amerindian civilizations. "Inca civilization was not permanent," explained the historian Lorente in 1860. "It was instead an ideal preparation for the superior culture of Christianity."[127] Columbus, proclaimed a Mexican writer three decades later, elevated Mexico from the "obscure chaos in which it slumbered and [brought] it to the beautiful sphere of cultured peoples."[128] The success of the conquest itself demonstrated the superiority of European civilization. "If [Aztec and Inca] civilizations had been at the level of Old World civilization . . . the discoveries, explorations and military efforts at conquering them would have failed," noted one Peruvian scholar.[129] Whereas during the independence era the conquest had provided evidence of Spanish brutality, now it indicated the merits of European civilization. The influence of Comtean positivism in many parts of Spanish America in the years after 1850 contributed toward a tendency to view the region's history as a series of developmental stages, each an improvement on its predecessor. But whatever their precise assessment of the colonial heritage that Spain had bequeathed to Spanish America, nineteenth-century intellectuals were in agreement that the arrival of Europeans in the Americas had been a move in the direction of greater civilization and progress. European civilization, in other words, was better than the homegrown varieties.

For writers generally unimpressed by preconquest peoples, such as hard-line conservatives, this was not a surprising position. Colombian conservatives of the late-nineteenth-century Regeneration thus argued that their nation's civilization was entirely Iberian. "The civilization which we enjoy came to us from Europe," insisted the conservative writer Soledad Acosta de Samper in 1883. The conquest and colonial eras, agreed fellow conservative (and future president) Miguel Antonio Caro, had provided the "origins of American civilization."[130] Nor was it surprising that Argentine liberals should insist that when compared with indigenous culture, Spanish traditions, however defective, were a vast improvement. Thus the anti-indigenous Sarmiento insisted that "*Spaniard*, endlessly uttered as a hateful synonym of impious, immoral abductor, swindler, is in truth synonymous with *civilization* [and] the *European tradition* brought by them to these countries."[131] But it was not only the writers unimpressed by pre-Columbian cultures who praised Spanish colonization for advancing the cause of civilization. The conquest, although sometimes condemned as cruel, was nonetheless acknowledged to have been a move in the direction of civilization even by writers generally positive about the achievements of preconquest peoples. "Did the immense accumulation of misfortunes suffered by the peoples of America bring any benefits in terms of civilization? We hasten to respond affirmatively . . . We will not enter into a detailed enumeration of each and every advantage brought by European civilization, because that would be little less than impossible," was how the Mexican scholar Manuel Orozco y Berra put it.[132] European superiority was regarded as so overwhelming that when discussing the effect of the conquest, even historians who had elsewhere described preconquest peoples as civilized sometimes contradicted themselves by insisting that the conquest had introduced civilization to an uncultured continent. The conquest was an "eruption of civilization over chaos," proclaimed the Colombian liberal José María Samper, although in the same text he elsewhere described the preconquest Muiscas as "very advanced in civilization, relatively speaking."[133] In the words of the five-volume Mexican historical compendium *Mexico through the Centuries*, "Spanish domination fell when it had fulfilled its destiny, and over its ruins arose a people new to the list of political societies, but bringing with them the ideas, habits, education and tendencies that they had inherited from the people who gave them *civilization* in return for independent life."[134] Thus although the authors of

Mexico through the Centuries had devoted an entire volume to the civilized nature of preconquest Mexico, they nonetheless stressed that colonial culture was the true source of independent Mexico's civilization.

The specific features of this superior Spanish civilization were enumerated far more frequently than were those of the earlier civilizations of the preconquest era. Writers often mentioned that the conquest had replaced paganism with Christianity, and many also cited the beautiful Spanish language as another positive contribution to the region's overall level of culture and civilization, notwithstanding the ongoing disputes between Peninsular and creole grammarians about the status of Spanish American vocabulary and syntax.[135] Yet at the same time writers also indicated, explicitly or implicitly, that this Spanish civilization had not always been of benefit to indigenous people themselves. The Guatemalan historian Antonio Batres Jaúregui, although repeating throughout his 1894 study of Guatemala's indigenous population that he did not wish to judge Spain's behavior, nonetheless provided a catalogue of abuses inflicted by the conquistadors and made clear that the quality of life enjoyed by the Maya had declined markedly since the conquest.[136] The superior civilization introduced by Spain, in other words, was often shown to have brought little if any gain to the indigenous population, even if the authors of such accounts declined to draw this conclusion from their own evidence. Far from noting the improvements that colonialism had brought to indigenous people, many writers instead dwelt obsessively on the annoying failure of indigenous people to adopt the features of this superior culture. Their refusal to learn Spanish was a particular source of complaint. These accounts thus implicitly reinforced a sequential version of the continent's history, in which indigenous culture (and indigenous peoples) had been replaced by a superior European culture (and superior European people). After ceding to this more advanced civilization, indigenous peoples stepped out of history into the realm of folklore.

CONCLUSIONS

I begin this chapter by noting the close connections between the composition of national histories, on the one hand, and the process of nation-building on the other. In the words of the historian Jean Meyer, "When we say 'national identity,' we are also saying 'history.'"[137] By including preconquest history—even as a preamble to genuinely "national" history—within discussions of the national past, historia patria helped make the pre-Columbian era part of the nation's heritage. The conversion of pre-colonial history into poetic folklore also helped incorporate the era into a broader category of national heritage. The importance of such literary representations to the enterprise of nation-building should not be under-estimated. As a number of scholars in addition to Sommer have noted, these more literary forms of writing can contribute to the construction of a national past alongside works of conventional history.[138] Narrating, telling stories, served to incorporate the past into the heritage of the nation; it helped make the *stories* of the past part of the patrimony of the nation-building elite, even if the past about which the stories were told was not quite their past. These stories made it possible for respectable elites to listen to Inca cantatas and eat Aztec puddings. Appreciating the preconquest past did not mean claiming a personal indigenous heritage, as the conservative Peruvian writer José de la Riva Agüero made clear. Although, as he noted in 1917, "Our nationality's most undeniable and glorious roots lie in the Inca empire," this did not make him an Indian. Rather, his comments were addressed to "all those white men capable of sublime thinking and feeling," a category in which he explicitly included himself.[139] It was thus quite possible for elite intellectuals to profess the European heritage discussed in the previous chapter at the same time that they admired the achievements of the distant preconquest peoples who had once inhabited their patrias. These achievements demonstrated themselves perhaps most strikingly in the imposing preconquest buildings present in many parts of Spanish America. In the next chapter I examine the importance of monuments and archaeology to the nationalization of the preconquest past.

 *Chapter 5*

Archaeology, Museums, and Heritage

In 1852 the Guatemalan historian Francisco de Paula García Peláez published his *Memoirs for the History of the Ancient Kingdom of Guatemala*. Although this three-volume work focuses primarily on the colonial period, a few dozen pages in the first volume address Guatemala's preconquest population. There, García Peláez's central concern was to demonstrate the superiority of Guatemala's indigenous ruins over those of Mexico, from which Guatemala had separated in 1823. Guatemala's importance vis-à-vis Mexico could be judged, he made clear, by comparing the quality of pre-Columbian monuments in each country: the greater the ruins, the greater the state in whose territory they lay. (Guatemala was at the time engaged in a protracted border dispute with Mexico, which may have helped focus García Peláez's mind on the territorial dimensions of Guatemala's national identity.) The remains of preconquest cities were a sign of Guatemala's importance, and hence a part of Guatemala's historia patria. Perhaps they were not as significant in shaping modern Guatemala as the colonial epoch to which García Peláez devoted the majority of his text, but they were nonetheless noteworthy. Those splendid ruined cities, however, had nothing whatsoever to do with Guatemala's contemporary Maya peoples, who at the time were actively supporting the government of Rafael Carrera, with whom García Peláez maintained an uneasy alliance. On the contrary, García Peláez insisted, they could not possibly have been constructed by the ancestors of these indigenes. They were instead the work of a mysterious people whose "very name is unknown."[1] In other words, García Peláez could accept that the ruins were of national significance but not that they had been built by the Maya. Preconquest civilization was part of national history yet possessed no direct connection either to Guatemala's contemporary Maya population or, for that matter, to García Peláez himself. García Peláez, an archbishop as well as a historian, made clear that the Guatemala to which he belonged was born in the colonial period. Preconquest ruins thus formed part of Guatemala's national heritage, although they were not part of the personal genealogy of any individual Guatemalan. They were instead physical manifestations of Guatemala's importance as a nation.

García Peláez's insistence that Maya ruins were simultaneously significant and disconnected from contemporary indigenous people exemplifies the process of appropriation and disassociation through which the preconquest past was incorporated into elite concepts of national heritage across Spanish America. In this chapter I examine the role of preconquest artifacts within elite discussions of the nation during the century after independence. The first section charts changing elite attitudes toward the collection and preservation of pre-Columbian artifacts. Subsequent sections explore the venues in which these items were displayed, looking in particular at Spanish American participation in world's fairs and the formation of national museums.

In considering the significance of monuments and museums to the articulation of nationality I draw on the growing body of research stressing the links between museums, historical ruins, and national identity. Ancient monuments, as Anthony Smith notes, can play an important role in the nationalist enterprise: "From the standpoint of a territorial nationalist it is quite legitimate to annex the monuments and artefacts of earlier civilizations *in the same place,* appropriating their cultural achievements to differentiate and glorify the territorial nation, which may (to date) lack achievements of its own."[2] Although the elite nationalisms studied here were not based on a fundamentally territorial vision of the nation, the display of pre-Columbian artifacts did provide opportunities to "differentiate and glorify" the nation. Monuments and museums, in other words, are places where nationalism may be embodied and made visible. In the previous chapter I began to explore the ways in which national elites imagined the preconquest era as part of national history. Here I consider the place of material culture within these imaginings.

PATRIMONY AND PRE-COLUMBIAN ARTIFACTS

Broadly speaking, until the eighteenth century the collecting of objects, whether in Europe or the Americas, was governed by a set of priorities and concerns quite different from those shaping that process in the nineteenth and twentieth centuries. Objects were gathered, displayed, and sorted not according to the scientific, natural, and historical classifications introduced in the eighteenth century but rather by an acquisitive urge accompanied by the desire to arouse wonder. This they might do by being surprising, outlandish, or rare.[3] Pre-Columbian artifacts, which demonstrated in particular the magnificent variety of God's creation, began to be incorporated into cabinets of curiosities in the decades after Columbus's arrival in the Americas. Duke Cosimo I of Florence owned an inlaid Aztec mask, while in France similar objects were installed in the royal Palais des Cabinets. The Vatican too acquired a collection of pre-conquest items.[4] Spanish monarchs and individuals connected with the colonial administration also assembled collections that included American curiosities. Peru's sixteenth-century Viceroy Francisco de Toledo, for example, collected Incaic textiles.[5] Preconquest artifacts were also seen as an appropriate subject for scholarly analysis, because antiquities of all sorts assisted the exploration of man's place in the universe. Moreover, as Jorge Cañizares-Esguerra has shown, eighteenth-century historians became increasingly interested in what nonalphabetic writing systems such as those used in preconquest America revealed about the development of the human capacity to reason.[6] The majority of the extant preconquest pictorial manuscripts, or codices, were collected in the eighteenth century, usually by Europeans such as the Italian Lorenzo Boturini, who assembled an enormous library of pre-Columbian and conquest-era codices in the 1730s and 1740s.[7]

Contrasting with this elite European interest in preconquest artifacts was the general disregard in which they were held by all but a handful of creoles.[8] For many creoles, preconquest objects were interesting primarily when they might be melted down into gold or silver ingots, or when they needed to be destroyed as part of an anti-idolatry campaign.[9] Filiberto de Mena, a Chilean creole, described the indifference with which such items were viewed by most creoles in his 1791 description of the "monuments from the time of the Incas" around Salta. Mena stressed both the presence in the area of substantial indigenous ruins and the disdain with which they were regarded. Commenting on a site containing preconquest tombs, he noted that he was unable to provide much information on them "because in the thirty-six years that I have lived here curiosity has stirred no one to request permission to excavate and explore those graves."[10] During

Alexander von Humboldt's visit to the preconquest ruins at Cañar in Ecuador he likewise noted that the local hacendado "prided himself on the role his ancestors had played in destroying such buildings."[11] Europeans wishing to purchase, or indeed simply take, preconquest artifacts thus met with few obstacles. Humboldt returned to Europe in 1804 with various pre-Columbian objects, some of which he presented to the king of Prussia.[12]

A subsection of educated creoles expressed a more scholarly interest in preconquest remains, which when viewed through the lens of creole patriotism provided evidence for the greatness of pre-Columbian empires, and therefore of the creoles themselves. Although the Inca empire perhaps played a less important role within Peruvian creole patriotism than did the Aztec state in Mexico, Peruvian chroniclers nonetheless celebrated the architectural achievements of the Incas. Following the lead established by Garcilaso de la Vega's 1609 *Comentarios reales de los Incas*, which had waxed eloquent on (among other things) Incaic architecture, most Peruvian chroniclers felt compelled to praise the construction of Inca roads and buildings.[13] These structures "disprove the false idea of *Peruvian* brutality or extreme barbarism," in the words of one eighteenth-century writer.[14] In late colonial Colombia, the creole scientist Francisco José de Caldas urged the viceregal government to "gather together and sketch" the preconquest ruins at San Agustín, so as to shed light on the people who built them, "of whom our historians have not transmitted to us the slightest information."[15] In New Spain, the preconquest ruins that dotted the landscape around central Mexico and the Yucatan occupied an even more important place within creole patriotism. In the eighteenth century Mexican creoles penned lengthy studies of Aztec monuments, and a number amassed considerable private collections of pre-Columbian items.[16] By the late eighteenth century such interest served an explicitly patriotic agenda. In 1788 José Antonio Alzate, the editor of the *Gaceta de Literatura de México*, promised that his journal would provide details about "the few antiquities that remain of the Mexican nation, and, if the printing costs can sustain it, they will be illustrated," because of the importance of conserving information about the "nature, character [and] customs of the Mexican nation."[17] Antonio de León y Gama likewise explained that he would publish information about two Aztec sculptures found in Mexico City in 1790 (the Coatlicue and the Piedra del Sol or "Aztec calendar") in order to "shed some light on ancient Literature, which in other countries is so encouraged."[18] León y Gama compared the excavation of these two statues with those undertaken in Pompeii and Herculaneum, while Alzate likened the pre-Columbian ruins of Xochicalco to the Egyptian pyramids.[19] The Jesuit Francisco Xavier Clavijero not only composed a multivolume *Ancient History of Mexico*, which detailed the achievements of preconquest peoples, but also stressed the need to "preserve the remains of the antiquity of our patria," by which he meant Aztec monuments.[20] In Guatemala, too, pre-Columbian remains were cited as a source of creole pride. Francisco Antonio de Fuentes y Guzmán, the creole author of a late-seventeenth-century chronicle, praised the stelae and other sculptures found in Maya sites such as Atitlán. Hieroglyphic writings in particular proved, in his view, that the preconquest Indians were not barbarous, "as some believe."[21] By the late colonial period, in other words, pre-Columbian artifacts had been incorporated into creole patriotism's celebration of creole heritage.

Even in Mexico the interest in the pre-Columbian past, while patriotic, was not necessarily revolutionary. León y Gama's defense of Aztec culture, for example, was aimed at proving "how falsely *Spain's enemies* slander [the Indians] by calling them irrational, in order to discredit the great deeds achieved in the conquest of these kingdoms."[22] On the surface, at least, the late colonial celebration of preconquest peoples served to celebrate Spain. For this reason Spanish monarchs approved and even financed archaeological explorations. Charles III sanctioned the exploration of Palenque and Charles IV similarly backed the exploration of sites such as Xochicalco, Monte Albán, and Mitla.[23] State interest in pre-Columbian ruins explains why Mexico's colonial government established an Antiquities Junta in 1808, which was intended to oversee future excavations.[24] Colonial Mexico was, however, unusual in possessing such a committee and such state-supported concern with preconquest remains. The colonial administrations in the other Spanish colonies showed no more regard for protecting preconquest items than was shown toward the protection of any other aspect of the region's material culture.

After independence, state interest in protecting preconquest artifacts manifested itself in two discrete bursts, the first in the 1820s and the second in the final decades of the nineteenth century. Both were linked in particular ways to the larger process of elite nation-building underway during the nineteenth century. Immediately after independence Peru and Mexico enacted laws aimed at keeping pre-Columbian artifacts within national boundaries. This legislation associated the preservation of preconquest antiquities with national pride. An 1822 Peruvian law requiring a government permit for the export of "mineral stones, ancient ceramics, fabrics and other objects found in Huacas [Andean graves]" explained (somewhat incoherently) that legislation was necessary as "the monuments which remain from Peru's antiquity are the property of the nation. They are part of the glory which they give to the nation. . . . We have watched with sorrow as, even here, priceless objects are sold and taken to places where their value is recognized, depriving us of the benefits of possessing what is ours."[25] Pre-Columbian ruins, in other words, were a sign of the greatness of preconquest civilizations, and therefore were important to the state. In Mexico, the first efforts by the independent government to prevent the export of pre-Columbian artifacts also date from 1822, when the colonial Antiquities Junta was reconstituted as a national body.[26] This was followed in 1827 by a law prohibiting the export of, inter alia, "monuments and Mexican antiquities."[27] Two years later the veteran pro-Aztec campaigner Servando Teresa de Mier successfully introduced a bill in the Chamber of Deputies "such that no ancient writings or monuments might be removed without the government having preferential rights to them."[28] Thus by the 1830s there were a series of laws and institutions in Peru and Mexico intended to prevent the removal of pre-Columbian artifacts because of their importance to the nation.

Whether these laws were enforced was another matter; in practice, few obstacles lay in the way of foreign collectors who wished to remove pre-Columbian artifacts from any part of Spanish America during the first half of the nineteenth century. Peruvian officials noted in 1837 that despite legislation requiring government permission to export preconquest artifacts, "with the exception of two or three people no one has requested this permission, and it is well known that these items are continuously exported to Europe."[29] Things were little different in Mexico. When in 1856 the British anthropologist Edward Tylor prepared to return to the United Kingdom after a four-month stay in Mexico, he reported matter-of-factly: "Our last day . . . was spent in packing up antiquities to be sent to England, the express orders of the Government against such exportation to the contrary notwithstanding."[30] Indeed, in the same years Mexican officials were giving preconquest artifacts as gifts to foreign visitors and merchants. "In the neglect of all antiquities in Mexico . . . every vestige of her former history will gradually pass to foreign countries," predicted one U.S. diplomat.[31] In Colombia, as Clara Isabel Botero has shown, travelers removed Quimbaya and Tairona gold figurines without the least impediment.[32] In Central America the appreciation occasionally expressed by individuals such as García Peláez for Maya monuments did not prevent North American explorers from purchasing entire preconquest cities. In 1839 John Stephens and Frederick Catherwood bought the Maya ruins at Copán for fifty dollars. Stephens reported that, in the view of the local landowner, "the property was so utterly worthless that my wanting to buy it seemed very suspicious."[33] The ease with which collectors removed artifacts is reflected in the holdings of the major European and U.S. museums, which acquired substantial collections of preconquest items during these years. By 1850, for example, the Louvre possessed enough pre-Columbian antiquities to open an entire gallery devoted to their display.[34]

The failure to enforce protective legislation in the regions where it existed illustrates both the weakness of the national state in the first half of the nineteenth century and also the still-uncertain place of the preconquest era within emergent historia patria. As I noted in the previous chapter, in most parts of Spanish America it was not until the 1840s that sustained scholarly efforts were made at composing national histories, and it was several decades before the fruits of these efforts were harvested. Indeed, it was not until the 1880s that even partially effective governmental efforts were made to protect preconquest artifacts anywhere in Spanish America. In Mexico, state support for archaeological research increased dramatically during the rule of Porfirio Díaz, and a body dedicated to the protection of pre-Columbian ruins—the office of Inspection and Conservation of Archaeological Monuments—was created in 1885. It was responsible for acts such as the conversion of the ruins at Mitla into a national monument allowing the public to "admire the beauty of its notable architecture."[35] The Díaz regime was also the first to post guards at archaeological sites, as Christina Bueno has noted, and in 1896 and 1897 new laws were passed protecting the "archaeological patrimony."[36] Foreign collectors, moreover, began to experience difficulties in gaining export permits. When in 1878 the French collector Auguste Le Plongeur tried to remove a Maya "Chac Mol" figure, the statue was confiscated and sent to the Yucatan Museum in Mérida.[37] Attempts in 1880 by another French archaeologist to export some of his finds from Palenque prompted a heated debate in the Mexican national congress, which resulted in the denial of the export permit and the deposit of the artifacts in the National Museum.[38] Enrique Florescano is thus incorrect in his claim that the Mexican state began to value pre-Columbian artifacts only after the Mexican Revolution.[39]

Peru followed a similar trajectory: after the attempts in the 1820s and 1830s at preventing unauthorized export, efforts at keeping artifacts in the country languished until the late nineteenth century, when interest in protecting these "national monuments" revived. Legislation issued in 1893 again prohibited the unauthorized exploration, extraction, and export of all preconquest remains, and more legislation followed in 1911.[40] Elsewhere pre-Columbian antiquities were generally granted protection as part of the national patrimony in the first decades of the twentieth century, at the same time that colonial and other artifacts were accorded protected status. In Honduras the export of archaeological remains was prohibited in 1900, sixty years after the (ultimately abortive) sale of Copán to Stephens and Catherwood, and a half century after such ruins had first been placed under state protection.[41] Guatemala established laws prohibiting the unauthorized export of pre-Columbian items in 1893.[42] In 1914 Venezuela prohibited the export of "official documents or other historical objects"—terms that presumably included pre-Columbian artifacts, unless they had been previously offered for sale to the government.[43] In the same years Argentines were still calling for laws to protect "properties and moveable items of historical interest," such as "landscapes and historical locations," including "Quechua cemeteries."[44] The Colombian government declared pre-Hispanic objects the property of the state in 1918, and in 1920 their unauthorized removal from the country was prohibited.[45] In Chile historic items of all sorts, including "anthropo-archaeological objects or items," were in 1925 placed under state control where their export was prohibited.[46]

"THOSE VENERABLE AND MYSTERIOUS RUINS"[47]

What prompted Spanish American governments to issue legislation protecting Pre-Columbian artifacts? In the case of laws enacted in the 1820s, the answer lies in the indianesque nationalism typical of the period. As the Peruvian 1822 legislation prohibiting such exports explained, Incaic artifacts belonged to Peru because they were part of its national glory. Peru, as a revindication of the Inca empire, needed to preserve the tangible relics of its glorious past.[48] Later laws did not view the Spanish American republics as reincarnations of preconquest empires, but like earlier legislation they reflected the need for a past inherent in the nation-building process. As I argued in the previous chapter, by the mid-nineteenth century the preconquest era had been incorporated into national history in most parts of Spanish America. Within historia patria, the preconquest period was described as part of the heritage of the nation, if not of the historians writing these histories. In such works the precolonial era was generally presented as a time of civilization, albeit a civilization inferior to that later introduced from Europe. Pre-Columbian ruins helped demonstrate the grandeur of this past, and therefore, as García Peláez realized, of the nation itself. Across Spanish America writers during the second half of the century thus lauded preconquest ruins for showing the high level of civilization attained in the Americas before the conquest. Mexican writers argued that the Aztecs' "magnificent monuments" proved the Aztecs to be "the most cultured people the Spaniards found in the New World."[49] The huge monolith known as the Piedra del Sol, which appeared regularly on commemorative medals during the Porfiriato, was particularly singled out in school history manuals as evidence for the high degree of civilization achieved by the Aztecs.[50] Monumental ruins showed that other cultures dwelling within Mexican territory had been civilized as well. "The scattered ruins, which are a living page of their glory and grandeur, . . . testify still to the level of civilization achieved [by the Toltecs]," noted the antiquarian Francisco Pimentel.[51] The sacred city of Mitla likewise demonstrated the cultured status of the Zapotecs, in the view of the politician and historian Justo Sierra.[52] In Guatemala, writers from the 1830s praised the civilized qualities of Maya ruins; the geographer Juan Galindo asserted that the details about indigenous ruins that he included in his 1834 *Atlas of the State of Guatemala* would "proclaim clearly to the world the high level of civilization of these countries in former times and save ancient America from the charge of barbarism."[53] "Mexican and Central American ruins demonstrate conclusively that in ancient times these lands were inhabited by an important civilization," agreed the scholar Antonio Batres Jaúregui sixty years later.[54] Muisca artifacts, insisted the Colombian academic Ezequiel Uricoechea in 1854, revealed the "degree of intellectual perfection of those peoples, the first inhabitants of America."[55] Incaic buildings too were lauded by scholars for illustrating the empire's grandeur. "These mute but eloquent witnesses reveal the history of past deeds and show us the intelligence, power and grandeur of the nation ruled by our Incas," insisted Mariano de Rivero, director of Peru's National Museum.[56] Such objects, elite writers across Spanish America agreed, were thus "national antiquities," part of "our ancient history."[57] Preconquest monuments formed part of the nation's heritage because they demonstrated the grandeur and significance of the nation's past.

The ability of elite nation-builders to appreciate preconquest artifacts was greatly facilitated by the development of archaeology as a scholarly discipline. During the second half of the nineteenth century, while Spanish American elites struggled to create satisfactory national pasts for their new states, scholars in other parts of the world were beginning to take a particular interest in those aspects of the Amerindian past that could be dug up and transported elsewhere: the years between 1860 and 1925 saw the emergence of modern archaeology. Investigators developed a series of new dating and excavation techniques, which were communicated through the emerging scholarly community via a growing number of archaeological journals and specialist congresses.[58] At the same time, archaeology, together with anthropology, were established as academic disciplines within leading universities in Europe and the United States. Harvard began teaching archaeology within its newly founded department of anthropology in 1886, while Oxford issued its first archaeology diploma in 1905. Prehistoric archaeology was taught at the University of Toulouse starting in 1890. Museums dedicated to archaeology and anthropology, such as Harvard's Peabody Museum or the Pitt Rivers Museum now in Oxford, were similarly established during these years and began to fund excavations and surveys.[59] Although during this period most excavations in Spanish America were carried out by foreigners—the famous "discovery" of Machu Picchu, for example, was undertaken in 1911 by the U.S. explorer Hiram Bingham—Spanish Americans such as the Mexican Leopoldo Batres (who under Porfirio Díaz held the post of Inspector and Conservator of Archaeological Monuments) or the Chilean Prudencio Valderrama (who in 1875 excavated ruins in the Punta de Teatinos) began to explore the region's archaeological heritage alongside their better-funded North American and European colleagues. Archaeological societies were also formed in a number of Spanish American countries in the years after 1850.[60]

The emergence of archaeology intersected with Spanish American nationalism in subtle ways, for the increasing international interest in archaeology encouraged Spanish American states to value pre-Columbian ruins and artifacts for their scientific merit. It is not a coincidence that the late-nineteenth-century upsurge in legislation designed to protect preconquest artifacts coincided with a period of particular foreign interest in pre-Columbian antiquities. From the 1880s European and U.S. museums and universities excavated an ever-growing number of preconquest sites across Spanish America. It was in these years that Pachacamac, Machu Picchu, Tiahuanaco, Chichén Itzá, Tikal, and Copán were explored by foreign archaeologists keen to export their findings to the broader scientific community.[61] In seeking to protect preconquest artifacts Spanish American governments were responding to this international attention, including the specific recommendations of organizations such as the International Congress of Americanistas, which in 1915 urged Spanish American nations to pass protective legislation.[62] The language of protective legislation itself reflects the increasing foreign and archaeological interest in these sites. Although the 1845 Honduran law that declared Copán to be the property of the state had described the ruins simply as "ancient monuments that exist in the Valley of Copán," in 1874 legislators were referring to the "ancient and very well-known ruins and notable historical monuments." By 1889 the site had become "ruins known as the 'Ruins of Copán,' which merit very special government attention because of their archaeological importance." When in 1900 legislation was passed completely forbidding the export of any preconquest artifacts, the Honduran congress justified the law by referring to their considerable archaeological and scientific interest.[63]

That foreigners showed more appreciation for preconquest artifacts than did the states in whose territory they lay was considered shameful by many nineteenth-century Spanish American intellectuals. "It is humiliating that Europeans and Anglo-Americans investigate the mysteries of our own archaeology with greater interest than we do ourselves," lamented a Colombian antiquarian.[64] The interest that foreigners took in preconquest artifacts was cited as good evidence that Spanish Americans ought to value these things. The pre-Columbian antiquities displayed at Costa

Rica's national museum, observed the modernist poet Rubén Darío, "will without doubt attract the attention of European science," which, he argued, meant that the region needed more protective legislation: "Many individuals, particularly foreigners, have filled entire museums with Central American antiquities, without this having so far provoked any controls over those more or less commercial currents that carry away the finest jewels of our ancient archaeological treasures to enrich and beautify distant lands."[65] Protective legislation helped address these concerns.

Archaeology also influenced the methods by which Spanish American elites evaluated preconquest cultures. Eighteenth-century European historians such as William Robertson had divided human history into stages based on their characteristic modes of subsistence: hunter-gatherer, pastoral, agricultural, and commercial. The earlier stages were classified as "savage'" and "barbarian." Civilized society was associated with the development of agriculture and trade.[66] The discipline of archaeology provided a new language for evaluating and assessing cultures that built on these eighteenth-century ideas at the same time as it introduced new methodologies for interpreting "prehistory," as the history of human existence before the development of writing came to be known. In 1836 the Danish curator Christian Jürgensen Thomsen published his theory that prehistory should be divided into what he called the Stone, Iron, and Bronze Ages, each of which represented a developmental advance over the previous age. Degrees of civilization were thus linked very explicitly to the types of artifacts produced by a given culture. Thomsen's classification proved influential, and in the 1860s further modifications were introduced, so that the Stone Age was divided into the Paleolithic and the Neolithic.[67] In addition, building on eighteenth-century ideas, archaeologists began specifying the distinct features associated with savage, barbaric, and civilized cultures. The English archaeologist Edward Tylor, writing in the 1860s to 1880s, described Savage society as lacking both agriculture and domesticated animals. Savage cultures were also often nomadic and belonged to the Stone Age. The transition to the Barbaric stage was marked by the development of agriculture and / or pastoralism. Civilization began with the development of writing.[68] The U.S. scholar Lewis Morgan developed these terms further in his 1877 *Ancient Society*. Morgan divided human development into seven stages: Lower, Middle, and Upper Savagery, Lower, Middle, and Upper Barbarism, and Civilization. The transition from one stage to another was marked by transformations in language, forms of subsistence, and a variety of other structures. In particular, the progression from Upper Savagery to Lower Barbarism was marked by the development of pottery. The domestication of animals and / or the development of irrigated agriculture differentiated Lower Barbarism from Middle Barbarism. Upper Barbarism was characterized by the manufacture of iron. With the invention of a phonetic alphabet true Civilization began.[69]

Individual societies could thus be classified according to the artifacts they generated as well as by the presence or absence of permanent settlements. The Egyptian pyramids, for example, demonstrated the civilized status of their builders, as did Egyptian hieroglyphic writing.[70] European and U.S. archaeologists employed these schema to order the cultures of the New World alongside those of the Old World. "The Village Indians who were in the Middle Status of barbarism, such as the . . . Aztecs and the Cholulans, manufactured pottery in large quantities," noted Morgan.[71] Spanish American scholars largely rejected the assignment of the Aztecs to the category of "Middle Barbarism," but they did employ the underlying ideas developed by U.S. and European archaeologists to classify the region's preconquest peoples. In particular, the correlation between a society's artifacts and its level of culture was used to argue that the Aztecs, Incas, Maya, and to a lesser degree, Muiscas, were civilized. The monumental structures built by these peoples were cited as good evidence for their builders' civilized status. The "artistic monuments" of the ancient Mexicans, insisted one Mexican orator in 1845, "reveal a degree of civilization and culture very distant from [barbarism]."[72] Moreover, the emphasis placed by nineteenth-century archaeologists on writing systems as a marker of civilization helps explain Mexican scholars' frequent mention of Aztec hieroglyphics. "In vain do some European writers attempt to portray them as submerged in barbarism: their hieroglyphs speak," noted the same speaker.[73]

On the other hand, the analytical categories developed by archaeologists did little to elevate the status of nomadic peoples such as the Mapuche. Lacking a written language and believed to possess neither an agricultural tradition nor a developed pastoral system, preconquest pampas dwellers appeared irremediably fixed in the age of Lower Barbarism. Such peoples might be important scientifically as representations of an early state in human evolution, but they were certainly not civilized. The language of archaeology, in other words, complimented the tendencies of nineteenth-century historia patria both in its affirmation of Aztec and Inca civilization and in its denial of that status to nomadic peoples who failed to construct monumental buildings. The nationalist importance of having a monumental and civilized preconquest past was acknowledged even by those who believed that, sadly, their nations lacked such a past. The conservative Colombian writer Ernesto Restrepo Tirado expressed particularly clearly the patriotic potential of pre-Columbian history at the same time as he denied that Colombia's preconquest population deserved the accolades they had received from other scholars. Although other savants such as Uricoechea had endowed the Muiscas (or Chibchas, as they were often called during the nineteenth century) with both writing and a calendar—two infallible markers of civilization—Restrepo unhappily concluded that they had possessed neither: "It pains us to contribute to the destruction of such poetic and appealing fictions. How much more pleasant it would be to interpret our stones as revealing inscriptions and fragments of ancient calendars! How much we would prefer to display before the eyes of the civilized world a Chibcha nation so advanced as to have mastered figurative writing and able to record on stone the division of time!"[74]

Restrepo's lament, located at the conclusion of his 1892 study of Colombia's pre-Columbian cultures, reveals clearly the appeal of having a civilized preconquest history that one could "display before the eyes of the civilized world." Presumably for this reason, the separate volume coedited by Restrepo in the same year to accompany the Colombian exhibition of Quimbaya gold work shown at the 1892 world's fair in Madrid placed considerably more emphasis on the artistic and aesthetic merit of preconquest artifacts than did his other works.[75] When the eyes of the civilized world were upon Colombia it was necessary to cast its ancient history in the best possible light.

SPANISH AMERICA AT THE WORLD'S FAIRS

World's fairs such as the 1892 exposition held in Madrid to mark the quatrocentenary of Columbus's arrival in the Americas provided particularly focused opportunities for states to exhibit their technical and artistic achievements "before the eyes of the civilized world." The Spanish American republics participated in many of these international exhibitions, for world's fairs offered the chance to attract commercial investment and much-desired foreign immigration. The fairs also served as forums for performances of nationalism. The nation-state was the central organizational principle at all world's fairs, and participant states viewed these events as occasions when "each nation opens publicly the great book that truthfully records its ways of life, its social, economic and industrial condition, its wealth and *its position among the other nations*."[76] Because of their importance as sites for the display of national identity, the pavilions of individual countries often included areas devoted to national history. The historical exhibits mounted by Spanish American states varied in size and quality both over time and from country to country. They nonetheless provide an interesting perspective from which to view elite nationalism's treatment of the preconquest past, for Colombia was not alone in exhibiting pre-Columbian antiquities: on some occasions, indigenous artifacts constituted the only historical material displayed at all.[77] In this section I examine the place of indigenous antiquities within these displays, looking particularly at the exhibits shown at the 1889 Universal Exposition held in Paris to mark the centenary of the French Revolution.[78]

Mexico, as Mauricio Tenorio Trillo has shown, housed its exhibition at the 1889 event in a specially constructed "Aztec palace" described by its architects as being in the "purest Aztec style" (see figure 18).[79] Its display at the Paris exhibition was intended to show Mexico as "a national entity with a glorious past but ready to adjust to the dictates of cosmopolitan nationalism and eager to be linked to the international economy."[80] The government of Porfirio Díaz, like all Latin American governments, hoped to use the fair to attract European immigration. To do this, it was felt necessary to correct the reigning European image of Mexico as a land of permanent disorder inhabited by backward savages. The Aztec palace contributed to this goal by illustrating the architectural achievements of "the most advanced races of Mexico," including, on center stage, the Aztecs.[81] This use of architectural styles derived from preconquest monuments was intended to communicate pride in Mexico's preconquest past. It was this style, rather than colonial architecture, that was hailed as "national" by (some) Mexican critics.[82] Nor was Mexico alone in presenting preconquest architecture as distinctively national. Ecuador, inspired by

Archaeology, Museums, and Heritage 147

Figure 18. Mexican Pavilion, Paris Universal Exposition, 1889. The Mexican Pavilion designed by Antonio Peñafiel for the 1889 Paris Exposition substituted two preconquest figures (based on statues from the Toltec site of Tula) for the usual Greco-Roman caryatids. The facade was decorated with images of Aztec gods and heroes and varied pre-Columbian motifs. *Source*: Picard, *Rapport Général*, 2: plate facing 226. Courtesy of the Bodleian Library.

news of the planned Aztec palace, arranged the construction of an "Inca palace" to serve as the Ecuadorian pavilion in Paris (see figure 2).[83] The pavilion, moreover, housed a selection of Incaic artifacts, which were compared in importance to the relics of the ancient Egyptians, thus once again underscoring the idea that the Inca empire was part of an American classical antiquity, as Blanca Muratorio has noted. Colombia's exhibit (housed in Uruguay's pavilion) likewise displayed pre-Columbian gold figures and other preconquest items.[84]

While the Mexican and Ecuadorian pavilions at the Paris Universal Exposition exalted preconquest architecture, the Argentine pavilion contained "no trace of Argentina's 'uncivilized' indigenous population, past or present," as Ingrid Fey has shown.[85] Offers of indigenous "curiosities" by provincial governors for display at the exposition were refused, and when French visitors to the pavilion asked to see some Argentine "savages," they were told politely but firmly that there were none.[86] The Argentine exhibit was thus consonant with the attitudes toward Argentina's principal preconquest cultures expressed in the historia patria discussed in the previous chapter. The Argentine government, possessed of no preconquest cultures displaying recognized characteristics of civilization (aside from the geographically marginal Incas), instead stressed Argentina's European heritage, and its advanced manufacturing potential, in the hope of encouraging French immigration and European consumption of Argentine chilled beef. Reports in the Argentine press on the Argentine presence at the exposition reveal an immense concern with their nation's image in Europe, and the author of the official publication informed readers that, during the construction of the pavilion, the Parisian public was surprised by the "martial appearance" and the "European-style uniforms" of Argentine soldiers, "which the people of this country did not expect to see." Argentine readers would also be pleased to learn that the pavilion succeeded in demonstrating that Argentina was just like a European country. "There are things just like we have here! There are trams, plazas, gardens like ours!" exclaimed Parisian visitors, to the delight of the Argentine organizers.[87] This single-minded emphasis on appearing European indeed attracted the criticism of some of the Argentine representatives at the exposition. Enrique Nelson, for example, maintained that instead of commissioning French artists to decorate the pavilion with typical Argentine scenes, the organizers should have chosen Argentine artists, even if they were less proficient technically. The result of hiring French artists to paint depictions of Argentine women, he complained, was that they appeared more Italian than American.[88] We might suspect, however, that this was precisely the point. In any event, Argentina's approach to attracting European migrants was more successful than that of Mexico. It appears that potential immigrants were more impressed by offers of good wages and a recognizably European culture than by an exotic, albeit monumental, past.[89]

The response of these countries to the 1889 Universal Exposition in Paris was largely typical of their responses to the other nineteenth-century international exhibitions. Argentina consistently excluded preconquest items from their displays at world's fairs. The Uruguayan historian Andrés Lamas made clear what sorts of historic material he felt should be exhibited when he complained that Argentina's entry to an 1882 international exhibition included only commercial and scientific displays rather than the independence-era mementoes he considered essential to understanding his country's heritage.[90] The Mexican display at the 1892 Columbian Exposition held in Madrid, on the other hand, included some ten thousand pre-Columbian antiquities as well as colored reproductions of codices.[91] The Colombian display at the same event included an outstanding collection of Quimbaya gold work subsequently presented to the Spanish queen regent. The Ecuadorian exhibit included over a thousand Inca and Cara artifacts in addition to photographs of Inca monuments. The exhibition catalogue stressed that the Caras, supposedly the earliest civilization in Ecuador, were closely related to the Inca Atahualpa, and its readers were reminded that the Inca empire was a "very advanced civilization."[92] Guatemala, whose Maya remains demonstrated its national importance (in the view of García Peláez), included in its display at the 1855 Paris Exhibition "a very ancient stone which the Indians used for sacrifices," which had the distinction of having been mentioned in Prescott's history of the conquest of Mexico. This was the only item that the Guatemalan government wanted returned after the conclusion of the exposition.[93]

MUSEUMS AND MEMORIES

The displays mounted at these international exhibitions mirror the contents of the national museums established across Spanish America after independence. National museums were founded in two waves that roughly paralleled the development of protective legislation discussed earlier. In many countries national museums were created in the first decade after independence. For example, the Mexican national museum dates from 1825, and the Peruvian national museum was founded in 1826. Elsewhere national museums were established in the last decades of the nineteenth century; Venezuela did not acquire a national museum until 1875 (see table 1). Regardless of when the first museums were founded, the last decades of the nineteenth century saw an accelerated rate of museum formation. In Argentina, for example, seven new museums were opened in the years between 1877 and 1905.[94] Existing museums also reopened in grander premises or with increased budgets. In the timing of their establishment, these Spanish American museums kept pace with the formation of

TABLE 1. The date of the foundation of national museums in Spanish America.

COUNTRY	1820S–1830S	1870S+
Argentina	[1823][1]	1883/1889[2]
Chile	1830	
Colombia	1823[3]	
Guatemala	1831[4]	1898[5]
Honduras		[1889][6]
Mexico	1825	
Peru	1826	
Venezuela		1875

1. Plans to create a museum were discussed in 1812, and the Museo Público de Buenos Aires opened in 1823.

2. Circa 1883 the Museo Público de Buenos Aires was renamed the Museo Nacional de Buenos Aires. The National Historic Museum was created 24 May 1889, inaugurated in 1890, and nationalized in 1891.

3. From its founding in 1823 until early 1826 the museum was known as the Museo de Historia Natural, or the Museo de Ciencias Naturales, rather than the Museo Nacional.

4. The Museo National de Guatemala was founded by decree on 24 October 1831, although legislation from 1851 suggests that the museum no longer existed at that date. Lindsay Brine, in *Travels amongst American Indians*, reported the existence of a museum in Guatemala City prior to 1894.

5. The museum was re-founded in 1898 and then again in 1935.

6. The first legislation creating a Museo Nacional dates from 1889, but no museum actually existed until 1932.

Sources: Oviedo, ed., *Colección de leyes*, 9:98–99; Burmeister, *Anales del Museo Público*, 2; Brine, *Travels*; Castill Ledón, *El Museo Nacional*, 10; Rubin de la Borbolla and Cerezo, *Guatemala*, 29, 31, 35–36, 49–52; Rubin de la Borbolla and Rivas, *Honduras*, 13, 17, 23, 28–30, 32–33; Tello and Mejía Zesspe, *Historia de los museos*, 3–4; Bernal, *A History of Mexican Archaeology*, 139; Rodríguez Villegas, *Museo Histórico Nacional*, 16; *Gaceta de Colombia*, Bogotá, 21 Sept. 1823; *Gaceta de Colombia*, Bogotá, 7 Dec. 1823; *Gaceta de Colombia*, Bogotá, 18 July 1824; *Gaceta de Colombia*, Bogotá, 15 Jan. 1826; *Gaceta de Colombia*, Bogotá, 5 March 1826; Calzadilla, "El olor de la pólvora," 113, 120; Beatriz González, "¿Un museo libre de toda sospecha?" in Memorias del Simposio Internacional, *Museo, memoria y nación*; and Andermann, "Reshaping the Creole Past," 147 n.1.

museums in Europe. There too the creation of national museums was primarily a nineteenth-century phenomenon.[95] If the formation of museums illustrates the development of elite national sentiment—and many intellectuals in nineteenth-century Spanish America believed that it did—then the process of museumification in Spanish America suggests that, as Benedict Anderson has argued, Spanish America was in the vanguard, not the rear guard, of the nationalist movement.[96]

A museum, insisted Santiago's mayor Benjamín Vicuña Mackenna, was a "history book," whose holdings constituted a "vast and varied collection of memories." National museums were therefore books of historia patria displaying national memories.[97] What then were these national memories? What did these museums contain and how were they organized? Both the contents and the methods of display evolved over the century, shaped by changing perceptions of what constituted national history and by developments within the disciplines that underpinned elite understanding of the past. For example, once archaeology became established as a discipline many Spanish American countries created separate museums of archaeology, or special sections devoted to archaeology within existing museums. The transformations undergone by Mexico's "national museum" illustrate this process very clearly. In 1790 Mexico City possessed a Museum of Natural History, which in fact contained not only items of natural history but also historical and archaeological material. With independence the government of the Federal Republic created a National Museum, to which the holdings of the Museum of Natural History were transferred. In 1831 the National Museum was reorganized into sections devoted to antiquities, industrial products, and natural history, as well as a botanical garden. In 1865 it was renamed the Museum of Natural History, Archaeology and History, and it was again reorganized to include a section on anthropology. In 1887 the Gallery of Ancient Monoliths was formed to display monumental pieces such as the Coatlicue and the Piedra del Sol. In 1909 it was divided into two separate museums: the National Museum of Archaeology, History, and Ethnology and the Museum of Natural History. Thus it was only in 1909 that national history and natural history were firmly disassociated.[98] Geological and botanical items in fact figured prominently in the holdings of virtually all national museums until at least the 1870s, as they did in Spanish American exhibits at international expositions.[99] Yet while displays of natural bounty formed an important part of museum holdings, all national museums also owned collections of historical material.

From its formation in 1825 Mexico's National Museum possessed pre-conquest artifacts, or at least artistic representations of such artifacts. At its opening the new museum incorporated the items previously contained in the colonial Museum of Natural History, including Luciano Casteñe-da's drawings of pre-Columbian ruins.[100] To these were added various "statues and stones sculpted by the heathens of this country," which were assembled by Lucas Alamán.[101] Indeed, the 1826 regulations governing the museum specifically required that it collect such items. Thus when the Scottish wife of Spain's first diplomatic envoy visited the museum in 1840 she could report that it contained "many curious Indian antiquities," including "upwards of two hundred historical manuscripts, some in hieroglyphical characters anterior to the conquest, and many in the different ancient languages of the country. Of the ancient sculpture, it possessed two colossal statues and many smaller ones, besides a variety of busts, heads, figures of animals, masks, and instruments of music or of war, curiously engraved, and indicating to whom they belonged."[102]

Preconquest items remained on display throughout the century; an 1857 print by Casimiro Castro, for example, depicts a selection of the impressive number of "Mexican antiquities" owned by the museum (see figure 19).[103] Outside Mexico City the provincial museums established in the last decades of the nineteenth century also displayed preconquest remains. For example, Mérida's Yucatan Museum (founded 1877) was mandated to help conserve "all the ruins that exist in the peninsula, preventing the removal therefrom of any object whatsoever." The museum was to display suitable pieces, such as the Chac Mol confiscated from the French archaeologist Le Plonguer in 1878.[104]

In other countries, too, newly founded museums collected preconquest artifacts. Shortly after the 1823 establishment of Colombia's national museum General Antonio José de Sucre donated to it a cloak allegedly worn by the Inca Atahualpa's wife. In fine indianesque style, he proclaimed it an "ancient monument worthy of the museum in the Colombian capital and much more worthy now that our patria's troops have avenged the blood of the innocent Incas and liberated their former empire."[105] A decade later, the museum contained, according to Augusto Le Moyne, "arms, fetishes and pottery of the ancient Indians."[106] Although both Colombians and

Figure 19. Casimiro Castro, *Mexican Antiquities from the National Museum of Mexico*, 1857. This print illustrates a number of the pre-Columbian artifacts owned by Mexico's National Museum in the mid-nineteenth century. The items include the circular Stone of Tizoc, displayed prominently at the right, and a brazier with the bust of the goddess Chalchiuhtlicue. *Source*: Ramírez, *Descripción*, frontispiece. Courtesy of the Bodleian Library.

foreigners were to complain for the remainder of the century about the decrepit state of the museum, and although it consistently failed to acquire the often considerable collections of preconquest items built up by private collectors, archaeological antiquities remained a core feature of the museum's holdings throughout the century, as Clara Isabel Botero has shown.[107] Indigenous objects and antiquities also formed a central part of the earliest collection of Chile's national museum, founded in 1830.

These items were displayed throughout the nineteenth century, and they constituted a key section of the National Historical Museum, which was formed in 1911 through an amalgamation of the historical holdings of the National Museum and various other museums. The preconquest holdings of the Chilean national museum was also considerably enriched by the material looted from Peruvian museums during the War of the Pacific.[108]

In Peru, independence-era leaders had from 1822 planned the creation of a national museum intended to house pre-Columbian relics, although it was not until 1826 that the government actually set about assembling a collection of objects, including "fabrics and precious things removed from Huacas."[109] Such items remained important elements of the museum's collections throughout the century, alongside objects of natural history.[110] The national museum was closed from 1882, following its destruction by invading Chilean forces, until its refounding as the Museum of National History in 1905.[111] The new museum again displayed archaeological artifacts, under the supervision of the noted archaeologist Max Uhle, its director. In 1913 the museum was further divided into museums of national history and of archaeology and anthropology, and in 1924 a Museum of Peruvian Archaeology was also created. Both archaeological museums contained preconquest collections, although never such complete ones as their directors desired.[112] Guatemala's national museum, created in 1831, contained by the 1890s "a good collection of Indian antiquities which had been found within the territories of the Republic, including several idols from Copán and Santa Cruz del Quiché," although it is not clear when these items entered the collection.[113] The archaeological holdings were transferred to a separate museum of archaeology in 1933.[114]

In short, in many Spanish American countries it was standard throughout this period for museums to display pre-Columbian artifacts, and conversely for pre-Columbian artifacts to be displayed in museums. In essence, preconquest remains meant "museum." The equivalence was recognized by the Peruvian writer Ventura García Calderón in a 1924 short story set in the Andes. When a character discovers a magnificent cache of "ancient vases" hidden in the mountains, he notes with delight: "It was a stupendous *museum* of grave-goods: Not even Berlin possessed anything similar!"[115]

A collection of preconquest items thus *was* a museum—but was it a *historical* museum? While the museums founded in the 1820s had displayed botanical, mineralogical, industrial, and pre- and postconquest material within a single institution (with preconquest items perhaps labeled "antiquities"), with the development of the discipline of archaeology, preconquest material began increasingly to be seen as part of "prehistory." According to this approach, only preconquest societies possessing an alphabet could be considered part of history, national or otherwise. By 1912 Colombia's national museum thus segregated its "historical" holdings from its indigenous ones. Postconquest nonindigenous material was listed in the museum guide in the section devoted to "history," preconquest material was classified as "archaeology," and contemporary indigenous artifacts were described in a further, separate section.[116] Similarly, the National Historical Museum created by the Argentine government in 1889 contained no indigenous material whatsoever, although both the earlier national museum and Argentine archaeological museums did. Argentina's first museum, the Public Museum of Buenos Aires (founded in 1823 and, circa 1883, renamed the National Museum of Buenos Aires) in the 1860s possessed not only a collection of Pleistocene fossils but also various Incaic vases, which were displayed in the "historical antiquities section" alongside two Peruvian mummies. Preconquest items were thus "historical antiquities." With the development of archaeology and theories of evolution they became prehistoric objects whose importance was scientific, not historical; in 1878 Buenos Aires acquired its first Anthropological and Archaeological Museum, which counted among its supporters some of the country's most noted scholars. The Museo de la Plata, as it was subsequently named, contained skulls of indigenous peoples, several Andean mummies, and thousands of preconquest and contemporary indigenous artifacts amid a vast array of zoological and paleontological items. In the view of the museum's founder Francisco Moreno, indigenous pottery, skeletons, and living representatives together demonstrated Argentina's evolutionary prehistory, as Mónica Quijada has shown.[117] By the late nineteenth century evolutionary theory had made it possible to convert the contemporary Indian into an evolutionary ancestor of the creole; Sarmiento thus referred to contemporary native peoples as "our prehistoric fathers."[118]

On the other hand the National Historical Museum, founded in 1889 and opened to the public in 1890, possessed a collection consisting solely of colonial and independence-era items. Indeed, it had been founded specifically to preserve the "traditions of the May Revolution and the war of independence," events declared to be "of transcendental national interest."[119] It displayed the furniture and other household possessions belonging to the independence-era ancestors of the very Porteño elite who established the museum. A particular coup was the acquisition in 1899 of the entire bedroom in which the independence hero José de San Martín had died.[120] As Jens Andermann has argued, this "national" museum was in fact a shrine to the creole, Porteño household.[121] This, the museum's designers asserted, was Argentina, or at least what Argentina ought to be. The "patriotic" nature of such displays was hailed by the Argentine sociologist Ernesto Quesada, who in 1897 delivered an enthusiastic lecture on the museum. As he commented, "The museum has not let pass a single patriotic opportunity without contributing to its commemoration."[122]

The view that the independence era represented patriotism above all else was shared by museums outside of Argentina. "If the archaeological section signifies science, the section devoted to the Republic signifies the patria," explained a 1906 guide to Peru's national museum.[123] Mementoes of the heroes of independence occupied an important place in all national museums. In Colombia, the national museum by 1825 possessed "the garland that General Antonio José de Sucre and the liberating army of Peru offered to the Colombian legislature."[124] Other mementoes of the war of independence followed rapidly, and by 1881 legislation explicitly declared that the museum's acquisitions policy should give preference to "possessions, portraits, weapons and in general any relic of the próceres of independence."[125] By 1912 the museum had an entire gallery devoted to "relics" of the leaders of independence.[126] In Chile, the Museo Nacional in 1849 acquired the Spanish flag captured by insurgent forces at the 1817 battle of Chacabuco. This and other independence-era flags were displayed prominently in a large case, to the disgust of the museum's new German director who complained that such items had no place in what he considered a museum of natural history.[127] Holdings of independence-era artifacts were such that by 1910, the organizers of Chile's Centennial Exhibition easily amassed a substantial exhibition of independence-era items such as military uniforms.[128] In Mexico, the 1910 celebrations marking the centenary of independence included the symbolic transfer to the national museum of the very font in which Miguel Hidalgo had been baptized.[129]

Most national museums also displayed at least some colonial artifacts. In Mexico, the national museum from its earliest days had contained colonial memorials and other manuscripts. When the U.S. diplomat Brantz Mayer visited the national museum in the 1840s it possessed portraits of the viceroys, colonial furniture, a collection of colonial coins, and the armour worn by Hernán Cortés in the conquest of Mexico.[130] In Colombia, the changing status of colonial artifacts illustrates well the changing position of the colonial period itself within the elite imagination. In 1825 the national museum had acquired the standard allegedly used by Pizarro in the conquest of Peru, which had been captured during the independence campaign. In the 1820s the flag was displayed—not to celebrate the colonial period but rather to mark the "glory of [America's] emancipation and the heroic achievements of the sons of Colombia in the land of the Incas."[131] In subsequent decades its meaning altered, so that Pizarro's flag ceased to represent the horrors of the conquest, gloriously avenged with independence, and instead came to symbolize simply another aspect of the country's heritage. In the first decades of the twentieth century it was blandly displayed alongside other "historical objects" such as the conquistador Gonzalo Jiménez de Quesada's spurs, the window through which Bolívar escaped an assassination attempt in 1828, and a vast number of portraits of viceroys and independence-era officers.[132] The colonial era thus had become merely part of Colombia's historical heritage, rather than a mark of infamy purged by independence.

CONCLUSIONS

I have suggested that in many parts of nineteenth-century Spanish America the appreciation of preconquest artifacts by elites was prompted by both the development of archaeology as a scientific discipline and by the demands of the nationalist process itself. These forces combined to encourage an elite appreciation of pre-Columbian monuments and other preconquest antiquities. What impact did this interest in preconquest history have on the status of contemporary indigenous peoples within elite imaginings of the nation? The comments by García Peláez at the opening of this chapter make clear that in his case little continuity was perceived between the builders of the admired pre-Columbian monuments and contemporary indigenous peoples. García Peláez's views were quite typical: elite celebration of preconquest artifacts was often facilitated by the absolute certainty that these items had nothing whatsoever to do with contemporary indigenous peoples. Whatever merits such pre-conquest civilizations had possessed, they were frequently declared to have vanished utterly: pre-Columbian monuments, proclaimed the Mexican liberal Ignacio Ramírez, revealed "a civilization unjustly lost."[133] The conservative Lucas Alamán expressed identical views in his *Historia de Méjico*, where he insisted that there remained no trace of "the nation which built Palenque and the other admirable constructions in the Yucatan Peninsula." Of the Toltecs there remained only "their pyramids at Cholula and Teotihuacán."[134] Mexican orators similarly praised the Maya ruins at Uxmal as revealing the "high level of civilization" achieved by preconquest peoples, while at the same time noting that all signs of this civilization had disappeared.[135] Likewise the marvelous artifacts left by the ancient Muiscas were declared to be the only remaining evidence of their existence, the study of which constituted "the last monument to the Indian."[136] The pre-Incaic ruins at Tiahuanaco were "broken links in the chain of prehistoric civilizations," utterly disconnected from any subsequent cultures.[137] Incaic monuments were evidence of the achievements of "great civilizations that have vanished."[138] In the last decades of the century, craniology and "scientific" discussions of race provided a new language to express the same ideas. When the Peruvian scholar Rómulo Cúneo-Vidal visited Tiahuanaco in the 1890s he noted that the indigenous people currently inhabiting the area around the ruins possessed neither "the clean facial angle typical of an evolved race with a broad culture nor the traits which ought to correspond to the possible heirs of the powerful lineage that left as a sign of its existence the earliest traces of civilization known in the American continent." He therefore concluded that they were unrelated to the builders of Tiahuanaco, which he regarded as one of the "most magnificent civilizations the world has ever known."[139]

Nineteenth-century elites thus stressed not the continuities linking the preconquest past with the contemporary indigenous population but rather the discontinuities separating one from the other. Pre-Columbian ruins were therefore available for the appreciation of anyone sensitive to their charms: "What does it matter that our fathers had Moorish blood and white skin?" asked José Martí. "The spirit of men floats over the land in which they once lived and we take it in with every breath."[140] It was not necessary to claim indigenous ancestry in order to savor the achievements of these past peoples. At the same time, where continuities were drawn

Archaeology, Museums, and Heritage 159

between the indigenous past and present this did not necessarily elevate elite estimation of contemporary indigenous peoples. On the contrary, considerations of preconquest archaeology might serve to highlight the degradation of contemporary Indians. Thus in 1878 the liberal Mexican writer José María Vigil urged his government to study the pre-Columbian past in order to understand how Indians had sunk to their current level of barbarism.[141] Writers across Spanish America regularly noted the distance that separated preconquest indigenous culture from contemporary indigenes. As Ventura García Calderón put it in 1927, "Without the evidence provided by [preconquest] cemeteries no one would believe this mournful and lethargic Indian race" capable of any artistic undertakings.[142] While preconquest monuments might (very) occasionally be described as the work of "our ancestors," postconquest Indians were emphatically not heirs to the civilizations that had created them.[143] In the next chapter I explore in greater detail the separation of the glorious indigenous past from what Mark Thurner has called the "'miserable' native present."[144]

Chapter 6

Citizenship and Civilization: The "Indian Problem"

In June 1888 the Argentine Cámara de Diputados debated whether to distribute land to the remnants of the indigenous groups defeated by the national army in the "conquest of the desert," as the government called its 1879 assault on the indigenous peoples settled south of the Río Negro. After its victory Argentina had occupied the vast expanse confiscated from its former inhabitants, who in return were to be offered small tracts of land in other parts of the country. The 1888 proposal to distribute land provoked the congressmen to a broader consideration of the treatment experienced by the conquered peoples at the hands of the state, which, in the view of several deputies, did not show Argentina in a particularly flattering light. Deputy Juan Carballido, representing Buenos Aires Province, denounced recent attacks on resettled Pampas indigenes: "Sir, I am unaware of any order or practice which places those indigenes in an inferior position relative to the other inhabitants of Argentine territory. I do know that the constitution says that all inhabitants are equal before the law, and if there were a law stating that indigenes who failed to keep their promises could be gunned down, then I say the Argentine congress should lose no time in erasing that law from Argentine legislation." Deputy Estanislao Zeballos, representing the capital, agreed with Carballido that Indians, although savages, "are nonetheless Argentine citizens, as the constitution and the citizenship law state, once they have accepted communal life."[1] Deputy Víctor Molina, representing the Comisión de Colonización y Tierras Públicas, the body behind the proposal to distribute land, although rejecting Carballido's and Zeballos's critique of the state, nonetheless affirmed that the indigenous inhabitants of the Pampas were Argentine citizens. "The Indians," Molina stated authoritatively, "are Argentine citizens, as the national constitution states."[2] Molina's belief that they were citizens did not alter his view that they were also uncivilized savages whose existence had brought only trouble to Argentina. When asked by Carballido whether the lands he was proposing to distribute possessed sufficient water, Molina responded petulantly, "there is enough water to drown all the tribes!"[3]

These affirmations that the Pampas Indians were Argentine citizens took place during a broader consideration of how to "civilize" them. Molina's Comisión de Colonización y Tierras Públicas maintained that this was best accomplished, short of drowning the unfortunate refugees, by obliging them to adopt a sedentary, Hispanic lifestyle. In that way they would slowly acquire the habits of civilization necessary to become useful members of the Argentine republic. This was considered to be a difficult but not impossible task, which the government sought to facilitate through both land grants and missionary activity. However, those native peoples who refused to become civilized could not participate in civil society and needed to be eliminated from the body politic. This was declared to be necessary for the survival of the very civilization that the savages rejected. As commentators observed, "The extinction of inferiors is one of the conditions of universal progress . . . It is like an amputation which, although painful, cures gangrene and saves the patient from death."[4] Civilizing the Indian was thus simultaneously redemptive and purgative. The Buenos Aires daily *La Prensa* captured this ambivalence in an 1878 editorial: "We are engaged in a racial struggle in which the dreadful curse of extinction, uttered in the name of civilization, hangs over the head of the indigene. Let us therefore destroy that race morally, let us annihilate its authority and political organization, may its tribes disappear, and if necessary let its families be divided. This dispersed and broken race will in the end embrace the cause of civilization."[5]

The Indian, in other words, would be both exterminated and civilized. The Argentine state's negotiation between these concepts (civilization and extermination) was particularly acute in the years after 1875, when the government announced its plans to "occupy the desert [i.e., the regions inhabited by independent indigenous groups] in a permanent fashion, thereby delivering rich and extensive areas of countryside to civilization and wealth." It referred to the planned expansion as a "crusade against barbarism," to be pursued until "the inhabitants of the desert accept either through kindness or force the benefits that civilization offers them." At the same time, government ministers insisted that the expansion wasn't planned as a violent attack: "In a word, . . . the intention of the executive power is to populate the desert, not to destroy the Indians."[6] Unwilling to admit that its version of civilization could be imposed through violence, the government presented the campaign as simultaneously martial and benign.

That the inhabitants of the Pampas were savages (or barbarians—writers used the terms interchangeably) was not in dispute. Argentine legislation routinely referred to them as the "barbarous Pampas Indians," whose defeat was a victory for civilization.[7] As a triumph over barbarism, it was a victory wrought by the forces of civilization itself, almost without the need for human intervention. The liberal historian Vicente Fidel López thus described the conquest of the desert as an irresistible natural process: "The savage lacks the traditional and psychological means which allow the Christian child to evolve into [a part of civilized society], and . . . it is this insurmountable failing which makes lifelong children or slaves of the masses of savages or indigenes who fall under the power of civilized nations."[8] Such rhetoric ultimately permitted the complete effacement of the military, whose efforts had actually defeated the barbarians of the Pampas. By 1910 writers could attribute the supposed disappearance of Argentina's native peoples to "the powerful forces of progress, civilization and culture."[9]

These remarks suggest that "civilization" functioned as a metaphor for the capacity to participate in civic life. Congress was, after all, the "center of civilization."[10] This is the reason why the Argentine congress's deliberations on how to civilize the Pampas Indians provoked a heated exchange over whether they were in fact citizens. Deputies were obliged by their own legislation to acknowledge that indigenous peoples were citizens of Argentina, but they were unable to accept them as civilized—and if they were not civilized then how could they participate in civic life? For the Argentine elite, indigenous citizenship was a paradox best solved, as Deputy Molina implied, by the complete elimination of these awkward "citizens," perhaps by drowning.

In this chapter I explore what nineteenth-century elites referred to as the "Indian problem"—that is, the belief that a large indigenous population weakened the state and impeded the development of national identity. I consider in particular the widely expressed view that contemporary native peoples were either essentially uncivilized or at best far less civilized than their preconquest ancestors. Such attitudes contrast with the elite interpretations of the preconquest past that I discussed in previous chapters, for although pre-Columbian indigenous cultures might be accorded the status of "civilizations," nineteenth-century indigenous peoples were rarely considered to be truly civilized. The nineteenth-century native American had somehow lost contact with his (the contemporary indigene was almost invariably coded as male) more civilized past. How had this happened? How had the culture of the preconquest world been converted into so much barbarism? To address these questions I examine the explanations offered by nineteenth-century elites to explain this process of decline. I then probe the consequences believed to ensue from this lack of civilization, looking in particular at its perceived impact on the nation as a coherent entity. In other words, in this chapter I contrast the role of preconquest and contemporary "Indians" within elite nationalism during the first century after independence.

"I HAVE TRIED TO BECOME AN INDIAN AND FORGET CIVILIZATION"

The term "civilization" is both ill defined and ubiquitous in nineteenth-century discourse. Consider, for example, the descriptions of civilization offered by Antonio Batres Jáuregui, a liberal Guatemalan lawyer, in an 1894 study. Citing various authorities he defined civilization as "the state of human advancement resulting from social order replacing the absolute individual independence and lack of laws typical of the barbarous life of the savage," or as "the development, more or less absolute, of the moral and intellectual faculties of men in society." He further added the utilitarian definition that civilization was "the greatest sum of morality and well-being in the greatest number of human beings," and that it was "advancement, progress and light."[11] What are we to make of Batres Jáuregui's definitions? As I noted in the previous chapter, nineteenth-century elites were influenced by anthropological models of human development that classified cultures as more or less civilized depending on the presence or absence of certain features such as a phonetic alphabet. In addition, for the continent's elites "civilization" was often associated with specific aspects of Hispanic culture, such as speaking Spanish. In principle, then, "civilization" could be tightly defined in anthropological or cultural terms. Batres Jáuregui's definitions, however, are strikingly vague and circular:

civilization emerges as the opposite of the barbarous life of the savage. Essentially, in nineteenth-century Spanish America "civilization," rather than being a well-defined concept, appeared as part of a binary pair consisting, in the words of Domingo Faustino Sarmiento's famous book, of civilization and barbarism. The one was needed to define the other.

The contemporary Indian might also function as civilization's defining opposite. In 1858 the Ecuadorian writer Juan León Mera published his *Indigenous Melodies,* a set of poems loosely inspired by the Andean world. In the prologue he explained that he had tried not merely to reflect indigenous life but to become truly indigenous himself, at least for the purposes of poetic inspiration. He expressed this in the following way: "I have tried to become an Indian as well and to forget civilization and the other conditions of modern life."[12] Although in other writings Mera had described the civilized nature of pre-Columbian societies, when he discussed contemporary indigenousness he stressed that being Indian meant being uncivilized. It is true that not all intellectuals displayed unalloyed enthusiasm for modernity; some splenetic *modernistas* viewed civilization as a tiresome curse and Mera himself implied that at times one might wish to forget the conditions of modern life. Being uncivilized, however, was from the elite perspective incompatible with participation in the civic life of the nation. In this section I survey the comparisons that nineteenth-century writers drew between the civilized preconquest past and the uncivilized indigenous present.

In Peru elite writers often contrasted the achievements of the Incas with the degraded condition of contemporary indigenous peoples. Peruvian Indians, "that race so great then as it is degraded today," had suffered the loss of "even the memory of their past greatness," lamented the liberal Limeño daily *El Comercio* in 1868.[13] Mark Thurner and Cecilia Méndez have shown that this distinction between the glorious indigenous past and the miserable indigenous present formed a significant part of elite discourse throughout the century.[14] For example, conservative opponents of the 1836–39 Peruvian-Bolivian Confederation simultaneously lauded the Inca past and attacked the Confederation's leader Andrés Santa Cruz as a barbarous Indian whose actions polluted the "sacred land of the Incas."[15] As Méndez notes, "the memory of the Incas is invoked in order to spurn and segregate the Indian."[16] At the same time, Santa Cruz's evident "civilization" (such as his knowledge of French) provoked outrage in his opponents precisely because it inverted what they regarded as the natural order in which creoles were civilized and contemporary indigenes—for so Santa Cruz was labeled—were savage. Native peoples who did not speak French were barbarians, and those who did were pretentious upstarts.

In Colombia government officials remarked throughout the century on "the state of imbecility in which [the Indians] today languish," and the need to "promote the civilization of indigenous tribes."[17] Liberals in particular (once the party formed in the 1840s) contrasted the current degradation of Colombia's indigenous population with the achievements of the region's pre-Columbian peoples. The geographer Agustín Codazzi, for example, following his extensive travels around Colombia in the 1850s, concluded that contemporary Indians were wholly incapable of equaling the achievements of their ancestors.[18] The moderate conservative historian José Antonio de Plaza agreed that although the Muiscas had been among "the most civilized in the New World," after the conquest they had degenerated sadly.[19] Hard-line conservatives, who had never accepted preconquest cultures as civilized in the first place, did not believe the Indians to have deteriorated since the conquest. They instead contrasted the (higher) levels of culture achieved during the colonial period with the indigenous population's current unhappy state, which they tended to blame on liberal misgovernance, a pattern followed by conservatives in many other parts of the continent as well.[20]

As in Peru and Colombia, in Mexico liberal elites both before and after the midcentury reforms stressed the distance that separated contemporary indigenous peoples from their pre-Columbian ancestors. Although, as Charles Hale has shown, pre-reform liberals were not particularly interested in indigenous affairs, when they did turn their attention to the indigenous population they were unimpressed by what they saw. From Paris, José María Luis Mora, the chief spokesman of pre-reform liberalism and sometime minister of education, described contemporary native peoples as a "reduced and degraded" remnant.[21] Newspapers contrasted the achievements of Mexico's preconquest peoples with the miserable Indians who populated the nineteenth-century republic. Writing in the midst of the substantial indigenous uprising known as the Caste War the liberal paper *El Siglo XIX* mourned: "The great qualities that once adorned the Indians have either disappeared entirely or, if they have been preserved, are hidden in a few individuals. In general the masses have degenerated, learning has been converted into ignorance, and the knowledge that was once possessed has been lost to such an extent that it is very difficult to recognize today's Indians as the descendents of the Mexicans of Moctezuma's empire."[22]

The radical Reform-era liberal Ignacio Ramírez agreed that indigenous peoples (a group in which he only occasionally included himself) had changed out of all recognition from their glorious preconquest ancestors: the former "would appear as unrecognizable animals to their emperors and caciques, were the latter to escape from the tomb."[23] In the last decades of the century, the same years that saw a resurgence of state interest in preconquest monuments, comments on the debased nature of Mexico's contemporary Indians came thick and fast. The rise of archaeology, far from elevating their status, merely highlighted their degradation: "The conquered race lost even its historical traditions. Today foreigners know more than the Indian about the past glories of our grandfathers," noted the liberal historian and future government minister Julio Zárate in 1870.[24] Legislation from 1891, moreover, specifically charged teachers with instructing schoolchildren in the "degradation of the Indian race."[25] Even the poets of the Cuauhtémoc Literary Society lamented that their namesake's modern descendants were "dull-witted, weak and abject."[26] Contemporary Maya peoples in the Yucatan, who had demonstrated their fundamentally savage nature in the Caste War, were similarly condemned as ignorant barbarians.[27]

Liberal elites in Guatemala also contrasted the ancient Maya with contemporary, brutish *indios*. The leaders of the breakaway Estado de los Altos, established in 1838 in the Guatemalan highlands, celebrated the glories of the preconquest past in their patriotic writings in a typically indianesque fashion, but when it came to contemporary indigenes they stood shoulder to shoulder with the elites in Guatemala City: both regarded the nineteenth-century Maya as frankly uncivilized.[28] The conservative elites who allied with Rafael Carrera did not hold substantially different views, although Carrera himself advocated policies at times more congenial to indigenous peoples themselves. After liberals regained control of the national government following Carrera's death in 1865, the Maya were viewed uniquely as a problem whose lack of civilization would weaken the state and undermine the planned expansion of the coffee economy. Indians, explained the *Diario de Centro América* in 1880, in the midst of the coffee boom, stood "immobile on the road of progress."[29] Consequently, Central America was a region "which the light of civilization never penetrates," whose indigenous population resembled "a great sleep-walking somnambulist."[30] While the preconquest Maya had been an opulent and proud people, the contemporary Maya population was poverty-stricken and debased; the exploration of ancient Maya cities merely highlighted this contrast. "There where a magnificent temple raised / its dazzling dome of stone / now disappears amid the ruins / a miserable hut of cactus or straw," mused the poet Juan Fermín Aycinena, scion of a powerful Guatemalan dynasty.[31] This situation was well summarized by a 1930 independence-day orator who noted that "the conquest-era Indian is described as having been a civilizing element and today's Indian as a dead weight impeding progress."[32]

In Chile, where elite writers were more divided on the merits of preconquest cultures, only some argued that pre-Columbian peoples had shown more civilization than contemporary indigenous peoples. The scholar and prolific bibliographer José Toribio Medina, for example, maintained that Chile's preconquest population had been "infinitely more advanced than the nomadic tribes that we know today."[33] Others, particularly during the years of Chile's occupation of Mapuche territory, stressed rather the continuing barbarism that characterized all indigenous people past and present. "The Pampas Indian," proclaimed the liberal congressman Benjamín Vicuña Mackenna in a speech to the Chilean parliament intended to justify the southward expansion, was "perhaps the most horrible member of the human race," while the Araucanian "is nothing other than an indomitable brute, the enemy of civilization." Neither, he insisted, had been any more civilized in past centuries.[34] Elite thinkers, moreover, disputed whether contemporary indigenous peoples were likely ever to become civilized.[35] In Argentina, too, few elite writers contrasted the achievements of the preconquest era with the decline of the nineteenth century, as most doubted the indigenous inhabitants of the Pampas had ever been civilized. Instead, liberals stressed the benefits that would accrue to the state with the elimination of autonomous indigenous savages. Domingo Faustino Sarmiento, for example, grew increasingly frank about the need to exterminate Argentina's indigenous population. While his earlier works, such as the 1845 *Facundo,* depicted an Argentine Republic trapped in a vast wilderness surrounded by "barbaric Indians" for whom at least some scholars detect traces of admiration, later writings

took a wholly unambivalent view.[36] "The occupation of such an extensive region must present many difficulties, but none of them compare
with the advantages to be gained from the extinction of the savage tribes,"
Sarmiento noted in the midst of the conquest of the desert.[37] The indigenous population, in other words, was a "black spot" in an otherwise civilized nation.[38]

"THE INDIAN LOST HIS CIVILIZATION WITH THE CONQUEST"

With the exception of scholars in Chile and Argentina as well as some
conservatives, elites in many parts of Spanish America believed that indigenous culture had deteriorated from pre-Columbian days. What was
thought to have caused this decline? Perhaps the blame for this situation
lay with the Spanish conquest. As the liberal Mexican daily *El Siglo XIX*
suggested in 1881, "The Indian . . . lost his own civilization with the conquest, without acquiring that of Europe."[39] On the other hand, more recent
causes might be behind indigenous backwardness. This was the conclusion reached by the young Antonio Batres Jáuregui. Batres Jáuregui, whose
views on civilization were cited in the previous section, was the winner of
a national competition held in Guatemala in 1892 in honor of the quatrocentenary of Columbus's arrival in the Americas. The competition offered
a cash prize for "the best system for the Republic to adopt, given its particular circumstances, to achieve the greatest advance in the civilization
of the Indians in the shortest amount of time, without violence and in
the most economical way." The Guatemalan government explained that
it was sponsoring the competition because the Indian majority "has not
been able to share the benefits of civilization, without which all progress
is impossible and all happiness illusory."[40] Batres Jáuregui's winning entry
described in considerable detail the unfortunate consequences of the conquest for Spanish America's native peoples, but when he came to account
for the miserable position of Guatemala's contemporary indigenous population he did not blame colonial rule. Rather, he denounced the *mandamiento*, a forced labor levy imposed on the indigenous population, which
had been reintroduced by the government in 1877. The mandamiento,
he insisted, was the equivalent of slavery, for it denied the Indian control
over his own labor. The very policies advanced by the liberal government

were thus partially responsible for Guatemala's backward population. But Batres Jáuregui did not blame the government alone. The Maya themselves bore some responsibility, through their unjustified commitment to communal landownership. Land that was communally held (rather than individually owned) prevented the development of the necessary capitalist spirit, in Batres Jáuregui's view. His essay therefore called for the complete abolition of communal land so as to "bring the aborigines along the road of civilization."[41] In this regard, his proposals fully endorsed the policies of Guatemala's post-1871 liberal governments, which had been systematically undermining the status of village landownership for the last two decades. Together, *El Siglo XIX* and Batres Jáuregui's essay summarize nearly all the explanations offered by nineteenth-century elite writers to explain the condition of the indigenous population. The legacy of colonial oppression, antidemocratic policies introduced by or continued under postindependence governments, and indigenous culture itself were all offered as reasons for the Indian's degraded state.

Spain was an easy target for those seeking to explain why contemporary indigenous people were so backward. The rhetoric of the independence years provided a framework for interpreting indigenous behavior in terms of colonial oppression; Spain had mistreated the Indians to such an extent that they had lost their links to the glorious preconquest past. This was the virtually universal interpretation of contemporary indigenous degradation offered by elites during the first decades after independence. In Colombia during the 1820s and 1930s the failure of the indigenous population to embrace the policies of the republican state was blamed on the continuing legacy of Spanish despotism. Their refusal to support the breakup of communal land, for example, was ascribed to the lingering effects of the "distrustful and mean-spirited policies of the Spanish government."[42] As the vice president Francisco de Paula Santander summed up the situation, "A long-standing habit of servitude has resulted in stupidity."[43] In 1830s Ecuador, the "ignorance and rusticity" of the indigenous population was similarly ascribed to Spanish colonialism.[44]

In many parts of Spanish America this tendency came to be associated particularly with the liberal party. In Colombia, the liberal writer Manuel Ancízar claimed in the 1850s that "the conquest produced no result in this unfortunate race other than humiliation and brutalization."[45] In Mexico, liberal writers blamed Spain for the abjection of the indigenous population well into the 1870s. Pre-Reform liberals such as Lorenzo de Zavala had criticized the laws of the Indies for the Indians' exclusion from the "rational world."[46] They had also attacked the behavior of the colonial church for its misguided emphasis on conversion. As Mora complained, "they focused solely on turning [the Indians] into Christians, without first troubling to make them men, and as a result did not manage to achieve either aim."[47] The condition of the contemporary indigenous population thus demonstrated the failure of colonial policies and the urgent need to adopt liberal reforms. Liberals of the Reforma continued these trends; the indigenous population, explained Tlalpam's independence-day orator in 1857, had within themselves "the germs of an honorable, hard-working or civilized people," but these seeds had not sprouted, because of mistreatment during the colonial period.[48] Even during the Porfiriato, when the tendency to blame Spain for Mexico's woes diminished as liberal intellectuals embraced their Hispanic roots, lingering traces nonetheless persisted. The politician and scholar Justo Sierra, for example, in an outline of a projected history of Mexico criticized Spain for maintaining Indians in a state of "incurable passivity."[49] The playwright (and politician) Gustavo Baz summarized this view in his 1874 biography of President Benito Juárez, in which he stated that "the indigenous race surely possessed brilliant qualities that an abjection of three centuries has in part destroyed."[50] In Guatemala, too, the inclination to blame Spain for indigenous degradation coexisted with the cultural Hispanism typical of the period of liberal rule inaugurated in the 1870s. Because of the "lamentable regime to which they have been subjected since their conquest," explained an 1879 law, the "aborigines . . . are in such a state of backwardness and abjection that they are incapable of sharing the many benefits offered by civilization."[51] In Peru, Thurner notes, "creole liberals would continue to blame the Spanish for having 'frozen' the Indians in a kind of primordial stupor which, they now rationalized, in effect rendered them incapable of assuming the responsibilities and privileges of full citizenship in the Peruvian Republic."[52] In Argentina, although most liberal scholars—unimpressed by the level of culture achieved by preconquest peoples—felt no need to explain the supposed nineteenth-century decline, those like Vicente Fidel López who had ascribed some degree of civilization to preconquest society likewise criticized the negative effects on the indigenous population of "three centuries of oppression and Catholicism."[53]

Abuses and errors from the colonial period—with Spain's alleged toler-ance of communal landholding practices being regarded as particularly unwise—were the most long-lived liberal explanation for indigenous de-cline. These criticisms of the colonial era are all the more striking given that, as noted in chapter 4, most elites described colonial culture as *more* civilized in global terms than preconquest culture. This highlights the ex-tent to which indigenous peoples were not included in elite visions of the nation; that the civilizing benefit of the conquest had not improved the well-being of the indigenous population was not a reason to doubt its existence, for indigenous peoples formed the periphery, not the center, of the nation.

Conservatives generally did not share this negative assessment of the colonial period, and they often looked elsewhere for explanations. Per-haps the decline in indigenous well-being had occurred principally af-ter independence rather than during the conquest, which, conservatives maintained, "did them a great and invaluable service."[54] During the co-lonial era, insisted the conservative Colombian historian José Manuel Groot, the Spanish monarchy had defended indigenous peoples, who had prospered far more than under the republic. In contrast, he insisted, con-temporary "Indians are the most miserable and unfortunate beings in the country."[55] The responsibility for this lay entirely with misguided liberal governments that had overturned centuries of sensible colonial policies. Liberals also were prepared to admit that behavior supported or tolerated by republican governments might have a negative impact on the indig-enous population. Batres Jáuregui's critique of the mandamiento was not unusual. Oppression at the hands of unscrupulous landowners and local officials was by midcentury often mentioned as a reason for Indian back-wardness. In Peru, for example, the landed oligarchy was singled out for criticism. Supporters of Peru's liberal *civilista* party created in 1871 went further, arguing that postindependence economic structures in particular, rather than mere abuse, lay behind the indigenous population's sad con-dition.[56] In Ecuador, too, liberal elites depicted an Indian brutalized not only by colonial rule but also by the forced labor systems that prevailed in many parts of the country.[57]

To these criticisms of the external forces shaping indigenous degrada-tion were joined others that located blame within the indigenous world itself. The persistence of communal landholding, along with other aspects of indigenous life believed to separate the Indian from the civilizing influences of creole culture, came under attack in all parts of Spanish America where indigenous villages retained control over communal lands, and even those who opposed the breakup of communal lands tended to agree that Indians ought to adopt other aspects—such as clothing or dietary habits—of Western culture.[58] It was also widely agreed that the cultural level of indigenous people would be vastly improved if they learned Spanish. Linguistic isolation, insisted a midcentury Peruvian official, explained why "our Indians, that is, almost the entirety of Peru, [today lie] in a torpor that differs little from barbarism." Until Peru's indigenous population abandoned Quechua, he asserted, "all of our efforts to civilize and instruct them will be in vain." Since Spanish was the language of "civilized Peru," he recommended that speaking Quechua be prohibited altogether.[59] Other cultural habits believed to be typically Indian—such as drunkenness—were likewise offered as explanations for indigenous backwardness, just as they had been during the colonial period.[60]

To suggest that indigenous people ought to adopt Western culture was essentially to suggest that they ceased being Indians, for throughout the nineteenth century racial classifications in Spanish America remained fundamentally cultural. Race was a flexible, malleable condition: "Anyone who stops being an Indian never wants to go back to being one," noted a Mexican newspaper in 1873.[61] In other words, it was possible to "stop being an Indian." Certainly "scientific" racism began to penetrate the language of some members of the intellectual elite in the last decades of the century, and explanations for perceived indigenous inferiority began to include references to physiology. Intellectuals sometimes bolstered their claims with anatomical details that supposedly proved beyond doubt that the Indians lacked this or that civilized quality. Thus the Bolivian social Darwinist Nicomedes Antelo argued that "the Indian and mestizo brains are incapable in cellular terms of grasping the idea of republican liberty."[62] Medical experts, moreover, employed new discourses on hygiene to articulate concerns about the inherent weakness of indigenous bodies. Nonetheless, elite views of what it meant to be "Indian" continued to involve a substantial element of culture, rather than simple physiology. In Bolivia, doctors insisted that the indigenous population was more susceptible to typhoid because of its special physiognomy, but they located the source of this distinctive physiognomy in indigenous culture rather than biology.[63]

Discussions of "blood" tended to slip into discussions of culture or environment, both of which were believed to affect bodies, constitutions, and character. As the liberal scholar Francisco García Calderón (son of a Peruvian president) argued, "detailed North American statistics show that the most unyielding races are altered by the actions of the American climate."[64] Rarely was "biology" presented in a pristine form separated from culture as an explanation for indigenous backwardness.

Nineteenth-century elites argued over whether the situation of the indigenous population could be remedied by state or private actions. Perhaps appropriate educational programs could counter the pernicious impact of Spanish colonialism, or perhaps the indigenous population was beyond redemption and the state should look to replace them with foreign immigrants. Or perhaps foreign immigration could transform inferior indigenous blood into hardier stock via mestizaje. Until these processes could take place, however, nineteenth-century elites were stuck with these disappointing Indians. Their existence was a source of considerable worry for these men (and occasionally women), who fretted that their nations would never progress while hampered with large, uncivilized populations. In the final section of this chapter I consider the relationship that nineteenth-century elites perceived between being civilized and being able to participate in the civic life of the nation. I conclude by comparing the civic roles accorded to preconquest and contemporary indigenous peoples.

CIVIC NATION OR CIVILIZED NATION?

In several recent studies the historian Mónica Quijada has contrasted early-nineteenth-century ideas about citizenship with those current in the late nineteenth century. Early-nineteenth-century views, she writes, were based on the idea of the "virtuous and enlightened citizen," whose right to participate in civic life was justified by his virtue and patriotism rather than by his race, class, or culture.[65] Quijada refers to this era of citizenship as that of the "civic nation." Only later, she argues, did citizenship become associated with the attainment of a particular level of civilization, which was thought to qualify the individual for participation in the rights and duties of citizenship. It was a lack of civilization, rather than a lack of virtue or patriotism, that disqualified the would-be citizen. This concept Quijada describes as the "civilized nation."

While Quijada usefully focuses attention on the changing ways in which ideas of citizenship were articulated during the nineteenth century, the contrasts between the early-nineteenth-century "civic nation" and the late-nineteenth-century "civilized nation" distract us from the underlying continuity in nineteenth-century elite concepts of citizenship, at least insofar as they relate to the perceived civic capacity of the indigenous population. In my view, concepts of civilization were embedded in all models of citizenship. During the early nineteenth century, although citizenship may have been discussed in terms of virtue and patriotism, elite commentators agreed that Indians were immune to these fine sentiments. As Andrés Guerrero has noted in the case of Ecuador in the first decades after independence, in de facto terms citizens were adult, Spanish-speaking white or mestizo men. "It was the colonial grouping that regarded itself as rational, civilized and white, *sensitive to the revolution of independence.*"[66] If Indians did not feel patriotism, if they were not "sensitive to the revolution of independence," this in itself made them less civilized, since patriotism was one of the markers of a civilized man. Ideas about virtue, in other words, were part of a larger discourse of both patriotism and civilization. Moreover, emotion was central to the articulation of ideas of citizenship in both periods. Peru's independence day, insisted a local official in 1833 Cuzco, should evoke "tender memories in the hearts of all good c[itizens]."[67] In 1899 Argentine nationalists made the similar argument that citizenship should be open only to those persons "who are capable of feeling the palpitations of the national soul."[68] Indeed, as Quijada herself notes, nationalism is generally constructed around a rhetoric of homogeneity, and throughout the century elites found it difficult to imagine themselves belonging to any group whose other members they considered uncivilized.

Sonia Alda offers a slightly different formulation of Quijada's dichotomy in her analysis of citizenship in nineteenth-century Guatemala. In the first decades after independence, Alda argues, intellectuals maintained that the indigenous population could become civilized through the acquisition of citizenship: citizenship functioned as a civilizing force. Thus to deny the Indian the right of citizenship would be to "seal off the route that constitutionality opened for him, which leads towards learning, employment and other public offices."[69] Citizenship, it was hoped, would lead to civilization. In later years, she argues, it was held that Indians needed to become civilized in order to assume the rights and duties of citizenship: civilization would lead to citizenship. In Alda's formulation, civilization and citizenship merge into each other. The direction of the flow changes, perhaps, but the interconnectedness remains. The conclusion of nineteenth-century elite discussions of the indigenous capacity as citizens was often that indigenous people could not be citizens because they were insufficiently civilized, or perhaps that they were insufficiently civilized because they were unable to be citizens.

In legal terms, however, there was no question about whether indigenous men were citizens: they were. During the wars of independence the constitutions and law codes composed by insurgents were clear in their acknowledgment of indigenous male citizenship. Juan Egaña's proposed 1811 constitution for Chile thus asserted that "there are no special taxes or privileges separating Indians and Spaniards. An Indian is a citizen as long as he fulfils the requirements established in the constitution."[70] The Colombian constitutions of the 1810s likewise stated that "the Indians enjoy all the rights of citizenship and may participate and vote in elections like any other citizen of the republic."[71] The 1819 Constitution of the United Provinces of South America noted explicitly that "as the Indians are equal in dignity and rights to the other citizens, they will enjoy the same pre-eminence and will be governed by the same laws."[72] Mexican codes also affirmed the equal status of indigenous and nonindigenous men.[73] In addition to enshrining the equality of all free men within their constitutions, insurgent bodies issued many ringing declarations of the legal equality that would reign between Indians and non-Indians once Spanish rule ended. The Cabildo of Buenos Aires, for example, proclaimed in 1810 that Indians and Spaniards were to be considered equal under the law.[74] The Chilean Senate agreed in 1819 that the constitution had "turned [the Indians] into citizens . . . These natives are now citizens like anyone else."[75] "Let there be no distinction between ladino and Indian, between black and white, between European and American," insisted the Central American insurgent José María Castilla in 1821.[76] These independence leaders made a point of affirming the equality between Indians and non-Indians in order to highlight the differences between the new republican states and the oppressive Spanish government, which had condemned Our Fathers the Indians as legal minors.

After independence these explicit acknowledgments of the Indians' legal equality were usually replaced with definitions of citizenship that stipulated the requirements for nationality and citizenship in nonracial terms, in line with the official abandonment of racial categories common in postindependence Spanish America (see the appendix).[77] The phrasing used in the Ecuadorian Constitution of 1845 is typical. Ecuadorians are defined as those men "born inside Ecuadorian territory," and citizens are defined as literate Ecuadorians older than twenty-one or married, with property worth over two hundred pesos (or a profession other than domestic servant or day laborer).[78] Racial status, in other words, was no longer discussed as part of the legal definition of citizenship. Although the requirements for literacy and property ownership included in many nineteenth-century constitutions effectively disenfranchised the majority of indigenous people (and were in some cases included for precisely that purpose), in legal terms being a male Indian was not in itself a bar to citizenship.[79]

This legal clarity was not, however, accompanied by any consistent belief in the indigenous capacity for citizenship on the part of the region's elites. On the contrary, when politicians and other public figures discussed whether indigenous people could actually function as citizens, they often concluded that they could not. Politicians from Mexico to the Andes agreed that most native Americans simply didn't understand the requirements of citizenship, although this did not mean they were exempt from obeying the laws of the state. Charles Walker has noted that in the extensive material he examined for his study on late colonial and early national Cuzco, "not a single author referred to the Indian as potentially rational or worthy of the rights and obligations of citizenship."[80] Even Peru's Friends of the Indians Society, established in 1867, argued that because of abuse by local elites indigenous people could not be considered "useful citizens"; although, like many others, the society believed that this situation could be altered.[81] In Ecuador, as Guerrero has shown, citizenship was widely regarded as an attribute of white or mestizo men who spoke Spanish.[82] In Bolivia, where citizenship as prescribed in the constitution generally required only birth on Bolivian soil, being male, and being over the age of twenty-one, neither elite politicians nor indigenous groups regarded such legal definitions as meaningful.[83] Indigenous groups struggled to redefine citizenship so that the payment of tribute in itself qualified the payer for citizenship, rejecting the view of citizenship contained in postindependence constitutions.[84] (Attitudes of indigenous groups in other parts of

Spanish America to republican concepts of citizenship are discussed later in this section.) Political elites in turn insisted that members of the indigenous population were not really citizens, regardless of the assertions of Bolivian constitutions. Indigenous men, proclaimed a government decree of 1882, should be exempted from military service, "given that they are not and never have been citizens."[85] Marta Irurozqui argues that the second half of the nineteenth century saw a "retreat from the vision of the Indian as a citizen," during which it became increasingly difficult for elites to envision indigenous people as functioning participants in civic life. She attributes this to the "revindicatory behavior" of Bolivia's indigenous population, shown particularly in the indigenous uprisings of 1869–71, and to elite fear of race war. "The result," she writes, "was the accentuation of the image of the Indian as backward, barbarous, and bestial, ever more difficult to imagine as a Bolivian citizen."[86] In Bolivia, in other words, the late nineteenth century saw a hardening of elite attitudes toward indigenous citizenship. In Argentina, the acknowledgment that in legal terms indigenous peoples were citizens did not prevent politicians and writers from dismissing them as incapable of civic acts. At the time of independence, argued the liberal historian Vicente Fidel López, indigenous peoples were "so degraded as to lack all the elements necessary for entry into an organic social body."[87] They would be capable of genuine participation in political life only after being reformed. Various ideas for accomplishing this transformation were proposed, particularly in the years after the conquest of the desert. Distribution of land, education schemes, and intermarriage with Irish immigrants were all suggested as methods for converting Argentina's indigenous population into productive citizens.[88]

In midcentury Guatemala, the conservatives aligned with Rafael Carrera criticized earlier liberal attempts at making Indians into citizens, which, they argued, were responsible for the Caste War in the Yucatan.[89] Liberals, complained the *Gaceta de Guatemala* in 1848, had called Indians to "participate in the splendid banquet of citizenship, whose delicacies they are unable to digest, and attempt to govern them with laws that they neither want nor understand."[90] This view was, ironically, shared by liberals, who themselves condemned Carerra's government as a futile charade in which barbarous Indians masqueraded as citizens. The triumph of liberalism in Guatemala in the 1870s did little to alter these perceptions. Alda argues that a consistent element of elite political thinking in postcolonial Guatemala was the belief that separate indigenous identity was incompatible with being a citizen: "The elite believed that the construction of a republic consisting of citizens required the assimilation of the indigenous population within Western parameters. 'Equality' for them meant not only legal but also cultural homogeneity, which implied the destruction of indigenous identity."[91] Different views prevailed as to whether the indigenous population would ever have the capacity to exercise the duties of citizenship. Perhaps through work they might acquire the ability to "be citizens capable of exercising their rights and fulfilling their duties." Other observers claimed that the indigenous population was forever separated from the world of citizenship.[92]

Mexican conservative and pre-Reform liberal elites also agreed in their negative assessment of the indigenous capacity for citizenship. *Omnibus,* a conservative paper, ridiculed the idea of Indian deputies appearing in the national Congress, and *El Siglo XIX,* Mexico's foremost liberal newspaper, argued that Indians were citizens in name only: "We believed that a pompous title was sufficient to change their sad fate; we gave them the name of citizens; we declared that they possessed rights equal to those of other Mexicans. Nonetheless if they lost nothing, neither did they gain anything from their new position: now, as before, and as it will be in the future, the poor Indians have carried all of society's weight, without enjoying any of its benefits." As a result, the paper explained in an article written in the midst of indigenous uprisings in the Sierra Gorda and the Yucatan, Indians were unable to participate in civic life. For them, "the terms *patria, independence, liberty, government* are empty words lacking any meaning."[93] This situation was made all the worse by the fact that the majority of Mexico's population was believed to be indigenous. Mexico was thus in the tragic position of possessing a large, civically incompetent population. Among Mexico's seven million inhabitants "there are not two million men capable of exercising the rights of citizenship," noted a liberal commentator three years later.[94] Indians were apparently capable only of formless rebellion.

The liberal Reform did not substantially alter elite assessment of indigenous capacity for citizenship—indigenous participation in the war of the Reforma and against the French intervention notwithstanding. Ignacio Ramírez, an outspoken advocate of radical liberalism, viewed the persistence of a separate indigenous identity as an obstacle to national unity. For

Ramírez many indigenous people were not really Mexican at all: "One of the many false beliefs with which we delude ourselves—one of the most destructive—is to imagine that our patria has a homogeneous population. Let us lift the thin veil of racial mixing that covers everything and we will find a hundred nations which, whatever our vain efforts, will not cohere to form one single nation."[95] Like Mora, Ramírez argued that the indigenous population was too degraded to exercise the rights of citizenship: "If we are to count them as citizens we must start by making them into men," he insisted.[96] During the Porfiriato, too, national elites agreed that the indigenous population lacked interest in government and citizenship. Indigenous peoples, complained the liberal journalist Faustino Estrada in 1894, were "of no political significance."[97]

The fact that elite intellectuals doubted indigenous capacity for citizenship by no means implies that indigenous groups shared this pessimistic view. Scholars have begun exploring the conceptions of citizenship held by indigenous communities during the nineteenth century. This research reveals a wide variety of responses to the idea of citizenship, ranging from complete rejection to wholehearted support. Studies of nineteenth-century Mexico and Guatemala have argued that some indigenous groups embraced the liberal model of citizenship and articulated a form of indigenous nationalism comparable, if not quite identical, to that expressed by nonindigenous liberals. In Guatemala, Greg Grandin has argued, leaders developed a nationalist language that both defended indigenous identity and at the same time demanded a political voice.[98] In the Mexican Sierra de Puebla, as Guy Thomson and Florencia Mallon have shown, indigenous communities developed a flourishing "popular liberalism." The language used by such groups stressed their contributions to the liberal party, and their entitlement to be treated as Mexican citizens. Thus when the indigenous villagers of Ixtacamaxtitlán composed a petition in 1871, the document was written in the name of "the resident citizens of Iztacamastitlan," who declared their entitlement to the same rights as other citizens in accordance with the constitution.[99] Sometimes such appeals to liberalism were part of a larger strategy of preserving aspects of indigenous identity enshrined in colonial legislation. In areas of highland Peru, as Thurner has demonstrated, local indigenous leaders adapted the language of citizenship to their own ends. Critiques of postcolonial developments and calls for a reduction in tribute levels were couched in references to the petitioners' status as "true citizens."[100] Similarly, some indigenous groups in the Colombian Cauca Valley insisted that they were "free citizens, like any other civilized Caucano," and then petitioned to retain the communal lands that midcentury elite liberalism declared to be obsolete and anti-liberal.[101]

Other indigenous groups clung to their colonial status as Indians, rejecting the model of citizenship offered by the postcolonial state. Tristan Platt's work on Chayanta has illustrated the lengths to which local indigenous groups went to preserve the relationship with the state established during the colonial era, when the payment of tribute had entitled them to a certain autonomy.[102] In other words, the very colonial structures blamed by many liberals for brutalizing the Indians were regarded by some indigenous people as protective measures whose loss after independence meant further abuse. Demands for a return to the colonial status of tribute payer might also be accompanied by a vigorous defense of the colonial era as a time of greater felicity for indigenous communities. "Today in the era of liberty we are more oppressed than when we were subjected. . . . because in those days they never took our properties away and today they deprive a community of them and do not act justly with us," insisted representatives of a community of Ópatas from northeast Mexico in 1836.[103] In other regions, too, indigenous groups sometimes called for the restoration of the tribute, although this did not always imply a thorough rejection of the status of citizen.[104] In brief, indigenous communities in Spanish America held many different attitudes toward the concept of citizenship, ranging from full endorsement to outright rejection. The largely negative assessment of the indigenous capacity for citizenship shared by many members of the creole elite did not reflect the varied indigenous views on the subject.

"THE TERRIBLE MISFORTUNE
THAT IS THE INDIAN"

What place, then, did the contemporary indigenous population occupy within elite constructions of nationalism during the nineteenth century? Despite the vigor with which many indigenous people embraced republican notions of citizenship, nineteenth-century elites generally regarded the impact of the indigenous population upon the nation as wholly negative. In particular, the indigenous population's supposed lack of nationalism was believed to weaken the state and impede progress. Indigenous people thus constituted "a powerful . . . obstacle to the progress of our institutions," a "danger in the heart of the country," "a force of inertia."[105] For the nation the Indian was, in the words of one Guatemalan writer, a "terrible misfortune."[106]

The damage done to the Spanish American republics by this cancerous group was in part economic; indigenous groups in Chile, for example, were viewed as an obstacle to modernization.[107] In Ecuador, they were blamed for interfering with export agriculture, in part through their inexplicable unwillingness to work as day laborers.[108] If Mexico's indigenous population were replaced by foreign immigrants the regions they inhabited would be thirty times richer, complained a Mexican post-Reform liberal in a study of "national problems," concluding that "the indigenous race hinders our progress."[109] The political implications of a large indigenous population were also serious. Many elite writers insisted that the presence of large indigenous populations impeded the development of national identity. They prevented their countries from becoming nations. As long as Mexico failed to incorporate the indigenous population into creole society, noted the scholar Francisco Pimentel in 1866, "it cannot aspire to the rank of true nation."[110] Central America's "ephemeral democracies . . . cannot live very long having in their breast the contradiction of a pariah people," warned a government official in Guatemala in 1878.[111] The fear that indigenous peoples were not only indifferent but actually hostile to the patria expressed itself particularly at times of war. In Peru, competing political groups agreed in blaming the indigenous population for the country's 1883 defeat by Chile in the War of the Pacific. Ricardo Palma, the director of Peru's National Library and a highly regarded author, noted that "the principal cause" of Peru's poor performance in the war "was that the majority of Peru consists of an abject and degraded race. . . . The Indian has no patriotic sentiments; he is the born enemy of whites and men from the coast, and man for man, he has no more objection to being Chilean than to being Turkish."[112] Supporters of the liberal Unión Nacional likewise laid Peru's defeat at the door of the indigenous population. "The Indian knows no patria because he has no property," insisted Manuel González Prada, spokesman for the party.[113] Similar complaints had been voiced decades earlier in highland Guatemala, where liberal elites blamed the collapse of the ephemeral Estado de los Altos on the lack of "patriotism" of the Maya population, itself due to their "scant intelligence."[114] In Mexico, too, newspapers regularly asked whether the indigenous population supported the patria in whatever struggle it happened to be engaged in at the time. In 1878, the liberal newspaper *El Monitor* went so far as to assert that "since the idea of patria does not exist in the indigenous past, it is impossible for the Indians to rise up in the name of this idea."[115]

The indigenous population was thus regarded by many nineteenth-century elites as an obstacle to nationalism. They prevented the development of "true nations." They constituted a "poisoned arrow" in the "heart of the Republic."[116] Contemporary indigenous peoples were regarded as at best only partially able to participate in the civic life of the nation. They had, moreover, lost contact with their more civilized preconquest pasts. The only regions in which liberal elites did not believe the indigenous population to have degenerated in the centuries since the conquest were those in which scholars doubted the civilized status of pre-Columbian cultures in the first place. That is, in all countries in which the preconquest past was believed to possess any merit elite writers insisted that contemporary indigenes had lost their connection thereto. The ties linking the pre-Columbian and contemporary Indian had been severed, whether by Spanish abuse or an inadequate diet. To whom, then, should that past belong but to the creole patria that understood how to appreciate it? During the independence era that "belonging" was expressed via a language of metaphorical ancestry; nationalizing elites and the nation itself were presented as the heirs to the empires of Moctezuma and Atahualpa. In subsequent years this genealogical linkage was replaced by a more generalized idea of "heritage" that allowed elites to view the preconquest epoch as part of the nation's past at the same time as they insisted their own ancestry was fundamentally Iberian. Constant throughout was the use of pre-Columbian history to construct national pasts that accorded little place to the contemporary indigenous population. In other words, preconquest Indians were good to build nations with, but contemporary Indians were not.

 *Chapter 7*

Indigenismo: The Return of the Native?

Many nineteenth-century elite thinkers, as I argued in chapter 6, perceived a deep gulf between the pre-Columbian period and the indigenous present. The conventional accounts of the social and cultural movement known as *indigenismo*, which flourished particularly in postrevolutionary Mexico and in Peru in the 1920s to 1940s, have presented indigenismo as the solution to this divided situation, as a source of healing for national cultures unable or unwilling to embrace the indigenous present. For example, Luis Villoro's pioneering study of indigenismo in Mexico argued that from the conquest to the twentieth century, creoles had viewed the Indian as either physically and chronologically near, and therefore as negative, or as physically and chronologically distant and therefore positive. The nineteenth-century elite displacement of the Indian to the distant past, he argued, allowed aspects of indigenous history to be reevaluated as positive and paved the way for the reintegration of the indigenous present.[1] Villoro thus saw twentieth-century Mexican indigenismo as a synthesis of previous responses to the Indian. In his view the twentieth-century appreciation of the Indian was possible only because of the nineteenth-century processes that displaced the Indian into the past, and thereby neutralized the negative assessment of indigenousness born of the conquest. In this final chapter I explore indigenismo's success in forging an intellectual synthesis between the preconquest past and the indigenous present. I conclude by exploring indigenismo's valorization of the mixed-race mestizo as an emblem for the new Spanish America.

INDIGENISMO

Indigenismo is a general term used to describe a movement that developed in a number of Spanish American countries from the second decade of the twentieth century. Martin Stabb has defined it as a "sympathetic awareness of the Indian."[2] Indigenismo was characterized by a concern with the well-being of contemporary indigenous peoples, often expressed as a desire to elevate Indians from their lowly position so that they might enjoy the benefits available to other citizens. Indigenistas formed political groupings dedicated to advancing the indigenous cause. They publicized the circumstances in which many indigenous people lived and called for governments to be more responsive to their needs. Where indigenismo was embraced by the state, official rhetoric was replete with references to the value and significance of the indigenous population and affirmations of the nation's commitment to improving their lot. The movement inspired an outpouring of literary works dedicated to exposing the contemporary indigenous world; writers from Mexico to Bolivia explored the grim realities faced by native peoples and offered critiques of the social and political forces that had created this oppressive situation.[3] Artistic works of other sorts also sought to depict the indigenous universe.

Individuals involved in indigenista-style activities did not always see eye to eye with their fellow indigenistas, and the movement's success in making meaningful improvements in the lives of indigenous people was disputed from its inception. José Carlos Mariátegui, the founder of the Peruvian Socialist Party, maintained that the problems facing Peru's indigenous people were primarily socioeconomic. For him, progress would come when the indigenous population embraced socialism.[4] Others stressed instead the need to improve indigenous health and hygiene, perhaps through increased access to education. Later scholars have been no more united on indigenismo's impact. Villoro believed that Mexican indigenismo did result in a new synthesis of indigenous past and present.[5] Others have argued that indigenismo failed to "return" the indigenous past to contemporary indigenes. Rita Eder, for example, has asserted that in Mexico "it is the mestizo who appropriates the cultural baggage of the prehispanic past."[6] Some Mexicanists have contrasted the limited nature of Mexican indigenismo with the more radical visions espoused by Peruvian indigenistas such as Mariátegui. Charles Hale, for example, has written that, unlike the Peruvian indigenistas, Mexico's premier indigenistas "assumed both the incorporation of the Indians into Mexican society and their ultimate Europeanisation."[7] Not all Peruvianists express such certainty about the radical nature of Peruvian indigenismo. Mark Thurner has noted the tendency of at least some branches of Peruvian indigenismo to "admire past Inka greatness while betraying contempt from contemporary Indians."[8] In this section I survey briefly the development of indigenismo in Peru, Mexico, and Central America. In the next I explore the place of the preconquest past within these movements.

In Peru the first decades of the twentieth century saw a flurry of elite concern with the health and well-being of the nation. As Pedro Dávalos y Lissón observed in 1919 in his four-volume assessment of Peru's moral and material decline, elite thinking during these years was characterized by a "reigning pessimism" in part prompted by the nation's crushing defeat at the hands of the Chilean army in the War of the Pacific in the 1880s.[9] Among the challenges facing Peru, most writers agreed, was "the Indian problem," which was widely seen, in the words of a 1918 doctoral thesis, as "the most painful and transcendental of our problems."[10] Continuing the nineteenth-century trends that I discussed in the previous chapter, these writers probed the question of what was wrong with Peru's Indians and what to do about it. Out of these discussions emerged a series of groups and individuals explicitly dedicated to improving the conditions of indigenous reality, usually in the belief that this improvement would benefit the nation as a whole. For example, Luis E. Valcárcel, an important Cuzco indigenista, argued that after centuries of oppression and deculturation the indigenous population was undergoing a process of revolutionary rejuvenation. "Culture will once again descend from the Andes," he proclaimed.[11] In his view, indigenous revival was driven by the moral and spiritual regeneration of the "New Indian," who eschewed subservience and alcohol and coca leaf addictions. At the same time a growing number of organizations such as the 1909 Asociación Pro-Indígena and the Cuzco-based Grupo Resurgimiento formed in 1926 (of which Valcárcel was a prominent member) dedicated themselves to studying contemporary indigenous culture.[12] The period also saw the publication of many specialist journals exploring indigenous reality; of these *Amauta*, edited by Mariátegui, and *La Sierra*, produced by Guillermo Guevara, were perhaps the most influential—although *Amauta*'s brief included far more than indigenous affairs only.[13] As Angel Rama has argued, many of the participants in these groups were members of the provincial lower middle classes, who championed indigenismo as part of their own critique of the landed elite.[14] These largely nonindigenous associations were joined by a few more radical indigenous organizations such as the Comité

Central Pro-Derecho Indígena "Tahuantinsuyo," which agitated for peasant landrights.[15]

These various groupings and associations were given official encouragement by the 4 July 1919 coup that propelled Augusto B. Leguía to the presidency for a second time. Leguía's "Patria Nueva," as he titled his new government, was supported primarily by middle-class groups and derived its economic strength from the growth of foreign investment. Leguía nonetheless encouraged the indigenista movement, partly because of indigenous mobilization prompted by economic problems, and partly because the highland landowners against whom these protests were directed were generally his political opponents. The growth of indigenismo among the urban middle classes—Leguía's support base—was surely also an influence.[16] A series of flowery speeches, backed up by new legislation, indicated the Patria Nueva's commitment to Peru's indigenous population. "The Indian," insisted Leguía in 1924, "is a great victim laid low by the accumulation of past servitudes and the indescribable abuses of the present . . . I therefore call for the reintegration of the Indian into national life."[17] The new 1920 constitution, moreover, declared explicitly that it would "protect the indigenous race and . . . issue special laws for its development and culture in accordance with its needs." Communal property was also accorded specific recognition.[18] The next year Leguía's government created the section of Indian Affairs in the Ministry of Development, and 1922 saw the formation of the Patronato de la Raza Indígena, a government institution similarly intended to protect and defend the indigenous population.[19] Although the influence of indigenismo on Leguía's government faded in subsequent years, the movement retained enough force to stimulate the naming of 24 June as the "Day of the Indian" in 1930, three months before Leguía fell from power and was replaced by a military government.[20]

In Mexico, as in Peru, the first decades of the twentieth century saw an increased focus on "great national problems," which in Mexico's case was prompted in part by the unraveling of the Díaz regime. In 1909, for example, Andrés Molina Enríquez published a three-hundred-page study of the reasons why Mexico "has not become a true nation."[21] Molina Enríquez singled out landowning patterns and agricultural structures as particularly problematic, although his critique encompassed many areas of Mexican life. For both Molina Enríquez and other writers on the "national problem," Mexico's supposedly incomplete, fragmentary nationality was a further cause of concern. As Manuel Gamio put it in his 1916 *Forjando patria:* "Can eight or ten million individuals of indigenous race, language, culture and civilization harbor the same ideals and aspirations, strive towards the same goals, worship the same patria and possess the same nationalist traits as the four or six million beings of European origin? We believe not."[22] The presence of partially autonomous indigenous communities was thus regarded as a challenge to Mexican nationality even by individuals such as Gamio, a noted archaeologist, anthropologist, and advocate of indigenous art. Although the indigenous population was acknowledged to be but one of Mexico's many problems, in Mexico as in Peru concerned individuals began to form organizations dedicated to "redeeming" the Indian.[23]

In Mexico, the growing middle-class disquiet about the state of the nation, combined with a groundswell of peasant concerns, exploded in 1910 into revolution that was to engulf the country for the next decade and that brought to power a series of leaders expressly committed to socializing Mexico. Part of that commitment involved addressing the problems faced by Mexico's large indigenous population. After the establishment of the first national revolutionary government a succession of state agencies were created to foment indigenous well-being. In 1917 the Dirección de Antropología, under the direction of Manuel Gamio, began to promote its vision of indigenous cultures as an important element of Mexican life. In 1920 the Dirección de Cooperativas Agrícolas was formed with the intention of supporting indigenous cooperatives. The Secretaría de Educación Pública (SEP), founded by José Vasconcelos in 1921, created rural schools for the indigenous and mixed-race peasantry, so as "to teach these creatures how to live."[24] The SEP subsequently established the so-called Cultural Missions, which sent teachers to isolated villages bearing a gospel of hygiene, athletics, and socialism. In 1926 the Casa del Estudiante Indígena was founded in Mexico City to demonstrate the educability of Mexico's indigenous population.[25]

Thus in Mexico, as in Peru, indigenismo became institutionalized during the 1920s. Alexander Dawson notes that between 1920 and 1940 indigenistas achieved a "uniquely powerful" position within Mexican society.[26] Although Mexican intellectuals had long discussed the possibility that the indigenous population might have been improved via programs of education and hygiene, the differences between the indigenismo of the 1920s and 1940s and the proposals of men such as Justo Sierra during the Porfiriato can be seen, Dawson observes, "in the sheer volume of resources devoted to Indian issues (rural education, land reform, credit and government bureaucracies)."[27] Indigenismo had by the mid-1920s become part of revolutionary Mexican nationalism: "To be truly Mexican," argues Rick López, "one was expected to . . . demonstrate a concern for the valorization and redemption of the Mexican Indian as part of the nation."[28] Valorizing the indigenous population meant, in addition to the programs discussed above, state support for the production of indigenous handicrafts and for the study and compilation of indigenous dances and music.[29] Much as Valcárcel argued that the new Peruvian Indian was reshaping his own destiny, so some government officials in Mexico began arguing that, far from being a dead weight on the Mexican nation, the indigenous population displayed a particular zeal for socialist reform.[30] In both countries, moreover, preconquest culture was cited to illustrate the contemporary indigene's innate inclination toward communism; in Peru indigenistas drew on a substantial nineteenth-century historical tradition of viewing the Incas as communists, while in Mexico writers such as Gamio presented communal landowning patterns as evidence for the indigenous population's instinctive communism.[31]

The apogee of indigenismo in Mexico is usually considered to be the 1934–40 presidency of Lázaro Cárdenas, the former governor of the state of Michoacán. In addition to establishing the Departamento de Asuntos Indígenas in 1936 and the Instituto Nacional de Antropología e Historia in 1938, he presided over a greatly increased program of agrarian reform that saw the creation of over forty-four million acres of *ejidos* (village-owned communal land). Cárdenas, like his predecessors, sought to incorporate the indigenous population into a larger "Mexican" whole. As he announced in 1938, "We will not be a complete nation so long as there exist in Mexico ethnic currents, separated by centuries and in a backward and abandoned state, that prevent national cohesion."[32] The goal of indigenismo under Cárdenas was therefore not to "indianize Mexico but to mexicanize the Indian."[33] The end of the Cárdenas presidency marked the end of the most vibrant stage of a state indigenismo actively concerned with contemporary indigenous people; subsequent presidents, in the words of Anne Doremus, "continued to encourage pride in Mexico's indigenous past, but emphasised mestizaje as key to the nation's social and economic welfare" (a matter to which I will return).[34]

A number of other countries initiated programs somewhat comparable in structure, although neither in scope nor purpose, to those inaugurated in Peru and Mexico. In Guatemala the government in 1920 established an Escuela Normal de Indígenas, which was intended to "disseminate knowledge among [the indigenous race]."[35] This built upon the legislation established in the 1890s during the presidency of José María Reina Barrios, who had created a series of "Indian schools" as well as the Instituto Agrícola de Indígenas (1894) to teach the indigenous population "modern" farming methods. Reina Barrios had also abolished the forced labor levy, or *mandamiento,* which the historian Batres Jáuregui had blamed for maintaining the indigenous population in a state of backwardness.[36] In Honduras, a series of Misiones Escolares ("Scholastic Missions") were created in 1914 with the goal of educating the indigenous population. The underlying nationalist purpose of these missions is revealed clearly in the enthusiastic report written in 1942 by a former pupil, who noted that while only some of the students attending these schools mastered reading and writing, "all learned to sing the National Anthem."[37]

As I noted above, the success of any of these programs in improving the conditions in which indigenous peoples lived remains a topic of historical debate, and in some cases there appears to have been little connection between isolated indigenista gestures and overall government policy. In Central America, for example, the period saw the wide-scale exploitation of the rural population by producers of bananas, coffee, and other export crops, with whom governments were often intimately linked. Moreover, a number of scholars have stressed the internal contradictions that beset indigenismo as an ideology or a policy. In the remainder of this chapter I explore neither the success nor the failure of indigenista-inspired governmental initiatives but rather the place that these movements accorded the preconquest past. Did the preconquest era become "closer," to use Villoro's metaphor? Did indigenismo "return" the pre-Columbian past to the indigenous population? How different were indigenista visions of the relationship between the indigenous past and present from those of the nineteenth-century elites discussed in previous chapters? I approach these questions via the somewhat oblique angle of indigenista artistic production, for it is there rather than in the realm of legislation that indigenismo came to full flower.

INCA THEATER AND MEXICAN MURALS

"Inca theater" was the invention of a group of indigenistas in early-twentieth-century Cuzco. As César Itier and Marisol de la Cadena have shown, members of the Cuzqueño elite formed a number of amateur theatrical troupes dedicated to performing plays about the Inca empire.[38] Groups included the Peruvian Company of Incaic Art, the "Huáscar" Incaic Company, the "Huáscar" Melodramatic Company, and a variety of other organizations with names similarly drawn from the Inca aristocracy. These groups performed both classic works, including the rediscovered colonial indigenous drama *Ollantay,* and newly composed pieces such as Mariano Rodríguez's 1917 *Wiraqucha* or Luis Ochoa Guevara's 1921 *Huarakko.*[39] Works were performed in Capac Simi, the version of Quechua allegedly spoken by the Inca elite, rather than "Runa Simi" as Cuzqueño elites called the vernacular Quechua of the day. Members dressed in elaborate costumes of supposedly great historical authenticity (see figure 4).[40]

The patriotic dimensions of Inca theater were stressed by its participants and admirers. Journalists declared that "*teatro incaico* represents today our only nationalism."[41] Continuing the trends already present in nineteenth-century historical writing, they insisted that the roots of Peruvian culture extended back to the days of the Inca empire. "Incaic art is for us the most comprehensible because it has shaped our nationality," wrote the Cuzco newspaper *El Sol* in 1913.[42] Inca theater in this way stressed its links to the preconquest past but not to the indigenous present of plebeian Quechua speakers. Indeed in the same years Quechua-language dramas that did not celebrate the Incas (such as those of Nemesio Zúñiga) were panned by elite critics. A similar fate befell Inca drama written by plebeians deemed insufficiently versed in the intricacies of Capac Simi.[43] As De la Cadena notes, Inca theater allowed the Cuzqueño elite to portray themselves "as the true descendants of the ancient Incas," without associating themselves with contemporary indigenes.[44] Nonetheless, as Zoila Mendoza has shown, Incaic theater and music in fact drew heavily from contemporary indigenous art forms. Elite visions of "Inca" culture were refracted through the lens of twentieth-century Andean life, even if its proponents at times preferred to downplay these influences.[45]

In his analysis Itier presents Inca theater as part of a specific Cuzco-based elite nationalism. Other scholars also have viewed the celebration of the Incas (whether in the nineteenth century or the twentieth) as a distinctly Cuzqueño phenomenon, said to contrast with the Limeño elite's general disregard for the Incas.[46] Certainly Cuzco has a particular claim on Inca history that could be exploited to further regionalist aims and to foment local identities. What I have been arguing, however, is that during the nineteenth century Peruvian elites began to view the Incas as an acceptable part of the *Peruvian* past. They were incorporated into a larger national history rather than left to remain simply part of a local patriotic tradition. Performances of Incaic theater indeed occurred outside Cuzco as well; in 1928, for example, Teodoro Valcárcel's *Poema coreográfico Sacsaihuamán* was performed before an assemblage of Lima's notables, including President Leguía. The principal roles were played by members of the Limeña aristocracy.[47] The indigenismo of these Inca-style theatrical troupes differed little from the attitudes of earlier generations of Peruvian elites, who had played the "cantata of Manco Capac" on their imported pianos and perused illustrated histories of the Incas but scorned suggestions that they were themselves *indios*. Inca theater, and indigenismo more generally, thus channeled trends already present in the nineteenth century—in the case of Peru, the celebration of the Incas as "national" and the identification of Cuzco as "the Rome of the Incas," Peru's own classical antiquity.[48] At the same time, indigenistas contrasted the grandeur of the Inca empire with the unfortunate situation of the contemporary indigenous population, concluding, in Luis Valcárcel's words, that most twentieth-century native peoples were an "ahistorical" group whose members had "forgotten their history" and were part of "a dead race," much as nineteenth-century elites had done. It was precisely for this reason that the Indian needed to be regenerated.[49] Other indigenista writers agreed that "the Indian" had lost access to his own history. "So as to deprive him of everything his memory has been torn from him and his sensibility had been squeezed out of him," wrote the historian and future politician Luis Alberto Sánchez in 1925.[50]

Similar views were expressed in Mexico; archaeologists such as Gamio noted that in the area around the great pyramids of Teotihuacán "the glorious architectural knowledge which had been handed down from the ancient builders of the famous City of the Pyramids had entirely disappeared . . . There were no traces of the former art industries except the making of a certain coarse pottery incomparably inferior to that which the tradition of the people might have led us to expect."[51] The sense of decline and deterioration that characterized much of twentieth-century indigenismo's assessment of the contemporary indigenous population thus continued the nineteenth-century trends discussed in the previous chapter. Moreover, these accounts of decline were frequently accompanied by romanticized images of the preconquest past as a time of virginal maidens and brave warriors, which themselves continued tropes established by nineteenth-century literature. When Gamio discussed the jade and pearl jewellery found at Teotihuacán he described it as belonging to "aristocratic Teotihuacanian virgins."[52]

We can see these similarities particularly clearly in the 1921 centenary celebrations held in Mexico to mark the centennial of Agustín de Iturbide's defeat of Spanish forces and in Peru to commemorate Lima's declaration of independence on 28 July 1821. The festivities in Peru appear on one level to reflect the reigning indigenismo of Leguía's government. In honor of the centenary the government erected statues to Túpac Amaru II and Manco Capac, the latter donated by Lima's Japanese community. The 1921 Primer Congreso Indígena Tawantinsuyu received government support as part of the official commemorations, and the Quechua drama *Ollantay* was performed during Cuzco's celebrations.[53] The festive parades that wound through the streets of Lima, moreover, included displays such as "Manco Capac's float," on which individuals dressed as Incas posed against an Inca-style archway (see figure 20). At the same time, other aspects of the celebrations painted a very different picture of Peru and its heritage. As Ascensión Martínez Riaza has shown, Leguía's government went to great efforts to include substantial Spanish representation at official events. Attempts were made to convince the Spanish monarch Alfonso XIII to attend the celebrations in Lima, although in the end the government was obliged to settle for a delegation of Spanish nobles. The speeches delivered by Leguía himself presented Peru as a Spanish-speaking nation whose culture derived entirely from Europe. Spain, he explained, was the "madre patria, the common patria of these peoples . . . We are blood of your blood, at one time your favorite sons. . . .

Indigenismo 193

Figure 20. *Manco Capac's Float*, Lima, July 1921. The Lima parade marking the centenary of Peruvian independence included a float celebrating Manco Capac, the first Inca. Individuals dressed as Incas lounge against a doorway reminiscent of the preconquest ruins that by the 1920s had become an important part of Peru's heritage. *Source: Mundial*, Lima, Aug. 1921, second supplement to the centenary edition.

We Peruvians are Spanish by blood, by tradition, by faith, by language, by everything that serves as the mark and distinction of a race."[54] The Limeño society newspaper *Mundial* similarly used the occasion of the centenary to stress Peru's Iberian heritage. On the arrival of the Spanish delegates, it editorialized, "a fervent tenderness of loving sons, proud of their lineage, caused us to feel a singular emotion in seeing that the mother from whom we emancipated ourselves politically extends her arms to us and affirms with us that spiritual continuity has not been lost."[55] Peru was thus the heir to Peninsular traditions and spirit. Leguía also proposed to erect a statue to Spain (the country that discovered America "and brought it civilization"), to be inaugurated on Columbus Day 1924 (1924 being an anagram of 1492).[56]

In Mexico the celebrations took place in a climate quite different from that of the 1910 centenary of Miguel Hidalgo's 1810 Grito de Dolores, but the government of Alvaro Obregón was no less aware than the Díaz regime had been of the opportunity such events provided to convey particular images of the nation and its past. Alongside the inevitable commemoration of the heroes of independence, and "popular" activities such as baseball games and horse races, the program included a number of events that referred directly to the preconquest past. The large number of visiting foreign dignitaries were taken to the ruins at Teotihuacán (as they had been during the 1910 festivities), where they were treated both to speeches exalting the Aztecs and to typical Mexican dishes such as tortilla soup and mole poblano. (In contrast, "not a single Mexican dish" had been served at the official banquets during the 1910 celebrations.)[57] The minister for education, José Vasconcelos, also commissioned from Carlos Chávez a ballet on an Aztec theme.[58] Floats at the official celebrations included an "Aztec war canoe," on which rode the winner of the India Bonita beauty contest.[59] In her study of these celebrations, Elaine Lacy discerns the influence of "at least a nominal *indigenismo*" in shaping official events.[60]

At the same time, as both Lacy and Annick Lempérière note, the centenary provided the opportunity to appreciate Mexico's colonial heritage. During the month of celebrations, "Mexico City's upper classes listened to poetry, classical music, and speeches extolling their Spanish ancestry . . . María Tapia de Obregón, the president's wife, attended some of these fiestas wearing typical Spanish dress."[61] The Mexico City town council inaugurated a park dedicated to Spain and renamed a street in the capital after Hernán Cortés. *El Universal* opined that the nation ought also to erect a statue to Cortés, the "racial father of Mexico."[62] The suggestion that Cortés was Mexico's father, so offensive in 1894, was no longer inflammatory in 1921. President Obregón himself observed that the conquistador had achieved great things, and he expressed willingness to erect such a statue, should the idea attract wider support.[63] Thus, in Mexico as in Peru the celebrations of the 1921 centennials, although incorporating elements of official indigenismo, nonetheless retained a substantial stratum of elite Hispanism, which located the nation's heritage not in the indigenous past but rather in the conquest and its consummation through independence. Similar views were articulated in Guatemala, which also celebrated its independence centennial in 1921. In Guatemala City the centenary speech delivered by the noted historian Antonio Batres Jáuregui incorporated the pre-Columbian period into a grand sweep of history that merged the preconquest, colonial, and independence periods into a single narrative.[64] Yet although Batres Jáuregui accepted the preconquest period as the "ancient civilization of our peoples," and the Indians as "our Indians," for him "our fathers" were the Spaniards.[65] In short, official indigenismo's treatment of the preconquest era represents not so much a radical departure from nineteenth-century elite nationalism as it does a coherent development of its underlying trends. Although official indigenismo was in part a response to popular mobilization, the particular contours of that response were shaped by a century's worth of creole discourse on "the Indian."

What was different about twentieth-century indigenismo's relationship with the preconquest past was the greatly increased level of *artistic* interest in pre-Columbian themes among national elites, in addition to the government support that such ventures received. While in the years after 1860 art students in Mexico had drawn preconquest scenes alongside illustrations of later events, by the 1920s the Mexican state was not only encouraging primary school students to study "Aztec" art but also was itself spending considerable sums commissioning works of public art that illustrated Mexico's precolonial heritage. From 1922 Adolfo Best Maugard added Aztec design motifs to the art curriculum of Mexico City public schools, in his capacity as head of the department of drawings, a subsection of the governmental department of schools.[66] Gamio, who established the governmental Department of Fine Arts, similarly encouraged Mexican artists to find inspiration in indigenous art forms.[67] Gamio's interest in indigenous artistry derived in part from his excavations of the preconquest ruins at Teotihuacán, which had both uncovered a vast quantity of information about preconquest craftsmanship and brought an influx of tourists to the site. Gamio encouraged the sale to tourists of native artworks loosely based on preconquest traditions, as these demonstrated the achievements of Mexico's peoples and also provided income for their producers.[68]

This emphasis on indigenous art as essentially Mexican differs from the nineteenth-century appreciation of "Aztec architecture" discussed in earlier chapters in that it sometimes embraced the artistic sensibilities of the contemporary indigenous population. Some indigenistas thus maintained that contemporary indigenous peoples possessed intimate connections to the spirit of preconquest art. In 1922 a group of Mexican artists including David Alfaro Siqueiros, Diego Rivera, and José Clemente Orozco issued a "Declaration of Social, Political and Aesthetic Principles," in which they stated that "the noble work of our race, down to its most insignificant spiritual and physical expressions, is native (and essentially Indian) in origin. With their admirable and extraordinary *talent to create beauty, peculiar to themselves, the art of the Mexican people is the most wholesome spiritual expression in the world* and this tradition is our greatest treasure."[69] The art of Diego Rivera illustrates well the ways in which Mexican indigenismo on occasion blended an appreciation of the preconquest past with an interest in contemporary indigenous peoples. After absorbing trends such as Cubism during an extended visit to Europe Rivera had become interested in indigenous motifs following his return to Mexico in 1921. He started collecting pre-Columbian art and his work began focusing on indigenous and peasant themes. His 1923–24 murals for the Ministry of Education, for example, showed indigenous laborers engaged in various revolutionary activities. In the late 1920s his murals also began depicting Mexico's indigenous past. In 1929 he started work on the vast murals in the National Palace that showed scenes of preconquest life alongside depictions of later historical moments (see figure 21). Rivera's murals in the Palace of Cortés in Cuernavaca, also begun in 1929, show scenes of the conquest and subsequent enslavement of the indigenous population. Nonetheless, Rivera's emphasis on the continuities between preconquest and contemporary indigenous life was not shared by all of his fellow muralists. Writings by Siqueiros, for example, suggest that he believed that worthwhile indigenous art was instead located solely in the ancient past.[70] As Leonard Folgarait has shown, the Mexican muralist movement was neither monolithic in outlook nor universally admired, but it was nonetheless closely integrated into the broader visions of postrevolutionary Mexican governments.[71]

In Peru the founding of the Escuela Nacional de Bellas Artes (ENBA) in 1919 created an institutional basis for an artistic focus on indigenous themes; the critic Mirko Lauer has described the 1920s as a period of "the visual epic of Incaic legends."[72] The ENBA itself was housed in a specially constructed building designed in "neo-Peruvian" style, combining colonial and pre-Columbian architectural elements.[73] Works by José Sabogal,

Figure 21. Diego Rivera, *The Ancient Indigenous World*, 1929. This section of Diego Rivera's mural for the Mexico City National Palace represents the Aztec empire as a vibrant, light-filled universe. *Source*: © 2006 Banco de México Diego Rivera & Frida Kahlo Museums Trust, México, D.F.

who taught at the E N B A from 1920 and became its director in 1932, exemplify the new focus on indigenous themes. Sabogal, whose art graced the covers of a number of issues of Mariátegui's journal *Amauta*, painted both Incaic and contemporary indigenous subjects. His preconquest figures were energetic and full of new vitality and life. His cover for the January 1927 issue of *Amauta*, for example, showed a stylized figure dressed in an *uncu* (the tunic worn during the period of Inca rule) striding through a field while sowing maize (see figure 22). The image combined an acknowledgment of Peru's Incaic (and agricultural) heritage with the sense of purposefulness and energy that indigenistas ascribed to the "new Indian." In the print a strong, healthy Indian looks fixedly into the future. The cover thus presents the preconquest Indian as vigorous, active, and in a sense modern—quite the opposite of the archaic Incas who appeared in nineteenth-century romantic fiction. Sabogal's 1929 "Incaic frieze" similarly depicted sturdy Incaic figures engaged in metal working and other activities, much as Diego Rivera's murals showed the bustle and energy of Tenochtitlán—Sabogal had in fact spent several months in Mexico studying the muralist movement (see figure 23).[74] Sabogal's focus on Andean and Incaic themes led Mariátegui to label him the first true "Peruvian painter."[75] Preconquest motifs were "national," truly Peruvian.

The embrace by the government of the preconquest past was particularly noticeable at the level of state iconography. Thus the Mexican president Cárdenas suggested in 1938 that a new street in Mexico City be named "Avenida Tenochtitlán" in honor of the Aztec capital.[76] On a more personal level, in 1934 Cárdenas named his son "Cuauhtémoc." Street nomenclature was but one area in which official indigenismo manifested itself. As I noted in chapter 2, during the independence era coins, flags, and state shields had made ample use of indigenous imagery, but after 1830 these images were largely removed from state symbols and were replaced either with the leaders of the independence movements themselves or with classically garbed feminine figures representing progress or some other national virtue. In the decades after 1910 the expunged indigenous figures returned to Spanish American stamps, coins, and other sites of official iconography. In Mexico the number of preconquest images appearing on stamps increased steadily from 1900 to 1940 (with the exception of the 1910s, when the Mexican Revolution seriously disrupted stamp production). Similar figures apply to Peru (with the curious exception of

Figure 22. Cover of the January 1927 issue of *Amauta*. José Sabogal's cover for this issue of Mariátegui's indigenista journal shows a stylized Incaic man striding through a field. The sturdy figure radiates determination and strength. *Source*: *Amauta*, Jan. 1927.

the 1920s, in which no indigenous images were used at all).[77] President Leguía, moreover, reestablished San Martín's indianesque Orden del Sol, of which he appears to have been the first recipient.[78] This trend influenced even governments displaying only a very weak commitment to indigenismo. For example, in 1926 the Honduran government renamed the country's currency the lempira, after the leader of the sixteenth-century Lenca resistance to the Spanish conquest. As Darío Euraque has shown, although Lempira had made a few appearances in nationalist rhetoric during the nineteenth century as an exemplar of Honduran heroism, the use of indigenous imagery on the national currency was unprecedented within Honduran state iconography.[79] The new currency was both named after Lempira and showed a stylized head of the hero on the obverse (see figure 24), whereas hitherto the currency had depicted the state shield and a classical figure representing Central America. Even more striking was that Honduran senators chose to call the currency the "lempira" in preference to naming it after Francisco Morazán, one of the heroes of Central American liberalism, who in the senate vote over renaming had come second behind the indigenous leader.

Euraque has linked this commemoration of Lempira with the official celebration of mestizaje; Hondurans, elite intellectuals began to argue, were a mixture of two valiant races—the indigenous and the Spanish— each of which was declared to possess its own virtues. Euraque notes that these years coincided with the official reclassification of the Honduran population as mestizo. In 1910, the official figures affirmed that mestizos constituted only about 10 percent of the population, and the (unpublished) 1916 census did not even include "mestizo" as a category but instead classifed Hondurans as either ladino or Indian. Yet by 1930 "mestizo" had become the majority category in population censuses. In Honduras, according to Euraque, the official celebration of preconquest figures formed part of a larger elite strategy of redefining the population as mestizo *rather than* indigenous. Far from indicating acceptance of the contemporary indigenous population into a broader sense of "Honduraness," official mestizaje instead signified the effacement of the indigenous population, whose position within contemporary Honduras was to be that of ancestor. Just as nineteenth-century elites in many parts of Spanish America had incorporated the preconquest past into the nation's history (if not into their personal ancestry) without accepting the contemporary indigenous population as a welcome part of the nation, so elites in 1920s Honduras accepted the preconquest past as part of their own heritage at the same time that they stated that Indians were no longer part of contemporary Honduras, whose population was now declared to be primarily mestizo.[80]

Euraque's interpretation of mestizaje as fundamentally anti-indigenous addresses issues also raised in the work of Jeffrey Gould, who has shown that in Nicaragua the rhetoric of mestizaje served precisely to efface the indigenous population. Gould has noted that in early-twentieth-century Nicaragua elite writers began to praise the mestizo as a "harbinger of progress." As in Honduras, in Nicaragua these celebrations of mestizaje also emphasised the "heroic (pre-Columbian) indigenous, component."[81] "From the fusion of the ancient American race with Spanish blood resulted this characteristic type which combines the energies of the soldier, the tenacity of the farmer and the dreams of the poet," insisted the Nicaraguan

Figure 23. José Sabogal, detail of *Inca Frieze*, 1929. Sabogal's *Inca Frieze* stresses the Inca empire's communal spirit, vigor, and industry. The upper panel, titled "The Inca," shows not the Inca himself but rather the close-knit group carrying the Inca's litter, while others prepare a ceremonial carpet and make obeisance. The lower panel depicts metalworking. *Source: Amauta,* April 1929.

Figure 24. A 1937 Honduran lempira. First used in 1931, the design depicts the conquest-era indigenous leader Lempira. Honduran currency was itself renamed the "lempira" in 1926. *Source*: Courtesy of Michael Shaw.

Guía Ilustrada in 1898.[82] At the same time, however, contemporary indigenous people were either criticized as obstacles to democracy or were declared to have disappeared altogether, replaced by hardy mestizos.[83] Indigenismo (and its paler spin-offs in Central America) could thus work to valorize the indigenous past just as nineteenth-century elite nationalism had done, but to whom did that past belong? In the final section of this chapter I examine the relationship between mestizaje, indigenousness, and elite nationalism.

INDIGENISMO, MESTIZAJE, AND THE NATION

J. Jorge Klor de Alva has defined mestizaje as a *"nation-building myth* that has helped link dark to light-skinned hybrids and Euro-Americans, often in opposition to both foreigners and the indigenous 'others' in their midst."[84] By defining mestizaje as a myth he usefully focuses attention away from understanding mestizaje as a simple process of biological mixing and toward an appreciation of mestizaje as an ideological construction. Myths of mestizaje don't have a single fixed meaning, as Klor de Alva notes, and recent research into the functioning of pro-mestizaje ideology in different parts of Spanish America has tended to stress precisely this variability; Gould, for example, stated that mestizaje excluded indigenous people in Central America but not in Mexico because of Mexico's history of popular liberalism.[85] Anne Doremus, on the other hand, has argued that in revolutionary Mexico advocates of mestizaje desired precisely "the Indians' extinction through racial mixing."[86] In this section I examine the applicability to other parts of Spanish America of Gould's and Euraque's claims that in Central America mestizaje served to efface contemporary native peoples. I also consider the relationship between indigenismo and mestizaje.

A number of scholars have argued that in Mexico and Peru the indigenismo of the 1920s gave way in the 1930s to a celebration of the mestizo. In Mexico, this process is sometimes said to have begun in the Porfiriato, when writers such as Justo Sierra had presented the mestizo as an improved version of the Indian.[87] Regardless of whether the rise of the mestizo began in the Porfiriato, by the mid 1930s the mestizo had been enthroned as the cultural icon of the Mexican Revolution, as Mary Kay Vaughan and others have shown.[88] Mestizos, the heirs to both European and indigenous culture, were the true Mexicans, the cosmic race, as José Vasconcelos named them. Marisol de la Cadena's research on indigenismo and its aftermath in Cuzco explores related themes. In *Indigenous Mestizos* De la Cadena shows how from the 1930s self-identified Cuzqueño mestizos were able to lay claim to indigenous culture without losing their mestizo identity.[89] Although the indigenistas of 1920s Cuzco had largely rejected the mestizo as "inauthentic," in the 1930s the preconquest past was converted by the so-called Neo-Indians into the heritage of Peru's mestizos, who began to participate in Inca-style dance troupes and religious ceremonies such as the Inti Raymi festival. "Neo-Indians" were defined as a moral entity rather than an ethnic group. "Today's Indian is not simply the historical Indian," insisted the neo-Indian Cuzqueño writer José Uriel García; "He is every man who lives in America with the same emotional or spiritual roots as those who once cultivated and benefited from it." Mestizos, he insisted, could be "even more indigenous than the Indians."[90] De la Cadena has stressed that in post-1930s Cuzco mestizo identity was not set in opposition to indigenousness. Celebrations of mestizo identity in 1930s Cuzco thus did not entail attempts at eliminating indigenousness, in contrast to the situation that Gould and Euraque describe for Central America. At the same time, by defining indigenousness in terms of ancient "emotional or spiritual roots," Cuzco's Neo-Indians reiterated nineteenth-century views that indigenousness was defined by practices linked to the distant past rather than to the present.

These studies share an interest in the dynamic between indigenismo and mestizaje. They illustrate the close links that bound the two even if the precise nature of the ties varies from account to account. Yet at the same time this dynamic also reveals the continuities between indigenismo and ideologies of mestizaje, and the nineteenth-century ideas discussed in this book. These continuities may be seen through a comparison of the writings of two early-twentieth-century nationalist thinkers, both of whom placed considerable emphasis on the mestizo, yet only one of whom operated in a clearly indigenista environment: the Mexican José Vasconcelos and the Argentine Ricardo Rojas.

José Vasconcelos played an important role in the educational reforms introduced in 1920s Mexico. First as rector of the National University and then as Minister for Education from 1921–24 he oversaw the restructuring of the educational system at the same time that he encouraged the muralist movement. While not a self-confessed indigenista, through his work at the Ministry for Education he helped create the institutionalized indigenismo of the 1920s. Although he subsequently became disaffected with the direction of postrevolutionary politics, in the years between 1918 and 1924 he was at the heart of the new Mexican regime. In 1925 he published *The Cosmic Race,* in which he argued that Spanish America's "ethnic mission" was the creation of a "synthetic race that shall gather all the treasures of History in order to give expression to universal desire."[91] This hybrid race was the future of the continent, for no single race was "capable of forging civilization by itself."[92] Vasconcelos maintained that Spanish America was the natural home of this new race, as there, in contrast with Anglo-America, the existing races had already begun the process of intermingling. Spanish American culture, he argued, drew on both "Cuauhtémoc and Atahualpa" and "our Hispanic fountainhead."[93]

But underlying this celebration of mestizaje was a fundamentally European outlook and a belief in the West as the fount of civilization. "The Spanish language is . . . the core of our nationality and the bond of union, the sign of intelligence of a hundred patrias across the planet," he insisted in a 1926 speech.[94] The cosmic race, although drawing on the good qualities of all races, was influenced most profoundly by white, European culture, which, Vasconcelos predicted, would predominate through its natural vigor. In Mexico, he noted approvingly, Spaniards had already spread "white ancestry through the soldier who begat a native family, and Occidental culture through the doctrine and example of the missionaries who placed the Indians in condition to enter into the new stage."[95] The primary contribution of indigenous peoples to the new race was their "countless number of properly spiritual capacities," the specific features of which Vasconcelos did not enumerate.[96] Beyond this, they had little to offer. "Say what one may," he noted, "the red men, the illustrious Atlanteans from whom Indians derive, went to sleep millions of years ago, never to awaken . . . No race returns . . . The Indian has no other door to the future but the door of modern culture, nor any other road but the road already cleared by Latin civilization."[97] Like the elite nineteenth-century nationalists who located acceptable indigenousness in the distant past, Vasconcelos saw the Indian as essentially obsolete. The role of the "Indian race" was to contribute its "tiny drop of blood" to a superior mixture in which European culture would dominate.

Vasconcelos elaborated on these views in his 1927 *Indología*, where he again stressed the obsolete nature of indigenous culture, which, he insisted, had already been in decline at the time of the conquest.[98] Moreover, like Gamio (and many others) he insisted that the indigenous population had remained entirely aloof from the wars of independence, itself "the first autochthonous manifestation" of the new mestizo race. Indeed, by the early nineteenth century the Indian scarcely existed at all, for with the conquest indigenous culture, and therefore identity, had already been replaced by European culture. Independence, he maintained, "could not have been a movement of Indian liberation, for the simple reason that the Indian had already ceased to exist; he perhaps never existed as a national entity, and at that time did not exist spiritually, given that all that he knows, all that he thinks, all that he is today is the result of the European invasion. His own identity disintegrated, just as the identity of all ancient cultures has disintegrated, never to return."[99] *Indología* placed somewhat more emphasis than had *La raza cósmica* on the extent to which the new mestizo America was distinct from both the Hispanic and the indigenous: "The European does not recognize us, nor do we recognize ourselves in him. Neither . . . do we recognize ourselves in the Indian, nor does the Indian recognize us."[100] The outcome was a picture of Spanish America's future that, like the one painted in *La raza cósmica*, accorded the indigenous population no place whatsoever.

In later years Vasconcelos became an outspoken defender of Mexico's Spanish heritage; his 1936 *Short History of Mexico* hailed the conquistador

Hernán Cortés as a savior, while in *Hernán Cortés: Creator of Our Nationality* (1941) he insisted (like Francisco Cosmes and *El Universal* before him) that "Cortés deserves, more than anyone else, the title that has so often been denied him of father of our nationality."[101] At the same time he began to use the word "Aztec" as a synonym of "barbarous." Benjamin Keen notes that Vasconcelos described Victoriano Huerta's murder of Francisco Madero as an "Aztec ritual," Emiliano Zapata's program as an example of "Aztec despotism," and Obregón's suppression of Adolfo de la Huerta's revolt as "Aztec cannibalism."[102] His rejection of the Aztecs as savages earned him little respect from intellectuals in post-1940s Mexico, but his subsequent ostracism should not obscure Vasconcelos's influence and importance in the 1920s. Although he did not always see eye to eye with fellow revolutionaries, his vision of a Mestizo America in which Indians, along with blacks, had been replaced by a modified version of the "white race" emerged from the center, not the periphery, of revolutionary Mexico.

In contrast with Vasconcelos's Mexico, the Argentina of Ricardo Rojas experienced neither social revolution nor institutionalized indigenismo. Elite Argentine culture was, however, influenced by criollismo, which stressed the importance of the nation's creole heritage in the face of European immigration. Rojas, who was born in the same decade as Vasconcelos and, like him, was at one time rector of his nation's most prestigious university, contributed to the development of criollista sentiment through a number of his writings. In *Blasón de Plata* (1910) and *Euríndia* (1924) he set out a vision of Argentina as a nation formed out of both Spanish and indigenous currents. In *Blasón de Plata* Rojas argued that the Indians, America's first "lineage," had created a folkloric underpinning to Argentine culture. Through the fund of place-names, words, and myths that they bequeathed to modern Argentina, "[they demonstrated to] us, the white . . . men . . . the nature of the bronze sons whom the sun of the Indies warmed in the heart of our maternal soil."[103] Rojas's use of the past tense ("warmed") signals the location of these indigenous heroes in a former time preceding the current age. Their role, in other words, was to symbolize the nation's past. With independence the Indians had been replaced by a newer, more active tribe—the creoles, the "second avatar of American consciousness"—much as Vasconcelos saw independence as the "first autochthonous manifestation" of the creolized mestizo.[104] "The destiny of America destroyed the original lineage, recasting its elements with those of another superior type," Rojas explained.[105] The indigenous contribution to Argentina was thus confined wholly to the past. At the same time indigenous artistic sensibilities formed part of national culture; indeed, from 1927 Rojas resided in a house specially built in the "neo-prehispanic" style, which combined features of colonial architecture with designs inspired by the preconquest ruins at Tiahuanaco.[106]

In his 1924 *Euríndia* Rojas stressed somewhat more the survival of indigenous cultures; during the colonial period, he noted, indigenous customs "indianized the Spaniard, while the Spaniard hispanicized the Indian."[107] Argentina was "a melting pot whose various elements were fused through the influence of the native soil, the Spanish language and democratic institutions."[108] This, he argued, was the essence of *argentinidad* (Argentineness). Thus, like Vasconcelos, Rojas conceived of mestizaje as a process leading essentially to an improved, superior version of the Spanish-speaking creole. Rojas's emphasis on the influence of "the native soil" provided him with a formula for the incorporation of recently arrived immigrants into Argentina. In contrast with the writers of the Generation of 1837, who had claimed, in the words of Alberdi, that "the patria is not the soil," Rojas linked the nation with a particular territory whose nationalizing effects were impressed upon all those who resided therein. "A spiritual kinship" thus linked all those who lived on "Argentine soil," he argued in both *Euríndia* and *Blasón de Plata:* "The Argentine soil, that was our common mother."[109] Rojas's view that national identity emanated from the soil led him to interpret the design of the Argentine flag as an image of the land itself, the radiant solar face a representation of the sun.[110] His emphasis on the nation as territory, in other words, entailed the erasure of the earlier indianesque nationalism that read Argentina as a reborn Inca empire whose solar deity therefore graced the nation's flag.

The similarities between Vasconcelos's and Rojas's visions make clear the continuities underlying elite views of the nation and the place of indigenous people therein, despite the considerable differences between early-twentieth-century Mexico and Argentina. For both men, indigenousness represented an earlier, distant stage in human (or national) evolution, destined for replacement by a superior culture, to which it nonetheless contributed some spiritual or aesthetic qualities. The connections between their views and those of the nineteenth-century elites that I discussed in earlier chapters should be clear. Just as romantic and modernist writers had viewed the indigenous past as a Spanish American antiquity, and just as elite nationalists had celebrated indigenous ruins at the same time that they denied the links between the monumental indigenous past and the contemporary indigenous present, so too did early-twentieth-century writers on mestizaje position indigenousness in opposition to modernity. Yet the writings of Vasconcelos and Rojas also illustrate that elite nationalism could not dismiss that ancient past altogether. It had become part of what made Spanish America distinctive—part of its heritage.

CONCLUSIONS

A conquistador who kills is in short a husband who loves. From there we sprang, from those dreadful nuptials. But we are neither Spaniards nor Indians, nor are we the combination of the two. . . . We come from the center of ourselves.
—ARTURO CAPDEVILA, *Los hijos del sol*

This, the Argentine writer Arturo Capdevila proclaimed in 1929, was the essential history of Spanish American creoles. Elite nationalists clung to the metaphors that had shaped the earlier expressions of national origin that I discussed in chapter 3, for Capdevila presented history as personal genealogy. Creole history thus originated in a sexual encounter between Spaniard and *india*. But while nineteenth-century romantic writers had likewise described the conquest as an amorous episode—"America, young and timid, with docility surrendered herself as a slave to those who had surprised her in her forgotten retreat," in the words of a Chilean writer in 1855—Capdevila dispensed with the delicacy that had cloaked these earlier accounts.[111] For Capdevila the mingling of conquistador and indigene was violent, indeed fatal; the moment of conception was also a moment of death, for in creating the new Spanish America, indigenous culture succumbed to the conquistador's sword: "A conquistador who kills is in short a husband who loves." The birth of the creole required the death of indigenous history. By now it should not come as a surprise that the outcome of a sexual encounter between a conquistador and an indigenous woman could be a creole rather than a mestizo. As we have seen, the boundary between mestizos and creoles was a slippery frontier. Capdevila, like Rojas and Vasconcelos, thus presented indigenousness simultaneously as part of creole heritage and as fundamentally obsolete.

In this book I have examined the place of the preconquest past in the sense of identity—both personal and national—articulated by the region's creole elites in the first century after independence. I have argued that elite understandings of the nation were bound up in the creole search for their own past, which sought to integrate the conflicting heritages bequeathed by preconquest, colonial, and republican history. During the independence era insurgents created a vision of the nation that stressed its privileged links to the pre-Columbian past, which they articulated through a language of genealogy. This earliest vision of Spanish American nationality was embedded in the state iconography invented to symbolize the new republics, as well as in the patriotic language born of the independence struggles. In subsequent decades elite interpretations of their own history accorded an ever more important place to the colonial era, while their view of the nation came to focus on the pivotal independence era, itself understood as an organic development of processes begun in the conquest. These transformations of the elite *imaginario* threatened to convert the preconquest period into an unwanted orphan era wholly disconnected from the modern republic. Forces inherent in the very idea of nationalism prevented such an outcome, for at the same time that elite thinkers were rediscovering their own Iberian ancestry they were reassessing the pre-Columbian era's potential as a building block of the national past. In many parts of Spanish America the preconquest period began to figure as an interesting and folkloric prelude to true national history, an indication of the nation's immense antiquity and an earlier stage in its development. Novels, historical writings, and archaeology all contributed to this process. At the same time they also helped separate that past from the contemporary indigenous population, which became an unwelcome and degraded residue of an earlier historical era lacking a place in the life of the modern republic. These developments, whose influence is visible in both the early-twentieth-century indigenismo of Mexico and Peru and the criollismo typical of Argentina in the same period, shaped the nationalism of creole elites across Spanish America in the century after independence.

This nationalism, while always focused on the intimate ties that bound the nation to its creole backers, nonetheless found space for the preconquest era within its conception of the national past. Its commitment to creating an equivalent space for the indigenous present was far more halting and equivocal. In the epilogue following I note briefly some of its more contemporary resonances.

 *Epilogue*

I am ready to concede that on the plane of factual being the past
existence of an Aztec civilization does not change anything very much
in the diet of the Mexican peasant of today . . . But it has been remarked
several times that this passionate search for a national culture which
existed before the colonial era finds its legitimate reason in the
anxiety shared by native intellectuals to shrink away from that
Western culture in which they all risk being swamped.
—FRANTZ FANON, *The Wretched of the Earth*

For the Caribbean writer Frantz Fanon the significance of the preconquest
past for Spanish America lay precisely in its (uncertain, ambiguous, partial) ability to counter the currents of Western culture, thereby contributing to the formation of an autonomous, anticolonial history. His contrast
between the "plane of factual being" and the realm of cultural anticolo-
nialism forms part of his larger analysis of the slippery nature of history
in colonial situations. Far from disowning the past as meaningless, Fanon,
along with other writers on postcoloniality, has stressed the significance,
indeed centrality, of the past to the process of postcolonial nation formation. It is also worth noting that he discusses the importance of the Aztecs
not only to elites but to the "Mexican peasant." Fanon's focus on the importance of the past to native intellectuals and peasants is a reminder that
the story I have related here—a story of elite engagement with the preconquest past—is by no means the only tale that could be told about nationalism and the pre-Columbian era. Scholars have for decades examined the
significance of Spanish America's preconquest history to the formation of
subaltern identities. John Rowe's seminal research on Inca nationalism, the
analyses of Alberto Flores Galindo, and a series of later works have helped
elucidate the significance of the Inca past both to members of the former
Inca nobility and to the Andean peasantry. These works have suggested
the importance of Inca history to the formation of indigenous identities
in the Andes and also its considerable revolutionary potential, especially

when coupled with messianic ideologies.[1] Scholars have likewise explored the importance of preconquest history to the identities of indigenous intellectuals in Mexico.[2] The growth of "Maya nationalism" in Central America further illustrates the vitality of indigenous history as a source of organizational and ideological identity outside channels sponsored by the state.[3] Thus as a parallel to this study a companion tale could be told about the use of the preconquest past by indigenous peoples themselves, drawing on such research and on other, less well-explored histories.

For example, in their interactions with the national state indigenous communities in nineteenth-century Mexico on occasion made enterprising use of preconquest history alongside the creole elites who sought to claim Cuauhtémoc for themselves. In 1826 the leaders of a Yaqui uprising in northern Mexico claimed to be defending "the crown of Moctezuma" to which end they carried "a flag with a figure painted on it, which they say is a portrait of him."[4] Indigenous rebels in the city of Tepic (in Nayarit) explained an 1873 revolt by noting that they were the "true sons of Anáhuac . . . descendents of the original Mexicans," while the nation's liberal rulers were merely the "bastard sons of our patria." Asserting that "for us independence has not existed," they swore that "if the blood of the intrepid Moctezuma flows through our veins, if the corruption and degradation in which we lie has not extinguished from our soul the nobility and valour which animated him, let us, the peoples of Nayarit, arise together with our brothers, and may we know how to die, so that the world should see that the invincible race of the descendents of our adored Tenochtitlán preserves undamaged both abnegation and heroism."[5] In late nineteenth-century Argentina the Araucanian commander Cipriano Catriel justified his position of leadership by noting that "I inherited the command that I exercise from my father, Old Catriel, who received it from the God of the Incas."[6] Thus indigenous groups along the Pacific and northern frontiers of Mexico and on the Argentine plains—regions that had not formed part of the Aztec and Inca empires—were at times as proficient at adapting and adopting the Aztecs and the Incas for their own purposes as were the Mexican liberals of the Porfiriato and creole revolutionaries in 1810 Buenos Aires. Creole elites are not the only ones who invent their own pasts. These are worthwhile stories that merit scholarly attention. Yet, as this book examines the use of the preconquest past not by Fanon's native intellectuals and Mexican peasants but rather by members of the national elite in nineteenth-century Spanish America, I end with some comments about the legacy of this nineteenth-century creole history for twentieth- and twenty-first-century Spanish America.

On the one hand, the incorporation of the preconquest past into official history is evident today in many parts of Spanish America. The metro stops in Mexico City named after Aztec emperors, mentioned in the introduction, are but one example. When metro line 1 opened in 1969 it included stops named "Moctezuma" and "Cuauhtémoc" alongside "Isabel la Católica" and "Insurgentes."[7] Although some writers would perhaps describe these stations as the fruit of the Mexican Revolution's commitment to indigenismo, in this book I have tried to remind readers that, as a number of other scholars have already argued, interest in the pre-Columbian era on the part of Mexican elites long predates the Revolution. Similarly, the introductory text to the pre-Columbian section of the Museo de Arte de Lima describes the artifacts on display as the work of "our distant ancestors."[8] The idea that Peruvian history predates the conquest and that national history is best described in terms of genealogy are themes present in nineteenth-century Peru as well. The fact that "our distant ancestors" is omitted from the English version of the same text further suggests that this particular vision of Peru is intended specifically to instruct Peruvians on their own ancestry. These examples of official history form part of a larger process of incorporation and acknowledgment of the preconquest past which this book has tried to explain. It would be pleasant to end with some cheerful comments about the slow but fundamentally positive changes that have taken place within elite nationalism, such that Mexico City now has Aztec-themed metro stops and Limeños have Inca ancestors. I could then conclude that these changes represent the long-postponed realization on the part of Spanish American states of their nations' fundamentally indigenous nature. This ending, however, would fit neither with the complexity of contemporary Spanish American state nationalism nor with the arguments of my book. I have tried to stress throughout not the inherent connections that in some natural way link the national past to the national present, but rather the constructed nature of all national pasts. In particular, I have emphasized that from the point of view of national elites there was no necessary connection between the preconquest past and the indigenous present, or at least that any such connection could be denied. It is with one example of that legacy that this book most appropriately ends.

In 1960 the military leaders then governing Guatemala declared Tecún Umán, the sixteenth-century Quiché warrior who had resisted the conquistador Pedro de Alvarado, to be a "national hero." The date 20 February was declared the Day of Tecún Umán, and various localities were named after him.[9] El Baúl hill in Quetzaltenango, for example, was renamed Tecún Umán hill so as to commemorate "the epic resistance of the Quiché people to foreign invasion in the sixteenth century, symbolized in a legendary name: Tecún Umán. Neither his heroism in the struggle for liberty, nor the sacrifice of his forces in an unequal combat on 20 February 1524, the day of the decisive battle at Llano del Pinal, were sufficient to prevent the conquest of his nation, but his example is preserved in popular memory and in the annals of national history."[10]

By 1980 newspapers, government officials, and representatives of the military were lauding Tecún Umán as a "symbol of American man," "a symbol of Guatemalan nationality," a representative of "our own national essence," and "our indigenous ancestor," as Carol Hendrickson has shown.[11] In the same decades, while the Guatemalan state exalted the achievements of the precolonial Maya and celebrated conquest-era indigenous warriors as symbols of nationality, the armed forces undertook a series of military campaigns against Guatemala's Maya population that many scholars have described as genocidal.[12] Tens of thousands of Quiché, Cakchiquel, and other Maya peoples were tortured and killed and hundreds of indigenous villages were destroyed. The nineteenth-century histories examined in this book should help make the intellectual genealogy of the Guatemalan military's behavior understandable, albeit never forgivable. The poets, politicians, and scholars whose ideas I have here discussed were by no means unanimous advocates of extermination; many spoke eloquently of the need to defend the indigenous population from abuse. Nonetheless, our understanding of their legacy should acknowledge not only the metro stops in Mexico City but also the more sombre history of twentieth-century Guatemala.

 *Appendix*

Abolishing the Indian?

During the wars of independence, insurgents in Mexico and Peru tried to abolish the term *indio*, as well as racial categories more generally, on the grounds that they were incompatible with republican concepts of equality. In Mexico a series of resolutions revoked colonial classifications. An 1822 law ordered that official documents should cease classifying people by racial origin, and in 1824 José María Luis Mora and Alonso Fernández proposed to the Mexican congress that "*indio*, in common acceptance as a term of opprobrium for a large portion of our citizens, be abolished from public usage."[1] Mora went so far as to assert that in legal terms "Indians no longer exist."[2] In Peru, Bernardo de Monteagudo was the first official to discard the term "Indian": in July 1822 he stated that in the future Indians "will be called Peruvians, names that they will justly value and whose worth they will appreciate more greatly with every passing day."[3] San Martín, who is often credited with the replacement of "Indian" with "Peruvian," in fact made his statement that "henceforth the aborigines will not be called Indians or natives; they are sons and citizens of Peru and should be known as Peruvians" a month later.[4] In other regions political leaders, without issuing legislation, simply began employing other words to replace the discredited colonial classifications.

A common replacement for *indio* (Indian) was *indígena* (indigene). In the 4 Oct. 1821 session of the Congress of Cúcuta, for example, representatives referred to "the Colombian indigenes called Indians in the Spanish [legal] codes," and then referred insistently to "indigenes" in the remainder of the session.[5] Mexican pamphleteers likewise referred to "the indigenes, that is, the Indians (so that everyone is clear whom we mean)."[6] In Peru officials began employing not only "indigene" but also "Peruvian," in keeping with the decrees cited above. Mark Thurner notes that in the early 1820s the term "Peruvian" was used to refer specifically to the "ex-indios" rather than to Peruvian nationals in general.[7] Just as often officials simply spoke of "the people formerly known as Indians." The 1815 constitution of the Colombian state of Mariquita and the Venezuelan 1811 constitution thus referred to "the section of citizens known until today as Indians."[8] In Mexico politicians alluded to "the so-called Indians."[9] San Martín similarly referred to "the Peruvians previously known as Indians or natives."[10] Only occasionally did committed liberals object that the retention of any sort of ethnic distinction—whatever the terms used to describe it—undermined the very basis of republicanism.[11] In general officials continued to view the world in caste terms, and they were therefore obliged—sometimes by their own legislation—to find euphemisms to allow them to continue to discuss the indigenous population as a discrete group without using the word "Indian."

Governmental commitment to this new nomenclature was short lived—rarely lasting beyond 1830. David Bushnell notes that in the case of Colombia, deputies' use of "indigene" was episodic, and that "despite the best of intention they even found it hard to eschew the word *salvaje* [savage]."[12] In Peru the impact of the attempted name change is revealed in an entry to an 1841 dictionary of Peruvian legislation. The index lists the following entry: "Indians—see *Peruvians—formerly Indians*."[13] The editor evidently assumed that readers would want to consult legislation relating to "Indians," despite the fact that this category had been legally abolished in 1822. In Mexico, government journals employed "Indian" and "indigene" side by side, and the unofficial newspapers were no more scrupulous.[14] Moreover, the continued existence in a number of countries of the Indian tribute further emphasizes the limited nature of these linguistic alterations, however much legislators tried to disguise this fact by endowing the tribute with vaguer titles. In 1827 Bolivia, for example, after the tribute was reestablished under the name of "personal contribution," the former Indians were defined as "the persons who pay the single personal contribution, which the Spanish called tribute, their fathers, wives and children."[15] Any abolition of the term "Indian" was unlikely to succeed as long as the category "Indian" remained.

In regions where no such independence-era abolition had been attempted, officials also continued throughout the century to employ racial distinctions in legislation. In Guatemala the legislation of the 1830s–1840s employed "indígena" in preference to "indio," but from the 1850s the term "indio" returned, to be replaced in the 1870s by "aborigines," or "the Indian race."[16] In Ecuador "indigene" was generally the preferred term in legislation until the end of the century, when laws began to mention "Indians," and, increasingly, "the Indian race."[17] Moreover, the idea of autochthonousness implicit in the term "indigene" began to annoy some creoles, who felt that the legitimacy of their own presence was subtly undermined by referring to "Indians" as the indigenous inhabitants. Creoles in late-nineteenth-century Argentina thus expressed dissatisfaction with the term "indigene" as a synonym for Indian, since "the children of Europeans who are born in the territory of the Republic are indigenous Americans."[18] The creoles, it seems, were the true natives.

 *A Note on Sources*

This study is based on material from libraries, museums, and archives in Argentina, Chile, Peru, Colombia, Mexico, Spain, Britain, and the United States.

Manuscript Material
I used manuscript material from the Archivo General de Indias in Seville, the Archivo General de la Nación in Mexico City, the Archivo General de la Nación in Buenos Aires, the Biblioteca Nacional de Perú, the Archivo Regional del Cuzco, the Rare Books and Manuscripts room of the Nettie Lee Benson Library at the University of Texas at Austin, and (via microfilm) the Archivo General de la Nación in Bogotá.

Newspapers
The Archivo General de Indias possesses a number of independence-era journals from across Spanish America; I made particular use of their collection of Chilean and Peruvian newspapers. I read later Chilean and Peruvian newspapers in the Biblioteca Nacional de Chile and the Biblioteca Nacional de Perú. Good collections of Mexican newspapers are held at the Hemeroteca Nacional, located within the Mexican Biblioteca Nacional, and at the Archivo General de la Nación, also in Mexico City; these also have some nineteenth-century Guatemalan journals. The Archivo General de la Nación in Buenos Aires has many nineteenth-century Argentine newspapers. I also read Mexican and Argentine newspapers at the Nettie Lee Benson Library. In addition, I consulted microfilms of nineteenth-century Colombian, Venezuelan, Peruvian, and Ecuadorian newspapers from the Colombian Archivo General de la Nación's Fondo Restrepo.

Other Printed Material
I consulted material from the Bodleian Library at Oxford University, the libraries of Cambridge University and Warwick University, the Nettie Lee Benson Library, the Archivo General de la Nación in Buenos Aires, the Biblioteca Nacional de Chile, the Peruvian Archivo General de la Nación, the Biblioteca Nacional de Perú, and the Biblioteca Nacional de México. I also read microfilmed

copies of many of the nineteenth-century texts held in the Colombian Archivo General de la Nación's Fondo Restrepo. Most of the Mexican *discursos cívicos* that I cite are located in Mexico City's Biblioteca Nacional, in the Colección Lafragua. The rare books and manuscripts room of the Nettie Lee Benson Library also has a substantial collection of Mexican and Guatemalan pamphlets; their Taracena Flores Collection is the source of all the Guatemalan *discursos cívicos* cited. The Fitzwilliam Museum in Cambridge allowed me to consult the library of its Numismatics Department, and the headquarters of the British Philatelic Society in London provided information on stamps from across Spanish America.

Artifacts

I refer to objects displayed in the Museo Histórico Nacional, Buenos Aires, the Museo Nacional de Arte, Mexico City, the Museo de Arte de Lima, the Museo Inka, Cuzco, and the Museo de Arte, Cuzco. I also studied the numismatic collections of the Museo Numismático "Dr. José Evaristo Uriburu" and the Museo Mitre, both in Buenos Aires.

 *Notes*

Abbreviations Used in the Notes

AGI   Archivo General de Indias, Seville

AGN (B)   Archivo General de la Nación, Bogotá

AGN (BA)   Archivo General de la Nación, Buenos Aires

AGN (MC)   Archivo General de la Nación, Mexico City

BN (CM)   Biblioteca Nacional del Perú, Lima, Colección Manuscrita

Introduction: On "Indians"

1. On "becoming Indian," see Serge Gruzinski, "The Net Torn Apart: Ethnic Identities and Westernization in Colonial Mexico, Sixteenth-Nineteenth Century," *Ethnicities and Nations*, ed. Guidieri, Pellizzi, and Tamiah; Urban and Sherzer, eds., *Nation-States and Indians in Latin America*; and Irene Silverblatt, "Becoming Indian in the Central Andes of Seventeenth Century Peru," *After Colonialism*, ed. Prakash. See also Martínez Pelaéz, *La patria del criollo*, esp. 471–72, 489–510.

2. Berkhofer, *The White Man's Indian*, xvii.

3. Blanca Muratorio, "Images of Indians in the Construction of Ecuadorian Identity at the End of the Nineteenth Century," *Latin American Popular Culture*, ed. Beezley and Curcio-Nagy, 107.

4. Mallon, *Peasant and Nation*, 14–15.

5. Brading, *Prophecy and Myth; The Origins of Mexican Nationalism;* and *The First America.* See also Keen, *The Aztec Image;* and Florescano, *Memory, Myth, and Time.*

6. "Creole" here refers to individuals of European heritage born in the Americas.

7. Anderson, *Imagined Communities*, chapter 11.

8. Vicente López y Planes, "Marcha patriótica," 1813, *La lira argentina.*

9. Goodman, ed., *Guatemala: The Postal History and Philately*, 1:78–82; and Eric Hobsbawm, "Mass-Producing Traditions: Europe, 1870–1914," *The Invention of Tradition*, ed. Hobsbawm and Ranger, 281 (for quote).

10. Sarmiento, "Review of *Investigaciones sobre el sistema colonial de los españoles*," 1844, *Obras*, 2:213.

11. Ramírez, "Discurso cívico pronunciado el 16 de setiembre de 1861," *Obras*, 1:136.

12. Blanca Muratorio, "Nación, identidad y etnicidad: Imagenes de los indios ecuatorianos y sus imagineros a fines del siglo XIX," *Imágenes e imagineros*, ed. Muratorio.

13. García Quintana, *Cuauhtémoc en el siglo XIX;* Itier, "Le théâtre moderne en Quechua"; and De la Cadena, *Indigenous Mestizos*, 72–78, 162–65.

14. Nora, ed., *Les Lieux de Mémoire*.

15. Fentress and Wickham, *Social Memory*, 128. See also Connerton, *How Societies Remember;* and Wertheimer, *Imagined Empires*, 7.

16. See, for example, Hobsbawm, "Nationalism and Nationality in Latin America," 313.

17. Stern, ed., *Resistance, Rebellion, and Consciousness;* Mallon, *Peasant and Nation;* Guardino, *Peasants, Politics, and the Formation of Mexico's National State;* Thurner, *From Two Republics to One Divided;* Walker, *Smoldering Ashes;* Thomson, with LaFrance, *Patriotism, Politics and Popular Liberalism;* Alda Mejías, *La participación indígena;* Irurozqui, "The Sound of the Pututos"; Grandin, *Blood of Guatemala;* and Sanders, *Contentious Republicans.*

18. Hobsbawm, "Nationalism and Nationality in Latin America," 313.

19. Hobsbawm, *Nations and Nationalism*, 37–38, 91.

20. Alberdi, *Autobiografía*, 118 (for quote); and Alberdi, *Bases*, 65.

21. Martha Bechis, "La 'organización nacional' y las tribus pampeanas en Argentina durante el siglo XIX," *Pueblos, comunidades y municipios*, ed. Escobar Ohmstede, Falcón, and Buve, 88.

22. Miller, *In the Shadow of the State*, 137.

23. Viroli, *For Love of Country*, 2.

24. Colonel Faez, Discurso de apertura, *El Progreso*, Santiago, 11 April 1843.

25. Larrabure y Unanue, "El himno nacional," Lima, 15 July 1874, *Manuscritos y publicaciones*, 1:227. On patriotic occasions, insisted another Peruvian, "an electric current of sweet emotions was felt to circulate through the veins of every patriot" (Juan Manuel Almesquita, "Alocución pronunciada con motivo de una función patriótica," Arequipa, 22 July 1864, BN [CM] D11811). The status of such nationalism as a sentiment, rather than an intellectual process, is revealed clearly by José de San Martín's 1822 insistence that women's greater emotional capacity made them natural patriots: "The more sensitive sex must naturally be the most patriotic" (Decree of San Martín, 11 Jan. 1822, Oviedo, *Colección de leyes*, 4:15–16).

26. McFarlane, "Identity, Enlightenment and Political Dissent"; Lomnitz, "Nationalism as a Practical System"; and Castro-Klarén and Chasteen, eds., *Beyond Imagined Communities*.

27. Gellner, *Nations and Nationalism*, 55.

28. Nora, ed., *Les Lieux de Mémoire*; Hobsbawm and Ranger, eds., *The Invention of Tradition*; and Le Goff, *History and Memory*, 86–87.

29. Bhabha, "Introduction: Narrating the Nation," *Nation and Narration*, ed. Bhabha, 1.

30. Smith, *National Identity*, 14.

31. JanMohamed, *Manichean Aesthetics*, 5 (for quotes), 40, 152, 182–84, 265, 279; and Fanon, *The Wretched of the Earth*, 166–99.

32. Bhabha, "Of Mimicry and Man: The Ambivalence of Colonial Discourse," *The Location of Culture*; and Bhabha, "Representation and the Colonial Text," 93–96. See also Hall, "Cultural Identity and Diaspora."

33. Constitución de la República de Tunja, 1811, cap. II; Constitución del Estado de Antioquia, 1812, sec. 3, art. 4; Constitución de la República de Cundinamarca, 1812, art. 28; Constitución del Estado de Mariquita, 1815, tít. II, art. 6; Constitución de la Provincia de Antioquia, 1815; Deberes del Cuidadano, art. 4, all in Pombo and Gutiérrez, eds., *Constituciones de Colombia*; and Constitución de Angostura, 1819, sec. 2, art. 5, *Actas del Congreso de Angostura*, ed. Cortázar and Cuervo, 148 (my emphasis in all cases). See also Earle, "Rape and the Anxious Republic."

34. Lissón quoted in Pagden, *Spanish Imperialism*, 136.

35. Widdifield, *The Embodiment of the National*, 153, 156–58, 160–61, 162 (for quote). Similarly, in the 1891 independence day parade held in Buenos Aires, "Liberty," "The Republic," and "The Provinces" were symbolized by costumed girls. The historic battalions that had actually fought in the wars of independence, on the other hand, were represented by schoolboys. See Bertoni, *Patriotas, cosmopolitas y nacionalistas*, 113.

36. See, for example, Harris, "Ethnic Identity and Market Relations," 354–55; and Antonio Escobar Ohmstede, "Los pueblos indios huastecos frente a las tendencias modernizadoras decimonónicas," *Pueblos, comunidades y municipios*, ed. Escobar Ohmstede, Falcón, and Buve, 172.

37. Cope, *The Limits of Racial Domination*, 5, 50, 53 (for quote), 6.

38. Ibid., 57 (for quote), 68–69.

39. Schiebinger, *The Mind Has No Sex* and *Nature's Body*; and Wheeler, *The Complexion of Race*.

40. Stepan, "The Hour of Eugenics," 64–101.

41. Peter Wade, "Afterword: Race and Nation in Latin America: An Anthropological View," *Race and Nation*, ed. Appelbaum, Macpherson, and Rosemblatt, 272 (for quote); and Knight, "Racism, Revolution, and *Indigenismo*," 72–78.

42. Thomas Holt, "The First New Nations," *Race and Nation*, ed. Appelbaum, Macpherson, and Rosemblatt, ix.

43. Quijada, "La ciudadanización del 'indio bárbaro' " and "Nación y territorio"; and Quijada, Bernand, and Schneider, *Homogeneidad y nación*.

44. Tenorio Trillo, *Mexico at the World's Fairs*; Muratorio, ed., *Imágenes e imagineros*; Poole, *Vision, Race, and Modernity*. See also Widdifield, *The Embodiment of the National*; Taracena Arriola, *Invención criolla*; Walker, *Smoldering Ashes*; Grandin, *Blood of Guatemala*; De la Cadena, *Indigenous Mestizos*.

45. Collier, *Ideas and Politics*; Gerbi, *The Dispute of the New World*; Keen, *The Aztec Image*; Pagden, "Identity Formation"; and König, *En el camino hacia la Nación*. For Brading, see *Prophecy and Myth*; *The Origins of Mexican Nationalism*; and *The First America*.

46. I use the nineteenth-century term "Araucanian" rather than "Mapuche" (the term preferred by the Mapuche themselves), to signal that my discussion refers to nineteenth-century elite imaginings of the preconquest past rather than conveying in any sense an indigenous vision.

47. Vicuña Mackenna, *Catálogo del Museo Histórico de Santa Lucia*, 4 (my emphasis); and *Revista Chilena*, Santiago, tomo I (1875).

CHAPTER 1. *Montezuma's Revenge*

1. *Correo Mercantil*, Lima, 18 May 1822, 25 May 1822, 5; and Balta Campbell, *Historia general del teatro*, 68–69.

2. Decree of Dec. 1821, Oviedo, ed., *Colección de leyes*, 3:10; and Tristan, *Les pérégrinations*, 326. The penalty was increased for recidivists.

3. "The theater of this capital, like all those of *civilised peoples*," begins an 1822 decree (Decree of Bernardo de Monteagudo, 30 May 1822, Oviedo, ed., *Colección de leyes*, 4:333 [my emphasis]).

4. See, for example, Brading, *The First America*, 420, 540.

5. Brading, *The Origins of Mexican Nationalism*, 3; Brading, "Patriotism and the Nation," 20; and Brading, *The First America*, 293–313, 343–90, 450–62.

6. Phelan, "Neo-Aztecism," 760–61.

7. Phelan, "Neo-Aztecism," 761; Keen, *The Aztec Image*, 190–91; and Pagden, *Spanish Imperialism*, 94.

8. These debates are discussed in Gerbi, *The Dispute of the New World*.

9. Pagden, *Spanish Imperialism*, 10.

10. Ocampo, *Las ideas de un día*, 228–29; Brading, *Prophecy and Myth*; Keen, *The Aztec Image*; and Florescano, *Memory, Myth, and Time*.

11. For varied examples of this rhetoric, see Rieu-Millan, *Los Diputados*, 96; Bustamante, *Cuadro histórico*, 1:620, 622; Brading, *The Origins of Mexican Nationalism*, 51; Exposición de José Ignacio Rayón al Congreso, 1813, *El Congreso de Anáhuac*, 114–17 —; P. A. J., *Los horrores de Cortés*; Un Americano, *A los ciudadanos militares*; J. C. M., "Soneto," *Noticioso General*, Mexico City, 12 Dec. 1821; *Marcha alusiva*; El Payo del Rosario, *Nuevas zorras de Sansón*; *El Ilustrador Mexicano*, Mexico City, 4 July 1823; and Connaughton, *Ideología y sociedad*, 148–50.

12. Brading, *Prophecy and Myth*, 42. See also Bustamante, *Cuadro histórico*, 1:623; Ortega, *México libre; Parangón patriótico*; and Herrejón Peredo, "Sermones y discursos," 162.

13. Bustamante alluded to Alvarado's massacre of thousands of Amerindians at Cholula in 1519. Bustamante, *Cuadro histórico*, 1:336. I have used Brading's translation from his *The First America*, 634–35. See also Carlos María de Bustamante, footnotes added to León y Gama, *Descripción histórica y cronológica*, 82–83n.

14. "Razonamiento del General Morales en la Apertura del Congreso de Chilpantzingo," Bustamante, *Cuadro histórico*, 1:622. I have modified Brading's translation from *Prophecy and Myth*, 42–43. Alternatively, see *Extracto del noticioso general*; and Bárcena, *Oración gratulatoria*.

15. Brading, *Prophecy and Myth*, 42–43.

16. Anderson, *Imagined Communities*, 44 (for quote); and Connerton, *How Societies Remember*, 6.

17. Minguet, in "El concepto de nación," refers to this as "archaeological patriotism." Martínez Peláez's related conceptions of the "creole patria" are set forth in his *La patria del criollo*.

18. McFarlane, "Identity, Enlightenment and Political Dissent," 331 (for quote); Brading, *Prophecy and Myth*; Brading, *Mexican Nationalism*; Brading, *The First America*, 3, 420, 540; Florescano, *Memory, Myth, and Time*, 191; and Florescano, *Etnia, estado y nación*, 334.

19. Salazar, "Elegía," 126.

20. Pedro Ignacio de Castro Barros, "Oración patriótica," Tucumán, 25 May 1815, Museo Historico Nacional, 1:114–15.

21. *Gazeta Ministerial Extraordinaria de Chile*, 21 Aug. 1821 (emphasis in the original). Atahualpa was executed by the Spanish at Cajamarca.

22. For "usurpation," see Bonilla, "Clases populares," 29; Explicación de la Función al cumple años del gobierno de la América del Sud, Buenos Aires, 1812, AGI, Diversos 2; *Gazeta Ministerial del Gobierno de Buenos Aires,* 17 March 1813; Proclama de los insurgentes del Cusco, 1814[?], Aparicio Vega, *El clero patriota,* 126; El cuidadano Juan Ramon Balcarce . . . , 31 Dec. 1815, *La revolución de mayo,* ed. Mallié, 2:563–64; *Los Andes Libres,* Lima, 18 Sept. 1821, *Periódicos,* ed. Tauro, 1:294, 296; Un americano, *A los ciudadanos militares;* Lagranda, *Consejo prudente;* Anonymous letter to Pedro Vicente Cañete, AGI, Diversos 3; *Correo Mercantil,* Lima, 4 June 1822; José María Salazar, "Canción nacional," *La guirnalda,* ed. Ortíz; Manuel Ferreyros, "Lima Independiente," 1822[?], and "Bosquejos de la tiranía y el Perú libre," both in *La poesía de la emancipación,* ed. Mira Quesada Sosa, 247–49, 401–4; and Chiaramonte, "Formas de Identidad," 83. "Vile usurper" is from Y. V. and J. P. A., "Contestación de los hijos del sol a la sombra de Atahuallpa," 1822, *La poesía de la emancipación,* ed. Mira Quesada Sosa, 356–57.

23. König, "Símbolos nacionales," 396–97.

24. José de la Torre Ugarte, "Canción Nacional del Perú," 1821, *La poesía de la emancipación,* ed. Mira Quesada Sosa, 293; and Monteagudo, "Oración inaugural," *La revolución de mayo,* ed. Mallié, 5:7. Monteagudo echoes Juan José Castelli's 3 April 1811 manifesto (Manifiesto de Castelli, Oruro, 3 April 1811, AGI, Diversos 2), which spread through the region in manuscript form: see the documents seized from José María Ladrón de Guevara and Vicente González in November 1814, AGI, Diversos 3. For other examples, see Francisco Xavier Iturre Patio, "Proclama del más perseguido americano a sus paysanos," 9 August 1810, *La revolución de Mayo,* ed. Mallié, 1:410; Acta de Independencia Absoluta de Cartagena, Cartagena, 11 Nov. 1811, *Documentos para la Historia de Cartagena,* ed. Arrazola, 185–91; Proclama de Santa Fe a los habitantes del Perú, 1812[?], AGI, Diversos 2; *La Aurora de Chile,* 13 August 1812; speech of Antonio Súarez, Santa Cruz de la Sierra, 25 May 1813, AGN (BA), Sala X: 44–8–29; Cabildo de Cuzco to Marqués de la Concordia, Cuzco, 17 Sept. 1814, *Conspiraciones y rebeliones,* ed. Villanueva Urteaga, 1:216–20; *El Censor,* Buenos Aires, 25 July 1816; "Patriotic Sermon delivered in Villeta," 28 Dec. 1819, AGN (B), Fondo Enrique Ortega Ricaurte, caja 184, carpetas 674–77; *Lima libre: Drama alegórica en un acto,* 1821, and Manuel López Lisson, "Loa en memoria del primer aniversario de la batalla de Ayacucho," 1825, both in *El teatro en la independencia,* ed. Ugarte Chamorro, 2:53, 271; *Columbia: Canción partiótica americana;* Salazar, "Elegía"; Fernández Madrid, "La

prisión de Atahualpa," *Elegías nacionales peruanas;* and *Canción patriótica a Simón Bolívar libertador.*

25. Torres y Peña, *Memorias,* 33–34. See also Manuel Pardo, "Memoria exacta," *Conspiraciones y rebeliones,* ed. Villanueva Urteaga, 1:258; Berístain de Souza, *Diálogos patrióticos,* 2; López Cancelada, *La verdad sabida,* viii; Carta Pastoral . . . [de] Don Manuel Abad Queipo, Valladolid, 26 September 1812, *Colección de Documentos,* ed. Hernández y Dávalos, 4:439; Berístain de Souza, *Discurso eucarístico;* and Zavala, *Ensayo histórico,* 1:54. After his arrest by royalist forces in 1811 the Mexican insurgent Miguel Hidalgo was specifically asked why he had claimed that Spain "has kept America enslaved for three hundred years" (Declaración del Cura Hidalgo, 7 June 1811, *Colección de Documentos,* ed. Hernández y Dávalos, 1:17).

26. *Manifiesto que hace a las naciones.*

27. *Correo Mercantil,* Lima, 18 May 1822.

28. José Joaquín de Olmedo, "Brindis a San Martín," *La poesía de la emancipación,* ed. Mira Quesada Sosa, 327. Olmedo also credited Bolívar with avenging the Incas: see José Joaquín de Olmedo, "Marcha," 1825, *La poesía de la emancipación,* ed. Mira Quesada Sosa, 487. For more vengeance, see "El observador americano a sus paisanos," 23 Dec. 1813, AGI, Diversos 3; *El Sol de Cuzco, Documentos,* ed. Blanco and Azpurua, 10:127; König, *En el camino,* 131–35, 236–41; Fernández Madrid, "La muerte de Atahualpa," *Elegías nacionales peruanas;* "Glosa," Ayacucho[?], 1820; Y. V. and J. P. A., "Contestación de los hijos del sol a la sombra de Atahuallpa," 1822; and F. S. M., "Himno," 1825, all in *La poesía de la emancipación,* ed. Mira Quesada Sosa, 195–96, 356–58, 488–90; *Los Andes Libres,* Lima, 7 Aug. 1821, 18 Sept. 1821, *Periódicos,* ed. Tauro, 1:269, 294; *Correo Mercantil,* Lima, 25 May 1822, 5; Miller, *Memoirs,* 2:215; *Gaceta de Colombia,* Bogotá, 15 Jan. 1826; and Villanueva Urteaga, "La idea de los Incas como factor favorable a la independencia," 157.

29. Andrés Bello, "La agricultura en la zona tórrida," *Repertorio Americano,* tomo 1, *Repertorio Americano,* 1:14, 8, 17 (for quote); and Pratt, *Imperial Eyes,* 172–80.

30. Gerbi, *The Dispute of the New World.*

31. Ibid., 297–98, 313.

32. König, *En el camino,* 225–26 (for quote); Carta pastoral de . . . Manuel Abad y Queipo, Valladolid, 26 Sept. 1812, *Colección de documentos,* ed. Hernández y Dávilos, 4:441–58; Torres y Peña, *Memorias,* 32–35; and Gregorio, Bishop of Cartagena, pamphlet, 3 Sept. 1819, AGI, Papeles de Cuba 743.

33. Walker, "The Patriotic Society," 294; and Walker, *Smoldering Ashes*, 115–17, discuss such exceptions.

34. Amunátegui, *Los precursores*, 1910 edition, 2:501.

35. Pinto, "Apuntes autobiográficos," 74. Note that Pinto describes himself as the descendant of the conquistadors, a matter to which I return in this chapter's penultimate section.

36. Collier, *Ideas and Politics*, 213–22.

37. *Gazeta Ministerial Extraordinaria de Chile*, 21 Aug. 1821 (for quote); and Amunátegui, *Los precursores*, 1872 edition, 3:567.

38. Collier, *Ideas and Politics*, 213; and Boccara and Seguel-Boccara, "Políticas indígenas en Chile," 746–47.

39. Amunátegui, *Los precursores*, 1910 edition, 2:512; and Torrente, *Historia*, 3:369.

40. Collier, *Ideas and Politics*, 264–66.

41. Egaña, *Cartas pehuenches*, section 4, letter 4, 2.

42. Ibid., section 1, letter 1, 2–3.

43. Zúñiga, *La Logia "Lautaro,"* 178.

44. For example, the Chilean journalist Camilo Henríquez, during his exile in Buenos Aires between 1814 and 1822, wrote a play called *Lautaro* for the Sociedad del Buen Gusto.

45. Cometta Manzoni, *El indio en la poesía de América Española*, 142–43.

46. The Logia Lautaro had links to the Cádiz-based Sociedad de Lautaro, also dedicated to American independence. See Zúñiga, *La Logia "Lautaro"*; and Eyzaguirre, "La Logia Lautarina," *La Logia Lautarina*.

47. Y. V., "La sombra de Atahuallpa a los hijos del sol," 1822[?], *La poesía de la emancipación*, ed. Mira Quesada Sosa, 355 (for quote; emphasis as in the original); Rosemberg, "La mención del indio," 306, 309; *El Monitor Araucano*, 15 June 1813; *Gazeta Ministerial Extraordinaria de Chile*, 23 Aug. 1821; *Los Andes Libres*, Lima, 31 July 1821, *Periódicos*, ed. Tauro, 1:264; and Collier, *Ideas and Politics*, 213.

48. Andrés Bello, "Noticia de una pintura histórica," *Repertorio Americano*, tomo 1, 1826, *El Repertorio Americano*, 1:71–73 (my emphasis). The painting was an earlier version of Henry Perronet Briggs, *The First Interview between the Spaniards and the Peruvians* (Tate Gallery, London).

49. Poole, *Vision, Race and Modernity*, 25.

50. Flores Galindo, *Buscando un Inca*, 211–23.

51. Rosemberg, "La mención del indio," 302–3 (for quote); *La lira argentina*, 163–73, 381–99; *Los Andes Libres*, Lima, 18 Sept. 1821, *Periódicos*, ed.

Tauro, 1:293–300; and *La poesía de la emancipación,* ed. Mira Quesada Sosa, 190–94, 265.

52. Juan Antonio Neirot, "Oración fúnebre . . . de los valientes soldados que murieron . . . el día 24 de Sept. de 1812," 1812, *La revolución de Mayo,* ed. Mallié, 5:125–26. Jorge Cañizares-Esguerra has argued that from the early nineteenth century the Inca empire was most commonly compared to the Orient rather than to ancient Greece and Rome (Cañizares-Esguerra, *How to Write the History of the New World,* 13, 39–44, 56). While this may be true of European writings, in Spanish America insurgent writers constantly likened the Incas to European classical antiquity.

53. *El Censor,* Buenos Aires, 12 Dec. 1816 (for quote); Fray Pantaleon García, "Proclama sagrada dicha . . . el 25 de mayo de 1814," Cordoba; and Julian Segundo de Agüero, "Oración patriótica," 25 May 1817, Buenos Aires, both in *El clero argentino,* Museo Historico Nacional, 1:91–92, 181–85; Panzos, *Letters on the United Provinces,* letter 1, letter 10, 72–76; Cabildo de Cuzco to Marqués de la Concordia, Cuzco, 17 Sept. 1814, *Conspiraciones y rebeliones,* ed. Villanueva Urteaga, 1:217; Francisco de Paula Castañeda, "Alocución o arenga patriótica . . . para la apertura de la nueva Academia de Dibujo," 10 Aug. 1814, Buenos Aires, *El clero argentino,* Museo Historico Nacional, 2:8; and "Antigüedades," *El Tribuno de la República Peruana,* 28 Nov. 1822, *Los ideólogos,* ed. Tamayo Vargas and Pacheco Vélez, 1:412.

54. José Bernardo Monteagudo, "Diálogo entre Atahualpa y Fernando VII en los Campos Eliseos," 1809, *El teatro en la independencia,* ed. Ugarte Chamorro, 1:253–61; and Francovich, "Un diálogo." See also Proclama de Ildefonso de las Muñecas, 1814[?], *Conspiraciones y rebeliones,* ed. Villanueva Urteaga, 2:384–85; Julian Segundo de Agüero, "Oración patriótica," 25 May 1817, Buenos Aires, *El clero argentino,* Museo Historico Nacional, 1:181–85; *Gazeta Ministerial de Chile,* 25 Aug. 1821; *Gazeta Ministerial Extraordinaria de Chile,* 21 Aug. 1821; *Gazeta Ministerial de Chile,* 25 Aug. 1821; *Gaceta de Colombia,* Bogotá, 16 Oct. 1825; Arenga del gobierno, 25 May 1825, AGN (BA), Colección Sánchez de Bustamante 3026 (leg. 2), doc. 90; Canción al Primer Congreso del Perú, *La poesía de la emancipación,* ed. Mira Quesada Sosa, 407; and Walker, *Smoldering Ashes,* 165–66. For Peru as the "land of the Incas," see José Manuel Arce, Oración, 8 Oct. 1821, *Obra de gobierno,* ed. Puente Candamo, 1:300; Macera, "El periodismo en la independencia," 1971, and "El indio visto por los criollos y españoles," 1965, both in *Trabajos de Historia,* 2:324, 338–39; *Gaceta de Colombia,* Bogotá, 6 Jan., 6 Feb., 13 March, 1 May, 4 Sept. 1825; and José Joaquín de Olmedo, "Introducción

a la función de teatro," 1825, *El teatro en la independencia,* ed. Ugarte Chamorro, 1:325.

55. José Bernardo Monteagudo, "Diálogo entre Atahualpa y Fernando VII en los Campos Eliseos," 1809, *El teatro en la independencia,* ed. Ugarte Chamorro, 1:261.

56. "Canción patriótica del ejército libertadora a los peruanos"; Marcha patriótica del Perú independiente, 1822; Felipe Lledías, "Canción patriótica," 1822; "Proclama de Huáscar Inca en su prisión," 1822; and "El prognóstico de Viracocha: Embajada de este príncipe al Inca su padre," 1822, all in *La poesía de la emancipación,* ed. Mira Quesada Sosa, 182–83, 307–10, 322–23, 359–61, 362–64; Mallet, *Diálogo;* Walker, "The Patriotic Society," 295; Rosemberg, "La mención del indio," 305; and König, "El indigenismo criollo," 755–56.

57. Raymond Buve has shown the difficulties that this celebration of the Aztecs posed to authorities in Tlaxcala, who had hitherto focused on the conquest-era Tlaxcalans' *support* of the conquistadors as a source of civic pride. See Buve, " 'Cádiz' y el debate sobre el estatus de una provincia mexicana: Tlaxcala entre 1780 y 1850," *Pueblos, comunidades y municipios,* ed. Escobar Ohmstede, Falcón, and Buve.

58. For ships, see Torrente, *Historia de la Revolución de Chile,* 369; and *Correo Mercantil,* Lima, 27 July 1822. See also Acta de Independencia del Alto Perú, 1825, *Las constituciones del Bolivia,* ed. Trigo, 159; *Canción patriótica;* José María Heredia, "Fragmentos descriptivos de un poema mejicano" (later published as "En el teocalli de Cholula"), 1825, *Repertorio Americano,* tomo 2, 1:37–40; and "Programme of the fiestas mayas of 1828," Zabala, *Historia de la pirámide de mayo,* 96–100.

59. José Fernández Madrid, *Guatimoc,* 1827, *Atala y Guatimoc.* Andrés Bello, in his review of this work, noted that the play's title alone "is enough to inspire Americans" (*El Repertorio Americano,* 2:306). *Xicontencatl* (1826), recounts in similar terms the resistance offered by the Tlaxcalan warrior Xicoténcatl the Younger to Hernán Cortés (José María Moreno y Buenvecino[?], *Xicotencatl: La novela del México colonial,* ed. Castro Leal, 1:79–177). For *Xicotencatl*'s author, see Pimentel, *Historia crítica de la literatura y de las ciencias en México,* 1885, *Obras,* 5:107. Luis Vargas Tejada, *Sugamuxi* (1826), set during the Spanish conquest of Colombia, is somewhat more ambivalent about the merits of the defeated Muisca civilization, but it shares with *Guatimoc* and *Xicotencatl* an unequivocally hostile attitude toward the conquistadors. (Luis Vargas Tejada, *Sugamuxi: Trajedia en cinco actos, Poesías de Caro i Vargas Tejada,* ed. Ortíz, vol 2: *Luis Vargas Tejada.*)

60. See also Fernández Madrid, "Fragmento de una oda a Iturbide en 1823," *José Fernández de Madrid y su obra*, 299.

61. Salazar, José María, "Elegía," 126; Salazar, *La campaña de Bogotá*; and König, "Símbolos nacionales," 395.

62. Colmenares, *Las convenciones contra la cultura*, 15–30; and Demélas-Bohy, *L'invention politique*, 335–36. Later reactions to indianesque nationalism are discussed in subsequent chapters.

63. Decree by Torre Tagle, 11 May 1822, Oviedo, ed., *Colección de leyes*, 4:354.

64. Curcio-Nagy, *The Great Festivals*, esp. 23–24, 27, 72.

65. Pedro de Peralta Barnuevo, "Júbilos de Lima y fiestas reales," 1723, cited in Périssat, "Les festivités dynastiques," 73.

66. Curcio-Nagy, *The Great Festivals*, 52.

67. Amunátegui, *Los precursores*, 1872 edition, 3:520.

68. Zabala, *Historia de la Pirámide de Mayo*, 29; and *Gazeta Ministerial del Gobierno de Buenos Aires*, Buenos Aires, 24 March 1813. Moreover, the Primera Escuadrilla Argentina, formed in 1811, included a ship named *25 de Mayo*, according to www.ara.mil.ar.

69. O'Gorman, "Discurso de Ingreso"; and Isabel Fernández Tejedo and Carmen Nava Nava, "Images of Independence in the Nineteenth Century: The *Grito de Dolores*, History and Myth," ¡*Viva Mexico!* ed. Beezley and Lorey, 31. For the 1825 celebrations in Mexico City, see Pantret, *Alusión*; Barquera, *Oración patriótica*; and *Función patriótica o gran solemnidad*.

70. Périssat, "Les festivités dynastiques," 76–77. See also Fee, "La Entrada Angelopolitana," 288, for indigenous people being paid four pesos each to participate, dressed as Chichimecs, in a 1640 festival. Indigenous participation in both civic and religious festivals, and the meaning of such participation, is discussed in Millones, "The Inka's Mask"; Dean, *Inka Bodies;* Cahill, "The Inca and Inca Symbolism"; Perissat, "Los Incas representados"; and Curcio-Nagy, *The Great Festivals*, 16–17, 41, 42, 49–50, 52, 79, 106–7.

71. Ocampo, *Las ideas de un día*, 15–17.

72. Zabala, *Historia de la Pirámide de Mayo*, 29. Or see *Descripción de las fiestas*, 9, for the performance of "the celebrated American tragedy entitled *Siripo, Cacique of the Timbues in Paraná*" and a dance performed by children "dressed in Indian style." (José Manuel de Labardén, an eighteenth-century Argentine writer, is the author of this drama.)

73. Halperín, *Politics, Economics and Society*, 164. See also Relación de los fiestas mayas de Buenos Aires en el present año de 1813, *La revolución de*

mayo, ed. Mallié, 2:233–36; and José Emilio Burucúa and Fabián Alejandro Campgane, "Los países del Cono Sur," *De los imperios a las naciones*, ed. Annino, Leiva and Guerra, 363.

74. Lomné, "Révolution française et rites bolivariens," 167–69.

75. Juan Estéban Soto, "Discurso patriótico," 25 May 1816, Buenos Aires, *El clero argentino*, Museo Historico Nacional, 1:166–67. Or see Fray Pantaleón García, "Proclama sagrada dicha . . . el 25 de mayo de 1814," Córdoba, and Julián Segundo de Agüero, "Oración patriótica," 25 May 1817, Buenos Aires, both in *El clero argentino*, Museo Historico Nacional, 1:91–92, 181–85; "Arenga," Buenos Aires, 25 May 1825, AGN (BA), Colección Sánchez de Bustamante, 3026 (leg. 2), doc. 90; Pando, *Elogio*; Tornel, *Oración*; and "Exhortación del cura de Umbita hecha a su pueblo el 29 de diciembre de 1819," AGN (B), Fondo Enrique Ortega Ricaurte, caja 184.

76. Pedro Ignacio de Castro Barros, "Oración patriótica . . . en el solemne 25 de mayo de 1815," Tucumán, *El clero argentino*, Museo Historico Nacional, 1:107–14 (for quote); Domingo Victorino de Achega, "Discurso pronunciado en la catedral de Buenos Aires," May 1813, *El clero argentino*, Museo Historico Nacional, 1:47; *El Censor*, Buenos Aires, 30 May 1818; "Tercera corrida de toros . . . en obsequio de . . . Simón Bolívar," 17 July 1825, *La poesía de la emancipación*, ed. Mira Quesada Sosa, 496; and König, *En el camino*; 245–47.

77. Miguel Luis Amunátegui, "18 de setiembre," *Revista de Santiago* 3 (Santiago, 1849), 288.

78. For examples, see Nariño, *La Bagatela*, no. 8, 1 Sept. 1811, *Nariño periodista*; and *La Abeja Poblana*, Puebla, 20 Sept. 1821. For discussion of familial imagery, see König, *En el camino*; Felstiner, "Family Metaphors"; and Ocampo, *Las ideas de un día*, 120–24. The broad contours of eighteenth-century republicanism's "family drama" are explored in Fliegelman, *Prodigals and Pilgrims*; and Hunt, *The Family Romance*.

79. Keen, *The Aztec Image*, 319; and Rozat, *Los orígenes de la nación*, 187. See also S. C., *Impugnación*; and *El Aguila Mexicana*, Mexico City, 3 April 1826, 28 Aug. 1826. For colonial claims that the creoles were the "true heirs" of the ancient American kingdoms, see Pagden, *Spanish Imperialism*, esp. chapter 4.

80. Collier, *Ideas and Politics*, 212–13.

81. Amunátegui, *Los precursores*, 1872 edition, 3:567 (for quote; my emphasis); *Monitor Araucano*, 6 April 1813; and *Aurora de Chile*, Santiago, 16 July 1812, 96.

82. Vicente López y Planes, "Loa," *El Censor*, Buenos Aires, 30 May 1818; and Rosemberg, "La mención del indio," 304. "Their father the Inca" is from Flores Galindo, *Buscando un Inca*, 217. See also Juan Ramon Rojas, "A las provincias del interior oprimidas," 1812, *La lira argentina*, 56; Paz Soldán, *Historia del Perú independiente*, 1:442; *Gazeta Ministerial Extraordinaria de Chile*, 21 Aug. 1821; Y. V., "La sombra de Atahuallpa a los hijos del sol," 1822[?], *La poesía de la emancipación*, ed. Mira Quesada Sosa, 354–55; and Rípodas Ardanaz, "Pasado incaico," 232.

83. Camilo Henríquez, *La Camila, o la patriota de Sud-América*, 1817, *Teatro drámatico nacional*, ed. Peña, 1:20.

84. José García Granados, "Canto a la independencia de Guatemala," *Repertorio Americano*, tomo 3, 1827, *Repertorio Americano*, 2:1–6.

85. Martínez Sarasola, *Nuestros paisanos los indios*, 169.

86. "La chicha," *Mundial*, Lima, 28 July, 1921.

87. Hidalgo, "Un gaucho de la Guardia del Monte contesta al manifiesto de Fernando VII," 1819, *Cielitos*, 33. Yierba mate, or *ilex paraguayensis*, is an herbal tea typical of Río de la Plata. The *cielito* is a poetic form associated with the world of the gauchos. Nicholas Shumway translates the term as "short ballad" (Shumway, *The Invention of Argentina*, 72).

88. Rosemberg, "La mención del indio," 290.

89. Shumway, *The Invention of Argentina*, 73; and, for a contrary view, Borges, "The Argentine Writer and Tradition."

90. Bosquejos de la tiranía y el Perú libre, *La poesía de la emancipación*, ed. Mira Quesada Sosa, 401–4 (for quote; my emphasis); *Los Andes Libres*, Lima, 21 Oct. 1821, *Periódicos*, ed. Tauro, 1:310–11; and König, *En el camino*, 242–43.

91. Manifiesto del Congreso, 6 Nov. 1813, *El Congreso de Anáhuac*, 110 (for quote); *El Despertador Americano*, 3 Jan. 1811; Rieu-Millan, *Los diputados*, 96; Bustamante, *Cuadro histórico*, 1:620, 622; Brading, *The Origins of Mexican Nationalism*, 51; Exposición de José Ignacio Rayón al Congreso, 1813, *El Congreso de Anáhuac*, 114–17; *El Aventurero*, no. 4, 1821; P. A. J., *Los horrores de Cortés*; Un Americano, *A los ciudadanos militares*; J. C. M., "Soneto," *Noticioso General*, Mexico City, 12 Dec. 1821; El Payo del Rosario, *Nuevas zorras de Sansón; Marcha alusiva a los heróicos hechos del exmo. sr. D. Agustín de Iturbide; El Ilustrador Mexicano*, Mexico City, 4 July 1823; Mateos, *Historia de la masonaría en México*, 17–21; and Connaughton, *Ideología y sociedad*, 148–50.

92. El cuidadano Juan Ramon Balcarce . . . , 31 Dec. 1815, *La revolución de Mayo*, ed. Mallié, 2:563–64 (for quote); Pedro Ignacio de Castro Barros, "Oración patriótica," 25 May 1815, *El clero argentina*, Museo Historico Nacional, 1:109; *El Censor*, Buenos Aires, 12 Dec. 1816; Hidalgo, "Un gaucho de la Guardia del Monte contesta al manifiesto de Fernando VII," 1819, *Cielitos*, 33; Mitre, *Historia de Belgrano*, 2:429; and José de la Torre Ugarte, "Canción Nacional del Perú," 1821, *La poesía de la emancipación*, ed. Mira Quesada Sosa, 293.

93. Brading, *Prophecy and Myth*, 40; and Acta de Independencia Mexicana, 28 Sept. 1821, *Leyes fundamentales de México*, ed. Tena Ramírez, 122.

94. Congreso Constituyente del Perú a los indios de las provincias interiores, Lima, 10 Oct. 1822, Martínez Sarasola, *Nuestros paisanos los indios*, 511. See also *Los Andes Libres*, Lima, 31 July 1821, *Periódicos*, ed. Tauro, 1:263.

95. *Aurora de Chile*, 16 July 1812.

96. Hernández, *Los indios de Argentina*, 204 (for quote), 205–6; Martínez Sarasola, *Nuestros paisanos los indios*, 157–58; López, *Historia de la República Argentina*, 5:528–29; and Navarro Floria, "Formar patria," 266–67, 279. For Guatemala, see Casey, "Indigenismo," 78; and "Proyecto de la historia de Guatemala escrito en 1825 por Don José Cecilio del Valle," Samayoa Guevara, *La enseñanza de la historia en Guatemala*, 106. For Chile, see *Aurora de Chile*, 16 July 1812. For Bolivia, see Rama, *Historia de las relaciones*, 42. For Venezuela, see Thibaud, *Repúblicas en armas*, 275.

97. Proclama de Castelli, Tiahuanacu, 25 May 1811, in Santos Vargas, *Diario*, ed. Mendoza, 424 (my emphasis).

98. Minguet, for example, insists that this rhetoric "does not in any sense reveal the desire to integrate the Indian population within the social body from which the creoles had just expelled the Spanish" ("El concepto de nación," 64). See also Pagden, *Spanish Imperialism*, 10; and Florescano, *Memory*, 192.

99. Panzos, *Letters on the United Provinces*, letter 1, letter 4, 45 (for quote), letter 10, 72–76; and Ocampo, *Las ideas de un día*, 64–65.

100. König, *En el camino*, 238 (for quote); *Discurso del señor diputado Navarrete* (also published as *Defensa de Méjico*); Pagden, "Identity Formation," 75; and Safford, "Race, Integration and Progress," 9.

101. Prospectus for *El Grito del Sud*, 14 July 1812, *La revolución de Mayo*, ed. Mallié, 5:114.

102. Decree of San Martín[?], 27 Aug. 1822, *Obra de gobierno*, ed. Puente Candamo, 1:350 (for quote); and the editorial in *La Gaceta*, 8 Sept. 1821, *El álbum de Ayacucho*, ed. Herrera, 55.

103. *El Argos Americano*, Cartagena, 6 May 1811, *Documentos para la Historia de Cartagena*, ed. Arrazola, 161.

104. Iturbide, *Proclama*, n.p. José María Tornel likewise insisted that the leaders of Mexico's insurgency were the "descendents of Cortés and Pizarro." See Tornel, *Manifiesto;* and also José María Tornel, *La Aurora de México*, Mexico City, 27 Sept. 1821. See also Rieu-Millan, *Los diputados americanos*, 93–98.

105. Mier, *Memorias*, 1:101. Elsewhere Mier described himself as a descendent of Cuauhtémoc (Brading, *The First America*, 595). See also *Aurora de Chile*, 16 July 1812; and Representación del Cabildo de la Suprema Junta Central de España, Santafe, 20 Nov. 1809, *Constituciones de Colombia*, ed. Pombo and Guerra, 1:62.

106. Pagden, *Spanish Imperialism*, 10.

107. Fernández Madrid, "La muerte de Atahualpa," *Elegías nacionales peruanas.*

108. "El Despertador," "Discursos o reflección que hace un patriota americano a sus hermanos," 1811, Peru[?], AGI, Diversos 2 and 3.

109. Torres y Peña, *Memorias*, 33.

110. Thus the anonymous author of one insurgent pamphlet explained that, after independence, "the term Indian will be erased from all archives and no titles will be recognised in the empire other than 'citizen,' 'American,' 'brothers'" ("El Despertador," "Discuros o reflección que hace un patriota americano a sus hermanos," 1811, Peru[?], AGI, Diversos 2 and 3). "In speaking of themselves, they use the word American, or Patriot," noted a British traveler in 1820s Chile (Hall, *Extracts*, 1:70). For further discussion of the term "americano," see Rieu-Millan, *Los Diputados*, 98. Rieu-Millan describes well the flexibility of this term, while at the same time bypassing the fact that this very flexibility accounted for much of its appeal.

111. Bolívar, "La carta de Jamaica," Kingston, 6 September 1815, *Escritos del Libertador*, 8:222–48. See also Viscardo y Guzmán, "Lettre aux Espagnols Americains," 1792, *Los escritos de Juan Pablo Viscardo y Guzmán*, ed. Simmons; Pedro Ignacio de Castro Barros, "Oración patriótica," 25 May 1815, *El clero argentina*, Museo Historico Nacional, 1:109; Juan Antonio Neirot, "Oración fúnebre . . . de los valientes soldados que murieron . . . el día 24 de Sept. de 1812," *La revolución de Mayo*, ed. Mallié, 5:125ff; Estéban de Luca, "Canción," 1823, *Antología poética de Mayo*, ed. Miri, 50; Manuel Ferreyros, "Lima Independiente," 1822[?], and José Manuel Valdez, "A Lima libre y triunfante," 1822[?], both in *La poesía de la emancipación*, ed. Mira Quesada

Sosa, 247–49, 250–55; *El Independiente*, Buenos Aires, 10 Jan. 1815; Isabel Fernández Tejedo and Carmen Nava Nava, "Images of Independence in the Nineteenth Century: The *Grito de Dolores*, History and Myth," *¡Viva Mexico!* ed. Beezley and Lorey, 18; and Ferrer Muñoz, "Las comunidades indígenas de la Nueva España," 516.

112. Manuel Belgrano, Tucumán, 27 July 1816, *El Censor*, Buenos Aires, 12 Sept. 1816; Proclama de Martín Güemes, Jujuy, 6 Aug. 1816, in *El Censor*, Buenos Aires, 12 Sept. 1816; Secret session of 6 July 1816, and session of 19 July 1816, both in *Asembleas Constituyentes Argentines*, ed. Ravignani, 1:237, 481–42; Mitre, *Historia del Belgrano*, 2:373–76, 418–32; López, *Historia de la República Argentina*, 5:462–66, 542–66; Rípodas Ardanaz de Mariluz Urquijo, "Fuentes Literarias," 1:295; and Rípodas Ardanaz, "Pasado incaico," 248.

113. See Francisco de Miranda, Esquisse de Gouvernement Federal, 1808, *Las constituciones de Venezuela*, ed. Mariñas Otero, 121; Robertson, *The Life of Miranda*, 1:192, 229, 2:135; and Thomas Maling to Viscount Melville, 18/20 March 1825, *Britain and the Independence of Latin America*, ed. Webster, 1:522.

114. *La Crónica Argentina*, Buenos Aires, 21 Sept. 1816.

115. *La Crónica Argentina*, Buenos Aires, 9 November 1816 (emphasis in the original).

116. *La Crónica Argentina*, Buenos Aires, 21 Sept. 1816. Bernardino de Rivadavia was equally unimpressed by Belgrano's proposals, commenting, "The more I think about them, the less I understand them" (see López, *Historia de la República Argentina*, 5:555–56).

117. *La Crónica Argentina*, Buenos Aires, 21 Sept. 1816.

118. *La Crónica Argentina*, Buenos Aires, 28 Sept. 1816. Atahualpa was in fact garroted.

119. *La Crónica Argentina*, Buenos Aires, 23 Nov. 1816.

120. *El Censor*, Buenos Aires, 19 Dec. 1816. See also *El Censor*, Buenos Aires, 19, 26 Sept. 1816; 2 Oct. 1816; 21, 28 Nov. 1816; 5, 12, 19 Dec. 1816; 9 Jan. 1817.

CHAPTER 2. *Representing the Nation*

1. "Relación de las extraordinarias demonstraciones de júbilo con que los patriotas de esta ciudad de Salta han celebrado el aniversario de nuestra regeneración política en los gloriosos días 24 y 25 de mayo de 1813," AGN (BA), Sala X: 44-8-29.

2. Hobsbawm, *Nations and Nationalism*, 37–38, 91; and Brading, "Nationalism and State-Building," 99.

3. José Guadalupe Romero, *Dictamen sobre los inconvenientes de mudar los nombres geográficos* (1860), cited in Craib, "A Nationalist Metaphysics," 59.

4. Session of 3 July 1823, *Historia parlamentaria*, ed. Mateos, 2:432; O'Gorman, ed., *Fray Servando Teresa de Mier*, xxxvi, 113; O'Gorman, *Historia de las divisiones territoriales*, 50–51, 61–62; and Brading, *The Origins of Mexican Nationalism*, 81.

5. Decreto de San Martín, Lima, 21 Sept. 1821, *El álbum de Ayacucho*, ed. Herrera, 60–61.

6. Solano Asta-Buruaga, *Diccionario geográfico*, 137–38, 359–60; Amunátegui, *Los precursores*, 1910 edition, 2:512; Torrente, *Historia de la Revolución de Chile*, 3:369; and www.armada.cl.

7. Meza Villalobos, *La conciencia política chilena*, 258–59.

8. Constitución de Cundinamarca, 1811, *Constituciones de Colombia*, ed. Pombo and Guerra, 1:126; Ley Fundamental de la República de Colombia, 17 Dec. 1819, *Actas del Congreso de Angostura, 1819–1820*, ed. Cortázar and Cuervo, 283–87; and König, "Símbolos nacionales," 394. Cartagena was likewise referred to poetically as "Calamar," after the region's preconquest name of Calamarí, meaning "crab." Crabs accordingly decorated the Estado de Cartagena's 1811 flag. See Salazar, *La campaña de Bogotá*; Restrepo Tirado, *Estudios*, 9; and König, *En el camino*, 250.

9. Daniel Milo, "Le nom des rues," *Les lieux de mémoire*, ed. Nora, vol. 2: *La Nation*, part 3, 287.

10. Hobsbawm, "Nationalism and Nationality," 315.

11. Manuel Belgrano to Superior Gobierno, Jujuy, 29 May 1812, AGN (BA), Sala X: 44–8–29. From their invention this flag and the matching *escarapela*, or rosette, were described as the "*national* flag" and the "*national* rosette"; see Manuel Belgrano to Superior Gobierno, Rosario, 13 Feb. 1812 and subsequent discussion in AGN (BA), Sala X: 44–8–29 (my emphasis).

12. José de San Martín, Pisco, 21 Oct. 1820, *Símbolos de la patria*, ed. Pons Muzzo, 3 (for quote); and Decree by Torre Tagle, 9 Feb. 1822, Oviedo, ed., *Colección de leyes*, 6:182–83. The insurgent Buenos Aires Asamblea similarly ordered in 1813 that the king's arms be replaced on all public buildings with the Assembly's new shield (Ingenieros, *La evolución de las ideas argentinas*, 2:34). See also Manuel Belgrano to Gobierno Superior, Jujuy, 29 May 1812, AGN (BA), Sala X: 44–8–29.

13. Encina, *Historia de Chile,* 7:392 (for quote); and Amunátegui, *Los precursores,* 1872 edition, 3:551.

14. Anita la Respondona, *Allá van esas frioleras,* n.p. The fleur de lys was a symbol of the Bourbons, while "fleeces" referred to the chivalric Order of the Golden Fleece, also associated with the Spanish monarchy.

15. Lomné, "Révolution française et rites bolivariens," 167; Lomné, "Les villes de Nouvelle-Grenade," 147; Ocampo, *Los ideas de un día* (cover reproduction of a pamphlet in the Biblioteca Nacional de México, Colección Lafragua 126); *Diario Independiente,* Mexico City, 27 Sept. 1821; El Payo del Rosario, *Nuevas zorras de Sansón;* and *La resurrección política de la América,* Biblioteca Nacional, Colección Lafragua 416. Sometimes the figure was further equipped with emblems of liberty drawn from other traditions, such as the Phrygian hat popularized by the French Revolution. See Lomné, "Révolution française et rites bolivariens"; and Burucúa, Jáuregui, Malosetti and Murilla, "Iconográficos de la Revolución Francesa," 149.

16. Honour, *The New Golden Land;* Fleming, "The American Image as Indian Princess," and Fleming, "From Indian Princess to Greek Goddess."

17. See K-78 in Grove, *Medals of Mexico,* vol. 1; or see F-5, from 1808, showing an Indian woman and an eagle flanking the coat of arms of Mexico City, F-31, F-52; and Taracena, *Invención criolla,* 223. The use of a noble Indian woman to represent Mexico in particular is discussed in Cuadriello, "La personificación de la Nueva España."

18. Nan, *Sueño alegórico.*

19. Grove, *Medals of Mexico,* vol. 1, F-21.

20. Hunt, *Politics, Culture and Class,* 88.

21. For discussion of these coins, see König, *En el camino,* 255–63.

22. Pedro Pérez Múñoz, Cartas, 1815, AGI, Diversos 42, letter 21. See also Earle, "Creole Patriotism."

23. Amunátegui, *Los precursores,* 1872 edition, 3:549; and Poirier, ed., *Chile en 1910,* plate facing 104. For another example, see Miguel Luis Amunátegui, "Apuntes sobre lo que han sido las bellas artes en Chile," *Revista de Santiago* 3 (Santiago, 1849), 41.

24. Grove, *Medals of Mexico,* vol. 2, no. 7, see also no. 75; Rosa, *Numismática,* 21, and, for Guatemala; and Castillo, *Al heróico pueblo.*

25. Platt, "Simón Bolívar," 169; and Session of 8 Aug. 1825, *Libro mayor de sesiones,* 44–46.

26. Camilo Henríquez, *La Camila, o La patriota de Sud-América,* 1817, *Teatro drámatico nacional,* ed. Peña, 1:1–39.

27. See Earle, "Rape and the Anxious Republic"; and Díaz, *Female Citizens*, 107–31.

28. Dousdebés, "Las insignias de Colombia," 460 (for quote); and Posada, "Heráldica colombiana." The medals designed to decorate insurgent Chilean soldiers depicted not only a sword but also an arrow in honor of the Araucanians; see *Monitor Araucano*, 10 April 1813.

29. Dousdebés, "Las insignias de Colombia," 460; König, "Símbolos nacionales," 395; Posada, "Heráldica colombiana"; Poirier, ed., *Chile en 1910*, plate facing 104; Grove, *Medals of Mexico*, vol. 2, nos. 7, 75; Rosa, *Numismática*, 21; Declaración del Cura Hidalgo, 7 June 1811, *Colección de documentos*, ed. Hernández y Dávalos, 1:13; Romero Flores, *Banderas históricas mexicanas*; and Session of 12 April 1823, Mateos, ed., *Historia parlamentaria*, 2:253–54.

30. For illustrations, see Poole, *Vision, Race and Modernity*, 34, 38, 39, 46, 47, 50.

31. Salazar, *La campaña de Bogotá*.

32. For this imagery in the Spanish world, see Bravo Arriaga, "De la fuente de las musas," 54–55; Fee, "La Entrada Angelopolitana," 312–13; *Júblios de Lima y glorias del Perú*, 1789, *El teatro en la independencia*, ed. Ugarte Chamorro, 1:23; Burkhart, "The Solar Christ"; and Curcio-Nagy, *The Great Festivals*, 72.

33. MacCormack, *Religion in the Andes*, 102, 107, 162–63. (Pedro Cieza de León's *Chrónica del Perú* was published in 1553–54.)

34. Frezier, *A Voyage to the South-Seas*, 272; Gisbert, *Iconografía*, 120–24, and color plate facing 210; Dean, *Inka Bodies*, 43, 126–27; Périssat, "Los Incas representados," 644; MacCormack, "Limits of Understanding," 217, 339; and MacCormack, *Religion in the Andes*, 261.

35. Gisbert, *La iconografía*, 29–30.

36. Letter of José Antonio Areche, Cuzco, 15 May 1781, reprinted in *La Prensa Argentina*, 24 Sept. 1816.

37. The currency was created by the Asamblea Constituyente on 13 April 1813. See Escudo Nacional of Asemblea General Constituyente de 1813, *La revolución de mayo*, ed. Mallié, 2:223; and Gumucio, *Las monedas de la independencia*, 73.

38. Museo Numismático, "Dr. José Evaristo Uriburu," Buenos Aires, numismatic display.

39. The decision to put an image of the sun on the "bandera de guerra" was taken on 26 Feb. 1818. For the development of the national flag, see AGN (BA), Sala X: 44-8-29; and López, *Historia de la República Argentina*, 4:118–19.

40. Insurgent documents, 1814, *Conspiraciones y rebeliones*, ed. Villanueva Urteaga, 2:556, 565; Bernardo O'Higgins, Proclama a los habitantes del Perú, Valparaíso, 5 May 1820, Paz Soldan, *Historia del Perú*, 1:442; Oficio de Sucre, Quito, 22 June 1822; Bernardo de Monteagudo, Exposición de las tareas administrativas del gobierno, Lima, 15 July 1822; *La Gaceta*, 10 Sept. 1823; and Proclamas de Bolívar, 15 Aug. 1824, all in *El álbum de Ayacucho*, ed. Herrera, 69–84, 122–23, 124–28, 139, 151–53; Memoria leída al congreso constituyente en la sesión pública del día 12 de feb. de 1825, Tamayo Vargas and Pacheco Vélez, eds., *Los ideológos*, 9:590. For poetic descriptions of Peruvians as the sons of the sun, see "Primera canción patriótica; Felipe Lledías, "Lima libre, canción patriótica," 1822; "Himno Patriótico," 1821; "Canción patriótica a los nobilisimos peruanos," 1821, Anon., "Canción patriótica"; Felipe Lledías, "Canción patriótica," 1822; José González, "Canción patriótica"; "Canción," 1824; J. M. Corbacho, "Canción patriótico," 1824; Dr. Fernández, "Canción," 1826; Andrés Bello, "Alocución a la poesía"; Canción al primer congreso del Perú; and José Joaquín de Olmedo, "Marcha," 1825; all in *La poesía de la emancipación*, ed. Mira Quesada Sosa, 295, 299–302, 306, 319, 320–21, 322–23, 475–79, 484–86, 500–1, 532, 407–8, 487; Estéban de Luca, "Canción," 1823, *Antología poética de Mayo*, ed. Miri, 50; and *Resúmen sucinto de la vida del Jeneral Sucre*, 18.

41. Establishment of Orden del Sol, 8 Oct. 1821, *El álbum de Ayacucho*, ed. Herrera, 74; and *Obra de gobierno*, ed. Puente Candamo, 1:379–84.

42. Ceremonial que se observará, 27 Dec. 1821, *Obra de gobierno*, ed. Puente Candamo, 1:397.

43. Decreto de San Martín, 27 Dec. 1821, *Símbolos de la patria*, ed. Pons Muzzo, 13.

44. José de San Martín, Bando, Pisco, 21 Oct. 1820, *Símbolos de la patria*, ed. Pons Muzzo, 3; and "Design for Uniforms," 15 Aug. 1821, Oviedo, ed., *Colección de leyes*, 4:47. For the use of the sun on Argentine uniforms, see Pedro Carrasco to Supremo Director del Estado, Sala de Congreso, 26 Feb. 1818, AGN (BA), Sala X: 44–8–29; see also the military dress coat belonging to Juan Antonio Avarez de Arenales on display in the Museo Histórico Nacional, Buenos Aires.

45. Sala i Vila, "De inca a indígena."

46. Congreso Constituyente del Perú a los indios de las provincias interiores, Lima, 10 Oct. 1822, Martínez Sarasola, *Nuestros paisanos los indios*, 511. A yaraví is a Quechua musical form typical of the Andes, and a *cachua* is an Andean dance.

47. Flores Galindo, *Buscando un Inca*; Walker, "The Patriotic Society"; and Walker, *Smoldering Ashes*, 103–5.

48. Bishop of Cuzco Juan Manuel Moscoso y Peralta to Visitador General Josef Antonio Areche, Cuzco, 13 April 1781, AGI, Audiencia de Cuzco 29.

49. Intendant Benito de Mata Linares to Minister for the Indies José de Gálvez, Cuzco, 6 Aug. 1785, AGI, Audiencia de Cuzco 35.

50. Such portraits are discussed in Rowe, "Colonial Portraits of Inca Nobles"; and Cummins, "We Are the Other." Examples may be viewed in the Museo Inka and the Museo de Arte in Cuzco.

51. The 1723 edition of the *Comentarios reales*, which contained a prologue by Gabriel de Cárdenas, was singled out as particularly pernicious. See Moscoso y Peralta to Areche, Cuzco, 13 April 1781; Josef Antonio Areche to Josef de Gálvez, Cuzco, 1 May 1781; Report by Jorge Escobedo, Aranjuez, 21 April 1782, all in AGI, Audiencia de Cuzco 29; Jose Antonio Areche, Cuzco 15 May 1781, reprinted in *La Prensa Argentina*, 24 Sept. 1816 (for quote); Walker, *Smoldering Ashes*, 53–54; Cahill, "The Inca and Inca Symbolism," 101–2; and (for Ecuador) Moreno Yánez, *Sublevaciones indígenas*, 410–11.

52. Jose Antonio Areche, Cuzco 15 May 1781, reprinted in *La Prensa Argentina*, 24 Sept. 1816.

53. For example, in 1659 a civic festival in Lima in honor of the city's artists had included floats with "figures of all the viceroys who had governed this kingdom, then eight costumed Incas"; see Mugaburu, *Chronicle of Colonial Lima*, ed. Miller, 51–52. Prior to the Túpac Amaru Rebellion, paintings as well as festivals had often traced a continuity between the Incas and the Hapsburgs. See Gisbert, *Iconografía*, especially images 116–19, 124, and the color plate following image 141; Millones, "The Inka's Mask"; Périssat, "Los Incas representados"; and Cahill, "The Inca and Inca Symbolism."

54. Antonio Samper and Josef Navarro to the Marqués Cavallero, Madrid, 6 Feb. 1807, summarizing earlier letters, AGI, Audiencia de Cuzco 29.

55. Flores Galindo, "Independencia y clases sociales," 138.

56. Declaración de María Ynes Ramos, Tarma, 1812, *Conspiraciones y rebeliones*, ed. Dunbar Temple, 1:133 (see also 134–43, 180); Molinari Morales and Ríos Burga, "'El 'messianismo inca' en la rebelión de 1812," 141; and Bonilla, "Clases populares," 26–27.

57. Proceso a Pumacahua, 1815; Bando de Pío de Tristan, Arequipa, 7 March 1815; Pío de Tristán to Bishop Luis Gonzaga de Encina, Arequipa, 9 March 1815, and Proclama de Pío de Tristán, Arequipa, 21 April 1815, all

in *Conspiraciones y rebeliones,* ed. Villanueva Urteaga, 1:304–16, 2:480 (for quote), 483–84, 604–7.

58. Brading, *The First America,* 420, 540 (for quote).

59. Méndez, "Incas sí, Indios no," 222; and Thurner, *From Two Republics to One Divided,* 9.

60. Flores Galindo, *Buscando un Inca,* 218 (for quote), 218–219.

61. For example, see *Los Andes Libres,* Lima, 31 July 1821, *Periódicos,* ed. Tauro, 1:263.

62. For statues, coins, and postage stamps, see Earle, "Sobre Héroes y Tumbas."

63. *El Abogado Nacional,* Buenos Aires, 24 Dec. 1818.

64. Decree of Riva Agüero, 6 June 1823, *El álbum de Ayacucho,* ed. Herrera, 246; Session of 11 Feb. 1824, *Historia parlamentaria,* ed. Mateos, 2:678; and Alamán, *Historia de Méjico,* 1968–69 edition, 5:484.

65. "Algunas cortas observaciones que hace un joven sobre el grito de los congresales," 21 June 1820, AGN (BA), Colección Andrés Lamas 2639 (leg. 36) (for quote); and the poem to 25 May written for the 1826 fiestas mayas in Zabala, *Historia de la pirámide,* 50.

66. Izunza, *Discurso,* 8.

67. *Toluca a la grata memoria de los héroes de Dolores.*

68. Palenzuela, *Primeros monumentos en Venezuela,* 148 (for quote); and Conway, *The Cult of Bolívar,* 18–45.

69. López, *Historia de la República Argentina,* 3:401–2 (for quote); and González, *La tradición nacional,* 161.

70. Mendoza, *Discurso,* 9 (for quote); Roa Barcena, *Discurso;* Francisco Granados Maldonado, "Elogio fúnebre que en memoria de los héroes de la independencia mexicana pronunció . . . en la Alameda de México el día 27 de septiembre de 1850," *Discursos pronunciados el 27 y 28 de septiembre de 1850;* and Juan Jáquez, "Oración cívica pronunciado en el palacio del gobierno de Durango . . . el día 16 de septiembre de 1850," *Composiciones en prosa y verso,* 157.

71. See, for example, Ignacio Manuel Altamirano, prologue to Prieto, *El romancero nacional.*

72. *El Comercio,* Lima, 9 Dec. 1858; and Majluf, *Escultura y espacio público.*

73. Calzadilla, "El IV centenario en Venezuela," 262; Calzadilla, "El olor de la pólvora"; and Krause and Mishler, *1994 Standard Catalog,* 2049–56.

74. Earle, "Sobre Héroes y Tumbas."

75. Acosta de Samper, *Biografías de hombres ilustres o notables*, 3. For varied discussion of the cult of the próceres elsewhere, see O'Gorman, "Discurso de Ingreso"; Carrera Damas, *El culto a Bolívar*; and *Caravelle: Héros et Nation en Amérique Latine* 72 (1999).

76. Escobar Ohmstede and Rojas Rabiela, eds., *La presencia del indígena*, 1:36, 39; and O'Gorman, *Historia de las divisiones territoriales*, 106, 130, 164.

77. Constitución de 1864, título I, art. 1; and Constitución de 1874, título I, art. 1, *Las constituciones de Venezuela*, ed. Mariñas Otero, 303, 325; Latzina, *Diccionario geográfico*, 435–37, 506–7; and Cohen, *The Columbia Gazetteer*.

78. These names honored Bolívar, Francisco de Paula Santander, Antonio Nariño, and Antonio José de Sucre. The first place in Colombia to be named after a prócer of independence was the municipality of Nariño, Cundinamarca, founded in 1833; the first named after Bolívar was established in 1844 (Gómez, *Diccionario geográfico*, 42, 44–45, 187, 263, 323, 328–29).

79. Solano Asta-Buruaga, *Diccionario geográfico*, 487.

80. Constitución de los Estados Unidos de Venezuela, 1901, título I, art. 2, *Las constituciones de Venezuela*, ed. Mariñas Otero, 423.

81. Isaacs, *Estudios*, 110.

82. *Aurora de Chile*, 16 July 1812.

83. Herrera, *Sermón*, 15 (my emphasis). Lucas Alamán similarly dismissed Carlos María de Bustamante's indianesque language as part of the independence era's "general delirium" (Alamán, "Noticios biográficos de . . . Carlos María Bustamante y juicio crítico de sus obras," 1849[?], *Documentos diversos*, 3:327). See also *"Que mueran los gachupines,"* for sarcastic commentary on the anti-Spanish attitudes of "the patriotic Anahuacan."

84. López, *Historia de la República Argentina*, 5:543–45 (my emphasis); and, for a Chilean example, Miguel Luis Amunátegui, "18 de setiembre," *Revista de Santiago* 3 (Santiago, 1849), 288.

85. López, *Historia de la República Argentina*, 5:462, 466, 542, 543, 545, 548. José Ingenieros described it as ridiculous; see his *La evolución de las ideas argentinas*, 2:104.

86. Sarmiento, *Facundo*, 54–55. For elite fears of the "folk," see Burns, *The Poverty of Progress*.

87. Georges Lomné, "El 'espejo roto' de Colombia: El advenimiento del imaginario nacional, 1825–1850," *De los imperios a las naciones*, ed. Annino, Leiva, and Guerra, 386. Or see Amunátegui, *Los precursores*, 1872 edition,

3:588–89, for the 1832 rejection of Chile's independence-era state shield on the grounds that it was "insignificant and premature."

88. Act of 4 Oct. 1821, *Actas del Congreso de Cúcuta, 1821*, ed. Restrepo Piedrahita, 3:207; and Restrepo Tirado, *Católogo general*, 105–6. See also Krause and Mishler, *1994 Standard Catalog of World Coins*, 476–7; König, "Símbolos nacionales," 398; and König, *En el camino*, 264.

89. Decree of Bolívar, 24 Feb. 1825; Abolition of Orden del Sol, 9 March 1825; Reglamento de la Legión de Honor Nacional, 15 Sept. 1836; and Abolition of the Legión de Honor Nacional, 22 Feb. 1839; all in Oviedo, ed., *Colección de leyes*, 3:7, 4:22, 35–38, 39–40. Sun imagery made a brief return to state iconography under Andrés Santa Cruz, but it was swiftly removed following his downfall; see Gisbert, *Iconografía*, 180.

90. Walker, *Smoldering Ashes*, 172.

91. One exception to this came after a series of victorious campaigns against the Mapuche in southern Chile in the 1880s when the Chilean military named several defensive forts along the new frontier after the heroes of *La araucana*. In so doing the Chilean state asserted its sovereignty over not only the territory of the Mapuche, but also over their past. See Silva, *Atlas de historia de Chile*, 96–97; and Solano Asta-Buruaga, *Diccionario geográfico*, 281.

92. See, for example, Miguel Cané, "Fiestas mayas," 1844, AGN (BA), Colección Andrés Lamas 2649 (leg. 46).

93. José de la Torre Ugarte, "Canción Nacional del Perú," 1821, *La poesía de la emancipación*, ed. Quesada Sosa, 293.

94. Primera canción patriótica, *La poesía de la emancipación*, ed. Quesada Sosa, 295–97.

95. Resolución suprema, Lima, 8 May 1901, and José Santos Chocano, "Himno Nacional," 1901, both in *Símbolos de la patria*, ed. Pons Muzzo, 233, 262–63. For Argentina, see Miri, ed., *Antología poética de Mayo*, 25; and Bertoni, *Patriotas, cosmopolitas y nacionalistas*, 180–84, 294–95.

96. Blanca Muratorio, "Images of Indians in the Construction of Ecuadorian Identity at the End of the Nineteenth Century," *Latin American Popular Culture*, ed. Beezley and Curcio-Nagy, 116; Blanca Muratorio, "Nación, identidad y etnicidad: Imagenes de los indios ecuatorianos y sus imagineros a fines del siglo XIX," *Imágenes e imagineros*, ed. Muratorio, 172; and *Inauguración de la estatua*.

97. *Stanley Gibbons Simplified Catalogue*, 3:771. Similarly, a temporary currency called the "inca" was introduced under Nicolás de Piérola between

1880 and 1883. See Grunthal, *The Coinage of Peru*; and Yábar Acuña, *El Inca de Oro*.

98. *El Siglo XIX*, Mexico City, 18 Sept. 1877; García Quintana, *Cuauhtémoc en el siglo XIX*, 22–26; Daniel Schávelzon, "Notas sobre Manuel Vilar y sus esculturas de Moctezuma y Tlahuicole," and Daniel Schávelzon, "El primer monumento a Cuauhtémoc (1869)," both in *La polémica del arte nacional*, ed. Schávelzon, 81–87, 109–11; Escobedo, ed., *Monumentos mexicanos*, 65, 118; and Tenenbaum, *Mexico and the Royal Indian*, 10–11.

99. Opatrný, "El papel de la historia," 60; and Opatrný, "La conciencia común en Cuba," 345. See also Gómez de Avellaneda, *Sab*, 100–2.

100. Santacilia, *Lecciones orales sobre la historia de Cuba*, 11 (for quote); and Opatrný, "La historia de Cuba."

101. Nápoles Fajardo, "Hatuey y Guarina," c.1856, *Poesías completas*, 154. In the same volume see also "Bartolomé de las Casas," 161–64.

102. Schmidt-Nowara, "Conquering Categories," 6–7.

103. Fuentes, *Sketches of the Capital of Peru*, 120 (emphasis in the original).

104. Juan Manuel Almesquita, "Alocución pronunciada con motivo de una función patriótica," Arequipa, 22 July 1864, BN(CM) D11811. For a Colombian example, see "Al 20 de julio—salutación," 1854, AGN (B), Archivo Restrepo, fondo XI, vol. 168; and "Otra," *Canción nacional para el 20 de julio*.

105. Velázquez, *Discurso*, n.p. (for quote); Porras, *Discurso*; *Oda lírica*; Vice President Vicente Santa Cruz, 15 Sept. 1845, Benson Library, Taracena Flores Collection, doc. 9348; Woodward, *Rafael Carrera*, 144–45; Sullivan-González, *Piety, Power and Politics*, 62; S. D. M. M., *Discurso*; Montúfar y Rivera Maestre, *Discurso escrito por el . . . XIL aniversario de la independencia, 15 Sept. 1862*; and, for later comment on such speeches, Montúfar y Rivera Maestre, *Discurso pronunciado . . . el 15 de setiembre de 1875*; and Montúfar y Rivera Maestre, *Discurso pronunciado . . . el 15 de septiembre de 1877*.

106. Brito, *Discurso*, n.p.; and *El Universal*, Mexico City, 30 Sept. 1851.

107. Enciso, *Oración*, 5. For additional examples, see Earle, "Padres del la Patria," 786–88.

108. Sánchez de Tagle and Mariano Elízaga, *Himno*; Guzmán, *Discurso*; Sánchez de Tagle, *Arenga*; poetry in *Aniversario del glorioso grito de libertad lanzado en Dolores el día 16 de sept. de 1810*; Aguilar de Bustamante, *Discurso*, 11; Olvera, *Oración*, 4; Juan Miguel de Lozada, "Gloria y libertad," *Poesías cívicas*, 5; and "Himno patriótico," *Composiciones en prosa y verso*, 218.

109. For a few Peruvian examples, see Rivero and Tschudi, *Antigüedades peruanas*, dedication, v, 101, 286–87; "Al Perú," *Miscelanea*, Lima, 23 Oct. 1832; and Lorente, *Historia antigua del Perú*, 4, 10. Charles Walker has, moreover, shown that the conservative caudillo Agustín Gamarra often referred to the Incas (Walker, *Smoldering Ashes*, 147–48, 167–70).

CHAPTER 3. *"Padres de la Patria"*

1. "Observador" (Francisco Cosmes), "¿A quien debemos tener patria?" *El Partido Liberal*, Mexico City, 15 Sept. 1894. The year 1810 saw Miguel Hidalgo's Grito de Dolores, which launched the independence movement, while 1821 was the year of Agustín de Iturbide's "consummation" of independence.

2. Cuauhtémoc, the last Aztec emperor, was tortured by Hernán Cortés in an attempt to learn the location of his treasure. Regarding the sea nymph Calypso, Cosmes probably had in mind her regret at Ulysses's departure from her island.

3. "Un artículo notable del 'Partido Liberal,'" *La Voz de México*, Mexico City, 18 Sept. 1894.

4. *El Siglo XIX*, Mexico City, 20 Sept. 1894.

5. Luis del Toro, "Boletín," *El Monitor Republicano*, Mexico City, 19 Sept. 1894.

6. *El Diario del Hogar*, Mexico City, 20, 23, 30 Sept. 1894.

7. Francisco Cosmes, "A mis contradictores sobre la cuestión de Cortés," *El Diario del Hogar*, Mexico City, 23 Sept. 1894.

8. See, in particular, "La nacionalidad mexicana," *El Diario del Hogar*, Mexico City, 30 Sept 1894; and Luis del Toro, "Boletín," *El Monitor Republicano*, Mexico City, 19 Sept. 1894.

9. Herrera, *Sermón*, 4, 7, 15–16.

10. Urrutia, *Discurso*, n.p.

11. Posada Gutiérrez, *Memorias*, 1:89 (for quote); Vergara y Vergara, *Historia de la literatura*, 418; and Caro, "La conquista," 386–88, 395–96.

12. Milla, *Esplicación*, 5. For a later, liberal, comment on the discourses of these years, see Montúfar, *Discurso pronunciado . . . el 15 de set. de 1877*; and Lorenzo Montúfar, "Discurso," San José de Costa Rica, 15 Sept. 1870, *Discursos del Dr. Lorenzo Montúfar*, 127.

13. Palacio, *Oración*, 7–8 (for quote); Vargas, *Discurso*, 6–7; P. Ruiz, "Editorial," *El Pájaro Verde*, Mexico City, 16 Sept. 1863; and Castillo y Lanzas, *Discurso*, 6.

14. José Ignacio Esteva, "Discurso pronunciado en la plaza principal de la H[eróica] Veracruz el 16 de septiembre de 1850," *Composiciones en prosa y verso*, 76–77 (for quote); *El Universal*, Mexico City, 30 Sept. 1851; Esteva, *Discurso;* Vargas, *Discurso*, 10; Palacio, *Oración*, 7–8; Castillo Negrete, *Discurso;* Patiño, *Discurso*, 8; Teófilo Carrasquedo, "Arenga cívica pronunciada . . . en la noche del 26 de setiembre de 1857, Ciudad de San Francisco de la Alta California," *El Siglo XIX*, Mexico City, 11 Nov. 1857; and the pro-Maximilian writings of Garay y Texada, *Discurso;* Fernández de Córdoba, *Discurso*, 9; Pastor, *Discurso*, 6; and P. Ruiz, "Editorial," *El Pájaro Verde*, Mexico City, 16 Sept. 1863. See also Rama, *Historia de las relaciones culturales*, 153.

15. Zaldaña, *Discurso* (for quote); Gómez Pedraza, *Oración*, 5; Anievas, *Discurso;* and González Suárez, *Historia*, 1:32.

16. Milla, *Esplicación*, 6 (for quote); Herrera, *Sermon*, 4, 7, 15–16; Arboleda, *Gonzalo de Oyon, Semana literaria de "El Porvenir,"* vol. 2 (Bogotá, 1858), 249; Valenzuela, "Colombia," *Poesías;* Caro, "La conquista," 387; Acosta de Samper, *Biografías de hombres ilustres*, 2, 4, 442; Jaramillo Uribe, *El pensamiento colombiano*, 83–94; and Martínez, *El nacionalismo cosmopolita*, 454, 460–61.

17. Vergara y Vergara, *Historia de la literatura*, 14.

18. Brading, *The First America*, 645–46 (for quote); and Hale, *Mexican Liberalism*, 18, 21, 217.

19. Alamán, *Disertaciones* 1:103 (for quote), 109–10; Ramírez de Arellano, *Oración*, 8; Barreda, *Oración;* Sánchez Facio, *Oración;* P. Ruiz, "Editorial," *El Pájaro Verde*, Mexico City, 16 Sept. 1863; and Vázquez de Knauth, *Nacionalismo y educación*, 68–69.

20. Piñol, *Discurso*, n.p. (for quote); Echeverría, *Discurso;* and Zaldaña, *Discurso.*

21. Andrés Bello, review of a biography of Columbus, *Repertorio Americano*, 2:191.

22. *El Universal*, Mexico City, 16 Sept. 1851 (for quote); Plan de Iguala, 24 Feb. 1821, *Leyes Fundamentales de Mexico*, ed. Tena Ramírez, 114; Espinosa, *Alocución*, 6; Pastor, "Discurso"; and Gutiérrez, *Discurso*, 12–13.

23. Caro, "La conquista," 396 (for quote); and Jaramillo Uribe, *El pensamiento colombiano*, 88–89.

24. Aycinena, *Discurso religioso pronunciado . . . el 15 de set. de 1855* (for quote); Aycinena, *Discurso pronunciado . . . el 15 de sept. de 1837;* García Peláez, *Discurso;* Aycinena, *Discurso religioso . . . el 15 de sept. de 1858;* Aycinena, *Discurso religioso pronunciado . . . el 15 de sept. de 1864;* and Sullivan-González, *Piety, Power and Politics.*

25. Earle, "Creole Patriotism."

26. "Proclama en favor de los indios," *Colección de documentos,* ed. Hernández y Dávalos, 4:766.

27. Berístain de Souza, *Diálogos patrióticos,* 2, 34, 35 (for quote); *Gaceta del Gobierno de México,* Mexico City, 6 Nov. 1810; Pedro Antonio de Cerradas to Viceroy Abascal, Cuzco, 26 April 1811, AGI, Diversos 2; Rieu-Millan, *Los Diputados,* 95–96; Carta Pastoral . . . [de] Don Manuel Abad Queipo, Valladolid, 26 September 1812; and Informe del Real Tribunal de Consulado de México, 27 May 1811, both in *Colección de documentos,* ed. Hernández y Dávalos, 4:439, 2:453, respectively; López Cancelada, *La verdad sabida,* viii; Berístain de Souza, *Discurso eucarístico;* and Zavala, *Ensayo,* 1:54.

28. Torres y Peña, *Memorias,* 33; and Aurrecoechea, *Memoria,* 25–26.

29. Bushnell and Macaulay, *The Emergence of Latin America,* 81.

30. Andrés Lamas, essay, 12 Nov. 1883 (for quote); Andrés Lamas, essay, 1880s; and Vicente Fidel López to Andrés Lamas[?], Buenos Aires, 30 May 1888; all in AGN (BA), Colección Andrés Lamas 2659 (leg. 56).

31. Quesada, *Alocución patriótica,* n.p. (for quote); and Avellaneda, *Centenario del Congreso de Tucumán.*

32. For an early example, see *El Censor,* Buenos Aires, 29 May 1817; and for the Generation of 1837, see Shumway, *The Invention of Argentina.*

33. Speech in honor of 25 May, José Rivera Indarte, 1844, in AGN (BA), Colección Andrés Lamas 2649 (leg. 46) (for quote); and José Rivera Indarte, "Melodias a mayo," *Cantos a mayo,* 59–80. See also Miguel Cané, "Fiestas mayas," 1844, AGN (BA), Colección Andrés Lamas 2649 (leg. 46).

34. Ruffini, "La trayectoria del discurso historiográfico de la Revolución de Mayo," 27 (for quote); Estéban Echeverría, "El 25 de mayo," 1844, *Cantos a mayo,* 16; and Echeverría, *Mayo y la enseñanza popular.* See also Alberdi, *Bases,* 65; and Shumway, *The Invention of Argentina,* 131, 135.

35. This is exactly how the conquest was presented in European painting and poetry of the period. See Delgado, "Hernán Cortés en la poesía española"; and Tudela, "Hernán Cortés en los grabados románticos."

36. José Rivera Indarte, "Melodias a mayo," *Cantos a mayo,* 69–70 (my emphasis).

37. Ibid., 81.

38. Sarmiento, review of *Investigaciones sobre el sistema colonial de los españoles,* 1844, *Obras,* 2:213. Or see Sarmiento, *Conflicto y armonía,* 107, 227, 409.

39. Sarmiento, review of *Investigaciones sobre el sistema colonial de los españoles*, 1844, *Obras*, 2:218 (for quote); and Sarmiento, *Conflicto y armonía*, 232. For Argentine liberals' frustration with the Spanish heritage, see Shumway, *Invention of Argentina*, 136–39, 144–45; Brading, *The First America*, 625; and Benítez, "El viaje de Sarmiento a España," 6–7.

40. Alberdi, *Bases*, 61 (for quote), 64; and Alberdi, *Autobiografía*, 118–28.

41. Criollismo was a late-nineteenth-century movement exalting the colonial and Latin roots of Argentine culture.

42. Gálvez, *El diario de Gabriel Quiroga*, 74–75, 92, 94 (for quote), 100, 200–1.

43. "I have the impression of having found myself in the family home where I resided prior to my birth," mused Bartolomé Mitre during a visit to Spain in the 1890s. See Rama, *Historia de las relaciones culturales*, 93 (for quote); Mitre, *Historia de Belgrano*, 2:418; Quesada, *Alocución patriótica*; Gálvez, *El solar de la raza*, 7; Quesada, *Nuestra raza*, 11–12, 14, 20–21; José E. Uriburu, "Brindis, *El Mercurio de Valparaíso*, Valparaíso, 22 Sept. 1890; Rock, "Intellectual Precursors," 277; Rojas, *La restauración nacionalista*, 158; Rojas, *Blasón de Plata*, 10, 216; and Meeting of Comisión Pro-Homenaje, 2 Aug. 1915, AGN (BA), Dardo Rocha 3001. For discussion of the relationship between the mid-nineteenth-century romantics and later cultural nationalists, see Delaney, "Imagining *El Ser Argentino*"; and for conflicts between "cosmopolitans" and "nationalists," see Bertoni, *Patriotas, cosmopolitas y nacionalistas*.

44. Lopez, *Historia de la República Argentina*, 1: opening sentence. This sentiment is expressed repeatedly throughout the entire preface.

45. Mitre, *Historia de San Martín*, 1:58–59. Bertoni discusses the late-nineteenth-century debate over whether the Argentine nation existed prior to 1810. Despite disagreeing about the moment in which the nation was born, most scholars agreed that the "formation of our nationality" occurred in the colonial era. See Bertoni, *Patriotas, cosmopolitas y nacionalistas*, 267–70 (270 for quote).

46. Andrés Lamas, introduction to Berro, *Poesías*, ix; Gutiérrez, "A la juventud argentina," 1852, *Poesías*, 101; Andermann, "Reshaping the Creole Past," 148; and Bartolomé Mitre, "Al 25 de Mayo," *Cantos a mayo*, 109.

47. Lugones, "Dedicatoria a los antepasados," *Poemas solariegos*, 1927, *Obras poéticas*, 809–10. "The history of the family thus melds with that of the nation," noted Gramuglio in "Literatura y nacionalismo," 17. A *maestre de campo* is the holder of Spanish military title roughly equivalent to brigadier, and an

encomendero is the recipient of an *encomienda,* a colonial structure granting indigenous labor and tribute rights.

48. *El Minero del año 34,* Serena, 24 Sept. 1834.

49. See, for example, Demélas-Bohy, "Héros et formation nationale," 7.

50. Barras Arana, review of Miguel L. Amunátegui, *Descubrimiento i conquista de Chile,* 1863, *Obras,* 8:132 (my emphasis).

51. Amunátegui, *Descubrimiento i conquista,* 7, 15 (for quote).

52. Bilbao, *Sociabilidad chilena,* 1844, *El pensamiento vivo de Francisco Bilbao.* See also *El Progreso,* Santiago, 10 April 1843; and Lastarria, "Investigaciones sobre la influencia de la conquista i del sistema colonial de los españoles en Chile," 206–7, 230–31, 270.

53. *El Mercurio,* Valparaíso, 28 March 1859 (for quote), 26 March 1860; Barros Arana, review of Miguel L. Amunátegui, *Descubrimiento i conquista de Chile,* 1863, *Obras,* 8:131; Amunátegui, *Los precursores,* 1910 edition, 1:5; and Woll, *A Functional Past,* 61–62.

54. García Calderón, *Memorias del cautiverio,* 163–64. The work was written prior to 1905, when García Calderón died, but it was first published (posthumously) in 1938. See also Vicuña Mackenna, "Primer discurso sobre la pacificación de Arauco," 9 Aug. 1868, and "Cuarto discurso sobre la pacificación de Arauco," 14 Aug. 1868, both in *Obras,* 12:396, 426, respectively. Chilean liberals' growing acceptance of the Spanish past is discussed in Yeager, *Barros Arana's Historia General de Chile,* x–xi.

55. Martínez, *El nacionalismo cosmopolita,* 460 (for quote); Samper, *Ensayo,* 6; Samper, *Apuntamientos,* 11–12, 17, 24, 27–30; and Segura, "Advertencia," *Ricaurte.*

56. Botero, "The Construction of the Pre-Hispanic Past," 72 (for quote), 148–49, 163, 234. For "our fathers" as the "degenerate sons" of the conquistadors, see "La Nueva Granada en 1839," *El Amigo del Pueblo,* Bogotá, 20 Jan. 1839.

57. José María Quijano Otero, 1872, cited in "El 20 de julio de 1810: Una cuestión histórica," 20.

58. González Prada, "Discurso en el Teatro Olímpico," *Páginas libres,* 27. See also Martínez, *El nacionalismo cosmopolita,* 188.

59. Sanders, *Nación y tradición,* 211.

60. Cisneros, "A la muerte del rey don Alfonso XII," 1886, *De libres alas,* 142. "To be a son of America: that is my glory!/And of Spanish race: that is my pride!," announced Cisneros in the same work.

61. Martínez Sobral, *Discurso,* n.p. (for quote); Goez, *Discurso;* Rodríguez Beteta, *Discurso,* 15 Sept. 1910; Vielman, *Discurso;* Mencos, *Discurso;* and Ra-

fael Arévalo Martínez, "Canto a las frases, los mares y las penínsulas," *Parnaso guatemalteca*, ed. Porta Mencos, 372. For a more critical view of the Spanish parent, see Salazar, *Discurso*; but see also Spínola, "Discurso pronunciado . . . en el Instituto Agrícola de Indígenas," 15 March 1896, *Artículos y discursos*, 125–40.

62. Rosa, "Centro-América," 1871, *Oro de Honduras*, 2:40–41, 45.

63. For liberal nationalism, see Vázquez de Knauth, *Nacionalismo y educación*.

64. Benigno Arriaga, "Discurso pronunciado en el templete de la Alameda," *Discursos y composiciones poéticas*. For additional Mexican examples, see Earle, "Padres de la Patria," 797; and, for a few non-Mexican examples of eroticization of the conquest, see Magariños Cervantes, *Celiar*, 56; D. Santamaría, "18 de setiembre," *Revista de Santiago* (Santiago, 1855); Urrutia, *Discurso pronunciado el 15 de setiembre de 1884*; and Pérez, *Discurso*.

65. See, for example, José María Acosta, "Discurso pronunciado . . . en el pueblo de Jilotepec . . . en la solemnidad del 16 de septiembre de 1850," and Manuel Semeria, "Discurso pronunciado el 16 de septiembre de 1850 en la plaza pública del Mineral de Catorce," both in *Composiciones en prosa y verso*, 24, 113.

66. See Earle, "Padres de la Patria," 797 n.81 for Mexicans as sons of the Aztecs.

67. Jacome, *Discurso*. For additional examples, see Earle, "Padres de la Patria," 798 n.82.

68. Ramírez, "Discurso cívico pronunciado el 16 de setiembre de 1861," "Discurso pronunciado en el puerto de Mazatlán la tarde de 16 de setiembre de 1863 en solemnidad de la independencia de México," and "Discurso pronunciado en el Teatro Nacional la noche del 15 de setiembre de 1867 por encargo de la Junta Patriótica," all in *Obras*, 1:136 (for quote), 152, 158, 177.

69. Sierra, "El Día de la Patria," 16 Sept. 1883, *Obras*, 9:108–10 (for quote); Sierra, "Política arqueológica," 8 Sept. 1910, *Obras*, 5:431; and Joaquín M. Alcalde, "Discurso pronunciado en el teatro de Iturbide la noche del 15 de setiembre de 1861," *Discursos pronunciados en la fiesta cívica del año de 1861*.

70. Riva Palacio, *Discurso pronunciado . . . en la capital de la República el 16 de set. de 1871*, 8 (for quote); and Carsi, *Discurso*, 9.

71. José María Vigil, "Necesidad y conveniencia de estudiar la historia patria," 1878, *Polémicas y ensayos*, ed. Ortega y Medina, 268.

72. Sierra, "El Día de la Patria," *Obras*, 9:108–9 (for quote); Sierra, "Proporciones humanas de Colón," 12 Oct. 1892, *Obras*, 5:160 (for Columbus as

Mexico's father); and Sierra, "España y América," 10 Nov. 1910, *Obras*, 5:273, 280, 283. Or see Vicente Riva Palacio, "Discurso pronunciado en las festividades cívicas del 16 de setiembre de 1867," *Discursos cívicos*, 27; Parada, *Discurso*, 8; Verdugo, *Discurso*, 11; Sosa, *Discurso*, 5; Morales, *Discurso*; Revilla, *Dos discursos*, 9; and Alonso Rodríguez Miramar, "Discurso pronunciado en el parque de la Alameda de México el 16 de septiembre de 1892," *Fiestas de septiembre de 1892*, 11.

73. Montesdeoca, *Oración*, n.p.

74. Bristol, "*'Hispanidad'* in South America"; Pike, *Hispanismo*; Rama, *Historia de las relaciones culturales*; Calzadilla, "El IV centenario en Venezuela"; Sergio Alejandro Cañedo Gamboa, "The First Independence Celebrations in San Luis Potosí, 1824–1847"; and Javier Rodríguez Piña, "Conservatives Contest the Meaning of Independence, 1846–1855," both in *¡Viva Mexico!*, ed. Beezley and Lorey, 82, 106–7, respectively; and Bertoni, *Patriotas, cosmopolitas y nacionalistas*, 174–77, 206.

75. Nineteenth-century historia patria's obsession with both the independence process and its origins is discussed in Colmenares, *Las convensiones contra la cultura*.

76. Valle, *Discurso*, n.p. See also Antonio Santibañez Rojas, "Discurso pronunciado . . . a la distribución de premios a los alumnos de las escuelas públicas el 18 de setiembre," *El Teléfono*, Melipilla, 23 Sept. 1883; Gould, *To Die in This Way*, 134; and Gould, "Gender, Politics, and the Triumph of Mestizaje," 9.

77. For celebrations of the quatrocentenary of Columbus's arrival in the Americas, see Batres Jáuregui, *La América Central*, 1:441; Muriá, "El cuarto centenario"; Miguel Rodríguez, "El 12 de octubre: Entre el IV y el V centenario," *Cultura e identidad nacional*, ed. Blancarte; Frédéric Martínez, "¿Como representar a Colombia? De las exposiciones universales a la Exposición del Centenario, 1851–1910," *Museo, memoria y nación*, Memorias des Simposio Internacional, 325–30; Botero, "The Construction of the Pre-Hispanic Past," 166–67; and Bertoni, *Patriotas, cosmopolitas y nacionalistas*, 177–79.

78. Périssat, "Les festivités dynastiques à Lima," 76–77.

79. Proposals of Comisión Pro-Centenario, 1906[?], AGN (BA), Colección Dardo Rocha 3001. See also Comisión Nacional del Centenario, caja 2, and Instrucción Pública y Bellas Artes, caja 363, both in AGN (MC); and Tenorio Trillo, "1910 Mexico City."

80. Pike, *Hispanismo*, 195.

81. Arango, Peinado, and Santa María, *Comunicaciones y correos*, 286; and Isaza and Marroquín, eds., *Primer centenario de la independencia de Colombia*, 151.

82. Tenorio Trillo, "1910 Mexico City," 187–88; Pike, *Hispanismo*, 195; Isaza and Marroquín, eds., *Primer centenario de la independencia de Colombia*; Proposals of Comisión Pro-Centenario, 1906[?], AGN (BA), Colección Dardo Rocha 3001; and Law 4369, 21 Oct. 1921, *Anuario de la legislación peruana*, 16:21–22.

83. The quote refers specifically to Venezuela. See Pike, *Hispanismo*, 195.

84. Isaza and Marroquín, eds., *Primer centenario de la independencia de Colombia*, viii (for quote), 29–33, 70–73, 123, 142, 151; and *Centenario de la independencia de la Provincia de Tunja*, 46, 51. See also Eduardo Talero, "El cóndor nuevo," *Chile en 1910*, ed. Poirier, 168–69; Rafael María Carrasquilla, "Discurso," *Primer centenario de la independencia de Colombia*, ed. Isaza and Marroquín; Monseñor Miguel de Andrea, *Oración*; and "Homenaje a España," *Chile en 1910*, ed. Poirier, 453.

85. Isaza and Marroquín, eds., *Primer centenario de la independencia de Colombia*, 70. For similar sentiments in Peru, see Riva Agüero, *Obras*, vol. 1: *Carácter de la literatura del Perú independiente*, 1905, 267.

86. Roberto Vargas Tamayo, "Discurso," *Centenario de la independencia de la Provincia de Tunja*, 46.

87. The official celebrations also included a trip to the ruins of Teotihuacán. Tenorio Trillo, "1910 Mexico City," 184–86; and Florescano, *Etnia, estado y nación*, 449.

88. Chueco, *La República Argentina en su primer centenario*, 1:5. Of the hundreds of photographs in these two volumes, only one, at the end of the second volume, shows an indigenous person (a "Patagonian Indian," labeled "remains of a dying race": 2:588).

89. Roberto Payro, "Criolla," *La Nación*, Buenos Aires, special centenary edition, 25 May 1910, 171.

90. Ramón Gómez Cuéllar, "Discurso," *Primer centenario de la independencia de Colombia*, ed. Isaza and Marroquín, 193 (for quote); Botero, "The Construction of the Pre-Hispanic Past," 230; and Frédéric Martínez, "¿Como representar a Colombia? De las exposiciones universales a la Exposición del Centenario, 1851–1910," *Museo, memoria y nación*, Memorias des Simposio Internacional, 325–30. Provincial celebrations occasionally mentioned pre-Columbian civilizations; see José Alejandro Ruiz, "Excelsior," *Centenario de la independencia de la Provincia de Tunja*, 52.

91. Gamio, *Forjando Patria*, 10. See also Maqueo Castellanos, *Algunos problemas nacionales*, 76.

92. Jaramillo Alvarado, *El indio ecuatoriano*, 1:229. For Argentine examples, see Mitre, *Historia de Belgrano*, 2:418; Bunge, *Nuestra América*, 136; Rojas, *La restauración nacionalista*, 160; José Ingenieros, "La formación de una raza argentina," *Revista de Filosofía* 1:6, 473–75. For Peru, see Riva Agüero, *Obras*, vol. 1: *Carácter de la literatura del Perú independiente*, 1905, 90. For Colombia, see Martínez, *El nacionalismo cosmopolita*, 92; and Guillermo Camacho, "Introducción," *Primer centenario de la independencia de Colombia*, ed. Isaza and Marroquín, vi. For Venezuela, see Harwich Vallenilla, "La génesis de un imaginario colectivo," 376.

93. Guevara, "Los araucanos en la revolución de la independencia," 230, 242–43 (for quote). For Chile, see also Amaunátegui, *Los precursores*, 1910 edition, 2:497–98; Vicuña Mackenna, "Cuarto discurso sobre la pacificación de Arauco," *Obras*, 12:426; and Vicuña Mackenna, *La guerra a muerte*, 312–21. For Colombia, see Groot, *Historia eclesiástica*, 1:229; Samper, *Ensayo*, 159, 161; Caro, "La conquista," 396; and Sañudo, *Estudios*, 65. For Mexico, see Alamán, *Historia de Méjico*, 1942 edition, 3:358. For Argentina, see Alberdi, *Autobiografía*, 128; Alazraki, "El indigenismo de Martí," 150–51; and López, *Historia de la República Argentina*, 3:343.

94. Batres Jáuregui, *La América Central*, 2:604–5 (emphasis as in the original). Nearly identical sentiments were expressed in Antonio Batres Jáuregui, "Guatemala," *Chile en 1910*, ed. Poirier, 260. See also Azurdia, *Discurso*, 15 Sept. 1923; and Azurdia, *Discurso*, 15 Sept. 1927.

95. Mónica Quijada, "¿Qué nación? Dinámicas y disotomías de la nación en el imaginario hispanoamericano del siglo XIX," *Imaginar la nación*, ed. Guerra and Quijada, 47.

CHAPTER 4. *Patriotic History and the Pre-Columbian Past*

1. José Manzanares, "Expediente sobre la petición presentada por el teniente de la Armada," Callao, April 1876, BN (CM), D.10409.

2. Mera, *Catecismo*; and Andrés Guerrero, "Una imágen ventrilocua: El discurso liberal de la 'desgraciada raza indígena' a fines del siglo XIX," *Imágenes y imagineros*, ed. Muratorio, 216–17, 222–23.

3. Burns, *The Poverty of Progress*, 38. For example, the Mexican historian Lucas Alamán served in the administrations of Guadalupe Victoria, Anastasio Bustamante, and Antonio López de Santa Anna; his political career spanned three decades. José Manuel Restrepo was minister of the interior

in Colombia during the 1820s, when he composed his *Historia de la revolución de la República de Colombia*. The liberal Guatemalan historian Lorenzo Montúfar was minister of foreign relations and of education in Costa Rica during the 1870s. Vicente Riva Palacio served as governor of the states of Mexico and Michoacán in the 1860s, and as secretary for development in the 1870s, before contributing to the influential *México a través de los siglos*. The Peruvian Manuel de Mendiburu, author of such encyclopedic works as the multivolume *Diccionario histórico-biográfico del Perú*, occupied a series of diplomatic posts in the 1840s and 1850s. Domingo Faustino Sarmiento, probably the most widely read and influential historian of the nineteenth century, was Argentina's president between 1868 and 1874. His compatriot and fellow historian Bartolomé Mitre preceded him as president, serving between 1862 and 1868. Some also had military experience; Mitre, for example, was a general.

4. Colmenares, *Las convenciones contra la cultura*; and Sánchez, *Historia comparada*, 2:381–429.

5. Pierre Nora, "Entre mémoire et histoire: La problémématique des lieux," *Les lieux de mémoire*, Nora, vol. 1: *La République*, xxxviii. I have used the translation in Nora, "Between Memory and History," 1:17.

6. *El Venezolano*, Caracas, 1840, cited in Harwich Vallenilla, "La génesis de un imaginario colectivo," 349 (my emphasis). See also Smith, *National Identity*, 66–67, 93, 128.

7. Woll, *A Functional Past*, 30.

8. Ibid., 29, 117, 152, 154.

9. "Medidas para favorecer la instrucción," *El Progreso*, Santiago, 14 Feb. 1843 (for quote); *El Progreso*, Santiago, 10 April 1843 (for history as "a link that joins the American individual to his patria"); *El Progreso*, Santiago, 11 April 1843; *El Ferrocarril*, Santiago, 13 June 1863; and Woll, *A Functional Past*, 150.

10. Woll, *A Functional Past*, 160–61; and Yeager, "Barros Arana."

11. Woll, *A Functional Past*, 150–71.

12. Emiro Kastros [Juan de Dios Restrepo], "Memorias para la historia de la Nueva Granada por el Señor José Antonio de Plaza," *Colección de artículos escojidos*, 38 (for quote); and Melo, "La literatura histórica," 2:591–663.

13. "Alpha" [presumably Manuel Ancízar], introduction to Pérez, *Gonzalo Pizarro*, xiv. See also Caro, "La conquista," 397: "A people who neither know nor esteem their history lack sustaining roots and have no consciousness of their destiny as a nation."

14. Juan Esté, *Lecciones primarias de la historia de Venezuela* (1858), cited in Harwich Vallenilla, "La génesis de un imaginario colectivo," 349–50.

15. Baralt and Díaz, *Resumen;* and Calzadilla, "El olor de la pólvora," 113.

16. Thurner, "Peruvian Genealogies," 144, 152, 168; and Decree of 5 Oct. 1853, Oviedo, ed., *Colección de leyes,* 9:108. See also Law of 25 Oct. 1892, Aranda, ed., *Leyes y resoluciones expedidas por los congresos ordinarios de 1891 y 1892,* 229; and Riva Agüero, *La historia en el Perú.*

17. Polo, *Historia nacional,* 8 (my emphasis). This work reprints a series of articles published in *El Comercio* in 1876.

18. "Acto de la inauguración oficial del Instituto Histórico," 1906; Tello and Mejía Zesspe, *Historia de los museos,* 62.

19. Ruffini, "La trayectoria del discurso historiográfico"; Shumway, *The Invention of Argentina,* chapter 8; and Bertoni, *Patriotas, cosmopolitas y nacionalistas,* 256. For an example of history's importance to political decisionmaking, see José Rivera Indarte to Andrés Lamas, 25 May 1844, AGN (BA), colección Andrés Lamas 2649 (leg. 46).

20. Ramos Mejía, *Las multitudes argentinas,* 254 (for quote), 253–55; Rojas, *La restauración nacionalista,* particularly 84, 147, 159–60, 195, 199, 212; Ramos Mejía, *Historia,* 1:148; Zabala and Gandía, *La enseñanza de la historia,* 13, 31; Bristol, "*Hispanidad,*" 92–93; Pike, *Hispanismo,* 193, 413; and Bertoni, *Patriotas, cosmopolitas y nacionalistas,* esp. 41–77, 117–20, 255–60.

21. "Proyecto de la historia de Guatemala escrito en 1825 por Don José Cecilio del Valle," Samayoa Guevara, *La enseñanza de la historia,* 10–11.

22. The commissioned work was *Documentos para la historia de las revoluciones de Centro-América.* Gálvez perhaps also sponsored Alejandro Marure, *Bosquejo histórico de las revoluciones de Centro América* (1837). See Taracena, *Invención criolla,* 224; Hawkins, "A War of Words," 513; and Woodward, *Rafael Carrera,* 44.

23. This work is also known as the *Memorias de Jalapa.* Vela, *Literatura guatemalteca,* 1:51–104; and Griffith, "The Historiography of Central America, 649–50.

24. Rosa, "Conciencia del pasado," 1880, *Oro de Honduras,* 1:191. See also Montúfar, *Discurso pronunciado ... el 15 de septiembre de 1877,* 16; Montúfar, *Reseña histórica,* 1:ii, vii-viii; Palmer, "A Liberal Discipline," 146; and Valle, "Historia intelectual de Honduras."

25. Tenorio-Trillo, *Mexico at the World's Fairs,* 68; Vázquez de Knauth, *Nacionalismo y educación,* 71; and Roldán Vera, "Conciencia histórica y

enseñanza," x, 87. See also Ramírez, "Instrucción Pública," 1868, *Obras*, 2:183.

26. Riva Palacio, Arias, Chavero, Vigil, and Zárate, *Resumen integral;* and Vázquez de Knauth, *Nacionalismo y educación*, 118–19.

27. Vázquez de Knauth, *Nacionalismo y educación*, 100–3, citing legislation from 1891.

28. José María Lacunza, "Discurso primero," 1844, *Polémicas y ensayos*, ed. Ortega y Medina, 81; Vázquez de Knauth, *Nacionalismo y educación*, 43; and Roldán, "Conciencia histórica y enseñanza," 8, 11.

29. Rozat, *Los orígenes de la nación;* Vázquez de Knauth, *Nacionalismo y educación;* and Roldán, "Conciencia histórica y enseñanza."

30. Brading, *The First America*, 645.

31. Ortega y Medina, ed., *Polémicas y ensayos;* Woll, "The Philosophy of History"; Colmenares, *Las convenciones contra la cultura;* and Stuven, *La seducción*, 221–50.

32. Manuel Larrainzar, "Algunas ideas sobre la historia; manera de escribir la de México, especialmente la contemporánea, desde la declaración de independencia en 1821, hasta nuestros días," 1865, Ortega y Medina, ed., *Polémicas y ensayos*, 158.

33. Riva Agüero, *La historia en el Perú*, 548 (for quote); and Gamio, *Forjando Patria*, 8.

34. Francisco García Calderón, *Obras escogidas*, 2:124 (for quote), 129.

35. Sierra, "Política arqueológica: Discurso en la sesión inaugureal del XVII Congreo Internacional de Americanistas, el 8 de septiembre de 1910," *Obras*, V:431 (my emphasis).

36. For example, Harwich Vallenilla has calculated that on average 60 percent of the discussion in nineteenth-century Venezuelan history texts concerned the independence era (Harwich Vallenilla, "La génesis de un imaginario colectivo," 358, 368–70). See also Colmenares, *Las convenciones contra la cultura*, 15, 21, 30–31. Vázquez de Knauth, *Nacionalismo y educación*, 67, asserts that prior to the 1880s Mexican textbooks devoted most space to the colonial era.

37. D'Alva Ixtililzóchitl, *Cruautés horribles*, ed. Bustamante.

38. See, for example, Icaza and Gondra, *Colección de las antigüedades mexicanas*.

39. Bustamante, *Mañanas de la Alameda;* Brading, *The First America*, 639 (for quote); and Rozat, *Los orígenes de la nación*, 21–195.

40. See, for example, Carlos María de Bustamante, footnotes added to Leon y Gama, *Descripción histórica y cronológica*, 40n.

41. Contemporaries acknowledged that the speeches delivered at civic festivals constituted a form of historical writing. See Rama, *Historia de las relaciones culturales*, 153.

42. Gutiérrez de Villanueba, *Discurso*; Terán, *Oración*; Orozco y Berra, *Oración*; Arenas, *Discurso*, 5; Torre, *Discurso*; and Anievas, *Discurso*.

43. Tornel, *Oración*, 5–7.

44. *Ensayos de poesía y elocuencia* (for quote); J. C. C., *Discurso*, 4; Rosa, *Discurso*; Brito, *Discurso*; and Ramon Prieto, "Discurso pronunciado en Tampico el 16 de septiembre de 1850"; Francisco España, "Poesía recitada en tarde del 17 de septiembre de 1850 . . . en Morelia: 'A Hidalgo'; and 'Canto épico,'" all in *Composiciones en prosa y verso*, 180–81, 230.

45. Brading, "Manuel Gamio," 75 (for quote), 6. For Lorenzo de Zavala's sentiments, see Zavala, *Ensayo*, 1:13; and Juan Ortega y Medina, "Indigenismo y hispanismo en la conciencia historiográfica mexicana," *Cultura e identidad nacional*, ed. Blancarte, 63. For José María Luis Mora, see Mora, *Méjico y sus revoluciones*, 1:196; [José María Luis Mora?], "Población de la República Mexicana," and [José María Luis Mora?], "Sobre la administración de Méjico bajo el régimen español," *El Indicador de la Federación Mexicana*, Mexico City, 4 Dec. 1833, 12 Feb. 1834. Hale discusses their attitudes toward indigenous peoples in his *Mexican Liberalism*, 215–47.

46. Keen, *The Aztec Image*, 415. See also Pimentel, *Memoria sobre las causas que han originado la situación actual de la raza indígena de México y medios de remediarla*, 1864, *Obras*, vol. 3, "Parte primera: Los indios en la antigüedad."

47. Orozco y Berro, *Historia antigua*, 1:111, 229; and Keen, *The Aztec Image*, 419–24. See also Rozat, *Los orígenes de la nación*, 230–31.

48. Mirafuentes, *Discurso*, 5; Montesdeoca, *Oración*; Mendoza, *Discurso*, 13; Julio Zárate, "La raza indígena," *El Siglo XIX*, Mexico City, 2 Dec. 1870, 1; Gustavo Baz, "Arqueología colonial," *El Domingo*, Mexico City, 10 Aug. 1873, *La crítica de arte*, ed. Rodríguez Prampolini, 2:177–79; Islas, *Discurso*, 4–6; Olaguibel and Mantiel y Duarte, *Discurso*; Payno, *Compendio de historia de México*, 76; Vicente Reyes, "El monumento a Cuauhtémoc," 1887, *La polémica del arte nacional*, ed. Schávelzon, 115; Sierra et al., *Mexico, Its Social Evolution*, vol. 1, part 1, 54–57; and Widdifield, *The Embodiment of the National*, 142. See also Ramírez, *Discurso pronunciado el día 27 de setiembre de 1856*, 6; and Ignacio Ramírez, "Discurso pronunciado en el teatro nacional de México

la noche del 15 de setiembre de 1867," *Discursos cívicos pronunciados en las festividades del 15 y 16 de setiembre de 1867*, 4, although these views contrast somewhat with those expressed in Ramírez, "Lecturas de historia política de Mexico," 1871, *Obras*, 1:230.

49. See, for example, Pimentel, "Los toltecas," *Obras*, 3:421; Rozat, *Los orígenes de la nación*, 211, 224–25; Riva Palacio, Arias, Chavero, Vigil, and Zárate, *México a través de los siglos*, vol. 1: *Historia antigua y de la conquista*, 1884[?], Alfredo Chavero, esp. 76; and Sierra, *Evolución política*, 22–34. See also Batres Jaúregui, *Los indios*, 79.

50. Samper, *Ensayo*, 19.

51. Rivero and Tschudi, *Antigüedades peruanas*, 210, 309 (for quote); Rivero, *Antigüedades peruanos: Primera parte*, 1, 12, 24–25; and Thurner, "Peruvian Genealogies of History and Nation," 143.

52. Choquehuanca, *Ensayo de estadística*, 57–58 (for quote); Rivero and Tschudi, *Antigüedades peruanas*, dedication, 307–9; Lorente, *Historia antigua del Perú*, 1–10; Vargas, *Indicaciones económicas*, 2; Larrabure y Unánue, *Cañate*, 17; Mera, *Catecismo*, 148–51; González Suárez, *Historia general*, 1:86–87, 93, 199, 334–35; Walker, *Smoldering Ashes*, 147–48; Thurner, "Peruvian Genealogies"; Zerda, *El Dorado*, 3; Uricoechea, *Memoria*, 28; and "Alpha" [presumably Manuel Ancízar], introduction to Pérez, *Gonzalo Pizarro*, xiv.

53. Thurner, *From Two Republics to One Divided*, 12, 131; and Thurner, "Peruvian Genealogies," 163–64. See also Riva Agüero, "Influencia de las instituciones incáicas en la civilización del Perú," 1902, *Obras*, vol. 5: *Estudios de historia peruana: Las civilizaciones primitivas y el imperio incáica*, 35–39; and Riva Agüero, "Sobre el monumento a Manco Capac," 1917, *Obras*, vol. 5: *Estudios de historia peruana: Las civilizaciones primitivas y el imperio incáica*, 53; Francisco García Calderón, *Obras escogidas*, 1:77–80, 82–83, 161; Gootenberg, *Imagining Development*, 196–97; and Keen, "The Inca Image," 165.

54. "Discurso de Mariano Ignacio Prado y Ugarteche," 29 July 1906, Tello and Mejía Zesspe, *Historia de los museos*, 64. See also Cúneo-Vidal, *Historia*, for not only the Incas but also earlier cultures as great civilizations.

55. Martínez Izquierdo and Cavero Egúsquiza, *Geográfica*, xv. Similarly, members of the Cuzco elite occasionally described themselves as "the noble Incas"; see Itier, "Le theatre moderne en Quechua," 96.

56. López, *Historia de la República Argentina*, 1:100, 103, 123, 601 (for quote), 136–37; López, *Les Races Aryennes*, 13–15; and Quijada Mauriño, "Las raíces indoeuropeas."

57. Andermann, "The Museo de la Plata."

58. Quijada, "Las raíces indoeuropeas," 184. See also Moreno, *Nicomedes Antelo*, 23, 25, for negative social-Darwinist comments about the Incas and the use of "Incaic" as a criticism.

59. Plaza, *Memorias*, vi–vii. See also "Tradiciones antiguas de Cundinamarca," *El Amigo del Pueblo*, Bogotá, 28 Oct. 1838, 36; Emiro Kastros [Juan de Dios Restrepo], "*Memorias para la historia de la Nueva Granada* por el Señor José Antonio de Plaza," *Colección de artículos escojidos*, 42; Samper, *Ensayo*, 19, 20, 27, 29, for the preconquest cultures of the Aztecs, Incas, Chibchas, and Maya as at least "relatively" civilized; and Zerda, *El Dorado*, 3.

60. See, for example, Cuervo, *Resumen*, 11; Uricoechea, *Memoria*, 21, 29, 32; Zerda, *El Dorado*, 3, 22, 48, 62–63, 65, 70; letter of Manuel Vélez to Liborio Zerda, 1882, postscript to Zerda, *El Dorado*, 98; Botero, "The Construction of the Pre-Hispanic Past," 105, 141, 157. For the Muisca as a "nascent civilization," see Codazzi, "Antigüedades indígenas," *Jeografía*, 2:406 (see also 2:410, 435–90). The Muisca possessed "a civilization that was advanced for those times and places," agreed Cuervo, *Resumen*, 12.

61. For discussion of the Chibcha calendar, see Botero, "The Construction of the Pre-Hispanic Past," 44, 110–11.

62. Botero, "The Construction of the Pre-Hispanic Past," 163; and González Suárez, *Historia*, 1:104, 119, 333, 337. For the preconquest Catíos as having begun to progress along the "road of civilization," see Uribe Angel, *Geografía*, 508, although he elsewhere describes them as occupying "the lowest possible rung in the relative ladder of civilization," because they were cannibals (510).

63. García Peláez, *Memorias*, 1:32 (for quote); Riva Palacio, Arias, Chavero, Vigil, and Zárate, *México a través de los siglos*, vol. 1: *Historia antigua y de la conquista*, 1884; Rozat, *Los orígenes de la nación*, 284–85; Sierra, *Evolución política del pueblo mexicano*, 16–19; Darío, "El viaje a Nicaragua," 1909, *Obras*, 3:1047; Palmer, "A Liberal Discipline," 179; Grandin, *Blood of Guatemala*, 282–83; Batres Jáuregui, *Los indios*, 19–26, 65; Batres Jáuregui, *La América Central*, 1:7; and, for later examples, Asturias, "El problema social del indio," 1923, *El problema social*, 40–45; Arriola, *Discurso*; Azurdia, *Discurso*; and Alvarado Tello, *Discurso*.

64. Milla, *Historia*, 2 (for quote), 102.

65. Euraque, "Antropólogos, arqueólogos, imperialismo."

66. Unsigned memoria, *Administraciones de Santander, 1820–25*, ed. López Domínguez, 1:79; "La Nueva Granada en 1839," *El Amigo del Pueblo*, Bogotá, 20 Jan. 1839; Samper, *Ensayo*, 20, 28; and Isaacs, *Estudios*, 145, 237. For "semi-

barbarous tribes" in Ecuador, see González Suárez, *Historia*, 1:54, 127–28, 142, 3:217–27.

67. Rozat, *Los orígenes de la nación*, 300–1.

68. Batres Jáuregui, *Los indios*, 18, 83.

69. *La Opinión*, Riosucio, 1911, cited in Applebaum, *Muddied Waters*, 170.

70. Lastarria, *Investigaciones*, 23.

71. Amunátegui, *Descubrimiento i conquista*, 21, 296; and Amunátegui, *Los precursores*, 1910 edition, 2:106, 498 (for quote).

72. *La Revista Católica*, Santiago, 4 June 1859 (for quote), 18, 25 June 1859, 16 July 1859; and *El Mercurio*, edición de Santiago, 10, 11, 24, 27, 30 May 1859, 7, 25, 30 June 1859, 29 July 1859, 27 Aug. 1859.

73. Barros Arana, *Historia jeneral*, 1:75. For further discussion of the Mapuche's savage lifestyle, see Barros Arana, *Historia jeneral*, 1:76, 83–4, 93–94, 104–5, 2:222, 225, 380, 406–7, and 3:8–9; and Yeager, *Barros Arana's Historia*, 72, 78, 85, 93, 94. See also Barros Arana, Importancia de los documentos históricos, 1873, *Obras*, 8:139; and Barros Arana, review of Miguel L. Amunátegui, *Descubrimiento i conquista de Chile*, 1863, *Obras*, 8:132.

74. Barros Arana, *Historia jeneral*, 2:127.

75. Ibid., 1:27, 33–34, 37, 40 (for quote), 71–72.

76. Vicuña Mackenna, "Tercero discurso sobre la pacificación de Arauco," 12 Aug. 1868, and "Cuarto discurso sobre la pacificación de Arauco," 14 Aug. 1868, both in *Obras*, 12:418–42, 427–29.

77. Vicuña Mackenna, *Lautaro*, x.

78. Shumway, *The Invention of Argentina*, 144.

79. Sarmiento, "Review of *Investigaciones sobre el sistema colonial de los españoles*," 1844, *Obras*, 2:216. See also Sarmiento, *Conflicto y armonía de las razas*, 103–4.

80. Sarmiento, "Review of *Investigaciones sobre el sistema colonial de los españoles*," 1844, *Obras*, 2:214.

81. Alberdi, *Bases*, 60–62.

82. Ibid. (emphasis as in the original). See also Shumway, *The Invention of Argentina*, 138.

83. López, *Historia de la República Argentina*, 1:xii, 100, 103, 123, 136–37, 200–1, 209–10, 601.

84. Francisco Moreno to Vicente G. Quesada, 8 June 1877, González, *Obras*, 14:128; Quijada, "Ancestros, ciudadanos, piezas de museo," 29 (for quote); Salgado and Azar, "Nuestro lugar entre los primates"; and Navarro Floria, Salgado, and Azar, "La invención de los ancestros."

85. Rojas, *La restauración nacionalista*, 84, 147, 159 (for quote), 195, 199, 212; and J. M. G., *Elemental*, 68, 82–83.

86. Luis María Torres cited in Andermann, "Total Recall," 25. For immigration statistics, see Míguez, "Introduction," xiii.

87. Restrepo, *Los chibchas*, 1, 7–10, 18, 60–61, 66–69. See also his son Ernesto Restrepo Tirado's *Estudios*, 49 (for the view that only the Muiscas had attained any "intellectual culture" whatsoever), 58, 59, 68, 83; Martínez, *El nacionalismo cosmopolita*, 85; and Acosta de Samper, *Biografías*, 2.

88. Sommer, *Foundational Fictions*, 7.

89. Fernández Madrid, *Elegías nacionales peruanas* (my emphasis).

90. Gutiérrez, "Caicobé: Leyenda guaraní," c.1840, *Poesías*, 113–20. Or see Gutiérrez, "Irupeya," 1843, *Poesías*, 121–35; Juan León Mera, "Las dos tórtolas," *Antología ecuatoriana*, ed. Mera, 2:131–33; and Pérez, "Vaganiona," *Fantasías indígenas*, 1877, *Obra poética*, 137–43.

91. Corominas, *Breve diccionario*, 398; and Corripio, *Diccionario*, 307.

92. Franco, *Spanish American Literature*, 55–56, 68; and Meléndez, *La novela indianista*.

93. For example, José María Roa Bárcena, *Leyendas mexicanas*, 1862; Salvador Sanfuentes, *Leyendas nacionales*, 1885, and Juan de Dios Peza and Vicente Riva Palacio, *Tradiciones y leyendas mexicanas*, 1900. For comment, see González, *La tradición nacional*, 24–25; and Rodó, "José María Gutiérrez y su época," *Obras*, vol. 4: *El mirador de Próspero*, 473.

94. José Joaquín Ortíz, "Al Tequendama," *La guirnalda*, ed. Ortíz, segunda serie, 60. Or see Ricardo Carrasquilla, "Al Funza," and José María Vergara i Vergara, "Popayán en un día de tempestad," both in *La guirnalda*, ed. Ortíz; Pereira Gamboa, "A Bogotá," 1848, *Poesías*, 82; and Juan León Mera, "El genio de Los Andes," *Antología ecuatoriana*, ed. Mera, vol. 2.

95. José María Heredia, "Fragmentos descriptivos de un poema mejicano" (later published as "En el teocalli de Cholula"), 1825, *Repertorio Americano*, 1:39–40.

96. Nápoles Fajardo, "El behique de Yarigua," c.1856, *Poesías completas*, 151. Or see Palma, "La gruta de las maravillas," 1875, "Palla-Huarcuna," 1872, and "La achirana del Inca," 1875, all in *Tradiciones peruanas completas*, 7–10; and Pérez, "Guarionex," "Toella," and "El último cacique," *Fantasías indígenas*, 1877, *Obra poética*, 113–14, 116–17, 153.

97. Henríquez Ureña, "José Joaquín Pérez," 1905, *Horas de estudio*, 1910, *Obra crítica*, 141 (my emphasis).

98. Darío, "Palabras liminares," *Poesías profanas*, 1896–1901, *Poesías completas*, 1:546; and Kristal, *The Andes*, 22.

99. Darío, "A Bolivia," *Entre el Río de la Plata y la Isla de Oro*, 1898–1907, *Poesías completas*, 2:1000–1. See also "Caupolicán," from *Sonetos aureos*, 1890, "A Colón," from *El canto errante*, 1907, "Canto a la Argentina," 1910, "Chinampa," and "El sueño del Inca," from *Sonetos americanos*, 1888, all in Darío, *Poesías completas*, 1:535, 2:703–4, 787–824, 888–89.

100. Santos Chocano, "Dedicatoria," *Alma América*. Another poem proclaimed: "The blood that beats in me is both Spanish and Incaic:/And were I not a poet I would perhaps have been a white Adventurer or an Indian Emperor!" (Santos Chocano, "Blason," *Alma América*). See also Santos Chocano, "La ñusta," *Alma América*.

101. Cornejo Polar, *Literatura y sociedad*, 44.

102. Montalvo, "Urcu, Sacha," 1888, *El Espectador*, 232.

103. Mera, *La virgen del sol*.

104. Pereira Gamboa, *Akímen Zaque*. Or see Gutiérrez, "Las flores de Lilpu," 1850, *Poesías*, 154–58. Other works on similar themes that I have not been able to consult include José Joaquín Ortiz, *Sulma* (1833); José María Lafragua, *Netzula* (1839); Juan José Nieto, *Yngermina o la hija de Calamar* (1844); José María Roa Bárcena, *Leyendas mexicanas* (1862); Eligio Ancona, *La cruz y la espada* (1866); Ireneo Paz, *Amor y suplicio* (1873); J. R. Hernández, *Azcaxóchitl o la flecha de oro* (1878); and Eulogio Palma y Palma, *La hija de Tutul-Xiu* (1884).

105. Rodríguez Galván, "La visión de Moctezuma," 1842, *Poesías*, 1:164–78. For similar plots, see Ortiz, *La Virgen del Sol*; Nápoles Fajardo, "El cacique de Maniabón," and "Narey y Coalina," c.1856, *Poesías completas*, 143–47, 155–61; Caicedo Rojas, *Jilma-episodio de la historia de los muiscas, La guirnalda*, ed. Ortíz, segunda serie, 188–90; Pérez, *Huayna Capac*; Pérez, *Atahualpa*; Pérez, *Jilma*; Julio Arboleda, *Gonzalo de Oyon, Semana literaria de "El Porvenir,"* vol. 2 (Bogotá, 1858); Eligio Ancona, *Los mártires del Anáhuac*, 1873, *La novela del México colonial*, ed. Castro Leal, 1:403–616; Palma, "Palla-Huarcuna," 1872, and Palma, "La achirana del Inca," 1875, both in *Tradiciones peruanas completas*, 8–10; Pérez, "Areitos," *Fantasías indígenas*, 1877, *Obra poética*, 194–97; and José Ramón Yepes's two novellas, *Iguaraya* and *Anaida*, both written around 1860 but not published until 1882 (both in Yepes, *Anaida*, 1–57, 63–83). Yepes's romantic tales are set among the "savages" of preconquest Venezuela, rather than among explicitly civilized peoples. See also Cometta,

El indio en la poesía, 151, 170–72; and García Quintana, *Cuauhtémoc en el siglo XIX*, 18.

106. José Joaquín Ortiz, introduction to Madiedo, *Poesías*, v. See also López, *La novia del hereje*, 328; and Meléndez, *La novela indianista*, 102, 137.

107. Berro, "Yandubayá y Liropeya," 1840, *Poesías*; and Eligio Ancona, *Los mártires del Anáhuac*, 1873, *La novela del México colonial*, ed. Castro Leal, 1:403–616.

108. Pérez, *Gonzalo Pizarro*; and Kristal, "The Incest Motif." In José Milla's novel *La hija del adelantado* the tragic love affair concerns a conquistador and the mestiza daughter of Pedro de Alvarado and the Tlaxcalan princess Jicotencal (Milla, *La hija del adelantado*, 1866, *Obras*, vol. 5).

109. Sanfuentes, "Inámi, o la laguna de Ranco (en Valdivia): Leyenda indígena," *Leyendas nacionales*. The poem is set in an indeterminate point in the colonial past, but the complete separation between indigenous and European cultures described in the poem makes it in many ways equivalent to other romantic dramas set in the conquest era, in that the narrative is driven by the intrusion of Spaniards into a pristine indigenous world.

110. Santos Chocano, *Los conquistadores*, 1906, *Obras*, 315–55. See also Santos Chocano's poem "La ñusta," *Alma América*, *Obras*, 426–31; and Palma, "La muerte en un beso," 1852, *Tradiciones peruanas completas*, 23–27.

111. Rodríguez Galván, "Profecía de Guatimoc," *La poesía mexicana del siglo XIX*, ed. Pacheco, 170. For Guatemalan examples, see Juan Fermín Aycinena, "Al pensativo" and "El indio," *Parnaso guatemalteca*, ed. Porta Mencos, 184–91. "But alas! The hour has sounded/which Destiny in his fateful book/ had marked as the end of that nation," runs "El indio" (188).

112. Caro, "En boca el último Inca," 1835, *Obras escogidas*. See also José María Vergara i Vergara, "Popayán en un día de tempestad," in *La guirnalda*, ed. Ortíz, 205.

113. See, for example, José Joaquín Pesado, "Vanidad de la gloria humana (canto de Netzahualcóyotl)," 1854, in *La poesía mexicana del siglo XIX*, ed. Pacheco, 145–48.

114. See Sánchez, *Historia comparada*, 2:381–82.

115. Widdifield, *The Embodiment of the National*, 119.

116. Ibid., 103; and Tenorio-Trillo, *Mexico at the World's Fairs*, 118–19.

117. Hutchinson, *Two Years in Peru*, 1:336; Majluf, "Republican and Contemporary Art," 129–30, 195; and Thurner, "Peruvian Genealogies," 170.

118. Majluf, "Republican and Contemporary Art," 134.

119. Ricardo Palma, "Relación de cuadros recibidos por el director de la Biblioteca Nacional," Lima, 8 May 1884, and "Relación de retratos, esculturas y otras obras de arte de artistas peruanos y extrangeros," Lima, 24 July 1892, both in BN(CM), D3893, D4631 respectively. The latter, although missing its first page, appears to be another list of works owned by the Biblioteca Nacional.

120. These works are now on display in the Museo de Arte de Lima. For comments about Chile, see Miguel Luis Amunátegui, "Apuntes sobre lo que han sido las bellas artes en Chile," *Revista de Santiago* 3 (Santiago, 1849), 42.

121. Martí, "Las ruinas indias," *La edad de oro*, vol. 1:2, 1889, *Obras*, 1:114 (my emphasis); and Martí, "Un viaje a México," 1889, *Obras*, 5:189.

122. Rozat, *Los orígenes de la nación*, 312, 323, 396.

123. Marcoy, *A Journey*, 1:8–9; and Marcoy, *Travels*, 1:240. See also Hutchinson, *Two Years in Peru*, 1:321.

124. Pilcher, *¡Que Vivan los Tamales!* 48, citing cookbooks from 1868 and 1877.

125. Manuel Alvarez, "Creación de una arquitectura nacional," 1900, *La polémica del arte nacional*, ed. Schávelzon, 161.

126. For Mexican speeches implying that the conquest was a step backward not only for the Aztecs personally but for civilization in general, see Pando, *Elogio*; Herrera, *Oración*; Dublan, *Oración*; Gonzaga Gordoa, *Discurso*; and Rosa, *Discurso*.

127. Lorente, *Historia antigua del Perú*, 6 (for quote), 8.

128. Medina y Ormaechea, *Iniciativa para celebrar el primer centenario*, 29. Or see Aguirre, *Discurso*; Muriá, "El cuarto centenario," 125–27.

129. Mendiburu, *Diccionario*, 1:2.

130. Acosta de Samper, *Biografías*, 2 (also 4, 442); and Caro, "La conquista," 387. See also Jaramillo Uribe, *El pensamiento colombiano*, 83–94. For Mexican examples, see Manuel García Aguirre, "Discurso," *El 16 de setiembre de 1851*; and Cortes y Esparza, *Oración*.

131. Cited in Alazraki, "El indigenismo de Martí," 143 (my emphasis). Alberdi and the historian-president Mitre also stressed that European civilization was in every way superior to preconquest barbarism. See Mitre, *Las ruinas de Tiahuanaco*, 59–61; Mitre, *Historia de Belgrano*, 1:20–21, 2:205; and Mitre, *Historia de San Martín*, 1:87. For examples from later writers, see Ruffini, "La Trayectoria del discurso historiográfico," 39; José Ingenieros, "La formación de una raza argentina," *Revista de Filosofía* 1:6 (Buenos Aires, 1915); and Corbiere, *El gaucho*, 6, 9, 11.

132. Orozco y Berro, *Historia antigua*, 4:578–82 (quotes from 578, 579). See also Riva Palacio, Arias, Chavero, Vigil, and Zárate, *Resumen integral*, vol. 2: *El virreinato*, 1886[?], Vicente Riva Palacio, 9; Muriá, "El cuarto centenario," 125; Faustino Estrada, "Discurso," 1894, García Quintana, *Cuauhtémoc en el siglo XIX*, 122–23; Powell, "Mexican Intellectuals and the Indian Question," 32; Tenorio-Trillo, *Mexico at the World's Fairs*, 69–70; and Roldán, "Conciencia histórica y enseñanza," 60, 71–79. See also Jaramillo Alvarado, *El indio ecuatoriano*, 1:214–15, 233; Calzadilla, "El IV centenario en Venezuela y el fin del matricidio," 265–67; Uricoechea, *Memoria*, 27; Martínez Sobral, *Discurso*; Batres Jáuregui, *Los indios*, vii, 19; Batres Jáuregui, *La América Central*, 1:15; and Alvarado Tello, *Discurso*.

133. Samper, *Ensayo*, 18, 19, 252. For the conquest as introducing the Chibchas to "the true civilization of today," see Zerda, *El Dorado*, 54.

134. Riva Palacio, Arias, Chavero, Vigil, and Zárate, *Resumen integral*, vol. 3: *La guerra de la independencia*, 1887?, Julio Zárate, 12 (my emphasis). Or see Pimentel, *Historia crítica de la literatura y de las ciencias en México*, 1885, *Obras*, 4:37; and Sierra, "Proporciones humanas de Colón," 12 Oct. 1892, *Obras*, 5:153.

135. For the role of language in relations between Spain and Spanish America, see Rama, *Historia de las relaciones culturales*, 98, 115–48. See also Bristol, "*Hispanidad*," 88–90; Stuven, *La seducción*, 173–94; and Osmundo Arriola, "En elogio del idioma," *Parnaso guatemalteca*, ed. Porta Mencos, 426.

136. See Batres Jáuregui, *Los indios*, 91–93, for comments on the impact of the conquest.

137. Meyer, "History as National Identity," 33.

138. See, for example, Treece, *Exiles, Allies, Rebels*, 10; Barr-Melej, *Reforming Chile*, 106; and Bertoni, *Patriotas, cosmopolitas y nacionalistas*, 255.

139. Riva Agüero, "Sobre el monumento a Manco Capac," 1917, *Obras*, 5:53.

CHAPTER 5. *Archaeology, Museums, and Heritage*

1. García Peláez, *Memorias*, 1:12. For García Peláez's relations with Carrera see Sullivan-González, *Piety, Power, and Politics*.

2. Smith, *National Identity*, 117 (emphasis as in the original). See also Anderson, *Imagined Communities*, 178–85; Martin Prösler, "Museums and Globalization," *Theorizing Museums*, ed. Macdonald and Fyfe, 32; Janowitz, *England's Ruins*, 1–7; and Beatriz González-Stepan, "Showcases of Consump-

tion: Historical Panoramas and Universal Expositions," *Beyond Imagined Communities,* ed. Castro-Klarén and Chasteen, 226.

3. On the sense of wonder, see Greenblatt, "Resonance and Wonder."

4. Bernal, *A History of Mexican Archaeology,* 131; Pieper, "Papageien und Bezoarsteine"; Pieper, "The Upper German Trade," 94; and Laura Laurencich-Minelli, "Museography and Ethnographical Collections in Bologna during the Sixteenth and Seventeenth Centuries"; Elisabeth Schneicher, "The Collection of Archduke Ferdinand II at Schloss Ambras: Its Purpose, Composition and Evolution"; Lorenz Seelig, "The Munich Kunstkammer, 1565–1807"; William Schupbach, "Some Cabinets of Curiosities in European Academic Institutions"; and Christian Feest, "Mexico and South America in the European *Wunderkammer*"; all in *The Origins of Museums,* ed. Imnpey and MacGreggor, 20–21, 44, 108, 232, 327–35, respectively; and Botero, "The Construction of the Pre-Hispanic Past," 27–29.

5. Julien, "History and Art." See also Bernal, *A History of Mexican Archaeology,* 131; Carbello Carro, "Amerikanische Sammlungen"; Humboldt, *Sitios de las cordilleras,* 188; and Botero, "The Construction of the Pre-Hispanic Past," 39.

6. Cañizares-Esguerra, *How to Write the History of the New World,* chapter 2.

7. Boturini Benaduci, "Catalogo del Museo Histórico Indiano," bound into *Idea de una nueva historia;* Glass, "A Survey"; and Humboldt, *Sitios de las cordilleras,* 187–96.

8. The appreciation of preconquest artifacts by indigenous peoples is an entirely different matter. A number of sources suggest that in parts of Spanish America such items continued to be venerated, or at least esteemed. See, for example, Humboldt, *Sitios de las cordilleras,* 252. For contrasting accounts of indigenous responses to the Aztec statues unearthed in Mexico City in 1790, see Poinsett, *Notes on Mexico,* 83; Bullock, *Six Month's Residence,* 336, 341–42; Mayer, *Mexico,* 114; Moxó, *Cartas méjicanas,* 42; and Florescano, *El patrimonio nacional,* 149.

9. For colonial Colombia, see Botero, "The Construction of the Pre-Hispanic Past," 15–20.

10. Filiberto de Mena, "Monumentos del tiempo de los Incas," Salta, 22 Nov. 1791, in AGN (BA), Colección Andrés Lamas, 2655 (leg. 52).

11. Humboldt, *Sitios de las cordilleras,* 247, 255.

12. Ibid., 80, 164, 192, 250.

13. Brading, *The First America*, 319, 395, 413, 415.

14. "Carta escrita a la Sociedad por el Doctor Don Pedro Nolasco Crespo," *Mercurio Peruano*, Lima, 19 Aug. 1792, 255 (for quote; emphasis as in the original); and "Idea general de los monumentos del antiguo Perú," *Mercurio Peruano*, Lima, 17 March 1791, 201–8.

15. Caldas, "Estado de la geografía del Virreinato de Santafe de Bogotá," 1808, *Obras*, 202. For the collecting of Mochica items in 1780s New Granada, see Ballesteros Gaibrois, "Spanische archäologische Forschungen," 188–89.

16. See Humboldt, *Sitios de las cordilleras*, 79; Brading, *The First America*, esp. 453–64; and Cañizares-Esguerra, *How to Write the History of the New World*, 300–5.

17. *Gazeta de Literatura de México*, 15 Jan. 1788.

18. León y Gama, *Descripción histórica y cronológica*, 4.

19. Ibid.; and José Antonio Alzate Ramírez, *Descripción de las antigüedades de Xochicalco*, 19 Nov. 1791, published as a supplement to vol. 2 of the *Gazeta de Literatura de México*.

20. Clavijero, *Historia antigua de México*, 1:4.

21. Brading, *The First America*, 306–10; and Martínez Pelaéz, *La patria del criollo*, 156 (for quote; paraphrasing Fuentes y Guzmán).

22. León y Gama, *Descripción histórica y cronológica*, 4 (my emphasis).

23. Keen, *The Aztec Image*, 312–13; Rosa Casanova, "Imaginando el pasado: El mito de la ruinas de Palenque–1784–1813," *Imaginar la nación*, ed. Guerra and Quijada; and Cañizares-Esguerra, *How to Write the History of the New World*, 322–45.

24. Bernal, *A History of Mexican Archaeology*, 134.

25. Decree of Marquis of Torre Tagle, 2 April 1822, *Obra de gobierno*, ed. Puente Candamo, 1:322. This legislation was reiterated in 1836, 1837, and 1841; see Tello and Mejía Zesspe, *Historia de los museos*, 9–11, 16, 19–20.

26. Bernal, *A History of Mexican Archaeology*, 134; and Elena Isabel Estrada de Gerlero, "La litografía y el Museo Nacional como armas del nacionalismo," *Los pinceles de la historia*, ed. Tovar, Estrada, Uriarte, Hernández Ramírez, and Torre, 155.

27. Lombardi de Ruiz, *El pasado prehispánico*, 30–31.

28. Carlos María de Bustamante, footnotes added to León y Gama, *Descripción histórica y cronológica*, 89n.

29. Decree of 26 Sept. 1837, Tello and Mejía Zesspe, *Historia de los museos*, 16. See also Tello and Mejía Zesspe, *Historia de los museos*, 34–47; and Zárate, *El Cuzco y sus monumentos*, 72. In 1874 Eugenio Larrabure y Unánue

complained that locals sold preconquest artifacts "for a paltry sum to foreigners who value these things" (Larrabure y Unánue, *Cañate,* 71). For an example, see Hutchinson, *Two Years in Peru,* 1:116, 127, 138, 162, 296, 2:82, 88–90, 95, 139, 185.

30. Tylor, *Anahuac,* 264. See also Lyon, *Journal,* 1:21, 57, 2:125–26; Bullock, *Six Month's Residence,* 326–42; Mier, *Memorias,* 1:53–56; and Keen, *The Aztec Image,* 339–40.

31. Mayer, *Mexico,* 84, 96, 106, 221–22, 227, 234–35, 251 (for quote), 257; Rodríguez Prampolini, ed., *La crítica de arte,* vol. 2; García Quintana, *Cuauhtémoc en el siglo XIX,* 17; and Ramírez, "Antigüedades mexicanas," 1868, *Obras,* 2:210.

32. For example, the substantial collection of preconquest items built up by the Colombian Romoaldo Cuervo Rubiano was bought after his death in 1871 by a traveling actor. Efforts at preventing the export of preconquest material were impeded by a piece of 1833 legislation that gave full ownership of buried preconquest items to their finders. Even after this legislation was discarded in 1918, European archaeologists continued to express astonishment over the ease with which preconquest artifacts could be removed from the country. See Botero, "The Construction of the Pre-Hispanic Past," 54–57, 66, 75, and chapter 4; and Uricoechea, *Memoria,* 20, 30, for criticism of the "complete lack of appreciation for the works of the ancient Neogranadans."

33. Stephens, *Incidents of Travel,* 1:126 (for quote), 127–29. Similarly, the preconquest Mayan artifacts excavated from the Guatemalan site of Santa Lucía in the 1860s ended up at a museum in Berlin, rather than in Guatemala (Batres Jáuregui, *La América Central,* 1:204–5, 436).

34. The British Museum established its American Room in 1890. See Vicuña Mackenna, *Católogo,* 6; Rojas, *La restauración nacionalista,* 195, 220–29; Ventura García Calderón, "Un loable esfuerzo por el arte incaico," 1927, *La polémica del indigenismo,* ed. Aquézolo Castro, 62–63; letter of Julio Tello, 20 March 1915, Tello and Mejía Zesspe, *Historia de los museos,* 99; Orellana Rodríguez, *Historia de la arqueología en Chile,* 58; Bernal, *A History of Mexican Archaeology,* 131–32; Elizabeth Williams, "Art and Artifact at the Trocadero: *Ars Americana* and the Primitivist Revolution," *Objects and Others,* ed. Stocking; and Botero, "The Construction of the Pre-Hispanic Past," 210.

35. *El Imparcial,* Mexico City, 17 Jan. 1902.

36. Enrique Florescano, "La creación del Museo Nacional de Antropología y sus fines científicos, educativos y políticos," *El patrimonio cultural,* ed. Florescano, 154; Florescano, *Etnia, estado y nación,* 447; Lombardi de Ruiz,

El pasado prehispánico, 33; and Bueno, "Centralising Memory." Lombardi de Ruiz and Florescano differ on the date of the 1897 legislation. On enforcement of this legislation, see Suárez Cortés, "Las interpretaciones positivas del pasado," 48; Keen, *The Aztec Image,* 417–18; and Powell, "Mexican Intellectuals and the Indian Question," 30.

37. Lombardi de Ruiz, *El pasado prehispánico,* 30.

38. Florescano, *Etnia, estado y nación,* 447; and Lombardi de Ruiz, *El pasado prehispánico,* 31–32. This is not to imply that the export of artifacts ceased completely; see Lumholtz, *Unknown Mexico,* 460. Moreover, Justo Sierra spoke in favor of permitting export, on the grounds that Mexico's preconquest history would become *better* known through being sent abroad (Sierra, "Exportación arqueológica," 28 Oct. 1880, *Obras,* 5:25–8).

39. Enrique Florescano, "La creación del Museo Nacional de Antropología y sus fines científicos, educativos y políticos," *El patrimonio cultural,* ed. Florescano, 160.

40. Decree of 27 April 1893; and Decree of 19 Aug. 1911, both in Tello and Mejía Zesspe, *Historia de los museos,* 47–48, 76–77. Additional legislation was issued in 1929: Law 6634, 13 June 1929, *Anuario de la legislación peruana,* 23:245–47.

41. Rubin de la Borbolla and Rivas, *Honduras,* 27–42.

42. The law of 15 Nov. 1893 prohibited the extraction of material from the "monuments and ruins of the palace of the ancient kingdom of the K'iche." This was followed by the law of 10 Jan. 1894, which stated that all such monuments and other objects found within Guatemala were the property of the state. Subsequent legislation prohibited the pursuit of agricultural activities in areas of archeological interest. Legislation from 1922 permitted "minor excavations" without state permit, while Decree 1376 of 1925 reaffirmed the state's ownership of archeological antiquities. Rubín de la Borbolla and Cerezo, *Guatemala,* 13–16, 32–42.

43. Decreto sobre documentos históricos, 24 Jan. 1914, *Historia de la historiografía,* ed. Carrera Damas, 278–79.

44. Rojas, *La restauración nacionalista,* 195, 220–29. See also Proyecto de ley: Parques y jardines nacionales," 1912, Moreno, *Perito en argentinidad,* 87–91.

45. Further legislation was issued in 1931 and 1936. See Botero, "The Construction of the Pre-Hispanic Past," 258–59, 284, 298.

46. Items of interest were to be placed in the national museum; see Montandon, *Chile,* 11, 29–36.

47. Barros Arana, *Historia jeneral*, 1:9.

48. See *Los Andes Libres*, Lima, 18 Sept. 1821, in *Periódicos*, ed. Tauro, 1:295; and José Faustino Sánchez Carrión, "Aptitud civil de la República Peruana," 22 Dec. 1822, *Los ideólogos*, ed. Tamayo Vargas and Pacheco Vélez, 1:397. For comparable attitudes in 1820s Mexico, see Castillo Ledón, *El Museo Nacional*, 23.

49. The quote is from the *Bulletin of the Instituto Nacional de Geografía y Estadística* (1850), cited in Keen, *The Aztec Image*, 412. "Magnificent monuments" is from Arenas, *Discurso*, 5. See also Ramírez, "Lecturas de historia políticas de México," 1871, *Obras*, 1:212; *La crítica de arte*, ed. Rodríguez Prampolini, 2:178; *La polémica del arte nacional*, ed. Schávelzon, 153, 200; Sierra, *Mexico: Its Social Evolution*, 1:25; and, for comment on Maya ruins, Riva Palacio, Arias, Chavero, Vigil, and Zárate, *Resumen integral*, 1:86.

50. Payno, *Compendio*, 70–71; and Grove, *Medals of Mexico*, 2: nos. 231–32, 287, 418, 467.

51. Pimentel, "Los toltecas," 1856, *Obras*, 3:428. Novels too described preconquest ruins as "annals of [a] noble, valiant, illustrious and artistic people" (Eligio Ancona, *La cruz y la espada* [1866], cited in Meléndez, *La novela indianista*, 102 [for quote], 106).

52. Sierra, *Obras*, 12:38.

53. García Peláez, *Memorias*, 1:10. "The ruins scattered across Central America bear witness not only to their remote antiquity but also to an advanced civilization," wrote José Milla (*Historia de la América Central*, 2).

54. Batres Jaúregui, *Los indios*, 24.

55. Uricoechea, *Memoria*, 28, 32. See also Botero, "The Construction of the Pre-Hispanic Past," 58.

56. Rivero and Tschudi, *Antigüedades peruanas*, dedication, 259. See also letter of Mariano de Rivero, 24 July 1845, Tello and Mejía Zesspe, *Historia de los museos*, 21–22; Lorente, *Historia antigua*, 7–9; Thurner, "Peruvian Genealogies," 143; Mera, *Catecismo*, 150; and Larrabure y Unánue, *Cañate*, 62, 71.

57. For example, see Thurner, "Peruvian Genealogies," 160; Botero, "The Construction of the Pre-Hispanic Past," 140; Discurso de Mariano Ignacio Prado y Ugarteche, 29 July 1906, Tello and Mejía Zesspe, *Historia de los museos*, 64; Rodríguez Prampolini ed., *La crítica de arte*, 2:257–63, 269–71; and Gamio, *Forjando Patria*, 57.

58. For example, the *American Journal of Archaeology* was founded in 1885, and by 1890 the Congrès International d'Anthropologie et d'Archéologie Préhistorique had met over a dozen times.

59. Stiebing, *Uncovering the Past*, 23–24, 49–54; and Bahn, ed., *The Cambridge Illustrated History of Archaeology*, 120–24, 131–32.

60. Examples include the Sociedad de Arqueología in Cuzco (founded 1869), and the Sociedad Arqueológica de Santiago (founded 1878). See González La Rosa, *Informe*, 42; and Orellana Rodríguez, *Historia de la arqueología en Chile*, 17.

61. Bingham, *Inca Land*; Brunhouse, *Pursuit of the Ancient Maya*; and Stiebing, *Uncovering the Past*, 195–97.

62. Comas, ed., *Los congresos internacionales de americanistas*, xxxviii–xxxix.

63. Acuedro no. 4, 28 Jan. 1845, Acuerdo, 28 Dec. 1874, Acuerdo, 24 July 1889, and legislation of 4 April 1900, Rubin de la Borbolla and Rivas, *Honduras*, 27–29, 36–37.

64. Liborio Zerda, cited in Isaacs, *Estudios*, 17. "European museums have and are anxious to possess [pre-Columbian artifacts], intelligent foreigners search diligently for them, and we in general disdain and destroy them without giving them the importance they deserve," sighed Manuel Uribe Angel, in his *Geografía general*, 504. See also Francisco P. Moreno to Vicente G. Quesada, 8 June 1877, González, *Obras*, 14:129–30; *Revista de la Sociedad Arqueológica de Santiago*, tomo 1, 14; Riva-Agüero, *Paisajes Peruanos*, 40; Botero, "The Construction of the Pre-Hispanic Past," 115, 182; Decreto no. 198, 15 March 1898, Rubin de la Borbolla and Rivas, *Honduras*, 32–33; and Schell, "Capturing Chile," 48.

65. Darío, "Exposición colombiana: Costa Rica," *Obras completas*, 1:732–34. See also González La Rosa, *Informe*, 41; and Lombardi de Ruiz, *El pasado prehispánico*, 1:23, 44.

66. O'Brien, *Narratives of Enlightenment*, 133–34; and Wheeler, *The Complexion of Race*, 35.

67. Stiebing, *Uncovering the Past*, 49. On "prehistory," see Chippindale, "The Invention of Words"; and Clermont and Smith, "Prehistoric, Prehistory, Prehistorian."

68. Tylor, *Anthropology*, 18; Tylor, *Primitive Culture*, 1:26–27; Fagan, *In the Beginning*, 285; and Stocking, *Victorian Anthropology*. See also Tylor, *Researches*.

69. Morgan, *Ancient Society*, 11–23.

70. Tylor, *Anthropology*, 16.

71. Morgan, *Ancient Society*, 19.

72. J. J. C., *Discurso*, 4. For general claims that the construction of large monuments in itself provided evidence of their constructors' civilized nature, see Barros Arana, *Historia jeneral*, 1:7–8, 27; and Riva Palacio, Arias, Chavero, Vigil, and Zárate, *México a través de los siglos*, 1:xviii-xix. For a later example, see Vasconcelos, *The Cosmic Race*, 47–48.

73. J. J. C., *Discurso*, 4; and Bueno, "Centralising Memory."

74. Restrepo Tirado, *Estudios*, 181. For Chilean examples, see Medina, *Los aborígenes de Chile*, 6, 54; and *Revista de la Sociedad Arqueológica*, tomo 1, 1. For Diego Barros Arana, the absence of monuments offered solid proof that before the Inca conquest Chile was inhabited by "barbarians who had not left the earliest stages of the stone age" (Barros Arana, *Historia jeneral*, 1:27).

75. *Exposición Histórico-Americana*, 9, 11.

76. Greenhalgh, *Ephemeral Vistas*; and Tony Bennett, "The Exhibitionary Complex," *Representing the Nation*, ed. Boswell and Evans, 353. The quotation is from "Exposición de 1889 en Paris," *El Orden*, Tucumán, 5 March 1888 (my emphasis).

77. This was the case, for example, with the Venezuelan display at the 1867 Paris exposition. See Thirion, *États-Unis de Vénézuela*.

78. I have focused on this fair because a number of Spanish American countries participated in it, and because Paris was generally regarded by Spanish American elites as the epicenter of the civilized world.

79. See Tenorio Trillo, *Mexico at the World's Fairs*. "Purest Aztec style" is from Antonio Peñafiel, "Explicación del Pabellón Mexicano en París de 1889," 1889, *La polémica del arte nacional*, ed. Schávelzon, 177.

80. Tenorio Trillo, *Mexico at the World's Fairs*, 64.

81. Ibid., 65.

82. Not all members of the Mexican elite approved of this "Mexican architecture." Key documents from the debate about national architecture are reproduced in *La polémica del arte nacional*, ed. Schávelzon.

83. The pavilion was designed by a French architect, with Ecuadorian approval. See Blanca Muratorio, "Images of Indians in the Construction of Ecuadorian Identity at the End of the Nineteenth Century," *Latin American Popular Culture*, ed. Beezley and Curcio-Nagy; and Blanca Muratorio, "Nación, identidad y etnicidad: Imagenes de los indios ecuatorianos y sus imagineros a fines del siglo XIX," *Imágenes e imagineros*, ed. Muratorio.

84. Frédéric Martínez, "¿Como representar a Colombia? De las exposiciones universales a la Exposición del Centenario, 1851–1910," *Museo, memoria*

y nación, Memorias del Simposio Internacional; and Botero, "The Construction of the Pre-Hispanic Past," 153–55.

85. Ingrid Fey, "Peddling the Pampas: Argentina at the Paris Universal Exposition of 1889," *Latin American Popular Culture*, ed. Beezley and Curcio-Nagy, 76 (for quote); and Alcorta, *La República Argentina*. For the Chilean pavilion, see Norambuena, "Imagen de la América Latina," 101–7.

86. Enrique Ortega, "Desde París," *La Prensa*, Buenos Aires, 13 July 1889.

87. Alcorta, *La República Argentina*, 1:9, 15.

88. Enrique Nelson to Eduardo Olivera, Paris, 20 Aug. 1889, in AGN (BA), Sala X: 43–9–7.

89. Tenorio Trillo, *Mexico at the World's Fairs*, 37.

90. Andermann, "Reshaping the Creole Past," 148–49.

91. *Homenaje a Cristóbal Colón*, i, vii, ix.

92. Blanca Muratorio, "Images of Indians in the Construction of Ecuadorian Identity at the End of the Nineteenth Century," *Latin American Popular Culture*, ed. Beezley and Curcio-Nagy, 110 (for quote); and Blanca Muratorio, "Nación, identidad y etnicidad: Imagenes de los indios ecuatorianos y sus imagineros a fines del siglo XIX," *Imágenes e imagineros*, ed. Muratorio, 126–27, 144.

93. *Suplemento al número 67 de la Gaceta de Guatemala*, Guatemala, 25 July 1855.

94. Podgorny, "Vitrinas y administración."

95. Le Goff, *History and Memory*, 88.

96. Anderson, *Imagined Communities*, chapter 4; Botero, "The Construction of the Pre-Hispanic Past," 145–50; and Godoy, "Franz Boas," 233.

97. Vicuña Mackenna, *Católogo*, 3.

98. Joaquín García-Bárcena, "El patrimonio paleontológico," and Enrique Florescano, "La creación del Museo Nacional de Antropología y sus fines científicos, educativos y políticos," both in *El patrimonio cultural*, ed. Florescano; and Luis Gerardo Morales-Moreno, "History and Patriotism in the National Museum of Mexico," *Museums and the Making of "Ourselves,"* ed. Kaplan. García-Bárcena and Florescano give different dates for the museum's renaming as the Museo de Historia Natural, Arqueología e Historia (120, 152).

99. The 1898 plans to create a Museo Nacional de Honduras, for example, called specifically for the proposed museum to house "natural, artistic and industrial products" (Decreto no. 198, 15 March 1898, Rubin de la Borbolla and Rivas, *Honduras*, 33). On the development of natural history museums

in Latin America, see Lopes and Podgorny, "The Shaping of Latin American Museums."

100. Keen, *The Aztec Image*, 313; and Bernal, *A History of Mexican Archaeology*, 133–35.

101. Castillo Ledón, *El Museo Nacional*, 11.

102. Calderón de la Barca, *Life in Mexico*, 126, 270 (for quote); Mayer, *Mexico*, 84–114; and Tylor, *Anahuac*, 222–29.

103. The museum was periodically closed by one or another Mexican government during the first four decades of its existence. See Castillo Ledón, *El Museo Nacional*, 30–31, 69, 77; Joaquín García-Bárcena, "El patrimonio paleontológico," *El patrimonio cultural*, ed. Florescano 120; and Bernal, *A History of Mexican Archaeology*, 138. For a description of key archaeological holdings in 1910, see Sierra, "Política arqueológica," 8 Sept. 1910, *Obras*, 5:433–34.

104. On Mexican museums outside Mexico City, see *El Imparcial*, Mexico City, 17 Jan. 1902; and Lombardi de Ruiz, *El pasado prehispánico*, 31–33 (for quote).

105. *Gaceta de Colombia*, Bogotá, 15 Jan. 1826.

106. Le Moyne, *Voyages et séjours*, 173. He traveled in the 1830s and 1840s.

107. Botero, "The Construction of the Pre-Hispanic Past," 140–44. See also Isaacs, *Estudio*, 202; Restrepo, *Los chibchas*, x; and Restrepo Tirado, *Católogo general*.

108. Philippi, "Algo sobre las momias peruanas"; *Revista de la Sociedad Arqueológica de Santiago*, tomo 1, 6; Medina, *Los aborígenes de Chile*, 7, 191; "Los indios chilenos," *La Revista Católica: Periódico quincenal*, número especial dedicada a celebrar el centenario de la independencia, 431–34; Philippi, "Historia del Museo Nacional de Chile," 16, 25, 34–35; Rodríguez Villegas, *Museo Histórico Nacional*, 16, 26; Tello and Mejía Zesspe, *Historia de los museos*, 49–50; and Orellana Rodríguez, *Historia de la arqueología en Chile*, 53, 76, 126–27.

109. Torre Tagle, 2 April 1822, *Obra de gobierno*, ed. Puente Candamo, 322; and Government circular, 8 April 1826, in Oviedo, ed., *Colección de leyes*, 9:98–99. The 1826 documents referred only to a "museum"; it appears not to have acquired the title of Museo Nacional until the 1830s, although for the next decade legislation referred with equal frequency to the Museo de Historia Natural. See Legislation of 3 June 1836, 6 June 1836, 16 April 1839, 27 Oct.

1840, 1 March 1841, and 26 Sept. 1845, all in Oviedo, ed., *Colección de leyes*, 9:100–2, 104–5, 106, 196–98, 108, respectively.

110. Fuentes, *Sketches of the Capital of Peru*, 53; Marcoy, *A Journey*, 1:92; Hutchinson, *Two Years in Peru*, 1:319, 333–34; Philippi, "Algo sobre las momias peruanas"; and Tello and Mejía Zesspe, *Historia de los museos nacionales del Perú*, 7–33, 40–42.

111. Tello and Mejía Zesspe, *Historia de los museos*, 59–69.

112. Ibid., 71; and Basadre, *Historia de la República del Perú*, 15:319–21.

113. Brine, *Travels*, 184.

114. Rubín de la Borbolla and Cerezo, *Guatemala*, 12–13, 29–31, 34, 43–49.

115. Ventura García Calderón, "La momia," *La venganza del cóndor*, 1924, *Obras escogidas*, 406 (for quote; my emphasis); Martí, "Las ruinas indias," *La edad de oro*, 1:2, 1889, *Obras*, 1:123; Darío, "Exposición colombiana: Costa Rica," *Obras completas*, 1:731; and Batres Jáuregui, *Los indios*, 20.

116. Restrepo Tirado, *Católogo general*.

117. The Museo de la Plata reopened in a new locale in 1888. For the Museo Público, see Burmeister, *Anales del Museo Público*, 5–6. For the Museo de la Plata see AGN (BA), sala VII, 2998 (Colección Dardo Rocha, leg. 298); Francisco Moreno to Vicente Quesada, 8 June 1877, González, *Obras*, 14:132–36; Decreto de Vicente Quesada, Buenos Aires, 13 Nov. 1877; and Francisco Moreno to Oficina de Estadística de la Provincia de Buenos Aires, La Plata, 24 Oct. 1882, both in AGN (BA), sala VII, leg. 3096 (Archivo Francisco Moreno, leg. 1); Quijada, "Ancestros, ciudadanos, piezas de museo," 28–29; Quijada, "Nación y territorio," 387–88; and Andermann, "Reshaping the Creole Past," 147.

118. Alazraki, "El indigenismo de Martí," 154.

119. Decree by the Intendente Municipal de Buenos Aires, 24 May 1889, cited in Ministerio de Educación de la Nación, *Catálogo del Museo Histórico Nacional*, 1:18.

120. Quesada, *El Museo Histórico Nacional*, 7–19; and Andermann, "Reshaping the Creole Past."

121. Andermann, "Reshaping the Creole Past," 147.

122. Quesada, *El Museo Histórico Nacional*, 7–19.

123. Tello and Mejía Zesspe, *Historia de los museos*, 73.

124. 21 April 1825, *Acuerdos del Congreso de Gobierno de la República de Colombia, 1825–27*, ed. López Domínguez, 1:42, 182–89; and *Gaceta de Colombia*, Bogotá, 5 March 1826.

125. Botero, "The Construction of the Pre-Hispanic Past," 144 (for quote); and Beatríz González, "¿Un museo libre de toda sospecha?" *Museo, memoria y nación*, Memorias del Simposio Internacional, 91.

126. Restrepo Tirado, *Católogo general.*

127. Philippi, "Historia del Museo Nacional de Chile," 19.

128. Rodríguez Villegas, *Museo Histórico Nacional*, 16; Muñoz Hernándes, "Los festejos del centenario," 54; and Schell, "Capturing Chile," 53. For Peru, see Tello and Mejía Zesspe, *Historia de los museos*, 70.

129. Luis Gerardo Morales-Moreno, "History and Patriotism in the National Museum of Mexico," *Museums and the Making of "Ourselves,"* ed. Kaplan, 182.

130. Mayer, *Mexico*, 90–91, 99, 108. See also Calderón de la Barca, *Life in Mexico*, 126, 270; and Elena Isabel Estrada de Gerlero, "La litografía y el Museo Nacional como armas del nacionalismo," *Los pinceles de la historia*, ed. Tovar, Estrada, Uriarte, Hernández Ramírez, and Torre, 160. Argentina's museums likewise possessed colonial artifacts, as did the Museo Histórico del Santa Lucia, which opened in Santiago in 1874. The national museum of Peru housed a series of viceregal portraits. See Francisco Moreno to Oficina de Estadística de la Provincia de Buenos Aires, La Plata, 24 Oct. 1882, AGN (BA), sala VII, leg. 3096 (Archivo Francisco Moreno, leg. 1); Quesada, *El Museo Histórico Nacional*, 7–19; Vicuña Mackenna, *Católogo*, 9–24; Rodríguez Villegas, *Museo Histórico Nacional*, 20; and Tello and Mejía Zesspe, *Historia de los museos*, 8–9.

131. *Gaceta de Colombia*, Bogotá, 12 June 1825; *Gaceta de Colombia*, Bogotá, 4 Sept. 1825; and König, *En el camino*, 384–85. The Colombian national museum was not alone in claiming to possess Pizarro's standard. When the Argentine liberal Juan Bautista Alberdi visited José de San Martín in Paris, he described seeing "the famous standard of Pizarro" in the general's house (interview with José de San Martín, Paris, 14 Sept. 1843, Alberdi, *Autobiografía*, 244–45).

132. Restrepo Tirado, *Católogo general.*

133. Ramírez, *Discurso pronunciado el día 27 de setiembre de 1856*, 6. See also García Icazbalceta, *Colección de documentos*, 1:vii.

134. Alamán, cited in Pimentel, *La economía política*, 186–87.

135. Mateos, *Discurso*, 7–9 (for quote); Olaguíbel and Mantiel y Duarte, *Discurso*, 7; Payno, *Compendio* 76; Juan de Dios Peza, "En las ruinas de Mitla," *La poesía mexicana*, ed. Pacheco, 335; Francisco Rodríguez ("Tepoztecocanetzin

Calquetzani"), "Bellas artes: Arquitectura y arqueología mexicanas," 1899, *La polémica del arte nacional,* ed. Schávelzon, 154, for Mexico's preconquest ruins as "the sacred relics of a people, a race, a civilization sacrificed in the dawn of their existence, now lost forever in eternity"; Widdifield, *The Embodiment of the National,* 92; and Pimentel, *Memoria sobre las causas que han originado la situación actual de la raza indígena de México y medios de remediarla,* 1864, *Obras,* 3:7.

136. Uricoechea, *Memoria,* 28–29, 32.

137. Mitre, *Las ruinas de Tiahuanaco,* 57 (for quote), 4.

138. Julio Tello, 17 April 1926, in Tello and Mejía Zesspe, *Historia de los museos,* 155.

139. Cúneo-Vidal, *Historia de la civilización peruana,* 10, 54.

140. Martí, "La América," April 1888, *Obras,* 24:302.

141. José María Vigil, "Necesidad y conveniencia de estudiar la historia patria," 1878, *Polémicas y ensayos,* ed. Ortega y Medina, 268. Or see González Campo, *Discurso.*

142. Ventura García Calderón, "Un loable esfuerzo por el arte incaico," 1927, *La polémica del indigenismo,* ed. Aquézolo Castro, 64 (for quote); Riva Agüero, *Carácter de la literatura del Perú,* 118; Kristal, *The Andes Viewed from the City,* 171; De la Cadena, *Indigenous Mestizos,* 66; and Thurner, "Peruvian Genealogies."

143. For the preconquest past as "our past," see the letter of Mariano de Rivero, 24 July 1845; and Discurso de Augusto Leguía, 13 Dec. 1924, both in Tello and Mejía Zesspe, *Historia de los museos,* 21–22, 129–30.

144. Thurner, "Peruvian Genealogies," 141.

CHAPTER 6. *Citizenship and Civilization: The "Indian Problem"*

1. *Congreso Nacional: Diario de Sesiones de la Cámara de Diputados, año 1888,* vol. 1, session of 15 June 1888.

2. Ibid., session of 18 June 1888.

3. Ibid.

4. Nicomedes Antelo, cited in Moreno, *Nicomedes Antelo,* 21.

5. "Guerra fronteriza," *La Prensa,* Buenos Aires, 1 March 1878.

6. *Congreso Nacional: Cámara de Senadores, Sesión de 1875,* session of 22 Sept. 1875 (for quote); and *Congreso Nacional: Diario de Sesiones de la Cámara de Diputados, año 1884,* vol. 2, session of 10 Sept. 1884. In the debate of 13 Sept. 1878 the minister of war explained that "there is thus no proposal to exterminate the race, obeying that law of progress and victory whereby the

weaker race, the race that does not work, must invariably succumb on contact with the more gifted race, the race best fitted for work. . . . Here the Indians disappear not precisely through destruction, but rather through absorption and assimilation, as is demonstrated by the mass of our population, which is largely a mixture of Indian and Spaniard. The executive power cannot therefore have any feelings towards the Indian other than those of benevolence and humanity, so long as he chooses to live under the shelter of our laws and abandons his life of robbery and pillage, and ceases to impede the realization of the great work which is underway" (*Congreso Nacional: Cámara de Diputados, Sesión de 1878*, vol. 2, session of 13. Sept. 1878).

7. *Congreso Nacional: Diario de Sesiones, Cámara de Diputados, año 1878*, vol. 1, session of 14 Aug. 1878; Law 947 of 4 Oct. 1878, in *Congreso Nacional: Cámara de Senadores, Sesión de 1878; Congreso Nacional: Cámara de Senadores, Sesión de 1879*, sessions of 5 May, 23 Aug., 26 Aug. 1879; *Congreso Nacional: Diario de Sesiones de la Cámara de Diputados, año 1884*, vol. 1, session of 9 Sept. 1884; *Congreso Nacional: Diario de Sesiones, Cámara de Senadores, Sesión de 1884*, session of 11 Sept. 1884; Mónica Quijada, "Indígenas: Violencia, tierras y ciudadanía," *Homogeneidad y nación*, ed. Quijada, Bernand, and Schneider; and Navarro Floria, "El salvaje y su tratamiento." See also Zeballos, *La conquista de quince mil leguas*, 296–97, 300; Olascoaga, *La conquête de la Pampa*, ix, xii-xiii, 3; and Walther, *La conquista del desierto*, 535–36. Even newspapers that criticized the treatment of survivors agreed that the campaign had been a triumph over savagery. See, for example, *La América del Sur*, Buenos Aires, 29, 30 Jan. 1879, 9, 27, 28 Feb. 1879, 7, 20 March 1879.

8. López, *Historia de la República Argentina*, 1:209–10. López here refers explicitly to the Spanish conquest, and implicitly to the recently completed conquest of the desert. (López, *Historia de la República Argentina*, vol. 1, preface, contains repeated comparisons of the sixteenth-century conquest to the conquest of the desert.)

9. Chueco, *La República Argentina*, 1:6.

10. Barros, "Memorial especial del Ministro de la Guerra," 1877, *Indios, fronteras y seguridad interior*, 357–58.

11. Batres Jáuregui, *Los indios*, 19, 177, 188.

12. Mera cited in Cometta, *El indio en la poesía*, 166–69.

13. Thurner, "Peruvian Genealogies," 146.

14. Thurner, *From Two Republics to One Divided*; Thurner, "Peruvian Genealogies"; and Méndez-Gastelumendi, "Incas Sí, Indios No." See also Riva

Agüero, *Carácter de la literatura del Perú,* 118; de la Cadena, *Indigenous Mestizos,* 66; Matto de Turner, *Aves sin nido,* 44; González Prada, "Discurso en el Politeama," 1888, and "Nuestros indios," 1904, both in *Páginas libres/ Horas de lucha,* 46, 340–41; and, for an overview of elite attitudes toward the indigenous population, see Kristal, *The Andes Viewed from the City.* For comparable comments from Bolivia, see Vargas, *Indicaciones económicas,* 2–5, 35; Irurozqui, "The Sound of the Pututos," 109; and Moreno, *Nicomedes Antelo,* 16 (for Bolivia's indigenous population as "an archaic race . . . which forgets even the names of its gods").

15. Méndez-Gastelumendi, "Incas Sí, Indios No," 209.

16. Ibid., 210.

17. Session of 23 April 1824, *Santander y el Congreso de 1824,* ed. Ocampo López, 1:115 (for quotes); session of 31 Jan. 1825, and Session of 11 Jan. 1825, both in *Santander y el Congreso de 1825,* ed. Ocampo López, 1:247, 4:57 (for quotes); Memoria del vice-presidente Santander, 15 Jan. 1821, and José Manuel Restrepo, 27 April 1824, both in *Administraciones de Santander,* ed. López Domínguez, 1:10–11, 26, 249; Safford, "Race, Integration and Progress," 12, 16; and James Sanders, "Belonging to the Great Granadan Family: Partisan Struggle and the Construction of Indigenous Identity and Politics in Southwestern Colombia, 1849–1890," *Race and Nation,* ed. Appelbaum, Macpherson, and Rosemblatt, 60–61.

18. Codazzi, "Antigüedades indígenas," 2:434–39; Ancízar, *Perigrinación de Alpha,* 26; Isaacs, *Estudio,* 17, 202–3; and Safford, "Race, Integration, and Progress," 25.

19. Plaza, *Memorias,* vi-viii (for quote); José Joaquín Ortíz, "Al Tequendama," *La guirnalda,* segunda serie, ed. Ortíz, 61; König, *En el camino,* 472; and Botero, "The Construction of the Pre-Hispanic Past," 60–61.

20. Groot, *Historia eclesiástica y civil,* 1:229–30; Vergara y Vergara, *Historia de la literatura,* 70; Caro, "La conquista," 397; Botero, "The Construction of the Pre-Hispanic Past," 102, 111; Ley 89, 25 Nov, 1890, *Legislación indigenista de Colombia,* ed. García, 64–69; and Appelbaum, *Muddied Waters,* 110, 159, 170.

21. Mora, *Méjico y sus revoluciones,* 1:61 (for quote), 3; Mora, "Reacción servil del General Santa Ana," 1837, *Obras sueltas,* 152; Zavala, *Ensayo,* 11–13; and Hale, *Mexican liberalism,* 215–47.

22. "Guerra de castas," *El Siglo XIX,* Mexico City, 8 July 1848 (for quote), 18 Sept. 1849.

23. Ramírez, "Instrucción pública," 1868, *Obras,* 2:183 (for quote); Payno, *Compendio,* 76; and Vázquez de Knauth, *Nacionalismo y educación,* 42. For

the views of moderate conservatives, see Pimentel, *Memoria,* 10, 195, 198–99, 226; and Rozat, *Los orígenes de la nación,* 219.

24. Julio Zárate, "La raza indígena," *El Siglo XIX,* Mexico City, 2 Dec. 1870, 1. Note that Zárate describes preconquest indigenes as his grandfathers but places himself and contemporary indigenous people in completely different categories. The Aztecs may have been his ancestors but contemporary *indios* were not his brothers. See also L. Agontía, "La academia nacional de San Carlos en 1877," 1878, *La crítica del arte,* ed. Rodríguez Prampolini, 2:410; Keen, *The Aztec Image,* 416–17; and Rozat, *Los orígenes de la nación,* 253–61.

25. Vázquez de Knauth, *Nacionalismo y educación,* 100.

26. Luis de la Breña, "Discurso," 1893, García Quintana, *Cuauhtémoc en el siglo XIX,* 107.

27. Joseph, *Rediscovering the Past,* 25–26; and Hale, *Mexican Liberalism,* 240–41.

28. Taracena, *Invención criolla,* 221; Alda Mejías, *La participación indígena,* 134, 138; and Joaquín Arellano al público, 2 April 1838; Carlos Salazar a sus conciudadanos, 22 Aug. 1838; Mariano Rivera Paz a la División de Sacatepeques, Guatemala, 8 Sept. 1838; and Carlos Salazar, Parte circunstanciado, 17 Sept. 1838; all in Benson Library, Taracena Flores Collection, docs 9908, 9927, 9930, 9931, respectively.

29. Palmer, "A Liberal Discipline," 179 (for quote); Decree of 6 Sept. 1879, Acuerdo de 9 Feb. 1880, Acuerdo de 4 Jan. 1881, Decree of 10 Oct. 1892, Decree of 23 Oct. 1893, all in *Legislación indígenista de Guatemala,* ed. Skinner-Klée, 42–43, 45, 49; Casaus Arzú, "Los proyectos de integración social," 779, 787, 794–95, 807; and Shelton Davis, "Agrarian Structure and Ethnic Resistance: The Indian in Guatemalan and Salvadoran National Politics," *Ethnicities and Nations,* ed. Guidieri, Pellizzi, and Tamiah, 80–81.

30. Montúfar, *Reseña histórica,* 1:xii; and Spínola, *Discurso,* n.p. (for quotes); and Rodríguez Beteta, *Discurso,* 15 Sept. 1924.

31. Juan Fermín Aycinena, "El indio," *Parnaso guatemalteca,* ed. Porta Mencos, 187–91 (for quote); Batres Jáuregui, *Los indios,* xi (for the Maya as "an orphan people who have lost even the memory of their glories"), 24, 177; and González Campo, *Discuros.*

32. Carrillo, *Discurso,* n.p. For Nicaragua, see Gould, *To Die in This Way,* 13, 26, 37–38, 48–50, 159.

33. Medina, *Los aborígenes de Chile,* 46–47, 58.

34. Vicuña Mackenna, "Primer discurso sobre la pacificación de Arauco," 9 Aug. 1868, and Vicuña Mackenna, "Tercer discurso sobre la pacificación de

Arauco," 12 Aug. 1868, both in *Obras*, 12:400, 407–8 (for quotes), 419–20, respectively. See also Lastarria, *Investigaciones*, 77; *El Mercurio*, Valparaíso, 10 May 1859, 27 May 1859, 30 May 1859, 7 June 1859; and Boccara and Seguel-Boccara, "Políticas indígenas," 749, 754–55.

35. For views that the Mapuche were potentially civilizable, see Amunátegui, *Descubrimiento i conquista*, 526; Amunátegui, "Discurso pronunciado . . . el 13 de set. de 1864," *Obras*, 1:29, 32; and Cuadra, *Ocupación y civilización*, 7–8, 29. For negative assessment, see "La conquista de Arauco," *El Mercurio*, Valparaíso, 24 May 1859; "La civilización y la barbarie," *El Mercurio*, Valparaíso, 25 June 1859; Mónica Quijada, "¿Qué nación? Dinámicas y disotomías de la nación en el imaginario hispanoamericano del siglo XIX," *Imaginar la nación*, ed. Guerra and Quijada, 46–47; Pinto Rodríguez, "Del antiindigenismo al pro-indigenismo," 147–49; and Pinto Rodríguez, "Mapuche, colonos nacionales y colonos extranjeros."

36. Shumway, *The Invention of Argentina*, 134, 141; and Sarmiento, *Facundo*, 9–10, 12, 54–55, 126, 134.

37. Sarmiento, "La expedición al Río Negro," *El Nacional*, Buenos Aires, 17 April 1879, *Obras*, 41:329. Similar views are expressed in Sarmiento's other journalistic writings for *El Nacional* in 1879. See also Navarro Floria, "Sarmiento y la frontera sur."

38. *Congreso Nacional: Diario de Sesiones de la Cámara de Diputados, año 1885*, vol. 1, session of 15 July 1885.

39. *El Siglo XIX*, Mexico City, 3 Feb. 1881.

40. Decree of 10 Oct. 1892, *Legislación indígenista de Guatemala*, ed. Skinner-Klée, 45.

41. Batres Jáuregui, *Los indios;* and Shelton Davis, "Agrarian Structure and Ethnic Resistance: The Indian in Guatemalan and Salvadoran National Politics," *Ethnicities and Nations*, ed. Guidieri, Pellizzi, and Tamiah, 78–79 (for quote). Batres Jáuregui also suggested that indigenous people might adopt Western clothes and abandon their native languages (Batres Jáuregui, *Los indios*, 177, 186–88).

42. José Manuel Restrepo, Memorias del secretario de estado y del despacho del interior, Unsigned Memoria, José Manuel Restrepo, Exposición . . . del secretario de estado del . . . interior, 2 Jan. 1826, José Manuel Restrepo, 16 Feb. 1827, José María del Castillo, 12 May 1827, and Alejandro Vélez, 2 March 1833, all in *Administraciones de Santander*, ed. López Domínguez, 1:10–11, 79, 111, 2:26–27, 295–96, 3:147 (for quote); Session of 4 Oct. 1821, *Actas del Congreso de Cúcuta, 1821*, ed. Restrepo Piedrahita, 201; T[omás]

C[ipriano de] Mosquera, "Indíjenas," *Gaceta de Colombia,* 9 Nov. 1828; and Safford, "Race, Integration and Progress," 12.

43. Memoria del vice-presidente Santander, 15 Jan. 1821, *Administraciones de Santander,* ed. López Domínguez, 1:10–11, 26 (for quote).

44. Decree of Juan José Flores, Quito, 16 Jan. 1832, and Decree of Congreso Constitucional del Estado del Ecuador, Quito, 5 Oct. 1833, both in *Legislación indigenista del Ecuador,* ed. Rubio Orbe, 25–27 (for quote), 27–28. For Bolivian examples, see Tristan Platt, "The Andean Experience of Bolivian Liberalism, 1825–1900: Roots of Rebellion in Nineteenth-Century Chayanta (Potosí)," *Resistance, Rebellion, and Consciousness,* ed. Stern, 286; and Vargas, *Indicaciones económicas,* 2. For 1820s Mexico, see *El Sol,* Mexico City, 9 March 1824; and *El Aguila Mexicana,* Mexico City, 3 April 1826, 28 Aug. 1826.

45. Ancízar, *Perigrinación de Alpha,* 26 (for quote); Safford, "Race, Integration and Progress," 25; "Alpha" [presumably Manuel Ancízar], Introduction to Pérez, *Gonzalo Pizarro,* vii; and König, *En el camino,* 472.

46. Zavala, *Ensayo,* 1:12–13 (for quote), 15; and Hale, *Mexican Liberalism,* 219–21, 237–38.

47. Mora, *Méjico y sus revoluciones,* 1: 59–68, 187, 196 (for quote); and [José María Luis Mora?], Población de la República Mexicana," and [José María Luis Mora?], "Sobre la administración de Méjico bajo el régimen español," both in *El Indicador de la Federación Mexicana,* Mexico City, 4 Dec. 1833, 12 Feb. 1834.

48. Díaz Covarrubias, *Discurso.* (He also blamed mistakes made under republican rule.) Or see Rosa, *Discurso,* 26, 36.

49. Sierra, "México social y político, apuntes para un libro," 1889, *Obras,* 9:126 (for quote); and Rozat, *Los orígenes de la nación,* 414.

50. Widdifield, *The Embodiment of the National,* 142 (for quote); and Saldaña, *Discurso,* 7.

51. Decree of 6 Sept. 1879, *Legislación indígenista de Guatemala,* ed. Skinner-Klée, 42 (for quote); Salazar, *Discurso;* Batres Jáuregui, *La América Central,* 1:444; and Palmer, "A Liberal Discipline," 179.

52. Thurner, *From Two Republics to One Divided,* 11 (for quote), 44, 132. See also Pesce, *Indígenas e inmigrantes,* 29; Kristal, *The Andes Viewed from the City,* 40–41; Gootenberg, *Imagining Development,* 196–97 (for a different interpretation of Luis Carranza's views); and de la Cadena, *Indigenous Mestizos,* 66.

53. López, *Les races aryennes,* 15 (for quote); and López, *Historia de la República Argentina,* 5:548, 563–64.

54. Posada Gutiérrez, *Memorias*, 1:99; and Hale, *Mexican Liberalism*, 241–44.

55. Groot, *Historia eclesiástica y civil*, 1:229–30.

56. Kristal, *The Andes Viewed from the City*; Bustamante, *Los indios del Perú* (for a critique that places blame equally on local officials and the army); and Pesce, *Indígenas e inmigrantes*, 31–33.

57. Guerrero, *La semántica de la dominación*, 56–57; and Williams, "Popular Liberalism," 698, 706, 708–9.

58. For suggestions that a more European diet would improve indigenous well-being, see Sierra, "México social y político, apuntes para un libro," 1889, *Obras*, 9:126; and Bulnes, *El porvenir de las naciones latinoamericanas*, 19–20.

59. González La Rosa, *Informe*, 16–17, 32.

60. For Bolivian, Mexican, Guatemalan, and Ecuadorian examples, see Irurozqui, "La guerra de civilización," 415; Pimentel, *Memoria*, 226; Watanabe, "Culturing Identities," 330; and Williams, "Popular Liberalism," 729.

61. *El Pájaro Verde*, Mexico City, 4 March 1873.

62. Moreno, *Nicomedes Antelo*, 22. See also Demelas, "Darwinismo a la criolla"; and Quijada, "En torno al pensamiento racial."

63. Zulawski, "Hygiene and 'The Indian Problem,'" 118.

64. Francisco García Calderón, *Obras escogidas*, 2:92.

65. Mónica Quijada, "¿Qué nación? Dinámicas y disotomías de la nación en el imaginario hispanoamericano del siglo XIX," *Imaginar la nación*, ed. Guerra and Quijada; and Mónica Quijada, "El paradigma de la homogenie-dad," *Homogeneidad y nación*, Quijada, Bernand, and Schneider, 47–51.

66. Andrés Guerrero, "El proceso de identificación: Sentido común ciudadano, ventriloquia y transescritura," *Pueblos, comunidades y municipios*, ed. Escobar Ohmstede, Falcón, and Buve, 35 (for quote; my emphasis), 61n.34.

67. Bando de Juan Angel Bujando, Cuzco, 25 July 1833, Archivo Regional del Cuzco, Tesorería Fiscal, legajo 316: Bandos, años 1814–1836.

68. Bertoni, *Patriotas, cosmopolitas y nacionalistas*, 207.

69. Alda Mejías, *La participación indígena*, 190. Somewhat similar interpretations are set forth by Appelbaum, Macpherson, and Rosemblatt, in their introduction to *Race and Nation*, 4–5.

70. Juan Egaña, Proyecto de Constitución para el Estado de Chile, 1811, arts. 65–66, 78–80, *Sesiones de los cuerpos legislativos de la República de Chile*, ed. Letelier, vol. 1. See also Reglamento Constitucional Provisional, 27 Oct. 1812, art. 24, in the same volume.

71. Constitución de la República de Cundinamarca Reformada, 17 April 1812, "De los derechos del hombre," art. 24, *Constituciones de Colombia*, ed.

Pombo and Guerra, 2:8. See also Constitución del Estado de Mariquita, 1815, tit. xxiii, art. 1, in the same volume.

72. *Constitución de las Provincias Unidas en Sud-América,* sec. 2, cap. 2, art. cxxviii.

73. For Mexico, see Sentimientos de la Nación, Chilpancingo, 31 Oct. 1814, *El Congreso de Anáhuac,* 15; Iturbide, *Plan del Señor Don Agustín de Iturbide,* art. 12 (this is listed as article 13 in Iturbide, *Proclama*); Reglamento Provisional Político del Imperio Mexicano, 18 Dec. 1822, sec. 1, art. 7, *Leyes fundamentales de México,* ed. Tena Ramírez; and Bases de gobierno decreed by Soberano Congreso Constituyente Mexicano, 24 Dec. 1822, Benson Library, Taracena Flores collection, box 1, doc. 10562.

74. Martínez Sarasola, *Nuestros paisanos los indios,* 156, 157; and Mónica Quijada, "Imaginando la homogeneidad: La alquimia de la tierra," *Homogeneidad y nación,* Quijada, Bernand, and Schneider, 196.

75. Resolution of Senate, 26 Feb. 1819, *Sesiones de los cuerpos legislativos,* ed. Letelier, vol. 2; and Encina, *Historia de Chile,* 8:40.

76. Castillo, *Al heróico pueblo de Guatemala.*

77. See García Belaúnde, ed., *Constituciones del Perú;* Pombo and Guerra, eds., *Constituciones de Colombia; El Congreso de Anáhuac; Constitución de las Provincias Unidas en Sud-América;* Mariñas Otero, ed., *Las constituciones de Venezuela;* García Belaúnde, ed., *Constituciones del Perú;* Restrepo Piedrahita, ed., *Actas el Congreso de Cúcuta;* Letelier, ed., *Sesiones de los cuerpos legislativos;* Gallardo, ed., *Las constituciones de la República Federal de Centro-América;* Mariñas Otero., ed., *Las constituciones del Guatemala; Constitución de la República Argentina;* Trigo, ed., *Las constituciones del Bolivia; Constitución para la República Peruana;* Trabucco, ed., *Constituciones de la República del Ecuador; Constitución Política de la República de Chile;* and Tena Rodríguez, ed., *Leyes fundamentales de México.* I am aware of only one only postindependence Spanish American constitution that offered different definitions of citizenship for Indians and non-Indians. In the Peruvian Constitution of 1839 citizens are defined as literate Peruvians either married or over the age of twenty-five, "with the exception of Indians and mestizos," for whom the literacy requirement was postponed until 1844 in areas lacking primary schools (Constitución Política de la República Peruana, 10 Nov. 1839, títs. III-IV, in *Constituciones del Perú,* ed. García Belaúnde, 240).

78. Constitución de la República del Ecuador Sancionada por la Convención Reunida en Cuenca, 1845, tít. 1, sec. 2, art. 5, tít. 2, arts. 9–12, *Constituciones de la República del Ecuador,* ed. Trabucco, 96–98.

79. Alda Mejías, *La participación indígena,* offers a helpful discussion of the impact of changing definitions of the electorate on indigenous access to political rights in the case of Guatemala. See also Sábato, ed., *Ciudadanía política.*

80. Walker, *Smoldering Ashes,* 194. See also Kristal, *The Andes Viewed from the City,* 40–41; and Thurner, *From Two Republics to One Divided,* 1.

81. Bustamante, *Los indios del Perú,* 8 (for quote), 84; and Demélas, *L'invention politique,* 362. See also Francisco García Calderón, *Obras escogidas,* 1:256; Luna, "El 'civilismo' y la sociedad nacional peruana," 76; Kristal, *The Andes Viewed from the City,* 173; Méndez, "Incas Sí, Indios No," 206; and Larson, *Trials of Nation Making,* 164.

82. Andrés Guerrero, "Una imágen ventrilocua: El discurso liberal de la 'desgraciada raza indígena' a fines del siglo XIX," *Imágenes e imagineros,* ed. Muratorio, 209–10; Guerrero, *La semántica de la dominación,* 56–57; and Andrés Guerrero, "El proceso de identificación: Sentido común ciudadano, ventriloquia y transescritura," *Pueblos, comunidades y municipios,* ed. Escobar Ohmstede, Falcón, and Buve. See also Peña, "Etnicidad, ciudadanía y cambio agrario," 44; and for Colombian examples, Vergara y Vergara, *Historia de la literatura,* 70; and Safford, "Race, Integration and Progress," 12, 16.

83. Literacy and/or property requirements were included only in the constitutions of 1839, 1861, 1871, and 1878. Domestic service also invalidated citizenship; see *Las constituciones del Bolivia,* ed. Trigo.

84. See Platt, "Liberalism and Ethnocide"; Tristan Platt, "The Andean Experience of Bolivian Liberalism, 1825–1900: Roots of Rebellion in Nineteenth-Century Chayanta (Potosí)," *Resistance, Rebellion, and Consciousness,* ed. Stern; Irurozqui, "The Sound of the Pututos"; and Irurozqui, "Las paradojas de la tributación."

85. Orden 24 de nov. de 1882, cited in Irurozqui, "Las paradojas de la tributación," 734. Vargas, writing some decades earlier, agreed that patriotism was "completely unknown to this unfortunate race," although he felt that performing military service would help develop this sentiment (Vargas, *Indicaciones económicas,* 34–35).

86. Irurozqui, "Las paradojas de la tributación," 730–31; Irurozqui, "Ebrios, vagos y analfabetos," 726; and Irurozqui, "La guerra de civilización," 424. See also Moreno, *Nicomedes Antelo,* 22–23.

87. López, *Historia de la República Argentina,* 5:548, 563–64; and for examples of inconclusive discussions about whether Indians could be citizens, *Congreso Nacional: Diario de Sesiones de la Cámara de Diputados, año 1885,*

vol. 1, sessions of 19 Aug. 1885 and 24 Aug. 1885. Or see Alberdi, *Autobiografía*, 120.

88. See Mónica Quijada, "Indígenas: Violencia, tierras y ciudadanía," *Homogeneidad y nación*, ed. Quijada, Bernand, and Schneider; and Barros, "Memorial especial del Ministro de la Guerra," 1877, *Indios, fronteras y seguridad interior*, 357–58. For examples from Chile, see Boccara and Seguel-Boccara, "Políticas indígenas," 749–55; and Vicuña Mackenna, "Quinto discurso sobre la pacificación de Arauco," 1 Sept. 1864 (presumably actually 1868), *Obras*, 12:435.

89. Taracena, *invención criolla*, 322, 372.

90. Ibid., 373–74.

91. Alda Mejías, *La participación indígena*, 26 (for quote), 27, 109, 134, 138. See also Palmer, "A Liberal Discipline," 188; and Asturias, "El problema social del indio," 1923, *El problema social del indio*, 60: "The Indian is unaware that Guatemala is a republic and is unaware of his rights and obligations as a citizen."

92. *Diario de Centroamérica*, 1920, cited in Casaus Arzú, "Los proyectos de integración social del indio," 807 (for quote); and Grandin, *Blood of Guatemala*, 130.

93. "Guerra de castas," *El Siglo XIX*, Mexico City, 8 July 1848. For pre-Reform liberal views, see also Mora, *Méjico y sus revoluciones*, 1:66, 196; [José María Luis Mora?], "Población de la República Mexicana," and [José María Luis Mora?], "Sobre la administración de Méjico bajo el régimen español," both in *El Indicador de la Federación Mexicana*, Mexico City, 4 Dec. 1833, 12 Feb. 1834; and Hale, *Mexican Liberalism*, 223. For conservative views, see *El Omnibus*, Mexico City, 28 Feb. 1852, 24 June 1852; and *Diario de Avisos*, Mexico City, 21 Oct. 1857. Only occasionally did conservative newspapers depict indigenous men as functioning members of Mexican civil society; for an example, see *El Pájaro Verde*, Mexico City, 30 Jan. 1867.

94. Flores, *Oración*, 15 (for quote); J. M. del Castillo Velasco, "Oración cívica pronunciada en la Alameda de México el 16 de septiembre de 1850," *Discursos pronunciados el 16 de septiembre de 1850*, 15; and Meyer, *Problemas campesinos*, 28.

95. Ramírez, "Congreso Constituyente: Discurso pronunciado en la sesión del 7 de julio de 1856," *Obras*, 1:190.

96. Ramírez, "Instrucción Pública," 1868, *Obras*, 2:183. See also Gómez Flores, *Discurso*, 4; and Hale, *The Transformation of Liberalism*, 238.

97. Faustino Estrada, "Discurso," 1894, García Quintana, *Cuauhtémoc en el siglo XIX*, 123 (for quote); Orozco y Berro, *Historia antigua*, 4:579–82; and Gamio, *Forjando patria*, 171.

98. Grandin, *Blood of Guatemala*, 130, 140–41, 165–66. See also Alda Mejías, *La participación indígena*, chapters 6–8; and Watanabe, "Culturing Identities," 331.

99. Guy Thomson, "Memoria y memorias de la intervención europea en la Sierra de Puebla, 1868–1991," *Pueblos, comunidades y municipios*, ed. Escobar Ohmstede, Falcón, and Buve, 153. See also Thomson with LaFrance, *Patriotism, Politics and Popular Liberalism;* and Florencia Mallon, *Peasant and Nation.*

100. Thurner, *From Two Republics to One Divided*, 99–136, 150–52; and legislation of 15 Oct. 1887, *Leyes y resoluciones expedidas por los congresos ordinarios y extraordinarios de 1887*, ed. Aranda, 191–92.

101. James Sanders, "Belonging to the Great Granadan Family: Partisan Struggle and the Construction of Indigenous Identity and Politics in Southwestern Colombia, 1849–1890," *Race and Nation*, ed. Appelbaum, Macpherson, and Rosemblatt, 61–66, (62 for quote); and Sanders, *Contentious Republicans*, 35–43.

102. See, for example, Tristan Platt, "The Andean Experience of Bolivian Liberalism, 1825–1900: Roots of Rebellion in Nineteenth-Century Chayanta (Potosí)," *Resistance, Rebellion, and Consciousness*, ed. Stern.

103. Cynthia Radding, "Naciones y territorios indígenas frente al Estado en el noreste de México y el oriente de Bolivia, siglo XIX," *Pueblos, comunidades y municipios*, ed. Escobar Ohmstede, Falcón, and Buve, 115.

104. For examples from the first decades of independence, see Grandin, *The Blood of Guatemala*, 72; letter to José Manuel Goyaneche, 10 Oct. 1812, AGI, Diversos 2 (which refers to the collection of tribute "in those places where the Indians have asked to pay it"); and Decree of Bolívar, Bogotá, 15 Oct. 1828, *Legislación indigenista del Ecuador*, ed. Rubio Orbe, 20–25.

105. *El Aguila Mexicana*, Mexico City, 3 April 1826, 28 Aug. 1826; Sr. San Ramon, *Congreso Nacional: Cámara de Diputados, Sesión de 1878*, vol. 2, session of 13 Sept. 1878; and *El Siglo XIX*, Mexico City, 3 Feb. 1881, respectively.

106. Rafael Arévalo Martínez, *Manuel Adano* (1922), cited in Lorand de Olazagasti, *El indio en la narrativa guatemalteca*, 40.

107. Boccara and Seguel-Boccara, "Políticas indígenas," 742.

108. Peña, "Etnicidad, ciudadanía y cambio agrario," 44.

109. Maqueo Castellanos, *Algunos problemas nacionales*, 78, 83. See also Meyer, *Problemas campesinos*, 28; and Powell, "Mexican Intellectuals and the Indian Question," 27.

110. Pimentel, *Memoria sobre las causas que han originado la situación actual de la raza indígena de México y medios de remediarla,* 1864, *Obras,* 3:133. See also José María Vigil, "Necesidad y conveniencia de estudiar la historia patria," 1878, in *Polémicas y ensayos,* ed. Ortega y Medina, 268; Maqueo Castellanos, *Algunos problemas nacionales,* 68.

111. Palmer, "A Liberal Discipline," 174 (for quote); Batres Jáuregui, *Los indios,* 155, 200; Asturias, "El problema social del indio," 1923, *El problema social del indio,* 37; and González Campo, *Discurso.* For Nicaragua, see Gould, "Gender, Politics, and the Triumph of *Mestizaje*," 18–19.

112. Palma, *Cartas a Piérola,* 20.

113. González Prada, *El tonel de Diógenes,* 220 (for quote); González Prada, "Discurso en el Politeama," 1888, and "Nuestros indios," 1904, both in *Páginas libres/Horas de lucha,* 44, 342, respectively. For a reinterpretation of indigenous nationalism in late-nineteenth-century Peru, see Florencia Mallon, "Nationalist and Antistate Coalitions in the War of the Pacific: Junín and Cajamarca, 1879–1902," *Resistance, Rebellion, and Consciousness,* ed. Stern.

114. Taracena, *Invención criolla,* 306–7.

115. Cited in Hale, *The Transformation of Liberalism,* 224.

116. Vicuña Mackenna, "Segundo discurso sobre la pacificación de Arauco," 11 Aug. 1868, *Obras,* 12:414.

CHAPTER 7. *Indigenismo: The Return of the Native?*

1. Villoro, *Los grandes momentos,* esp. 235–37.

2. Stabb, "Indigenism and Racism," 405.

3. For discussion of literary indigenismo, see Cowie, *El indio;* Casey, *Indigenismo,* chapter 4; Cornejo Polar, *Literatura y sociedad;* and Kristal, *The Andes Viewed from the City.*

4. Mariátegui, "The Problem of the Indian," 1928, *Seven Interpretive Essays.*

5. Dawson similarly argues that Mexican indigenistas "connected the living Indians to that past, and acclaimed them for the first time as an integral part of the modern nation." See Dawson, "From Models of the Nation," 279–80.

6. Eder, "Las imágenes de lo prehispánico," 76. See also Friedlander, *Being Indian,* xiv.

7. Hale, *The Transformation of Liberalism,* 260. This view of the Mexican case is shared by Knight, "Racism, Revolution, and *Indigenismo.*"

8. Thurner, *From Two Republics to One Divided,* 12.

9. Dávalos y Lissón, *La primera centuria,* 1: introduction.

10. Tord, *El indio en los ensayistas*, 56. See also Mega, "Prológo," i; José Carlos Mariátegui, "El problema primario del Perú," *Mundial*, Lima, 1924, special edition for the centenary of the Battle of Ayacucho; José Carlos Mariátegui, "Peruanicemos al Perú," *Mundial*, Lima, 9 Oct. 1925; Valcárcel, *Tempestad en los Andes*, 118; Luis Carranza, "El problema indígena," *Amauta*, 2:10 (Dec. 1927); *La polémica del indigenismo*, ed. Aquézolo Castro; and Pease, *Peru*, 3:106.

11. Valcárcel, *Tempestad en los Andes*, 23 (for quote), 111.

12. These are discussed in Tord, *El indio en los ensayistas*, 146–52; and Kristal, *The Andes Viewed from the City*, 22–24. See also Casimiro Rado, "Estatutos del Grupo Resurgimiento," 1926, *El Proceso del Gamonalismo*, 1:1 (Jan. 1927), 2, in *Amauta*, 2:5 (Jan. 1927).

13. Others included *Boletín Titikaka, Inti, Inca, Wira Cocha*, and *Chasqui*; see Tord, *El indio en los ensayistas*, 153–59.

14. Rama, "El area cultural andina, 147–51; and Cornejo Polar, *Literatura y sociedad*, 14, 16.

15. De la Cadena, *Indigenous Mestizos*, 87–130.

16. Klarén, *Peru*, 241–55.

17. Tord, *El indio en los ensayistas*, 149–50.

18. Constitution of 1920, arts. 41, 58, *Constituciones del Perú*, ed. García Belaúnde, 351, 353.

19. Chevalier, "Official *Indigenismo*," 186; and Tord, *El indio en los ensayistas*, 149–50.

20. Decreto Supremo of 23 May 1930, Tord, *El indio en los ensayistas*, 163.

21. Molina Enríquez, *Los grandes problemas nacionales*, introduction.

22. Gamio, *Forjando patria*, 9. Or see Maqueo Castellanos, *Algunos problemas nacionales*, 68, 78, 83.

23. An example is the Indianist Society of Mexico formed in 1910 by Francisco Belmar; see Powell, "Mexican Intellectuals," 33.

24. Moisés Sáenz, 1928, cited in Vaughan, *Cultural Politics in Revolution*, 28.

25. Dawson, "From Models for the Nation," 286 n.30; and Dawson, "'Wild Indians.'"

26. Dawson, "From Models for the Nation," 279 (for quote), 80.

27. Ibid., 291 n.54. See also Knight, "Racism, Revolution, and *Indigenismo*," 79–83.

28. López, "The India Bonita Contest," 295.

29. Vaughan, *Cultural Politics in Revolution*, 29, 45; and Becker, *Setting the Virgin on Fire*, 71–73.

30. Dawson, "From Models for the Nation," 295–305.

31. Gamio, *Introducción, síntesis y conclusiones,* lxxxiii; Brading, "Manuel Gamio," 81–82; César Antonio Ugarte, "El comunismo de los antiguos peruanos," *Mundial,* Lima, Aug. 1921; Valcárcel, "La vida económica," 1922, *Del ayllu al imperio,* 166–87; Mariátegui, "prólogo" to Valcárcel, *Tempestad en los Andes,* 10; and Mariátegui, "The Problem of Land," *Seven Interpretive Essays,* 74–76.

32. Brian Hamnett, "Los pueblos indios y la defensa de la comunidad en el México independiente, 1824–1884: El caso de Oaxaca," *Pueblos, comunidades y municipios,* ed. Escobar Ohmstede, Falcón, and Buve, 193. See also Sáenz, "Las escuelas rurales," 73; Palacios, "Postrevolutionary Intellectuals," 318; and Dawson, "'Wild Indians,'" 334.

33. Peña, "Etnicidad, ciudadanía y cambio agrario," 41.

34. Doremus, "Indigenismo," 377 (for quote), 387–88.

35. Decree of 24 Dec. 1920, *Legislación indígenista de Guatemala,* ed. Skinner-Klée, 93.

36. Decreto Gubernativo no. 471 and Acuerdo Gubernativo de 20 de enero de 1894, both in *Legislación indígenista de Guatemala,* ed. Skinner-Klée, 49–50, 52–68; Casey, "Indigenismo," 99; and Grandin, *Blood of Guatemala,* 114, 283.

37. Martínez Landero, "Aspectos del indigenismo," 43.

38. Itier, "Le théâtre moderne en Quechua"; and De la Cadena, *Indigenous Mestizos,* 72–78.

39. Other works included José Lucas Caparó Muñoz, *T'itu Q'usñipa* (1896), Nicanor Jara, *Sumaq T'ika* (1898), José María Valle Riestra, *Ollanta* (1900), Daniel Alomía Robles's operas *Illa Cori* (1912) and *El condor pasa* (1913), and Mariano Rodríguez, *Utqha Mayta* (1914). See Tord, *El indio en los ensayistas,* 161–62; Itier, "Le théâtre moderne en Quechua"; and De la Cadena, *Indigenous Mestizos.*

40. For other examples of early-twentieth-century provincial elites dressing as Amerindians, see Poole, "An Image of 'Our Indian,'" 77–78; and Grandin, "Can the Subaltern Be Seen?" 108.

41. De la Cadena, *Indigenous Mestizos,* 78.

42. Itier, "Le théâtre moderne en Quechua," 50, 62, 94–98, 99 (for quote); and Discurso de Augusto Leguía, 13 Dec. 1924, Tello and Mejía Zesspe, *Historia de los museos,* 129–30.

43. Itier, "Le théâtre moderne en Quechua," 81–93, 128, 206; and, for additional comment on the relationship between race, class, and Quechua, see De la Cadena, *Indigenous Mestizos,* 162–65.

44. De la Cadena, *Indigenous Mestizos*, 73.

45. Mendoza, "Crear y sentir lo nuestro."

46. See, for example, Walker, "The Patriotic Society"; and Walker, *Smoldering Ashes*, 103–5.

47. Basadre, *Historia de la República del Perú*, 16:138. Or see Roberto MacLeam Estenós, "El indio está de moda," 1927, *La polémica del indigenismo*, ed. Aquézolo Castro, 106.

48. Zárate, *El Cuzco y sus monumentos*, 9, 77–78; Cosio, *Cuzco*, plates facing pages 14, 19; Santos Chocano, "Resumen de los siete cantos de 'El hombre-sol,'" 1924, *Obras*, 518; Discurso de Augusto Leguía, 13 Dec. 1924, Tello and Mejía Zesspe, *Historia de los museos*, 129–30; García, *Guía histórica-artística*, 5, 25, 34–35; and de la Cadena, *Indigenous Mestizos*, 72.

49. Valcárcel, *Tempestad en los Andes*, 21–22.

50. Luis Alberto Sánchez, "El documento y el hecho en la historia," *Mundial*, Lima, 9 Oct. 1925 (for quote); Tello, *Introducción a la historia antigua del Perú*, 47; and the somewhat comparable comments in Mariátegui, "The Problem of the Indian," 1928, *Seven Interpretive Essays*, 29.

51. Manuel Gamio, "The New Conquest," *Survey*, 1 May 1924, 146. For indigenous decadence around Teotihuacán, see Gamio, *Introducción, síntesis y conclusiones*, xix, lviii, lxxiii, lxxxvi.

52. Gamio, *Introducción, síntesis y conclusiones*, lxxviii.

53. Basadre, *Historia de la República del Perú*, 13:91; Itier, "Le théâtre moderne en Quechua," 63; Sanders, *Nación y tradición*, 169; and De la Cadena, *Indigenous Mestizos*, 98–92.

54. Martínez Riaza, "El Perú y España durante el Oncenio," 349. *Madre patria* means the "mother-fatherland," hence Spain.

55. *Mundial*, Lima, 28 July 1921.

56. Law 4369, 21 Oct. 1921, *Anuario de la legislación peruana*, 16:21–22.

57. Pilcher, *¡Que Vivan los Tamales!* 65 (for quote); Folgarait, *Mural Painting and Social Revolution*, 18; and Elaine Lacy, "The 1921 Centennial Celebration of Mexico's Independence: State Building and Population Negotiation," *¡Viva Mexico!*, ed. Beezley and Lorey, 209, 210.

58. Keen, *The Aztec Image*, 560.

59. Elaine Lacy, "The 1921 Centennial Celebration of Mexico's Independence: State Building and Population Negotiation," *¡Viva Mexico!* ed. Beezley and Lorey, 216 (also 218); and López, "The India Bonita Contest," 316–21.

60. Elaine Lacy, "The 1921 Centennial Celebration of Mexico's Independence: State Building and Population Negotiation," ¡Viva Mexico! ed. Beezley and Lorey, 210.

61. Ibid., 214 (for quote), 215.

62. Ibid., 230 n.73 (for quote), 230 n.77; and Lempérière, "Los dos centenarios," 348.

63. Elaine Lacy, "The 1921 Centennial Celebration of Mexico's Independence: State Building and Population Negotiation," ¡Viva Mexico! ed. Beezley and Lorey, 229 n.71.

64. Batres Jáuregui, Discurso; and Grandin, Blood of Guatemala, 282–83.

65. Batres Jáuregui, La América Central, 1:7, 22–23, 102, 440. Batres viewed independence as a triumph of Guatemala's Spanish heritage: Batres Jáuregui, La América Central, 2:604–5; and Batres Jáuregui, "Guatemala," Chile en 1910, ed. Poirier, 260.

66. Vaughan, The State, Education, and Social Class, 259; and Folgarait, Mural Painting and Social Revolution, 20. I was unable to locate a copy of Adolfo Best Maugard, Método de dibujo, Editorial de la Secretaria de Educación (Mexico City, 1923).

67. Gamio, Forjando patria, 51–52; and Brading, "Manuel Gamio," 79.

68. Manuel Gamio, "The New Conquest," Survey, New York, 1 May 1924, 192; and Brading, "Manuel Gamio," 80.

69. Syndicate of Technical Workers, Painters and Sculptors, "A Declaration of Social, Political and Aesthetic Principles," 1922, Siqueiros, Art and Revolution, 24 (for quote; emphasis as in the original); and Brading, "Manuel Gamio," 86.

70. Siqueiros, "The Historical Process of Modern Mexican Painting," 1947, "A New Direction for the New Generation of American Painters and Sculptors," 1921, and "New Thoughts on the Plastic Arts in Mexico," 1933, all in Siqueiros, Art and Revolution, 17, 22, 31. Or see Orozco, An Autobiography, 107.

71. Folgarait, Mural Painting and Social Revolution.

72. Lauer, Introducción a la pintura peruana, 65, 99.

73. Majluf, "Republican and Contemporary Art," 136. For other examples of "neoprehispanic" architecture, see Gutiérrez and Gutiérrez Viñueles, "Fuentes prehispánicas"; and Gutiérrez Viñuales, "La arquitectura neoprehispánica."

74. Juan de Ega, "De regreso de México, Sabogal cuenta . . ." Mundial, Lima, 10 June 1923.

75. José Carlos Mariátegui, "José Sabogal," *Amauta* 2:6 (Feb. 1927).

76. Cárdenas, *Obras: I-Apuntes*, 393.

77. *Stanley Gibbons Simplified Catalogue*, 3:369–72, 771–73.

78. Law 4634, 8 March 1923, *Anuario de la legislación peruana*, 17:75; and law 4685, 24 Aug. 1923, *Anuario de la legislación peruana*, 18:4. He also made (unsuccessful) efforts to repatriate from Spain the body of Garcilaso de la Vega, the author of the seventeenth-century *Comentarios reales de los Incas*; see Martínez Riaza, "El Perú y España," 345.

79. Euraque, "La creación de la moneda nacional."

80. Euraque also stresses the exclusion of blacks from this vision of Honduras.

81. Gould, "Gender, Politics, and the Triumph of *Mestizaje*," 10–11 (for quote), 19.

82. Ibid., 9.

83. Ibid., 18–19, 23.

84. J. Jorge Klor de Alva, "The Postcolonization of the (Latin) American Experience: A Reconsideration of 'Colonialisms,' 'Postcolonialism,' and 'Mestizaje,'" *After Colonialism*, ed. Prakash, 257 (for quote; my emphasis); and Gould, *To Die in This Way*, 135.

85. Gould, "Gender, Politics, and the Triumph of *Mestizaje*," 23–24.

86. Doremus, "Indigenismo," 380.

87. Basave Benítez, *México mestizo*, 25 (for quote), 36. Stabb's "Indigenism and Racism" also discusses Porfirian attitudes toward the mestizo.

88. Vaughan, *Cultural Politics in Revolution*. See also Knight, "Racism, Revolution, and *Indigenismo*," 85–98; and Doremus, "Indigenismo." Doremus stresses particularly the contradictory nature of the celebration of the mestizo. See also Becker, *Setting the Virgin on Fire*, 73.

89. De la Cadena, *Indigenous Mestizos*.

90. García, *El nuevo indio*, 5–8, 76, 96, 108–10 (quotes from 6, 76); and De la Cadena, *Indigenous Mestizos*, 143.

91. Vasconcelos, *The Cosmic Race*, 16, 18 (for quote), 38–40.

92. Ibid., 32.

93. Ibid., 11–12.

94. Vasconcelos, José, "El nacionalismo en la América Latina," *Amauta*, 2:5 (Jan. 1927). See also Vasconcelos, *The Cosmic Race*, 14; and Vaughan, *The State, Education, and Social Class*, 252.

95. Vasconcelos, *The Cosmic Race*, 16, 17 (for quote), 32.

96. Ibid., 32.

97. Ibid., 16.

98. Vasconcelos, *Indología, Obras,* 2:1123, 1170, 1186.

99. Ibid., 2:1177.

100. Ibid., 2:1208.

101. Beardsell, *Europe and Latin America,* 13.

102. Keen, *The Aztec Image,* 486.

103. Rojas, *Blasón de Plata,* 81.

104. Ibid., 196.

105. Ibid., 113, 117–18, 237 (for quote).

106. Gutiérrez Viñuales, "El papel de las artes," 381–82.

107. Rojas, *Euríndia,* 102.

108. Ibid., 134.

109. Rojas, *Blasón de Plata,* 163, 236.

110. Ibid., 257.

111. D. Santamaría, "18 de setiembre," *Revista de Santiago* (Santiago, 1855).

Epilogue

1. Rowe, "El movimiento nacional inca"; Flores Galindo, *Buscando un Inca;* Stern, ed., *Resistance, Rebellion, and Consciousness;* and Cahill, "The Inca and Inca Symbolism."

2. Gutiérrez, *Nationalist Myths and Ethnic Identities.*

3. Fischer and McKenna Brown, eds., *Maya Cultural Activism.*

4. *El Aguila Mexicana,* Mexico City, 30 July 1826.

5. *El Pájaro Verde,* Mexico City, 4 March 1873.

6. Martha Bechis, "La 'organización nacional' y las tribus pampeanas en Argentina durante el siglo XIX," *Pueblos, comunidades y municipios,* ed. Escobar Ohmstede, Falcón, and Buve, 96.

7. Lowe, "Mexico's Metro," 30–35.

8. Explanatory panel, pre-Columbian section, Museo de Arte de Lima, April 2004.

9. Dirección General de Cartografía, *Diccionario geográfico de Guatemala,* 1:85, 2:326; Carol Hendrickson, "Images of the Indian in Guatemala: The Role of Indigenous Dress in Indian and Ladino Constructions," *Nation-States and Indians,* ed. Urban and Sherzer, 290; and Grandin, *Blood of Guatemala,* 289. In the 1930s Jorge Ubico's dictatorial regime erected a statue to Tecún Umán; see Martínez Peláez, *La patria del criollo,* 510.

10. Dirección General de Cartografía, *Diccionario geográfico de Guatemala,* 2:326.

11. *El Gráfico*, 1980, cited in Carol Hendrickson, "Images of the Indian in Guatemala: The Role of Indigenous Dress in Indian and Ladino Constructions," *Nation-States and Indians*, ed. Urban and Sherzer, 290–91.

12. See, for example, Handy, *Gift of the Devil*, 165–83, 255–81; Carmack, ed., *Harvest of Violence*; Falla, *Massacres in the Jungle*; and Recovery of Historical Memory Project, *Guatemala*.

Appendix

1. Soberano Congreso Constituyente, 17 Sept. 1822, cited in González Navarro, "Instituciones indígenas en México independiente," 116; Brading, *First America*, 578–79; and José Rojas Garciadueñas, "El indigenismo en la literatura de México del siglo XVIII al XIX," *La polémica del arte nacional*, ed. Schávelzon, 73 (for quote). I have used the translation in Hale, *Mexican Liberalism*, 218.

2. Hale, *Mexican Liberalism*, 218 (for quote), 228.

3. Bernardo de Monteagudo, "Exposición de las tareas administrativas del gobierno, Lima, 15 July 1822," *El álbum de Ayacucho*, ed. Herrera, 73.

4. Decree of San Martín, 27 Aug. 1821, *Obra de gobierno*, ed. Puente Candamo, 1:350.

5. Restrepo Piedrahita, ed., *Actas del Congreso de Cúcuta*, 201; and Bushnell, *Santander Regime*, 174–82.

6. *Defensa de Méjico y justa causa de su independencia.*

7. Thurner, *From Two Republics to One Divided*, 24–28; Méndez-Gastelumendi, "The Power of Naming," 154; and, for an example, Bando de Agustín Gamarra, Cuzco, 22 Nov., 1826, Archivo Regional del Cuzco, Tesorería Fiscal, legajo 316: Bandos, años 1814–1836.

8. Constitución del Estado de Mariquita, 1815, tit. XXIII, art. 1, *Constituciones de Colombia*, ed. Pombo and Guerra, 2:330–31; and Constitución Federal para los Estados de Venezuela, 1811, cap. IX, art. 200, *Las constituciones de Venezuela*, ed. Mariñas Otero, 156–57.

9. Hale, *Mexican Liberalism*, 218. For an example, see *El Aguila Mexicana*, Mexico City, 10 Oct. 1824.

10. Decree of San Martín, 28 Aug. 1821, Oviedo, ed., *Colección de leyes*, 4:83.

11. For example, see the article by "J. M. M." [presumably José María Mora], *El Aguila Mexicana*, Mexico City, 28 Aug. 1836; *Diario del Gobierno de la República Mexicana*, Mexico City, 19 Oct. 1838; and González Navarro, "Instituciones indígenas en México independiente," 116.

12. Bushnell, *Santander Regime*, 182. Bushnell cites an 1826 Act in which the word "savage" was not edited out until the third reading. See also Session of 3 October 1821, *Actas del Congreso de Cúcuta*, ed. Restrepo Piedrahita, 3:190; and Consejo ordinario de gobierno of 11 March 1822, *Acuerdos del Congreso de Gobierno de la República de Colombia, 1821–24*, ed. López Domínguez, 1:30–31.

13. Santos de Quirés, *Colección de leyes, decretos y órdenes*, 400.

14. For example, see "Noticias estadísticas de Acayúcan," *Diario del Gobierno de la República Mexicana*, Mexico City, 6 March 1840.

15. Irurozqui, "Las paradojas de la tributación," 712, 725.

16. Skinner-Klée, ed., *Legislación indigenista de Guatemala*; and Palmer, "A Liberal Discipline," 58.

17. See, for example, Decree of 12 April 1899, *Legislación indigenista del Ecuador*, ed. Rubio Orbe, 65–67. Andrés Guerrero states that from 1857 the terms "indio" and "indígena" disappeared from official documents in the capital, although both terms were still widely used in texts produced in the periphery. (Andrés Guerrero, "El proceso de identificación: Sentido común ciudadano, ventriloquia y transescritura," *Pueblos, comunidades y municipios*, ed. Escobar Ohmstede, Falcón, and Buve, 48–49.) *Legislación indigenista del Ecuador* does not appear to support this claim.

18. In 1885 the Argentine National Congress suggested "tribe of Indians" as a possible replacement for "indigene." Sesión de 24 Aug. 1885, *Congreso Nacional: Diario de Sesiones de la Cámara de Diputados, año 1885*, 1:498 (for quotes); Mitre, *Historia de San Martín*, 1:87–88; and Mitre, *Historia de Belgrano*, 1:9–10, 202, 204, 240.

 *Bibliography*

ABBREVIATIONS

CDIP   *Colección documental de la independencia del Perú*
HAHR   *Hispanic American Historical Review*
HM   *Historia Mexicana*
JLAS   *Journal of Latin American Studies*
RI   *Revista de Indias*

MANUSCRIPT MATERIAL
Archivo General de Indias, Seville
  Audiencia de Cuzco 29, 35.
  Diversos 2, 3, 42.
  Papeles de Cuba 743.
Archivo General de la Nación, Bogotá
  Archivo Restrepo, fondo XI, vol. 168.
  Fondo Enrique Ortega Ricaurte, caja 184.
Archivo General de la Nación, Buenos Aires
  Archivo Francisco Moreno 3096 (leg. 1).
  Colección Andrés Lamas 2639 (leg. 36), 2649 (leg. 46), 2655 (leg. 52), 2659
    (leg. 56).
  Colección Dardo Rocha 2998 (leg. 298), 3001 (leg. 301).
  Colección Sánchez de Bustamante 3026 (leg. 2).
  Sala X: 43–9–7.
  Sala X: 44–8–29: "Escarapela nacional/bandera nacional/banda presiden-
    cial (1812–18)."
Archivo General de la Nación, Mexico City
  Comisión Nacional del Centenario, caja 2.
  Instrucción Pública y Bellas Artes, caja 363.
Archivo Regional del Cuzco, Cuzco
  Tesorería Fiscal, legajo 316: Bandos, años 1814–1836.
Biblioteca Nacional del Perú, Lima
  Colección Manuscrita.

Biblioteca Nacional de México, Mexico City
Colección Lafragua.
Nettie Lee Benson Library, University of Texas at Austin
Taracena Flores Collection.

NEWSPAPERS AND MAGAZINES
Abeja Poblana, Puebla, 20 Sept. 1821.
Abogado Nacional, Buenos Aires, 24 Dec. 1818.
Aguila Mexicana, Mexico City, 10 Oct. 1824, 3 April 1826, 30 July 1826, 28 Aug. 1826, 28 Aug. 1836.
Amauta: Revista Mensual de Doctrina, Literatura, Arte, Polémica, Edición en facsimile, 6 vols., Empresa Editorial Amauta (Lima, 1976 [?]).
América del Sur, Buenos Aires, 29, 30 Jan. 1879, 9, 27, 28 Feb. 1879, 7, 20 March 1879.
Amigo del Pueblo, Bogotá, 28 Oct. 1838, 20 Jan. 1839.
Aurora de Chile, 1812–1813: Reimpresión paelográfica a plana y renglón, ed. Julio Vicuña Cifuente, Imprenta Cervantes (Santiago, 1903).
Aurora de México, Mexico City, 27 Sept. 1821.
Aventurero, Puebla, no. 4, 1821.
Censor, Buenos Aires, 25 July 1816, 12, 19, 26 Sept. 1816, 2 Oct. 1816, 21, 28 Nov. 1816, 5, 12, 19 Dec. 1816, 9 Jan. 1817, 29 May 1817, 9, 30 May 1818.
Comercio, Lima, 9 Dec. 1858.
Correo Mercantil, Político y Literario, Lima, 18, 25 May 1822, 4 June 1822, 27 July 1822.
Crónica Argentina, Buenos Aires, 21, 28 Sept. 1816, 9, 23 Nov. 1816.
Despertador Americano: Primer periódico insurgente, Instituto Jalisciense de Antropolgia e Historia (Guadalajara, 1968).
Diario de Avisos, Mexico City, 21 Oct. 1857.
Diario del Gobierno de la República Mexicana, Mexico City, 19 Oct. 1838, 6 March 1840.
Diario del Hogar, Mexico City, 20, 23, 30 Sept. 1894.
Diario Independiente, Mexico City, 27 Sept. 1821.
Extracto del Noticioso General de México del lunes de julio de 1822 (Puebla, 1822).
Ferrocarril, Santiago, 13 June 1863.
Gaceta de Colombia, facsimile edition, 5 vols., Banco de la República (Bogotá, 1974).
Gaceta del Gobierno de México, Mexico City, 6 Nov. 1810.

Gacetas de Literatura de México de José Antonio Alzate Ramírez, CD-ROM, Benemérita Universidad Autónoma de Puebla/Sociedad Mexicana de Historia de la Ciencia y de la Tecnología (Mexico City, 1999).

Gazeta Ministerial de Chile, 25 Aug. 1821.

Gazeta Ministerial del Gobierno de Buenos Aires, Buenos Aires, 17 March 1813.

Gazeta Ministerial Extraordinaria de Chile, 21, 23 Aug. 1821.

Ilustrador Mexicano, Mexico City, 4 July 1823.

Imparcial, Mexico City, 17 Jan. 1902.

Independiente, Buenos Aires, 10 Jan. 1815.

Indicador de la Federación Mexicana, Mexico City, 4 Dec. 1833, 12 Feb. 1834.

Mercurio Peruano, Lima, 17 March 1791, 19 Aug. 1792.

Mercurio, Valparaíso, 28 March 1859, 10, 11, 24, 27, 30 May 1859, 7, 25, 29, 30 June 1859, 27 Aug. 1859, 26 March 1860, 22 Sept. 1890.

Minero del año 34, La Serena, 24 Sept. 1834.

Miscelanea, Lima, 23 Oct. 1832.

Monitor Araucano, 6, 10 April 1813, 15 June 1813.

Monitor Republicano, Mexico City, 19 Sept. 1894.

Mundial, Lima, 28 July 1921 (special centenary edition), Aug. 1921 (second supplement to the centenary edition), 10 June 1923, 1924 (special edition for centennial of Battle of Ayacucho), 9 Oct. 1925.

Nación, Buenos Aires, 25 May 1910 (special centenary edition).

Noticioso General, Mexico City, 12 Dec. 1821.

Omnibus, Mexico City, 28 Feb. 1852, 24 June 1852.

Orden, Tucumán, 5 March 1888.

Pájaro Verde, Mexico City, 16 Sept. 1863, 30 Jan. 1867, 4 March 1873.

Partido Liberal, Mexico City, 15 Sept. 1894.

Prensa Argentina, Buenos Aires, 24 Sept. 1816.

Prensa, Buenos Aires, 1 March 1878, 13 July 1889.

Progreso, Santiago, 14 Feb. 1843, 10, 11 April 1843.

Repertorio Americano, Londres, 1826–1827, ed. Pedro Grases, 2 vols., Edición de la Presidencia de la República (Caracas, 1973).

Revista Católica, Santiago, 4, 18, 25 June 1859, 16 July 1859, 1911 (special issue dedicated to the centenary of independence).

Revista Chilena, Santiago, vol. 1 (1875).

Revista de Filosofía, vol. 1:6 (Buenos Aires, 1915).

Revista de la Sociedad Arqueológica de Santiago, vol. 1 (Santiago, 1880).

Revista de Santiago, Santiago, 1849, 1855.

Semana Literaria de "El Porvenir," vol. 2 (Bogotá, 1858).

Siglo XIX, Mexico City, 8 July 1848, 18 Sept. 1849, 11 Nov. 1857, 2 Dec. 1870, 18 Sept. 1877, 3 Feb. 1881, 20 Sept. 1894.

Sol, Mexico City, 9 March 1824.

Suplemento al número 67 de la Gaceta de Guatemala, Guatemala, 25 July 1855.

Survey, New York, 1 May 1924.

Teléfono, Melipilla, 23 Sept. 1883.

Universal, Mexico City, 16, 30 Sept. 1851.

OTHER MATERIAL

Acosta de Samper, Soledad. *Biografías de hombres ilustres o notables: Relativas a la época de descubrimiento: Conquista y colonización de la parte de América denominada actualmente EE. UU. de Colombia*. Bogotá: 1883.

Afinsa Auctions. Sale catalogue for 30 October 2001 auction of the collection of F. W. Lange. Barcelona, 2001.

Aguilar de Bustamante, José María. *Discurso pronunciado en la plazuela principal de la Alameda de la capital de la República Mexicana . . . el 16 de septiembre de 1836*. Mexico City, 1837.

Aguirre, Regino. *Discurso pronunciado en la plaza de la constitución de Veracruz en la noche del 15 de setiembre de 1869*. Veracruz, 1869.

Alamán, Lucas. *Documentos diversos (inéditos y muy raros)*. 4 vols. Mexico City: Editorial Jus, 1946.

———. *Disertaciones*. Mexico City: Editorial Jus, 1969 [1844–45].

———. *Historia de Méjico*. 5 vols. Mexico City: Editorial Jus, 1968–69 [1849–52].

———. *Historia de Méjico*. 5 vols. Mexico City: Editorial Jus, 1942 [1849–52].

Alazraki, Jaime. "El indigenismo de Martí y el antindigenismo de Sarmiento." *Cuadernos Americanos* 140:3 (1965).

Alberdi, Juan Bautista. *Autobiografía: La evolución de su pensamiento*. Buenos Aires, n.d.

———. *Bases y puntos de partida para la organización política de la República Argentina*. Buenos Aires: Editorial Universitaria de Buenos Aires, 1966 [1852].

Alcorta, Santiago. *La República Argentina en la Exposición Universal de Paris de 1889: Colección de informes reunidos*. 2 vols. Paris, 1890.

Alda Mejías, Sonia. *La participación indígena en la construcción de la república de Guatemala. s. XIX*. Madrid: Ediciones de la Universidad Autónoma de Madrid, 2000.

Alvarado Tello, Bernardo. *Discurso oficial. 15 Sept., 1925.* Guatemala, 1925.

Americano, Un. *A los ciudadanos militares que componen la división del Sr. D. Vicente Guerrero. 28 Sept., 1821.* Mexico City, 1821.

Amunátegui, Miguel Luis. *Descubrimiento i conquista de Chile.* Santiago, 1862.

———. *Obras.* Vol. 1: *Discursos parlamentarias.* Santiago, 1906.

———. *Los precursores de la independencia de Chile.* 3 [?] vols. Santiago de Chile, 1909–10 [1870–72].

———. *Los precursores de la independencia de Chile.* 3 vols. Santiago, 1870–72.

Ancízar, Manuel. *Peregrinación de Alpha por las provincias del norte de la Nueva Granada en 1850–51.* Bogotá: Biblioteca de la Presidencia de Colombia, 1956.

Andermann, Jens. "The Museo de la Plata, 1877–1906." Available online at Relics and Selves: Iconographies of the National in Argentina. Brazil and Chile, 1880–1890, www.bbk.ac.uk/ibamuseum/texts/Andermann04.htm.

———. "Reshaping the Creole Past: History Exhibitions in Late Nineteenth-Century Argentina." *Journal of the History of Collections* 13:2 (2001).

———. "Total Recall: Texts and Corpses: The Museums of Argentinian Narrative." *Journal of Latin American Cultural Studies* 6:1 (1997).

Anderson, Benedict. *Imagined Communities: Reflections on the Origins and Spread of Nationalism.* London: Verso, 1991.

Anievas, José Ignacio de. *Discurso patriótico pronunciado en la Alameda de México la mañana del 16 de septiembre de 1854.* Mexico City, 1854.

Anita la Respondona. *Allá van esas frioleras al Pensador Mexicano.* Mexico City, 1821.

Aniversario del glorioso grito de libertad lanzado en Dolores el día 16 de septiembre de 1810. Durango, 1832.

Annino, Antonio, Luis Castro Leiva, and François-Xavier Guerra, eds. *De los imperios a las naciones: Iberoamérica.* Zaragoza: IberCaja, 1994.

Anuario de la legislación peruana, edición oficial: tomo XVI: *Legislatura de 1921,* Lima, 1923; tomo XVII: *Legislatura de 1922,* Lima, 1924; tomo XVIII: *Legislatura de 1923,* Lima, 1924; XXIII: *Legislatura de 1928,* Lima, 1929.

Aparicio Vega, Manuel Jesus. *El clero patriota en la revolución de 1814.* Cusco: n.p. 1974.

Appelbaum, Nancy. *Muddied Waters: Race, Region, and Local History in Colombia, 1846–1948.* Durham, N.C.: Duke University Press, 2003.

Appelbaum, Nancy, Anne Macpherson, and Karin Alejandra Rosemblatt, eds. *Race and Nation in Modern Latin America.* Chapel Hill: University of North Carolina Press, 2003.

Aquézolo Castro, Manuel, ed. *La polémica del indigenismo*. Lima: Mosca Azul, 1987.

Aranda, Ricardo, ed. *Leyes y resoluciones expedidas por los congresos ordinarios y extraordinarios de 1887*. Lima, 1889.

———, ed. *Leyes y resoluciones expedidas por los congresos ordinarios de 1891 y 1892*. Lima, 1893.

Arango, Mario, Augusto Peinado, and Juan Santa María. *Comunicaciones y correos en la historia de Colombia y Antioquia*. Santafé de Bogotá, 1996.

Arenas, Pascual. *Discurso pronunciado en la Alameda de la ciudad de México en el día 16 de septiembre de 1850*. Mexico City, 1850.

Arrazola, Roberto, ed. *Documentos para la historia de Cartagena, 1810–1812*. Cartagena: Editorial Oficial, 1963.

Arriola, Manuel. *Discurso oficial pronunciado . . . el 15 de septiembre de 1922*. Guatemala, 1922.

Asturias, Miguel Angel. *El problema social del indio y otros textos*. Ed. Claude Couffon. Paris: Centre de Recherches de l'Institut d'Ètudes Hispaniques, 1971.

Aurrecoechea, José María de. *Memoria geográfico-económico-política del Departamento de Venezuela*. Cádiz, 1814.

Avellaneda, Nicolas. *Centenario del Congreso de Tucumán: Discurso pronunciado el día 9 de julio de 1916*. Tucumán, 1916.

Aycinena, Juan José de. *Discurso pronunciado . . . el 15 de septiembre de 1837*. Guatemala, 1837.

———. *Discurso religioso pronunciado . . . el 15 de septiembre de 1858*. Guatemala, 1858.

———. *Discurso religioso pronunciado . . . el 15 de septiembre de 1855*. Guatemala, 1855.

———. *Discurso religioso pronunciado . . . el 15 de septiembre de 1864*. Guatemala. n.d.

Azurdia, José. *Discurso oficial. 15 Sept., 1923*. Guatemala, 1923.

Bahn, Paul, ed. *The Cambridge Illustrated History of Archaeology*. Cambridge: Cambridge University Press, 1996.

Ballesteros Gaibrois, Manuel. "Spanische archäologische Forschungen in Amerika im 18. Jahrhundert." *Tribus* 4 (1960).

Balta Campbell, Aida. *Historia general del teatro en el Perú*. Lima: Universidad de San Martín de Porres, 2001.

Baralt, Rafael María, and Ramón Díaz. *Resumen de la historia de Venezuela*. 3 vols. Curaçao, 1887 [1841].

Bárcena, Manuel de la. *Oración gratulatoria a Dios que por la independencia mejicana dijo en la catedral de Valladolid de Michoacán.* Mexico City [?], 1821 [?].

Bárquera, Juan Wenceslao. *Oración patriótica. 16 Sept. 1825.* Mexico City, 1825.

Barreda, Cástulo. *Oración cívica pronunciada en la noche del 15 de setiembre de 1853.* Mexico City, 1853.

Barr-Melej, Patrick. *Reforming Chile: Cultural Politics, Nationalism, and the Rise of the Middle Class.* Chapel Hill: University of North Carolina Press, 2001.

Barros, Alvaro. *Indios: Fronteras y seguridad interior.* Buenos Aires: Solar, 1975.

Barros Arana, Diego. *Historia jeneral de Chile.* Santiago, 1884–1902.

———. *Obras completas.* Vol. 8: *Estudios histórico-bibliográficos.* Santiago, 1910.

Basadre, Jorge. *Historia de la República del Perú, 1822–1933.* 17 vols. Lima: Editorial Universitaria, 1970.

Basave Benítez, Agustín F. *México mestizo: Análisis del nacionalismo mexicano en torno a la mestizofilia de Andrés Molina Enríquez.* Mexico City: Fondo de Cultura Económica, 1993.

Batres Jáuregui, Antonio. *La América Central ante la historia.* 2 vols. Guatemala, 1915–20.

———. *Discurso oficial. 15 Sept., 1921.* Guatemala, 1921.

———. *Los indios: Su historia y su civilización.* Guatemala, 1894.

Beardsell, Peter. *Europe and Latin America: The Identity of the Other.* Manchester: Manchester University Press, 1996.

Becker, Marjorie. *Setting the Virgin on Fire: Lázaro Cárdenas, Michoacán Peasants, and the Redemption of the Mexican Revolution.* Berkeley: University of California Press, 1995.

Beezley, William, and David Lorey, eds. *¡Viva Mexico! ¡Viva la Independencia! Celebrations of September 16.* Wilmington: SR Books, 2000.

Beezley, William, and Linda Curcio-Nagy, eds. *Latin American Popular Culture: An Introduction.* Wilmington: SR Books, 2000.

Benítez, Ruben. "El viaje de Sarmiento a España." *Cuadernos Hispanoamericanos* 406 (1984).

Berístain de Souza, José Mariano. *Diálogos patrióticos.* Mexico City, 1810–11.

———. *Discurso eucarístico . . . en la muy solemne acción de gracias celebrado por el Real Consulado de México.* Mexico City, 1814.

Berkhofer, Robert. *The White Man's Indian: Images of the American Indian from Columbus to the Present.* New York: Vintage, 1979.

Bernal, Ignacio. *A History of Mexican Archaeology.* London: Thames and Hudson, 1980.

Berro, Adolfo. *Poesías.* Montevideo, 1842.

Bertoni, Lilia Ana. *Patriotas, cosmopolitas y nacionalistas: Construcción de la nacionalidad argentina a fines del siglo XIX.* Buenos Aires: Fondo de Cultura Económica, 2001.

Bhabha, Homi. *The Location of Culture.* London: Routledge, 1994.

———, ed. *Nation and Narration.* London: Routledge, 1990.

———. "Representation and the Colonial Text: A Critical Exploration of Some Forms of Mimeticism." In *The Theory of Reading.* Ed. Frank Gloversmith. Sussex: Harvester Press, 1984.

Bilbao, Francisco. *El pensamiento vivo de Francisco Bilbao.* Ed. Armando Donoso. Santiago, 1940.

Bingham, Hiram. *Inca Land: Explorations in the Highlands of Peru.* Washington: National Geographic Adventure Classics, 2003 [1922].

Blancarte, Roberto, ed. *Cultura e identidad nacional.* Mexico City: Fondo de Cultura Económica, 1994.

Blanco, José Félix, and Ramón Azpurua, eds. *Documentos para la historia de la vida pública del Libertador.* 15 vols. Caracas: Ediciones de la Presidencia de la República, 1977–79 [1875].

Boccara, Guillaume, and Ingrid Seguel-Boccara. "Políticas indígenas en Chile (Siglos XIX y XX) de la asimilación al pluralismo (el caso mapuche)." *RI* 59:217 (1999).

Bolívar, Simón. *Escritos del Libertador.* 23 vols. Caracas: Sociedad Bolivariana de Venezuela, 1964–80.

Bonilla, Heraclio. "Clases populares y estado en el contexto de la crisis colonial." In *La independencia en el Perú.* Ed. Heraclio Bonilla, Pierre Chaunu, Tulio Halperín, Pierre Vilar, Karen Spalding, and E. J. Hobsbawm. Lima: Instituto de Estudios Peruanos, 1972.

Borges, Jorge Luis. "The Argentine Writer and Tradition." *Labyrinths.* London: Penguin, 1979.

Boswell, David, and Jessica Evans, eds. *Representing the Nation: A Reader. Histories. Heritage, and Museums.* London: Routledge, 1999.

Botero, Clara Isabel. "The Construction of the Pre-Hispanic Past of Colombia: Collections. Museums and Early Archaeology, 1823–1941." Ph.D. dissertation, Oxford University, 2001.

Boturini Benaduci, Lorenzo. "Catalogo del Museo Histórico Indiano." Bound into Lorenzo Boturini Benaduci. *Idea de una nueva historia general de la América Septentrional.* Madrid, 1746.

Brading, David. *The First America: The Spanish Monarchy, Creole Patriots, and the Liberal State, 1492–1867.* Cambridge: Cambridge University Press, 1991.

————. "Manuel Gamio and Official Indigenismo in Mexico." *Bulletin of Latin American Research* 7:1 (1988).

————. "Nationalism and State-Building in Latin American History." In *Wars, Parties and Nationalism: Essays on the Politics and Society of Nineteenth-Century Latin America.* Ed. Eduardo Posada-Carbó. London: Institute of Latin American Studies, 1995.

————. "Patriotism and the Nation in Colonial Spanish America." In *Constructing Collective Identities and Shaping Public Spheres.* Ed. Luis Roniger and Mario Sznajder. Brighton: Sussex Academic Press, 1998.

————. *Prophecy and Myth in Mexican History.* Cambridge: Cambridge University Press, 1984.

————. *The Origins of Mexican Nationalism.* Cambridge: Cambridge University Press Cambridge, 1985.

Bravo Arriaga, María Dolores. "De la fuente de las musas a la ribera de la laguna de México." *Carvelle* 73 (1999).

Brine, Lindesay. *Travels amongst American Indians: Their Ancient Earthworks and Temples; Including a Journey in Guatemala, Mexico and Yucatán.* London, 1894.

Bristol, William. "*Hispanidad* in South America, 1936–1945." Ph.D. dissertation, University of Pennsylvania, 1947.

Brito, José María. *Discurso pronunciado . . . el 16 de septiembre de 1851.* Mexico City, 1851.

Brunhouse, Robert. *Pursuit of the Ancient Maya: Some Archaeologists of Yesterday.* Albuquerque: University of New Mexico Press, 1975.

Bueno, Christine. "Centralising Memory: Amassing Ancient Artefacts in Porfirian Mexico City." Unpublished paper, 2003.

Bullock, William. *Six Month's Residence and Travels in Mexico.* London, 1824.

Bulnes, Francisco. *El porvenir de las naciones latinoamericanas ante las recientes conquistas de Europe y Norteamérica.* N.p., 1899.

Bunge, Carlos Octavio. *Nuestra América.* Buenos Aires: Ministerio de Cultura y Educación de la Nación, 1994 [1903].

Burkhart, Louise. "The Solar Christ in Nahuatl Doctrinal Texts of Early Colonial Mexico." *Ethnohistory* 35:3 (1988).

Burmeister, German. *Anales del Museo Público de Buenos Aires.* Buenos Aires, 1864.

Burns, E. Bradford. *The Poverty of Progress: Latin America in the Nineteenth Century.* Berkeley: University of California Press, 1980.

Burucúa, José Emilio, Andrea Jáuregui, Laura Malosetti, and María Líu Murilla. "Iconográficos de la Revolución Francesa en los paises del Plata." *Cahiers des Ameriques Latines* 10 (1990).

Bushnell, David. *The Santander Regime in Gran Colombia.* Newark: University of Delaware, 1954.

Bushnell, David, and Neil Macaulay. *The Emergence of Latin America in the Nineteenth Century.* New York: Oxford University Press, 1994.

Bustamante, Carlos María de. *Cuadro histórico de la revolución mexicana.* 3 vols. Mexico City: Ediciones de la Comisión Nacional para la Celebración del Sesquicentenario de la Proclamación de la Independencia Nacional, 1961 [1821–27].

———. *Mañanas de la Alameda: Publicadas para facilitar a las señoritas el estudio de la historia de su país.* 2 vols. Mexico City: Instituto Nacional de Bellas Artes, 1986 [1835–36].

Bustamante, Juan. *Los indios del Perú.* Lima, 1867.

Cahill, David. "The Inca and Inca Symbolism in Popular Festive Culture: The Religious Processions of Seventeenth-Century Cuzco." In *Hapsburg Peru: Images, Imagination and Memory.* Ed. Peter Bradley and David Cahill. Liverpool: Liverpool University Press, 2000.

Caldas, Francisco José de. *Obras completas.* Bogotá: Imprenta Nacional, 1966.

Calderón de la Barca, Frances. *Life in Mexico during a Residence of Two Years in that Country.* New York: E. P. Dutton, 1937 [1843].

Calzadilla, Pedro Enrique. "El IV centenario en Venezuela y el fin del matricidio." In *Los grandes períodos y temas de la historia de Venezuela V Centenario.* Ed. Luis Cipriano Rodríguez. Caracas: Instituto de Estudios Hispanoamericanos, 1993.

———. "El olor de la pólvora: Fiestas patrias, memoria y Nación en la Venezuela guzmancista, 1870–1877." *Caravelle* 73 (1999).

Canción nacional para el 20 de julio. Bogotá, 1836.

Canción patriótica a Simón Bolívar libertador. Cartagena, 1828.

Cañizares-Esguerra, Jorge. *How to Write the History of the New World: Histories, Epistemologies, and Identities in the Eighteenth-Century Atlantic World.* Stanford: Stanford University Press, 2001.

Cantos a mayo: Leidos en la sesión del Instituto Histórico-Geográfico Nacional el 25 de mayo de 1844. Montevideo, 1844.

Capdevila, Arturo. *Los hijos del sol*. Buenos Aires: Labaut and Cia, 1929.

Carbello Carro, Paz. "Amerikanische Sammlungen des 18. Jahrhunderts." In *Gold und Macht: Spanien in der Neuen Welt*. Munich: Kremayr and Scheriau, 1987.

Cárdenas, Lázaro. *Obras: I-Apuntes 1913–1940*. Mexico City: Nueva Biblioteca Mexicana, 1972.

Carmack, Robert, ed. *Harvest of Violence: The Maya Indians and the Guatemalan Crisis*. Norman: University of Oklahoma Press, 1992 [1988].

Caro, José Eusebio. *Obras escogidas de José Eusebio Caro*. Bogotá, 1873.

Caro, Miguel Antonio. "La conquista." 1881. In *Obras completas*. Vol. 2: *Estudios literarios*. Bogotá: Imprenta Nacional, 1920.

Carrera Damas, German. *El culto a Bolívar*. Caracas: Universidad Central de Venezuela, 1969.

———, ed. *Historia de la historiografía venezolana textos para su estudio*. Caracas: Universidad Central de Venezuela, 1961.

Carrillo, Alfonso. *Discurso oficial. 15 Sept., 1930*. Guatemala, 1930.

Carsi, Manuel. *Discurso pronunciado en el gran teatro de Guerrero la noche del 15 de setiembre de 1885*. Puebla, 1885.

Casaus Arzú, Marta. "Los proyectos de integración social del indio y el imaginario nacional de las élites intelectuales guatemaltecas, siglos XIX y XX." *RI* 59:217 (1999).

Casey, Dennis. "Indigenismo: The Guatemalan Experience." Ph.D. dissertation, University of Kansas, 1979.

Castillo, José María. *Al heróico pueblo de Guatemala*. Guatemala, 1821.

Castillo Ledón, Luis. *El Museo Nacional de Arqueología, Historia y Etnografía, 1825–1925*. Mexico City: Talleres Gráficos del Museo Nacional de Arqueología, Historia y Etnografía, 1924.

Castillo Negrete, José del. *Discurso que en el aniversario de nuestra independencia nacional del día 27 de setiembre de 1854 pronunció en Guadalajara*. Guadalajara, 1854.

Castillo y Lanzas, Joaquin María de. *Discurso pronunciado en la Alameda de México el 15 de setiembre de 1863*. Mexico City, 1863.

Castro-Klarén, Sara, and John Charles Chasteen, eds. *Beyond Imagined Communities: Reading and Writing the Nation in Nineteenth-Century Latin America*. Baltimore, Md.: Johns Hopkins University Press, 2003.

Castro Leal, Antonio, ed. *La novela del México colonial.* 2 vols. Mexico City: Aguilar, 1964.

Centenario de la independencia de la Provincia de Tunja. Tunja, 1913.

Chevalier, François. "Official *Indigenismo* in Peru in 1920: Origins, Significance, and Socioeconomic Scope." In *Race and Class in Latin America.* Ed. Magnus Mörner. New York: Columbia University Press, 1970.

Chiaramonte, José Carlos. "Formas de Identidad en el Río de la Plata luego de 1810." *Boletín del Instituto de Historia Argentina y Americana "Dr. E. Ravignani,"* Third series, 1 (1989).

Chippindale, Christopher. "The Invention of Words for the Idea of 'Prehistory.'" *Proceedings of the Prehistoric Society* 54 (1988).

Choquehuanca, José Domingo. *Ensayo de estadística completa de los ramos económico-políticos de la Provincia de Azangaro en el Departamento de Puno de la República Peruana del quinquenio contado desde 1825 hasta 1829 inclusivos.* Lima, 1833.

Chueco, Manuel. *La República Argentina en su primer centenario.* 2 vols. Buenos Aires, 1910.

Cisneros, Luis Benjamín. *De libres alas: Poesías completas.* Lima: E. Rosay, 1939 [?].

Clavijero, Francisco Javier. *Historia antigua de México.* 4 vols. Mexico City: Editorial Porrua, 1958 [1780].

Clermont, Norman, and Philip Smith. "Prehistoric, Prehistory, Prehistorian . . . Who Invented the Terms?" *Antiquity* 64 (1990).

Codazzi, Agustín. "Antigüedades indígenas." In *Jeografía física i política de las provincias de la Nueva Granada.* Comisión Corográfica. 4 vols. Bogotá: Banco de la República, 1954 [1858–59].

Cohen, Saul. *The Columbia Gazetteer of the World.* 3 vols. New York: Columbia University Press, 1998.

Collier, Simon. *Ideas and Politics of Chilean Independence, 1808–1833.* Cambridge: Cambridge University Press, 1967.

Colmenares, Germán. *Las convenciones contra la cultura.* Bogotá: Tercer Mundo, 1987.

Columbia: Canción partiótica americana. Cartagena, 1815.

Comas, Juan, ed. *Los congresos internacionales de americanistas: Síntesis histórica e índice biliográfica general, 1875–1952.* Mexico City: Instituto Indigenista Inter-Americano, 1953.

Cometta Manzoni, Aida. *El indio en la poesía de América Española.* Buenos Aires: Instituto Indigenista Inter-Americano, 1939.

Composiciones en prosa y verso pronunciados en varios puntos de la república. Mexico City [?], 1850 [?].

Congreso de Anáhuac, 1813. Mexico City: Cámara de Senadores, 1963.

Congreso Nacional: Cámara de Senadores. Sesión de 1875, Buenos Aires, 1875. *Sesión de 1878,* Buenos Aires, 1878. *Sesión de 1879,* Buenos Aires, 1879. *Sesión de 1884,* Buenos Aires, 1884.

Congreso Nacional: Diario de Sesiones de la Cámara de Diputados. Año 1878, 2 vols., Buenos Aires, 1879. *Año 1884,* 2 vols., Buenos Aires, 1885. *Año 1885,* 2 vols., Buenos Aires, 1886. *Año 1888,* 2 vols. Buenos Aires, 1889.

Connaughton, Brian. *Ideología y sociedad en Guadalajara (1788–1853).* Mexico City: Universidad Nacional Autónoma de México, 1992.

Connerton, Paul. *How Societies Remember.* Cambridge: Cambridge University Press, 1989.

Constitución de la República Argentina. Buenos Aires, 1826.

Constitución de las Provincias Unidas en Sud-América. Buenos Aires, 1819.

Constitución del Estado de Cartagena de Indias. Cartagena, 1812.

Constitución para la República Peruana. Lima, 1826.

Constitución política de la República de Chile jurada y promulgada el 25 de mayo de 1833 con las reformas efectuadas hasta el 26 de junio de 1893. Santiago, 1909.

Conway, Christopher. *The Cult of Bolívar in Latin American Literature.* Gainesville: University Press of Florida, 2003.

Cope, Douglas. *The Limits of Racial Domination: Plebeian Society in Colonial Mexico City, 1660–1720.* Madison: University of Wisconsin Press, 1994.

Corbiere, Emilio. *El gaucho desde su orígen hasta nuestros días.* Seville: Editorial Renacimiento, 1998 [1929].

Cornejo Polar, Antonio. *Literatura y sociedad en el Perú: La novela indigenista.* Lima: Lasontay, 1980.

Corominas, Joan. *Breve diccionario etimológico de la lengua castellana.* Madrid: Editorial Gredos, 1987.

Corripio, Fernando. *Diccionario etimológico general de la lengua castellana.* Barcelona: Editorial Bruguera, 1973.

Cortázar, Roberto, and Luis Augusto Cuervo, eds. *Actas del Congreso de Angostura, 1819–1820.* Bogotá: Biblioteca de la Presidencia de la República, 1989 [1921].

Cortes y Esparza, José María. *Oración cívica que . . . pronunció el 16 de septiembre de 1851.* Mexico City, 1851.

Cosio, José Gabriel. *Cuzco: The Historical and Monumental City of the Incas: Traveler's Guide.* Lima: Editorial Incazteca, 1924 [?].

Cowie, Lancelot. *El indio en la narrativa contemporánea de México y Guatemala.* Mexico City: Instituto Nacional Indigenista, 1976.

Craib, Raymond. "A Nationalist Metaphysics: State Fixations, National Maps, and the Geo-Historical Imagination in Nineteenth-Century Mexico." *HAHR* 82:1 (2002).

Cuadra, Luis de la. *Ocupación y civilización de Arauco.* Santiago, 1870.

Cuadriello, Jaime. "La personificación de la Nueva España y la tradición de la iconografía de 'Los Reinos.'" In *Del libro de emblemas a la ciudad simbólica, Actas del III Simposio Internacional de Emblemática Hispánica.* Vol. 1, ed. Víctor Mínguez, *Colecció "Humanitats,"* no. 3. Castellón, 2000.

Cuervo, Antonio B. *Resumen de la jeografía histórica, política, estadística i descriptiva de la Nueva Granada para el uso de las escuelas primarias superiores.* [Bogotá], 1852.

Cummins, Thomas. "We Are the Other: Peruvian Portraits of Colonial *Kurakakuna.*" In *Transatlantic Encounters: Europeans and Andeans in the Sixteenth Century.* Ed. Kenneth Andrien and Rolena Adorno. Berkeley: University of California Press, 1991.

Cúneo-Vidal, Rómulo. *Historia de la civilización peruana.* Barcelona: Maucci, c.1920.

Curcio-Nagy, Linda. *The Great Festivals of Colonial Mexico City: Performing Power and Identity.* Albuquerque: University of New Mexico Press, 2004.

D'Alva Ixtililzóchitl, Fernando. *Cruautés horribles des conquérants du Méxique.* Ed. Carlos María de Bustamante. Paris, 1838.

Darío, Rubén. *Obras completas.* 5 vols. Madrid: Colección Paradilla del Alcor, 1950–55.

———. *Poesías completas.* Ed. Alfonso Méndez Plancarte and Antonio Oliver Belmes. Madrid: Aguilar, 1967.

Dávalos y Lissón, Pedro. *La primera centuria: Causas geográficas, políticas y económicas que han detenido el progreso moral y material del Perú en el primer siglo de su vida independiente.* 4 vols. Lima: Imprenta Gil, 1919–22.

Dawson, Alexander. "From Models for the Nation to Model Citizens: *Indigenismo* and the 'Revindication' of the Mexican Indian, 1920–40." *JLAS* 30 (1998).

———. "'Wild Indians,' 'Mexican Gentlemen,' and the Lessons Learned in the Casa del Estudiante Indígena, 1926–1932." *Americas* 57:3 (2001).

De la Cadena, Marisol. *Indigenous Mestizos: The Politics of Race and Culture in Cuzco. Peru, 1919–1991.* Durham, N.C.: Duke University Press, 2000.

Dean, Carolyn. *Inka Bodies and the Body of Christ: Corpus Christi in Colonial Cuzco, Peru.* Durham: Duke University Press, 1999.

Defensa de Méjico y justa causa de su independencia. Mexico City, 1821 [?].

Delaney, Jeane. "Imagining *El Ser Argentino:* Cultural Nationalism and Romantic Concepts of Nationhood in Early Twentieth-Century Argentina." *JLAS* 34:3 (2002).

Delgado, Jaime. "Hernán Cortés en la poesía española de los siglos XVIII y XIX." *RI* 9 (1948).

Demélas-Bohy, Marie-Danièle. "Darwinismo a la criolla: El darwinismo social en Bolivia, 1880–1910." *Historia Boliviana* 1:2 (1981).

———. "Héros et formation nationale." *Caravelle: Héros et Nation en Amérique Latine* 72 (1999).

———. *L'invention politique: Bolivie, Equateur, Pérou au XIXe siècle.* Paris: Éditions Recherches sur les Civilisations, 1992.

Descripción de las fiestas cívicas celebradas en Montevideo: Mayo de 1816. Ed. Edmundo Narancio. Montevideo: Universidad de la República, 1951.

Díaz, Arlene. *Female Citizens, Patriarchs, and the Law in Venezuela, 1786–1904.* Lincoln: University of Nebraska Press, 2004.

Díaz Covarrubias, Juan. *Discurso cívico pronunciado en la ciudad del Tlalpam la noche del 15 de setiembre de 1857.* Mexico City, 1860.

Dirección General de Cartografía. *Diccionario geográfico de Guatemala.* 2 vols. Guatemala: Tipográfica Nacional, 1961.

Discurso del señor diputado Navarrete a favor de los indios. Mexico City, 1821.

Discursos cívicos pronunciados en las festividades del 15 y 16 de setiembre de 1867. Mexico City, 1867.

Discursos pronunciados el 16 de septiembre de 1850 en la Alameda de México. Mexico City [?], [1850?].

Discursos pronunciados el 27 y 28 de septiembre de 1850 en la capital de México. Mexico City [?], [1850?].

Discursos pronunciados en la fiesta cívica del año de 1861 en la capital de la República. Mexico City, 1861.

Discursos y composiciones poéticas que se leyeron en las festividades cívicas del 15 y 16 de setiembre del presente año. San Luis Potosí, 1869.

Doremus, Anne. "Indigenismo, Mestizaje, and National Identity in Mexico during the 1940s and the 1950s." *Mexican Studies/Estudios Mexicanos* 17:2 (2001).

Dousdebés, Pedro Julio. "Las insignias de Colombia." *Boletín de Historia y de Antigüedades* 24:274 (1937).

Dublan, Manuel. *Oración patriótica. 16 Sept. 1831.* Mexico City, 1831.

Dunbar Temple, Ella. ed. CDIP. Tomo 3: *Conspiraciones y rebeliones en el siglo XIX: La Revolución de Huánuco, Panatahuas y Huamalíes de 1812.* 5 vols. Lima: Comisión Nacional del Sesquicentenario de la Independencia del Perú, 1971.

Earle, Rebecca. "Creole Patriotism and the Myth of the Loyal Indian." *Past and Present* 172 (2001).

————. "Padres de la Patria and the Ancestral Past: Celebrations of Independence in Nineteenth-Century Spanish America." *JLAS* 34:4 (2002).

————. "Rape and the Anxious Republic: Revolutionary Colombia, 1810–1830." In *Hidden Histories of Gender and the State in Latin America.* Ed. Maxine Molyneux and Elizabeth Dore. Durham, N.C.: Duke University Press, 2000.

————. "*Sobre Héroes y Tumbas:* National Symbols in Nineteenth-Century Spanish America." *HAHR* 85:3 (2005).

Echeverría, Estéban. *Mayo y la enseñanza popular en la Plata.* Montevideo, 1845.

Echeverría, Manuel. *Discurso [pronunciado] . . . el 15 de setiembre de 1844.* Guatemala, 1844.

Eder, Rita. "Las imágenes de lo prehispánico y su significación en el debate del nacionalismo cultural." In *El nacionalismo y el arte mexicano.* Mexico City: Universidad Nacional Autónoma de México, 1986.

Egaña, Juan. *Cartas pehuenches: O correspondencia de dos indios naturales del Pire-Mapu, o sea la cuarta thetrarquía de los Andes, el uno residente en Santiago i el otro en las cordilleras pehuenches.* Printed pamphlets in the Sala Medina, Biblioteca Nacional de Chile, [1819?]

"El 20 de julio de 1810: Una cuestión histórica." *Boletín de Historia y de Antigüedades* 24:267 (1937).

Encina, Francisco A. *Historia de Chile desde la prehistoria hasta 1891.* 20 vols. Editorial Nascimento Santiago, 1969–70 [c.1940+].

Enciso, Francisco. *Oración cívica . . . [pronunciada] en la capital . . . de Oaxaca el 16 de septiembre de 1846.* Oaxaca, 1846.

Ensayos de poesía y elocuencia leídos por sus autores: Alumnos del Colegio de esta capital. Guadalajara, 1849.

Escobar Ohmstede, Antonio, and Teresa Rojas Rabiela, eds. *La presencia del indígena en la prensa capitalina del siglo XIX.* 4 vols. Tlalpan: Instituto Nacional Indigenista/CIESAS, 1992–93.

Escobar Ohmstede, Antonio, Romana Falcón, and Raymond Buve, eds. *Pueblos, comunidades y municipios frente a los proyectos modernizadores en América Latina, siglo XIX.* Mexico City: Colegio de San Luis/Centro de Estudios y Documentación Latinoamericanos, 2002.

Escobedo, Helen, ed. *Monumentos mexicanos: De las estatuas de sal y de piedra.* Mexico City: Grijalbo, 1992.

Espinosa, Rafael. *Alocución . . . [pronunciado el] 27 de septiembre de 1842.* Mexico City, 1842.

Esteva, José Ignacio. *Discurso pronunciado en la plaza principal de la Heróica Ciudad de Veracruz el día 27 de setiembre de 1853.* Veracruz, 1853.

Euraque, Darío. "Antropólogos, arqueólogos, imperialismo y la mayanización de Honduras: 1890–1940." *Revista de Historia* (San José) 45 (2002).

———. "La creación de la moneda nacional y el enclave bananero en la costa caribeña de Honduras: ¿En busca de una identidad etnico-racial?" *Yaxkin: Revista del Instituto Hondureño de Antropología e Historia* 14:1–2 (1996).

Exposición Histórico-Americana: Catálogo especial de la República de Colombia. Madrid, 1892.

Eyzaguirre, Jaime. *La Logia Lautarina y otros estudios sobre la independencia.* Buenos Aires: Editorial Francisco de Aguirre, 1973.

Fagan, Brian. *In the Beginning: An Introduction to Archaeology.* Boston: Little, Brown, 1972.

Falla, Ricardo. *Massacres in the Jungle: Ixcán, Guatemala, 1975–1982.* Boulder: Westview Press, 1992.

Fanon, Frantz. *The Wretched of the Earth.* London: Penguin, 1990 [1961].

Fee, Nancy. "La Entrada Angelopolitana: Ritual and Myth in the Viceregal Entry in Puebla de los Angeles." *Americas* 52:3 (1996).

Felstiner, Mary Lowenthal. "Family Metaphors: The Language of an Independence Revolution." *Comparative Studies in Society and History* 25 (1983).

Fentress, James, and Chris Wickham. *Social Memory.* Oxford: Blackwell, 1992.

Fernández de Córdoba, Manuel. *Discurso pronunciado en el gran teatro nacional la noche de 15 de setiembre de 1863.* Mexico City, 1863.

Fernández [de] Madrid, José. *Atala y Guatimoc.* Bogotá: Biblioteca Aldeana de Colombia, 1936.

———. *Elegías nacionales peruanas.* Cartagena, 1825.

———. *José Fernández de Madrid y su obra en Cuba.* Havana: Consejo Nacional de Cultura, 1962.

Fiestas de septiembre de 1892. Mexico City, 1892.

Fischer, Edward, and R. McKenna Brown, eds. *Maya Cultural Activism in Guatemala.* Austin: University of Texas Press, 1996.

Fleming, E. McClung. "The American Image as Indian Princess, 1765–1783." *Winterthur Portfolio* 2 (1965).

———. "From Indian Princess to Greek Goddess: The American Image, 1783–1815." *Winterthur Portfolio* 3 (1966).

Fliegelman, Jay. *Prodigals and Pilgrims: The American Revolution against Patriarchal Authority, 1750–1800.* Cambridge: Cambridge University Press, 1982.

Flores, Sabino. *Oración cívica pronunciado en la capital del Estado de Guanajauto el día 27 de setiembre de 185.* Guanajuato, 1851.

Flores Galindo, Alberto. *Buscando un Inca: Identidad y utopía en los Andes.* Lima: Instituto de Apoyo Agrario, 1987.

———. "Independencia y clases sociales." In *Independencia y revolución, 1780–1840.* Ed. Alberto Flores Galindo. Lima: Instituto Nacional de Cultura, 1987.

Florescano, Enrique. *Etnia, estado y nación: Ensayo sobre las indentidades colectivas en México.* Mexico City: Aguilar, 1996.

———. *Memory, Myth, and Time in Mexico from the Aztecs to Independence.* Austin: University of Texas Press, 1994 [1987].

———, ed. *El patrimonio cultural de México.* Mexico City: Fondo de Cultura Económica, 1993.

———, ed. *El patrimonio nacional de México.* Mexico City: Fondo de Cultura Económica, 1997.

Folgarait, Leonard. *Mural Painting and Social Revolution in Mexico, 1920–1940: Art of the New Order.* Cambridge: Cambridge University Press, 1998.

Franco, Jean. *Spanish American Literature since Independence.* London: Ernest Benn, 1973.

Francovich, Guillermo. "Un diálogo de Monteagudo, 1809." In *El pensamiento universitario de Charcas y otros ensayos.* Sucre: Universidad de San Francisco Xavier, 1948.

Frezier, Amadé. *A Voyage to the South-Seas, and Along the Coasts of Chili and Peru in the Years 1712, 1713 and 1714.* London, 1717.

Friedlander, Judith. *Being Indian in Hueyapan: A Study of Forced Identity in Contemporary Mexico.* New York: St. Martin's Press, 1975.

Fuentes, Manuel A. *Sketches of the Capital of Peru: Historical, Statistical, Administrative, Commercial and Moral.* London: Trübner and Co., 1866.

Función patriótica o gran solemnidad para celebrar el aniversario del glorioso grito de la independencia mexicana n.p., 1825. Benson Library, Austin. Discursos Cívicos. serv. 2–5, Reel 313.

Gallardo, Ricardo, ed. *Las constituciones de la República Federal de Centro-América.* 2 vols. Madrid: Instituto de Estudios Políticos, 1958.

Gálvez, Manuel. *El diario de Gabriel Quiroga.* Buenos Aires: Taurus, 2001 [1910].

————. *El solar de la raza.* Buenos Aires: Editores Tor, 1936 [1913].

Gamio, Manuel. *Forjando patria.* Mexico City: Editorial Porrua, 1960 [1916].

————. *Introducción: Síntesis y conclusiones de la obra "La población del Valle de Teotihuacán."* Mexico City: Secretaria de Educación Pública, 1922.

Garay y Texada, Francisco de. *Discurso patriótico pronunciado el día 16 de setiembre de 1863 en la ciudad de Toluca.* Toluca, 1863.

García, Antonio, ed. *Legislación indigenista de Colombia.* Mexico City: Instituto Indigenista Inter-Americano, 1952.

García, José Uriel. *Guía histórica-artística del Cuzco: Homenaje al centenario de Ayacucho.* Ed. Alberto Giesecke. Lima, 1925.

————. *El nuevo indio: Ensayo indianista sobre la sierra surperuana.* Cuzco: H. G. Rozas Sucesores, 1937 [1930].

García Belaúnde, Domingo, ed. *Constituciones del Perú.* Lima: Ministerio de Justicia, 1993.

García Calderón, Francisco. *Memorias del cautiverio.* Lima: Librería Internacional del Perú, 1949.

García Calderón, Ventura. *Obras escogidas.* Ed. Luis Alberto Sánchez. Lima: Ediciones Edubanco, 1986.

García Calderón Rey, Francisco. *Obras escogidas.* Vol. 1: *El Perú contemporánea* [1907]. Vol. 2: *La creación de un continente* [1912]. Lima: Fondo Editorial del Congreso del Perú, 2001.

García Icazbalceta, Joaquín. *Colección de documentos para la historia de México.* 2 vols. Mexico City: Editorial Porrua, 1971 [1858–66].

García Peláez, Francisco de Paula. *Discurso pronunciado el 15 de setiembre de 1856.* Guatemala, 1856.

————. *Memorias para la historia del antiguo Reyno de Guatemala.* 3 vols. Guatemala, 1851–52.

García Quintana, Josefina. *Cuauhtémoc en el siglo XIX.* Mexico City: Universidad Nacional Autónoma de México, 1977.

Gellner, Ernest. *Nations and Nationalism.* Oxford: Basil Blackwell, 1983.

Gerbi, Antonello. *The Dispute of the New World: The History of a Polemic, 1750–1900*. Pittsburgh: University of Pittsburgh Press, 1973 [1955].

Gisbert, Teresa. *Iconografía y mitos indígenas en el arte*. La Paz: Gisbert, 1980.

Glass, John. "A Survey of Native Middle American Pictorial Manuscripts." In *Handbook of Middle American Indians*, vol. 14. Ed. Robert Wauchope. Austin: University of Texas Press, 1975.

Godoy, Ricardo. "Franz Boas and His Plans for an International School of American Archaeology and Ethnology in Mexico." *Journal of the History of the Behavioural Sciences* 13 (1977).

Goez, Eduardo. *Discurso oficial pronunciado . . . el 15 de septiembre de 1909*. Guatemala, 1909.

Gómez, Eugenio. *Diccionario geográfico de Colombia*. Bogotá: Banco de la República, 1953.

Gómez de Avellaneda, Gertrudis. *Sab*. Ed. Catherine Davies. Manchester: Manchester University Press, 2001 [1841].

Gómez Flores, Francisco. *Discurso pronunciado en el puerto de Mazatlán el 17 de setiembre de 1869*. n.d.

Gómez Pedraza, Manuel. *Oración encomiástica que . . . dijo el día 16 de setiembre de 1842*. Mexico City, 1842.

Gonzaga Gordoa, Luis. *Discurso patriótico [pronunciado] en la plaza mayor de San Luis Potosí . . . el 15 de setiembre de 1831*. San Luis Potosí. Benson Library, Austin, n.d.

González, Joaquín V. *Obras completas*. Buenos Aires: Imprenta Mercatali, 1935.

———. *La tradición nacional*. Buenos Aires: Ministerio de Cultura, 1936 [1888].

González Campo, José. *Discurso oficial*. Guatemala, 15 Sept. 1929.

González La Rosa, Manuel T. *Informe que el inspector especial de todos los establecimientos departamentales de instrucción y beneficencia . . . presenta al señor ministro del ramo*. Lima, 1869.

González Navarro, Moises. "Instituciones indígenas en México independiente." In *Métodos y resultados de la política indigenista en México*. Ed. Alonso Caso, Silvio Zavala, José Miranda, Moises González Navarro, Gonzalo Aguirre Beltrán, and Ricardo Pozas. *Memorias del Instituto Nacional Indigenista* 6 (Mexico City, 1954).

González Prada, Manuel. *Páginas libres/Horas de lucha*. Ed. Luis Alberto Sánchez. Caracas [?]: Biblioteca Ayacucho, 1976.

———. *El tonel de Diógenes*. Mexico City: Edición Tezontle, 1945.

González Suárez, Federico. *Historia general de la República del Ecuador.* 3 vols. Quito: Editorial Casa de la Cultura, 1969–70 [1890–1913].

Goodman, Roland, ed. *Guatemala: The Postal History and Philately.* 2 vols. London: Robson Lowe Publishers, 1969.

Gootenberg, Paul. *Imagining Development: Economic Ideas in Peru's "Fictitious Prosperity" of Guano, 1840–1880.* Berkeley: University of California Press, 1993.

Gould, Jeffrey. "Gender, Politics, and the Triumph of *Mestizaje* in Early Twentieth Century Nicaragua." *Journal of Latin American Anthropology* 2:1 (1996).

———. *To Die in This Way: Nicaraguan Indians and the Myth of Mestizaje, 1880–1965.* Durham, N.C.: Duke University Press, 1998.

Gramuglio, María Teresa. "Literatura y nacionalismo: Leopoldo Lugones y la construcción de imágenes de escritor." *Hispamérica: Revista de literatura* 64/65 (1993).

Grandin, Greg. *The Blood of Guatemala: A History of Race and Nation.* Durham, N.C.: Duke University Press, 2000.

———. "Can the Subaltern Be Seen? Photography and the Affects of Nationalism." *HAHR* 84:1 (2004).

Greenblatt, Stephen. "Resonance and Wonder." In *Exhibiting Cultures: The Poetics and Politics of Museum Display.* Ed. Ivan Karp and Steven Lavine. Washington, D.C.: Smithsonian Institution Press, 1991.

Greenhalgh, Paul. *Ephemeral Vistas: The Expositions Universelles, Great Exhibitions and World's Fairs, 1851–1939.* Manchester: Manchester University Press, 1988.

Griffith, William. "The Historiography of Central America since 1830." *HAHR* 40 (1960).

Groot, José Manuel. *Historia eclesiástica y civil de Nueva Granada.* 5 vols. Bogotá: Imprenta Fonción Mantilla, 1869.

Grove, Frank. *Medals of Mexico.* Vol. 1: *Medals of the Spanish Kings.* Vol. 2: *Medals of Mexico, 1821–1971.* San José: Prune Tree Graphics, 1970–74.

Grunthal, Henry. *The Coinage of Peru.* Frankfurt: Numismatischer Verlag P. N. Schulten, 1978.

Guaman Poma de Ayala, Felipe. *El primer nueva corónica y bueno gobierno, 1615–16.* www.kb.dk/elib/mss/poma/frontpage.htm.

Guardino, Peter. *Peasants, Politics, and the Formation of Mexico's National State: Guerrero, 1800–1857.* Stanford: Stanford University Press, 1996.

Guerra, François Xavier, and Mónica Quijada, eds. *Cuadernos de Historia Latinoamericana.* No. 2: *Imaginar la Nación* (1994).

Guerrero, Andrés. *La semántica de la dominación: el concertaje de indios.* Quito: Ediciones Libri Mundi, 1991.

Guevara, Tomás. "Los araucanos en la revolución de la independencia." *Anales de la Universidad: número estraordinario publicado para conmemorar el primer centenario de la independencia de Chile, 1819–1910.* Santiago, 1911.

Guidieri, Remo, Francesco Pellizzi, and Stanley Tamiah, eds. *Ethnicities and Nations: Process of Interethnic Relations in Latin America, Southeast Asia, and the Pacific.* Austin: University of Texas Press, 1988.

Gumucio, Fernando Baptista. *Las monedas de la independencia, 1808–1827.* La Paz: Editorial Cervecería la Taquiña, 1995.

Gutiérrez, Juan María. *Poesías.* Buenos Aires, 1869.

Gutiérrez, Manuel. *Discurso pronunciado en la vila de Tacubaya el 16 de setiembre de 1864.* Mexico City, 1864.

Gutiérrez, Navidad. *Nationalist Myths and Ethnic Identities: Indigenous Intellectuals and the Mexican State.* Lincoln: University of Nebraska Press, 1999.

Gutiérrez, Ramón, and Rodrigo Gutiérrez Viñuales. "Fuentes prehispánicas para la conformación de un arte nuevo en América." *Temas de la Academia: Arte Prehispánico: creación, desarrollo y presistencia.* Ed. Romualdo Bruguetti et al. Buenos Aires: Academia Nacional de Bellas Artes, 2000.

Gutiérrez de Villanueba, José. *Discurso que en el aniversario del memorable día 20 de abril de [1]834 dijo en la plaza de armas de la ciudad de Orizaba.* Mexico City, 1836.

Gutiérrez Viñuales, Rodrigo. "La arquitectura neoprehispánica: Manifestación de identidad nacional y americana—1877/1921." *Arquitextos: Texto especial* 199 (2003). www.vitruvius.com.br/arquitextos/arq000/esp199_e.asp.

———. "El papel de las artes en la construcción de las identidades nacionales en Iberamérica." *HM* 53:2 (2003).

Hale, Charles. *Mexican Liberalism in the Age of Mora, 1821–1853.* New Haven, Conn.: Yale University Press, 1968.

———. *The Transformation of Liberalism in Late Nineteenth-Century Mexico.* Princeton, N.J.: Princeton University Press, 1989.

Hall, Basil. *Extracts from a Journal Written on the Coasts of Chili, Peru, and Mexico in the Years 1820, 1821, 1822.* 2 vols. Upper Saddle River, N.J.: Gregg Press, 1968 [1824].

Hall, Stuart. "Cultural Identity and Diaspora." In *Identity: Community, Culture, Difference.* Ed. Jonathan Rutherford. London: Lawrence and Wishart, 1990.

Halperín Donghi, Tulio. *Politics, Economics and Society in Argentina in the Revolutionary Period.* Cambridge: Cambridge University Press, 1975.

Handy, Jim. *Gift of the Devil: A History of Guatemala.* Boston: South End Press, 1984.

Harris, Olivia. "Ethnic Identity and Market Relations: Indians and Mestizos in the Andes." In *Ethnicity, Markets, and Migration in the Andes: At the Crossroads of History and Anthropology.* Ed. Brooke Larson and Olivia Harris with Enrique Tandeter. Durham, N.C.: Duke University Press, 1995.

Harwich Vallenilla, Nikita. "La génesis de un imaginario colectivo: La enseñanza de la historia de Venezuela en el siglo XIX." *Boletín de la Academia Nacional de la Historia* (Venezuela) 282 (1988).

Hawkins, Timothy. "A War of Words: Manuel Montúfar, Alejandro Marure, and the Politics of History in Guatemala." *Historian* 64:3–4 (2002).

Henríquez Ureña, Pedro. *Obra crítica.* Mexico City: Fondo de Cultura Económica, 1960.

Heredia, José María. *Oración pronunciada en el último aniversario del grito de independencia nacional.* Tlalpam, 1828.

Hernández, Isabel. *Los indios de Argentina.* Madrid: MAPFRE, 1992.

Hernández y Dávalos, J. E., ed. *Colección de documentos para la historia de la Guerra de Independencia de Mexico.* 6 vols. Mexico City: Kraus Reprint, 1968 [1880].

Herrejón Peredo, Carlos. "Sermones y discursos del primer imperio." In *Construcción de la legitimidad política en México.* Ed. Brian Connaughton, Carlos Illades, and Sonia Pérez Toledo. Zamora: Colegio de Michoacán, 1999.

Herrera, Bartolomé. *Sermón pronunciado . . . el dia 28 de julio de 1846 aniversario de la independencia del Perú.* Lima, 1846.

Herrera, José Hipólito, ed. *El álbum de Ayacucho: Colección de los principales documentos de la guerra de la independencia del Perú, y de las cantes de victoria y poesías relativas a ella.* Lima, 1862.

Herrera, José María. *Oración patriótica.* Mexico City, 1829.

Hidalgo, Bartolomé. *Cielitos y diálogos patrióticos.* Buenos Aires: Centro Editorial de América Latina, 1967.

Hobsbawm, Eric. "Nationalism and Nationality in Latin America." In *Pour une histoire économique et sociale internationale: Mélanges offerts à Paul Bairoch.* Ed. Bouda Etemad, Jean Baton, and Thomas David. Geneva: Éditions Passé Présent, 1995.

———. *Nations and Nationalism since 1780: Programme, Myth, Reality.* Cambridge: Cambridge University Press, 1990.

Hobsbawm, Eric, and Terence Ranger, eds. *The Invention of Tradition.* Cambridge: Cambridge University Press, 1992.

Homenaje a Cristóbal Colón: Antigüedades mexicanas publicadas por la Junta Colombiana de México en el cuarto centenario del descubrimiento de América. Mexico City, 1892.

Honour, Hugh. *The New Golden Land: European Images of America from the Discoveries to the Present Time.* London: Allen Lane, 1976.

Humboldt, Alexander von. *Sitios de las cordilleras y monumentos de los pueblos indígenas de América.* Buenos Aires: Solar/Hachette, 1968.

Hunt, Lynn. *The Family Romance of the French Revolution.* Berkeley: University of California Press, 1993.

———. *Politics, Culture and Class in the French Revolution.* London: Methuen, 1986.

Hutchinson, Thomas. *Two Years in Peru, with Exploration of Its Antiquities.* 2 vols. London, 1873.

Icaza, Isidro Ignacio de, and Isidro Rafael Gondra. *Colección de las antigüedades mexicanas que existan en el Museo Nacional.* facsimile edition. Mexico City: Talleres Gráficos del Museo Nacional de Arqueología, Historia y Etnografía, 1927 [1827].

Imnpey, Oliver, and Arthur MacGreggor, eds. *The Origins of Museums: The Cabinet of Curiosities in Sixteenth- and Seventeenth-Century Europe.* London: House of Stratus, 2001.

Inauguración de la estatua del Mariscal don Antonio José de Sucre en Quito, el 10 de agosto de 1892. Quito, 1892.

Ingenieros, José. *Obras completas.* Ed. Aníbal Ponce. Vol. 13: *La evolución de las ideas argentinas.* Buenos Aires: Tallers Gráficos Argentinos, 1937 [1918].

Irurozqui, Marta. "Ebrios, vagos y analfabetos: El sufragio restringido en Bolivia, 1826–1952." *RI* 56 (1996).

———. "'La guerra de civilización': La participación indígena en la Revolución de 1870 en Bolivia." *RI* 61 (2001).

———. "Las paradojas de la tributación. Ciudadanía política estatal indígena en Bolivia, 1825–1900." *RI* 59:217 (1999).

———. "The Sound of the Pututos: Politicisation and Indigenous Rebellion in Bolivia, 1825–1921." *JLAS* 32:1 (2000).

Isaacs, Jorge. *Estudios sobre las tribus indígenas del Magdalena.* Bogotá: Ministerio de Educación Nacional, 1951 [1884].

Isaza, Emiliano, and Lorenzo Marroquín, eds. *Primer centenario de la independencia de Colombia, 1810–1910.* Bogotá, 1911.

Islas, Emilio. *Discurso pronunciado . . . en la función cívica que tuvo lugar en la Alameda de México el 16 de setiembre de 1874.* Mexico City, 1874.

Itier, César. "Le théâtre moderne en Quechua a Cuzco 1885–1950: Ètude et Anthologie." Thèse de doctorat de nouveau régime, Université de Provence, Aix-Marseille I, 1990.

Iturbide, Agustín de. *Plan del Señor Don Agustín de Iturbide.* Puebla, 24 Feb. 1821.

———. *Proclama.* Iguala. Mexico City, 4 March 1821.

Izunza, José Rafael. *Discurso . . . en la festividad nacional de Puebla del 16 de septiembre de 1833.* Mexico City [?], 1833.

Jacome, J. *Discurso pronunciado . . . en el teatro principal la noche del 15 de sbre de 1869.* Puebla, 1869.

JanMohamed, Abdul. *Manichean Aesthetics: The Politics of Literature in Colonial Africa.* Amherst: University of Massachusetts Press, 1983.

Janowitz, Anne. *England's Ruins: Poetic Purpose and the National Landscape.* Cambridge, Mass.: Basil Blackwell, 1990.

Jaramillo Alvarado, Pío. *El indio ecuatoriano: Contribución al estudio de la sociología nacional.* Quito: Imprenta Nacional, 1925.

Jaramillo Uribe, Jaime. *El pensamiento colombiano en el siglo XIX.* Bogotá: Editorial Temis, 1964.

J. J. C. *Discurso . . . en la solemnización del aniversario del glorioso día 16 de setiembre de 1845 [pronunciado] en la universidad de este capital.* Guadalajara, 1845.

J. M. G. *Elemental del continente americano desde su descubrimiento hasta su Independencia para uso de las escuelas y colegios.* Buenos Aires, 1877.

Joseph, Gilbert. *Rediscovering the Past at Mexico's Periphery: Essays on the History of Modern Yucatán.* Tuscaloosa: University of Alabama Press, 1986.

Julien, Catherine. "History and Art in Translation: The *Paños* and Other Objects Collected by Francisco de Toledo." *Colonial Latin American Review* 8 (1999).

Kaplan, Flora, ed. *Museums and the Making of "Ourselves": The Role of Objects in National Identity.* London: Leicester University Press, 1994.

Keen, Benjamin. *The Aztec Image in Western Thought.* New Brunswick, N.J.: Rutgers University Press, 1985.

———. "The Inca Image in Western Thought." *Essays in the Intellectual History of Colonial Latin America.* Boulder: Westview Press, 1998.

Klarén, Peter Flindell. *Peru: Society and Nationhood in the Andes.* Oxford: Oxford University Press, 2000.

Knight, Alan. "Racism, Revolution, and *Indigenismo:* Mexico, 1910–1940." In *The Idea of Race in Latin America, 1870–1940.* Ed. Richard Graham. Austin: University of Texas Press, 1990.

König, Hans-Joachim. "El indigenismo criollo: ¿Proyectos vital y político realizables, o instrumento político?" *HM* 46 (1996).

———. *En el camino hacia la Nación: Nacionalismo en el proceso de formación del Estado y de la Nación de la Nueva Granada, 1750 a 1856.* Santafé de Bogotá: Banco de la República, 1994.

———. "Símbolos nacionales y retórica política en la independencia: El caso de la Nueva Granada." In *Problemas de la formación del estado y de la nación en Hispanoamérica.* Ed. Inge Buisson, Günter Kahle, Hans-Joaquim König, and Horst Pietschmann. Cologne: Böhlau Verlag, 1984.

Krause, Chester, and Clifford Mishler. *1994 Standard Catalog of World Coins.* Iola, Wisc.: Krause Publications, 1993.

Kristal, Efraín. *The Andes Viewed from the City: Literary and Political Discourse on the Indian in Peru, 1848–1930.* New York: Peter Lang, 1987.

———. "The Incest Motif in Narratives of the United States and Spanish America." In *Internationalität nationaler Literatur: Beiträge zum ersten Symposion des Göttinger Sonderforschungsbereichs 529.* Ed. Udo Schöning. Göttingen: Wallstein Verlag, 2000.

Lagranda, Francisco. *Consejo prudente sobre una de las garantías.* Mexico City, 1821.

Larrabure y Unánue, Eugenio. *Cañate: Apuntes geográficos, históricos y arqueológicos.* Lima, 1874.

———. *Manuscritos y publicaciones.* 3 vols. Lima, 1934–36. Vol. 1: *Literatura y crítica literaria.*

Larson, Brooke. *Trials of Nation Making: Liberalism, Race and Modernity in the Andes, 1810–1910.* Cambridge: Cambridge University Press, 2004.

Lastarria, José Victorino. "Investigaciones sobre la influencia de la conquista i del sistema colonial de los españoles en Chile." *Anales de la Universidad de Chile correspondientes al año de 1843 i al año de 1844.* Santiago, 1846.

Latzina, Francisco. *Diccionario geográfico argentino.* Buenos Aires, 1891.

Lauer, Mirko. *Introducción a la pintura peruana del siglo XX.* Lima: Mosca Azul, 1976.

Le Goff, Jacques. *History and Memory.* New York: Columbia University Press, 1992.

Le Moyne, Augusto. *Voyages et séjours dans l'Amérique du Sud.* Paris, 1880.

Lempérière, Annick. "Los dos centenarios de la independencia mexicana 1910–1921: De la historia patria a la antropología cultural." *HM* 45:2 (1995).

León y Gama, Antonio de. *Descripción histórica y cronológica de las dos piedras.* Ed. Carlos María de Bustamante. Mexico City, 1832.

Letelier, Valentín, ed. *Sesiones de los cuerpos legislativos de la República de Chile, 1811–1845,* Santiago, 1886–93.

Libro mayor de sesiones de la Asamblea de Representantes del Alto Perú. La Paz: Litografías e Imprentas Unidas, 1926.

Lira argentina o colección de las piezas poéticas dadas a luz en Buenos-Ayres durante la guerra de su independencia. Buenos Aires, 1824.

Lombardi de Ruiz, Sonia. *El pasado prehispánico en la cultura nacional (memoria hemerográfica, 1877–1911).* Vol. 1: *El Monitor Republicano (1877–1896).* Mexico City: Instituto Nacional de Antropología e Historia, 1994.

Lomné, Georges. "Révolution française et rites bolivariens: Examen d'une transposition de la symbolique républicaine." *Cahiers des Ameriques Latines* 10 (1990).

———. "Les villes de Nouvelle-Grenade: Théâtres et objets des jeux conflictuels de la mémoire politique (1810–1830)." In *Mémoires en devenir: Amérique Latine, 1492–1992.* Ed. François-Xavier Guerra. Bordeaux: Maison des Pays Ibériques, 1994.

Lomnitz, Claudio. "Nationalism as a Practical System: Benedict Anderson's Theory of Nationalism from the Vantage Point of Spanish America." *Deep Mexico, Silent Mexico: An Anthology of Nationalism.* Minneapolis: University of Minnesota Press, 2001.

Lopes, Maria Margaret, and Irina Podgorny. "The Shaping of Latin American Museums of Natural History, 1850–1990." *Osiris* 15 (2001).

López Cancelada, Juan. *La verdad sabida y buena fe guardada.* Cadiz, 1811.

López Domínguez, Luis Horacio, ed. *Acuerdos del Congreso de Gobierno de la República de Colombia, 1821–24.* Bogotá: Biblioteca de la Presidencia de la República, 1988.

———, ed. *Acuerdos del Congreso de Gobierno de la República de Colombia, 1825–27.* 2 vols. Bogotá: Biblioteca de la Presidencia de la República, 1988.

———, ed. *Administraciónes de Santander.* 5 vols. Bogotá: Biblioteca de la Presidencia de la República, 1990.

López, Rick. "The India Bonita Contest of 1921 and the Ethnicization of Mexican National Culture." *HAHR* 82:2 (2002).

López, Vicente Fidel. *Historia de la República Argentina: Su orígen, su revolución y su desarrollo político hasta 1852*. 10 vols. Buenos Aires: Carlos Casavalle Editor, 1888–93.

―――. *La novia del hereje*. Buenos Aires, 1917 [1846].

―――. *Les Races Aryennes du Pérou: Leur Langue, Leur Religion, Leur Histoire*. Paris, 1871.

Lorand de Olazagasti, Adelaida. *El indio en la narrativa guatemalteca*. Barcelona: Editorial Universitaria, Universidad de Puerto Rico, 1968.

Lorente, Sebastian. *Historia antigua del Perú*. Lima, 1860.

Lowe, Arbon Jack. "Mexico's Metro." *Américas* 22:7 (1970).

Lugones, Leopoldo. *Obras poéticas completas*. Madrid: Aguilar, 1948.

Lumholtz, Carl. *Unknown Mexico: A Record of Five Years' Exploration among the Tribes of the Western Sierra Madre; in the Tierra Caliente of Tepic and Jalisco; and among the Tarascos of Michoacan*. London: Macmillan, 1903.

Luna, Pablo. "El 'civilismo' y la sociedad nacional peruana." In *El indio como sujeto y objeto de la historia latinoamericana*. Ed. Hans-Joachim König. Frankfurt: Vervuert Verlag, 1998.

Lyon, G. F. *Journal of a Residence and Tour in the Republic of Mexico in the Year 1826*. 2 vols. London: Kennikat Press, 1971 [1828].

MacCormack, Sabine. "Limits of Understanding: Perceptions of Greco-Roman and Amerindian Paganism in Early Modern Europe." In *America in European Consciousness, 1493–1750*. Ed. Karen Ordahl Kupperman. Chapel Hill: University of North Carolina Press, 1995.

―――. *Religion in the Andes: Vision and Imagination in Early Colonial Peru*. Princeton: Princeton University Press, 1991.

Macdonald, Sharon, and Gordon Fyfe, eds. *Theorizing Museums: Representing Identity and Diversity in a Changing World*. Oxford: Blackwell, 1996.

Macera, Pablo. *Trabajos de Historia*. 4 vols. Lima: Instituto Nacional de Cultura, 1977.

Madiedo, Manuel María. *Poesías*. Bogotá, 1859.

Magariños Cervantes, Alejandro. *Celiar, leyenda americana en variedad de metros*. Madrid. c.1852.

Majluf, Natalia. *Escultura y espacio público. Lima, 1850–1879*. Lima: IEP Ediciones, 1994.

―――. "Republican and Contemporary Art." In *Art in Peru: Works from the Collection of the Museo de Arte de Lima*. Ed. Natalia Majluf, Cristóbal Makowski, and Francisco Stastny. Lima: Promperú, 2001.

Mallet, Mr. *Diálogo: Colón y Fray Bartolomé de las Casas*. Mexico, 1821.

Mallié, Augusto E., ed. *La revolución de mayo a través de los impresos de la época:* Primera *serie, 1809–1815.* 6 vols. Buenos Aires: Comisión Nacional Ejecutiva del Sesquicentenario de la Revolución de Mayo, 1965.

Mallon, Florencia. *Peasant and Nation: The Making of Postcolonial Mexico and Peru.* Berkeley: University of California Press, 1995.

Manifiesto que hace a las naciones el Congreso General Constituyente de las Provincia Unidas en Sud América. Sobre el tratamiento y crueldades que han sufrido de los españoles. Y motivado la declaración de su independencia. 25 Oct. 1817 Buenos Aires, 1817.

Maqueo Castellanos, Eusebio. *Algunos problemas nacionales.* Mexico City, 1910.

Marcha alusiva a los heróicos hechos del exmo. Sr. D. Agustín de Iturbide. Puebla, 1821.

Marcoy, Paul Laurent Saint-Cricq. *A Journey across South America.* 2 vols. London, 1873.

———. *Travels in South America: From the Pacific Ocean to the Atlantic Ocean.* 2 vols. London, 1857.

Mariátegui, José Carlos. *Seven Interpretive Essays on Peruvian Reality.* Trans. Marjory Urquidi. Austin: University of Texas Press, 1971.

Mariñas Otero, Luis. ed. *Las constituciones del Guatemala.* Madrid: Instituto de Estudios Políticos, 1958.

———, ed. *Las constituciones de Venezuela.* Madrid: Ediciones Cultura Hispánica, 1965.

Martí, José. *Nuestra América* (1891). *Grandes escritores de América.* Vol. 3. Ed. Pedro Henríquez Ureña. Buenos Aires: Losada, 1939.

———. *Obras completas.* 25 vols. Havana: Editorial Tierra Nueva, 1961.

Martínez, Frédéric. *El nacionalismo cosmopolita: La referencia europea en la construcción nacional en Colombia, 1845–1900.* Bogotá: Banco de la República, 2001.

Martínez Izquierdo, Simón, and Justiniano Cavero Egúsquiza. *Geográfica de los Estados Unidos Perú Bolivianos o sea República de los Incas.* Lima, 1880.

Martínez Landero, Francisco. "Aspectos del indigenismo en Honduras." *América Indígena* 2:1 (1942).

Martínez Peláez, Severo. *La patria del criollo: Ensayo de interpretación de la realidad colonial guatemalteca.* Mexico City: Fondo de Cultura Económica, 1998 [1970].

Martínez Riaza, Ascensión. "El Perú y España durante el Oncenio: El hispanismo en el discurso oficial y en las manifestaciones simbólicas (1919–1930)." *Hispánica* 18:2 (1994).

Martínez Sarasola, Carlos. *Nuestros paisanos los indios*. Buenos Aires: Emecé Editores, 1992.

Martínez Sobral, Enrique. *Discurso oficial. 15 Sept., 1897* Guatemala, 1897.

Mateos, José María. *Historia de la masonaría en México, 1806–1884*. Mexico City (undated facsimile of 1884 edition).

Mateos, Juan Antonio. *Discurso oficial pronunciado en el aniversario del 16 de setiembre de 1810*. Mexico City, 1872.

———, ed. *Historia parlamentaria de los Congresos Mexicanos*. 11 vols. Mexico City, 1878.

Matto de Turner, Clorinda. *Aves sin nido*. Buenos Aires: Solar, 1968 [1889].

Mayer, Brantz. *Mexico: As It Was and As It Is*. Philadelphia: G. B. Zieber and Co, 1847.

McFarlane, Anthony. "Identity, Enlightenment and Political Dissent in Late Colonial Spanish America." *Proceedings of the Royal Historical Society* 8 (1998).

Medina, José Toribio. *Los aborígenes de Chile*. Santiago: Fondo Historia y Bibliografía José Toribio Medina, 1952 [1882].

Medina y Ormaechea, Antonio A. de. *Iniciativa para celebrar el primer centenario de la independencia de México con una exposición universal*. Mexico City, 1893.

Mega, Ladislao F. "Prológo." In Hildebrando Castro Pozo, *Nuestra comunidad indígena*. Lima: Editorial El Lucero, 1924.

Meléndez, Concha. *La novela indianista en Hispanoamérica 1832–1889*. Madrid: Editorial Hernando, 1934.

Melo, Jorge Orlando. "La literatura histórica en la República." *Manual de literatura colombiana*. 2 vols. Bogotá: Planeta, 1988.

Memorias del Simposio Internacional y IV Cátedra Anual de Historia "Ernesto Tirado Restrepo." *Museo, memoria y nación: Misión de los museos nacionales para los ciudadanos del futuro*. Bogotá: Ministerio de Cultura, 2000.

Mencos, Ernesto. *Discurso oficial pronunciado . . . el 15 de septiembre de 1916*. Guatemala, 1916.

Méndez-Gastelumendi, Cecilia. "Incas Sí, Indios No: Notes on Peruvian Creole Nationalism and Its Contemporary Crisis." *JLAS* 28:1 (1996).

———. "The Power of Naming, or The Construction of Ethnic and National Identities in Peru: Myth, History and the Iquichanos." *Past and Present* 171 (2001).

Mendiburu, Manuel de. *Diccionario histórico-biográfico del Perú*. 8 vols. Lima, 1931 [1874–90].

Mendoza, Eufemio. *Discurso cívico pronunciado . . . en el Teatro Degollado en [el] . . . aniversario del glorioso grito de la independencia nacional.* Guadalajara, 1868.

Mendoza, Zoila. "Crear y sentir lo nuestro: La Misión Peruana de Arte Incaico y el impulso de la producción artístico-folklórica en Cusco." *Latin American Music Review* 25:1 (2004).

Mera, Juan León, ed. *Antología ecuatoriana: Cantares del pueblo ecuatoriano.* 2 vols. Quito, 1892.

————. *Catecismo de geografía de la República del Ecuador.* Quito, 1875.

————. *La virgen del sol: Leyenda indiana.* Quito, 1861.

Meyer, Jean. "History as National Identity." *Voices of Mexico* (Oct.–Dec. 1995).

————. *Problemas campesinos y revueltas agrarias (1821–1910).* Mexico City: Secretaría de Educación Pública, 1973.

Meza Villalobos, Néstor. *La conciencia política chilena durante la monarquía.* Santiago: Universidad de Chile, 1958.

Mier, Servando Teresa de. *Memorias.* Vol. 1. Ed. Antonio Castro Leal. Mexico: Editorial Porrua, 1971.

Míguez, Eduardo José. "Introduction: Foreign Mass Migration to Latin American in the Nineteenth and Twentieth Centuries—An Overview." In *Mass Migration to Modern Latin America.* Ed. Samuel Baily and Eduardo José Míguez. Wilmington: SR Books, 2003.

Milla, José. *Esplicación de algunos de los conceptos contenidos en el discurso pronunciado en el salón del Supremo Gobierno de Guatemala el 15 de setiembre de 1846.* Guatemala, 1846.

————. *Historia de la América Central.* Guatemala: Piedra Santa, 1976 [1879].

————. *Obras completas de Salomé Jil (José Milla).* Vol. 5: *La hija del adelantado y Memorias de un abogado.* Guatemala: Tipográfica Nacional [?], 1936.

Miller, John. *Memoirs of General Miller in the Service of the Republic of Peru.* 2 vols. New York: AMS Press, 1973 [1829].

Miller, Nicola. *In the Shadow of the State: Intellectuals and the Quest for National Identity in Twentieth-Century Spanish America.* London: Verso, 1999.

Millones, Luis. "The Inka's Mask: Dramatisation of the Past in Indigenous Colonial Processions." In *Andean Art: Visual Expression and Its Relation to Andean Beliefs and Values.* Ed. Penny Dransart. Aldershot, U.K.: Avebury, 1995.

Minguet, Charles. "El concepto de nación: Pueblo, estado, y patria en las generaciones de la Independencia." *Recherches sur le monde hispanique au 19ème siècle.* Lille: Université de Lille III, 1973.

Ministerio de Educación de la Nación. *Catálogo del Museo Histórico Nacional.* 2 vols. Buenos Aires, 1951.

Mirafuentes, Juan N. *Discurso para la noche de 15 de setiembre de 1862.* Mexico City, 1862.

Mira Quesada Sosa, Aurelio, ed. CDIP. Tomo 24: *La poesía de la emancipación.* Lima: Comisión Nacional del Sesquicentenario de la Independencia del Perú, 1971.

Miri, Hector, ed. *Antología poética de Mayo.* Buenos Aires: Ediciones Antonio Zamora, 1960.

Mitre, Bartolomé. *Historia de Belgrano y de la independencia argentina.* 3 vols. Buenos Aires, 1887 [1857].

———. *Historia de San Martín y de la emancipación sud-americana (según nuevos documentos).* 3 vols. Buenos Aires, 1887–90.

———. *Las ruinas de Tiahuanaco (recuerdos de viaje)* Buenos Aires, 1879.

Molina Enríquez, Andrés. *Los grandes problemas nacionales.* Mexico City: Imprenta de A. Carranza e Hijos. Mexico City, 1909.

Molinari Morales, Tirso Anibal, and Jaime Ríos Burga. "El 'messianismo inca' en la rebelión de 1812: Ideología caciquil y desborde indígena." *Patria, nación y mesianismo inca, en las ideologías de los próceres anti coloniales en el Perú, 1780–1814. Cuadernos de Historia* (Lima) 10 (1990).

Monseñor Miguel de Andrea. *Oración patriótica de acción de gracias por el éxito de las fiestas del centenario.* Buenos Aires, 1910.

Montalvo, Juan. *El Espectador.* Paris: Casa Editorial Garnier Hermanos, 1927.

Montandon, Roberto. *Chile: Monumentos históricos y arqueológicos.* Mexico City: Instituto Panamericano de Geografía e Historia, 1952.

Montesdeoca, Demetrio. *Oración cívica pronunciada . . . el 16 de setiembre de 1862 en el salón de la Plaza de la Constancia (Guanajuato).* Guanajuato, 1862 [?].

Montúfar y Rivera Maestre, Lorenzo. *Discursos del Dr. Lorenzo Montúfar.* Ed. Rafael Montúfar. Guatemala: Talleres Sánchez & De Guise, 1922.

———. *Discurso escrito por el . . . XII aniversario de la independencia, 15 Sept. 1862.* San Salvador, n.d.

———. *Discurso pronunciado . . . el 15 de setiembre de 1875.* Guatemala, 1875.

———. *Discurso pronunciado . . . el 15 de setiembre de 1877.* Guatemala, 1877.

———. *Reseña histórica de Centro-América.* 7 vols. Guatemala, 1878.

Mora, José María Luis. *Méjico y sus revoluciones.* Mexico City: Fondo de Cultura Económica, 1986 [1836].

———. *Obras sueltas.* Mexico City: Editorial Porrua, 1963.

Morales, Reynaldo. *Discurso patriótico que en conmemoración del LXXVII aniversario del grito de independencia pronunció . . . en San Luis Potosí.* San Luis Potosí, 1887.

Moreno, Francisco P. *Perito en argentinidad.* Buenos Aires: Artes Gráficas Yerbal, 1998.

Moreno, Gabriel René. *Nicomedes Antelo, 1885.* Santa Cruz de la Sierra: Publicaciones de la Universidad Gabriel René Moreno, 1960.

Moreno Yánez, Segundo. *Sublevaciones indígenas en la Audiencia de Quito desde comienzos del siglo XVIII hasta finales de la Colonia.* Quito: Ediciones de la Pontífica Universidad Católica del Ecuador, 1985.

Morgan, Lewis. *Ancient Society.* Cambridge, Mass.: Belknap Press of Harvard University Press, 1964 [1877].

Moxó, Benito María de. *Cartas méjicanas escritas . . . en 1805,* Genoa, 1837.

Mugaburu, Joseph, and Francisco Mugaburu. *Chronicle of Colonial Lima.* Ed. Robert Miller. Norman: University of Oklahoma Press, 1975.

Muñoz Hernándes, Luis Patricio. "Los festejos del centenario de la independencia: Chile en 1910." Tesis de licenciatura, Pontífica Universidad de Chile, 1999.

Muratorio, Blanca, ed. *Imágenes e imagineros: Representaciones de los indígenas ecuatorianos, siglos XIX y XX.* Quito: Flasco, 1994.

Muriá, José María. "El cuarto centenario del descubrimiento de América." In *El descubrimiento de América y su sentido actual.* Ed. Leopoldo Zea. Mexico City: Fondo de Cultura Económica, 1989.

Museo Historico Nacional. *El clero argentino de 1810 a 1830.* Vol. 1: *Oraciones patrióticas.* Buenos Aires, 1907.

Nan, María Francisca de. *Sueño alegórico . . . dedicado a la religión.* Mexico City, 1809.

Nápoles Fajardo, Juan Cristóbal. *Poesías completas.* Havana: Editorial de Arte y Literatura, 1974.

Nariño, Antonio. *Nariño periodista.* Ed. Carlos Restrepo Canal. Bogotá: Academia Colombiana de Historia, 1960.

Navarro Floria, Pedro. "'Formar patria a hombres que no la tienan': Pedro Andrés García, entre la frontera colonial y la política de conquista." *Revista Complutense de Historia de América* 25 (1999).

————. Leonardo Salgado and Pablo Azae. "La invención de los ancestros: El "patagón antiguo" y la construcción discursiva de un pasado nacional remoto para la Argentina 1870–1915." *RI* 64:231 (2004).

————. "El salvaje y su tratamiento en el discurso político argentino sobre la frontera sur, 1853–1879." *RI* 61 (2001).

————. "Sarmiento y la frontera sur argentina y chilena: De tema antropológico a cuestión social 1837–1856." *Jahrbuch für Geschichte Lateinamerikas* 37 (2000).

Nora, Pierre. "Between Memory and History." In *Realms of Memory*. Ed. Pierre Nora. 3 vols. New York: Columbia University Press, 1992.

————, ed. *Les Lieux de Mémoire*. 3 vols. Paris: Gallimard, 1984–92.

Norambuena Carraso, Carmen. "Imagen de América Latina en la Exposición Universal de París de 1889." *Dimensión Histórica de Chile* 17–18 (2002–3).

O'Brien, Karen. *Narratives of Enlightenment: Cosmopolitan History from Voltaire to Gibbon*. Cambridge: Cambridge University Press, 1997.

Ocampo López, Javier, ed. *Santander y el Congreso de 1824: Actas y Corespondencia*. 5 vols. Bogotá: Biblioteca de la Presidencia de la República, 1989.

————, ed. *Santander y el Congreso de 1825: Actas y Corespondencia*. 5 vols. Bogotá: Biblioteca de la Presidencia de la República, 1989.

Ocampo, Javier. *Las ideas de un día: El pueblo mexicano ante la consumación de su Independencia*. Mexico City: Colegio de México, 1969.

Oda lírica. 15 Sept. 1843 n.p., 1844. Benson Library, Austin. Taracena Flores Collection.

O'Gorman, Edmundo. "Discurso de Ingreso: Hidalgo en la historia." *Memorias de la Academia Mexicana de Historia* 23:3 (1964).

————, ed. *Fray Servando Teresa de Mier: Antología del pensamiento político americano*. Mexico City: Imprenta Universitaria, 1945.

————. *Historia de las divisiones territoriales de México*. Mexico City: Editorial Porrua, 1973.

Olaguibel, Manuel de, and Julian Mantiel y Duarte. *Discurso pronunciado en la Alameda de México . . . y prosa leida . . . en el aniversario del 16 de setiembre de 1875*. Mexico City, 1875.

Olascoaga, Manuel J. *La conquête de la Pampa: Recueil des documents relatifs a la campagne du Río Negro*. Buenos Aires, 1881.

Olvera, Pedro José. *Oración cívica pronunciada en el palacio de gobierno de Durango el 16 de septiembre de 1845.* Victoria de Durango, 1845.

Opatrný, Josef. "La conciencia común en Cuba, siglo XIX." In *Nation Building in Nineteenth Century Latin America: Dilemmas and Conflicts.* Ed. Hans-Joachim König and Marianne Wiesebron. Leiden: Leiden University, 1998.

———. "La historia de Cuba en la argumentación nacional: Lecciones orales de Pedro Santacilla." *Actas del XI Congreso Internacional de AHILA.* Vol. 2. Liverpool, 1996.

———. "El papel de la historia en la formación de la conciencia de una identidad particular de la comunidad criolla en Cuba." In *Identidad nacional y cultural de la Antilles hispanoparlantes: Ibero-Americana Pragensia.* Supplement 5. Prague, 1991.

Orellana Rodríguez, Mario. *Historia de la arqueología en Chile.* Santiago: Bravo y Allende Editores, 1996.

Orozco, José Clemente. *An Autobiography.* Trans. Robert Stephenson. Austin: University of Texas Press, 1962.

Orozco y Berra, Manuel. *Historia antigua y de la conquista de México.* 4 vols. Mexico City: Editorial Porrua, 1960 [1880].

———. *Oración cívica que . . . pronunció en esta ciudad el 16 de septiembre de 1846.* Puebla, 1846.

Ortega, Francisco Luis. *México libre: Melodrama heróica en un acto.* Mexico City, 1821.

Ortega y Medina, Juan A., ed. *Polémicas y ensayos mexicanos en torno a la historia.* Mexico City: Universidad Nacional Autónoma de México, 1970.

Ortíz, José Joaquín, ed. *La guirnalda: Colección de poesías i cuadros de costumbres.* Bogotá, 1855.

———, ed. *La guirnalda: Colección de poesías i cuadros de costumbres.* Segunda serie. Bogotá, 1856.

———, ed. *Poesías de Caro i Vargas Tejada.* 2 vols. Bogotá, 1857.

Ortiz, Juan Francisco. *La Virgen del Sol: O la sacerdotisa peruana.* Bogotá, 1830.

Oviedo, Juan, ed. *Colección de leyes: Decretos y ordenes publicadas en el Perú desde el año de 1821 hasta 31 de diciembre de 1859.* 16 [?] vols. Lima, 1861–63.

Pacheco, José Emilio, ed. *La poesía mexicana del siglo XIX.* Mexico City: Empresas Editoriales, 1965.

Pagden, Anthony. "Identity Formation in Spanish America." In *Colonial Identity in the Atlantic World, 1500–1800.* Ed. Nicholas Canny and Anthony Pagden. Princeton, N.J.: Princeton University Press, 1987.

Pagden, Anthony. *Spanish Imperialism and the Political Imagination: Studies in European and Spanish-American Social and Political Theory, 1513–1830.* New Haven, Conn.: Yale University Press, 1990.

P. A. J. *Los horrores de Cortés: Los confundió O-Donojú.* Mexico City, 1821.

Palacio, Antonio G. del. *Oración cívica pronunciada en el palacio del gobierno de Durango . . . el día 16 de setiembre de 1846.* Victoria de Durango, 1846.

Palacios, Guillermo. "Postrevolutionary Intellectuals: Rural Readings and the Shaping of the "Peasant Problem" in Mexico: *El Maestro Rural, 1932–34.*" *JLAS* 30:2 (1998).

Palenzuela, Juan Carlos. *Primeros monumentos en Venezuela a Simón Bolívar.* Caracas: Academia Nacional de Historia, 1983.

Palma, Ricardo. *Cartas a Piérola (sobre la ocupación chilena de Lima).* Lima: Editorial Mille Batres, 1964.

———. *Tradiciones peruanas completas.* Ed. Edith Palma. Madrid: Aguilar, 1964.

Palmer, Steven. "A Liberal Discipline: Inventing Nations in Guatemala and Costa Rica, 1870–1900." Ph.D. dissertation, Columbia University, 1990.

Pando, José María. *Elogio patriótico . . . [pronunciado] el 16 de septiembre de 1827.* Oaxaca, 1827.

Pantret, Andrés. *Alusión al grito de Dolores: Bailes alegóricos. 16 Sept. 1825* Mexico City, 1825.

Panzos, Vicente. *Letters on the United Provinces of South America addressed to the Hon. Henry Clay.* New York, 1819.

Parada, Manuel. *Discurso cívico pronunciado en el teatro nacional . . . la noche del 15 de setiembre de 1876.* Mexico City, 1876.

Parangón patriótica que por disposición de los gefes de la fábrica de puros y cigarros de esta capital . . . dijeron . . . con el plausible motivo de la jura de al independencia del Imperio Mexicano. Mexico City, 1821.

Pastor, Juan N. *Discurso pronunciado en la Alameda de esta capital el día 27 de setiembre de 1863.* Mexico City, 1863.

Patiño, Pomposo. *Discurso pronunciado el día 16 de setiembre de 1856 en la ciudad de Pachuca.* Puebla, 1856.

Payno, Manuel. *Compendio de historia de México para el uso de los establecimientos de instrucción pública.* Mexico City, 1902 [c.1870].

Payo del Rosario, El. *Nuevas zorras de Sansón que su autor dedica al impávido y benemérito general D. Antonio López de Santana.* N.p., 1823.

Paz Soldan, Mariano Felipe. *Historia del Perú independiente.* 2 vols. Lima, 1868–70.

Pease, Franklin. *Peru: Hombre e historia.* Vol. 3: *La república.* Lima: Ediciones Edubanco, 1993.

Peña, Guillermo de la. "Etnicidad, ciudadanía y cambio agrario: Apuntes comparativos sobre tres paises latinoamericanos." In *La construcción de la nación y la representación ciudadana en México, Guatemala, Perú, Ecuador y Bolivia.* Ed. Claudia Dary. Guatemala, 1998.

Peña Nicolás, ed. *Teatro drámatico nacional.* Santiago, 1912.

Pereira Gamboa, Próspero. *Akímen Zaque o la conquista de Tunja.* Bogotá, 1858.

————. *Poesías.* Bogotá, 1854.

Pérez, Fabián. *Discurso oficial. 15 Sept. 1896.* Guatemala, 1896.

Pérez, Felipe. *Atahualpa.* Bogotá 1856.

————. *Gonzalo Pizarro.* Bogotá, 1857.

————. *Huayna Capac.* Bogotá, 1856.

————. *Jilma.* Bogotá, 1858.

Pérez, José Joaquín. *Obra poética.* Santo Domingo: Universidad Nacional Pedro Henríquez Ureña, 1970.

Périssat, Karine. "Les festivités dynastiques à Lima: La célébration d'une histoire locale." *Caravelle* 73 (1999).

————. "Los Incas representados Lima—siglo XVIII: ¿Supervivencia o renacimiento?" *RI* 60:220 (2000).

Perú en el primer centenario de su independencia. Buenos Aires: Société de Publicité Sud-Américaine Monte Domecq, [1922].

Pesce, Luis. *Indígenas e inmigrantes en el Perú.* Lima, 1906.

Phelan, John Leddy. "Neo-Aztecism in the Eighteenth Century and the Genesis of Mexican Nationalism." In *Culture in History: Essays in Honor of Paul Radin.* Ed. Stanley Diamond. New York: Columbia University Press, 1960.

Philippi, Rodulfo Amadeo. "Algo sobre las momias peruanas." *Revista Chilena* (Santiago) 1 (1875).

————. "Historia del Museo Nacional de Chile." *Boletín del Museo Nacional* 7 (1914).

Picard, Alfred. *Rapport Général sur l'Exposition Universelle Internationale de 1889 à Paris.* 5 vols. Paris, 1891.

Pieper, Renate. "Papageien und Bezoarsteine: Gesandte als Vermittler von Exotica und Luxuserzeugnissen im Zeitalter Philipps II." In *Hispania-Austria II.* Vol. 5: *Die Epoche Philipps II.* Ed. Friedrich Edelmayer. Munich, 1999.

Pieper, Renate. "The Upper German Trade in Art and Curiosities before the Thirty Years' War." In *Art Markets in Europe, 1400–1800*. Ed. Michael North and David Ormrod. Aldershot: Ashgate, 1998.

Pike, Fredrick. *Hispanismo, 1898–1936: Spanish Conservatives and Liberals and Their Relations with Spanish America*. Notre Dame, Ind.: University of Notre Dame Press, 1971.

Pilcher, Jeffrey. *¡Que Vivan los Tamales! Food and the Making of Mexican Identity*. Albuquerque: University of New Mexico Press, 1998.

Pimentel, Francisco. *La economía política aplicada a la propiedad territorial en México*. Mexico City, 1866.

———. *Memoria sobre las causas que han originado la situación actual de la raza indígena de México y medios de remediarla*. Mexico City, 1864.

———. *Obras completas de D. Francisco Pimentel*. 5 vols. Mexico City: Tipográfica Económica, 1903–4.

Piñol, Bernardo. *Discurso pronunciado en la Santa iglesia catedral el 15 de setiembre de 1849*. Guatemala, 1849.

Pinto, Francisco Antonio. "Apuntes autobiográficos del General Don Francisco Antonio Pinto." *Boletín de la Academia Chilena de la Historia* 8:17 (1941).

Pinto Rodríguez, Jorge. "Del antiindigenismo al proindigenismo en Chile en el siglo XIX." In *La reindianización de América, siglo XIX*. Ed. Leticia Reina. Mexico City: Siglo XXI, 1997.

———. "Mapuche, colonos nacionales y colonos extranjeros en la Araucanía: Conflictos y movilizaciones en el siglo XIX." In *Los ejes de la disputa: Movimientos sociales y actores colectivos en América Latina, siglo XIX*. Ed. Antonio Escobar Ohmstede and Romana Falcón. *Cuadernos de Historia Latinoamericana* 10 (2002).

Platt, Tristan. "Liberalism and Ethnocide in the Southern Andes." *History Workshop Journal* 17 (1984).

———. "Simón Bolívar, the Sun of Justice, and the Amerindian Virgin: Andean Conceptions of the Patria in Nineteenth-Century Potosí." *JLAS* 25:1 (1993).

Plaza, José Antonio de. *Memorias para la historia de la Nueva Granada desde su descubrimiento hasta el 20 de julio de 1810*. Bogotá, 1850.

Podgorny, Irina. "Vitrinas y administración. Los criterios de organización de las colecciones antropológicas del Museo de La Plata entre 1897 y 1930." Available online at Relics and Selves: Iconographies of the National in Argentina. Brazil and Chile, 1880–1890, www.bbk.ac.uk/ibamuseums.

Poesías cívicas en honor de los aniversarios de la independencia de México.
Mexico City [?], 1850[?].

Poinsett, Joel Roberts. *Notes on Mexico Made in the Autumn of 1822.* New York: Praeger, 1969 [1824].

Poirier, Eduardo, ed. *Chile en 1910: Edición del centenario de la independencia.* Santiago de Chile, 1910.

Polo, José Toribio. *Historia nacional: Crítica del Diccionario histórico-biográfico del Perú del señor general Mendiburu.* Lima, 1891.

Pombo, Manuel Antonio, and José Joaquín Gutiérrez, eds. *Constituciones de Colombia.* 4 vols. Bogotá: Ministerio de Educación Nacional, 1951.

Pons Muzzo, Gustavo, ed. *CDIP.* Tomo 10: *Símbolos de la patria.* Lima: Comisión Nacional del Sesquicentenario de la Independencia del Perú, 1974.

Poole, Deborah. "An Image of "Our Indian": Type Photographs and Racial Sentiments in Oaxaca, 1920–1940." *HAHR* 84:1 (2004).

———. *Vision, Race, and Modernity: A Visual Economy of the Andean Image World.* Princeton, N.J.: Princeton University Press, 1997.

Porras, Basilio. *Discurso de ley pronunciado en el Salón de Sesiones de la Asamblea Constituyente el 15 de setiembre de 1841.* Guatemala, 1841.

Porta Mencos, Humberto, ed. *Parnaso guatemalteca: Segunda edición corregida y aumentada (1750–1930).* Barcelona: Casa Editorial Maucci, 1931 [?].

Posada, Eduardo. "Heráldica colombiana." *Boletín de Historia y de Antigüedades* 26:291–302 (1939).

Posada Gutiérrez, Joaquín. *Memorias histórico-políticas.* 4 vols. Bogotá: Imprenta Nacional, 1929 [1865].

Powell, T. G. "Mexican Intellectuals and the Indian Question, 1876–1911." *HAHR* 48 (1968).

Prakash, Gyan, ed. *After Colonialism: Imperial Histories and Postcolonial Displacements.* Princeton, N.J.: Princeton University Press, 1995.

Pratt, Mary Louise. *Imperial Eyes: Travel Writing and Transculturation.* London: Routledge, 1992.

Prieto, Guillermo. *El romancero nacional.* Mexico City, 1885.

Puente Candamo, José A. de la, ed. *CDIP.* Tomo 13: *Obra de gobierno y epistolario de San Martín.* 2 vols. Lima: Comisión Nacional del Sesquicentenario de la Independencia del Perú, 1974.

"Que mueran los gachupines y la patria será libre" (así se espresa el ignorante) Puebla, 1827.

Quesada, Ernesto. *Alocución patriótica pronunciada en la fiesta annual del Ateneo.* Buenos Aires, 1895.

Quesada, Ernesto. *El Museo Histórico Nacional y su importancia patriótica*. Buenos Aires, 1897.

———. *Nuestra raza*. Buenos Aires, 1900.

Quijada, Mónica, Carmen Bernand, and Arnd Schneider. *Homogeneidad y nación con un estudio de caso: Argentina, siglos XIX y XX*. Madrid: Consejo Superior de Investigaciones Científicas, 2000.

Quijada Mauriño, Mónica. "Ancestros, ciudadanos, piezas de museo: Francisco P. Moreno y la articulación del indígena en la construcción nacional argentina." *Estudios Interdisciplinarios de América Latina y el Caribe* 9:2 (1998).

———. "La ciudadanización del 'indio bárbaro': Políticas oficiales y oficiosas hacia la población indígena de la Pampa y la Patagonia, 1870–1920." *RI* 59:217 (1999).

———. "En torno al pensamiento racial en Hispanoamérica: Una refleción bibliográfica." *Estudios Interdisciplinarios de América Latina y el Caribe* 3:1 (1992).

———. "Nación y territorio: La dimensión simbólica del espacio en la construcción nacional argentina, siglo XIX." *RI* 60:219 (2000).

———. "Las raíces indoeuropeas de los incas: O los usos de la historia en el siglo XIX." In *Historia y universidad: Homenaje a Lorenzo Mario Luna*. Ed. Enrique González González. Mexico: Universidad Nacional Autónoma de México, 1996.

Rama, Angel. "El area cultural andina (hispanismo, mesticismo, indigenismo)." *Cuadernos Americanos* 33 (1974).

Rama, Carlos. *Historia de las relaciones culturales entre España y la América Latina*. Mexico City: Fondo de Cultura Económica, 1982.

Ramírez, Ignacio. *Discurso pronunciado el día 27 de setiembre de 1856*. Puebla, 1856.

———. *Obras*. 2 vols. Mexico City: Editorial Nacional, 1966.

Ramírez, José. *Descripción de algunos objetos del Museo Nacional de Antigüedades de México*. Mexico City, 1857.

Ramírez de Arellano, Manuel. *Oración cívica en la Alameda de México el día 27 de setiembre de 1859*. Mexico, 1859.

Ramos Mejía, José María. *Historia de la instrucción primaria en la República Argentina, 1810–1910 (Atlas escolar)*. 2 vols. Buenos Aires: Jacobo Peuser Editorial, 1910.

———. *Las multitudes argentinas*. Buenos Aires: La Cultura Popular, 1934 [1899].

Ranney, Edward, and Publio López Mondéjar, eds. *Martín Chambi: Photographs, 1920–1950*. Washington, D.C.: Smithsonian Institution Press, 1993.

Ravignani, Emilio, ed. *Asembleas Constituyentes Argentines seguidas de los textos constitucionales legislativos y pactos interprovinciales*. Vol. 1: *1813–33*. Buenos Aires: Talleres Jacobo Preuser, 1937.

Recovery of Historical Memory Project. *Guatemala: Never Again! The Official Report of the Human Rights Office*. London: Archdiocese of Guatemala, Latin America Bureau, etc. London, 1999.

Restrepo, José Manuel. *Historia de la revolución de Colombia*. 6 vols. Medellín: Bolsilibros Bedout, 1974 [1824–27].

Restrepo, Juan de Dios [Emiro Kastros]. *Colección de artículos escojidos*. Bogotá, 1859.

Restrepo, Vicente. *Los chibchas antes de la conquista española*. Bogotá, 1895.

Restrepo Piedrahita, Carlos, ed. *Actas del Congreso de Cúcuta, 1821*. 3 vols. Bogotá, 1989.

Restrepo Tirado, Ernesto. *Católogo general del Museo de Bogotá*. Bogotá, 1912.

———. *Estudios sobre los aborígenes de Colombia*. Bogotá, 1892.

Resúmen sucinto de la vida del Jeneral Sucre. Lima, 1825.

Resurrección política de la América n.p., 1821. Biblioteca Nacional (Mexico City) Colección Lafragua 416.

Revilla, Manuel G. *Dos discursos cívicos*. Mexico City, 1891.

Rieu-Millan, Marie Laure. *Los diputados americanos en la Cortes de Cadiz: Igualdad o independencia*. Madrid: Consejo Superior de Investigaciones Científicas, 1990.

Rípodas Ardanaz de Mariluz Urquijo, Daisy. "Fuentes literarias hispano-indianas del 'Plan del Inca.'" *Cuarto Congreso Internacional de Historia de América*. Vol. 1. Buenos Aires, 1966.

———. "Pasado incaico y pensamiento político rioplatense." *Jahrbuch für Geschichte Lateinamerikas* 30 (1993).

Riva Agüero, José de la. *La historia en el Perú: Tesis para el doctorado en letras*. Lima: Imprenta Nacional, 1910.

———. *Obras completas*. 18 vols. Lima: Instituto Riva-Agüero, 1962–66.

———. *Paisajes Peruanos*. Lima: Imprenta Santa María, 1955.

Riva Palacio, [Vicente]. *Discurso pronunciado . . . en la capital de la República el 16 de setiembre de 1871*. Mexico City, 1871.

Riva Palacio, Vicente, Juan de Dios Arias, Alfredo Chavero, José María Vigil, and Julio Zárate. *México a través de los siglos*. 5 vols. Mexico City and

Barcelona, 1884–89. Vol. 1: *Historia antigua y de la conquista*, Alfredo Chavero, 1884 [?]. Vol. 2: *El virreinato*, Vicente Riva Palacio, 1886 [?]. Vol. 3: *La guerra de la independencia*, Julio Zárate, 1887 [?].

Riva Palacio, Vicente, Juan de Dios Arias, Alfredo Chavero, José María Vigil, and Julio Zárate. *Resumen integral de México a través de los siglos.* 5 vols. Mexico City: Compañía General de Ediciones, 1968 [1884–89].

Rivero, Mariano de, and Juan Diego [Jacob von] Tschudi. *Antigüedades peruanas.* Vienna, 1851.

Rivero, Mariano Eduardo de. *Antigüedades peruanos: Primera parte.* Lima, 1841.

Roa Barcena, José María. *Discurso cívico pronunciado en Jalapa el 16 de setiembre de 1848.* Jalapa, 1848.

Robertson, William Spence. *The Life of Miranda.* 2 vols. New York: Cooper Square Publishers, 1969 [1929].

Rock, David. "Intellectual Precursors of Conservative Nationalism in Argentina, 1900–1927." *HAHR* 67:2 (1987).

Rodó, José E. *Obras completas.* Vol. 1: *El mirador de Próspero.* Ed. José Pedro Segundo. Montevideo: Ministerio de Instrucción Pública y Prevision Social, 1958.

Rodríguez Beteta, Virgilio. *Discurso oficial. 15 Sept. 1910.* Guatemala, 1910.

———. *Discurso oficial. 15 Sept. 1924.* Guatemala, 1924.

Rodríguez Galván, Ignacio. *Poesías.* 2 vols. Veracruz, 1883.

Rodríguez Prampolini, Ida, ed. *La crítica de arte en México en el siglo XIX.* 3 vols. Mexico City: Imprenta Universidad, 1964.

Rodríguez Villegas, Hernán. *Museo Histórico Nacional.* Dirección de Bibliotecas. Santiago: Archivos y Museos, 1982.

Rojas, Ricardo. *La restauración nacionalista: Crítica de la educación argentina y bases para una reforma en el estado de las humanidades modernas.* Buenos Aires: A. Peña Lillo, 1971 [1909].

———. *Obras de Ricardo Rojas.* Vol. 1: *Blasón de Plata.* Buenos Aires: Librería La Facultad, 1922 [1910].

———. *Obras de Ricardo Rojas.* Vol. 5: *Euríndia.* Buenos Aires: J. Roldan Editores, 1924.

Roldán Vera, Eugenia. "Conciencia histórica y enseñanza: Un analisis de los primeros libros de texto de historia nacional, 1852–1894." Tesis de licenciatura, Universidad Nacional Autónoma de México, 1995.

Romero Flores, Jesus. *Banderas históricas mexicanas.* Mexico City: Costa-Amic, 1973.

Rosa, Alejandro. *Numismática: Independencia de América.* Buenos Aires, 1904.

Rosa, Luis de la. *Discurso pronunciado en la Alameda de esta capital en el solemne aniversario de la proclamación de independencia nacional . . . el 16 de setiembre de 1810.* Mexico City, 1846.

Rosa, Ramón. *Oro de Honduras: Antología de Ramón Rosa.* 3 vols. Tegucigalpa: Universidad Nacional Autónoma de Honduras, 1993.

Rosemberg, Fernando. "La mención del indio en la poesía de la revolución." *Boletín de la Academia Argentina de Letras* 30 (1965).

Rowe, John Howland. "Colonial Portraits of Inca Nobles." In *Selected Papers of the XXIXth International Congress of Americanists.* Ed. Sol Tax. New York, 1949.

———. "El movimiento nacional inca del siglo XVIII." *Revista Universitaria* (Peru) 107 (1954).

Rozat, Guy. *Los orígenes de la nación: Pasado indígena e historia national.* Mexico City: Universidad Iberoamericana, 2001.

Rubín de la Borbolla, Daniel F., and Hugo Cerezo. *Guatemala: Monumentos históricos y arqueológicos.* Mexico City: Instituto Panamericano de Geografía e Historia, 1953.

Rubin de la Borbolla, Daniel F., and Pedro Rivas. *Honduras: Monumentos históricos y arqueológicos.* Mexico City: Instituto Panamericano de Geografía e Historia, 1953.

Rubio Orbe, Alfredo, ed. *Legislación indigenista del Ecuador.* Mexico City: Instituto Indigenista Inter-Americano, 1954.

Ruffini de Grané, Martha. "La trayectoria del discurso historiográfico de la Revolución de Mayo." In *Mayo de 1810: Entre la historia y la ficción discursivas.* Ed. Nelda Pilia de Assunção and Aurora Ravina. Buenos Aires: Editorial Biblos, 1999.

Sábato, Hilda, ed. *Ciudadanía política y formación de las naciones: Perspectivas históricas de América Latina.* Mexico City: Colegio de México, 1999.

Sáenz, Moisés. "Las escuelas rurales y el progreso del indio." *Mexican Folkways* 4:1 (1928).

Safford, Frank. "Race, Integration, and Progress: Elite Attitudes and the Indian in Colombia, 1750–1870." *HAHR* 71:1 (1991).

Said, Edward. *Orientalism.* London: Vintage, 1979 [1978].

Sala i Vila, Nuria. "De inca a indígena: Cambio en la simbología del Sol a principios del siglo XIX." *Allpanchis* 35–36:2 (1991).

Salazar, José María. *La campaña de Bogotá.* Bogotá, 1820.

Salazar, José María. "Elegía a las víctimas de Cundinamarca." In *Como nació la República de Colombia*. Segunda series documental: *1812–1817*. Ed. Guillermo Hernández de Alba. Bogotá: Banco de la República, 1981.

Salazar, Ramón. *Discurso pronunciado . . . el 15 de septiembre de 1881*. Guatemala, 1881.

Saldaña, Mariano. *Discurso cívico pronunciado . . . en celebridad del 16 de setiembre de 1871 en la plaza principal de la villa de Mexquitic*. San Luis Potosí, 1871.

Salgado, Leonardo, and Pablo Azar. "Nuestro lugar entre los primates: Un resúmen de las principales ideas de Florentino Ameghino sobre la evolución humana." *Saber y Tiempo* 15 (2003).

Samayoa Guevara, Hector Humberto. *La enseñanza de la historia en Guatemala (desde 1832 hasta 1852)*. Guatemala: Imprenta Universitaria, 1959.

Samper, José María. *Apuntamientos para la historia política i social de la Nueva Granada desde 1810, i especialmente de la administración del 7 de marzo*. Bogotá, 1853.

———. *Ensayo sobre las revoluciones políticas y la condición social de las repúblicas colombianas hispanoamericanos*. Paris, 1861.

Sánchez, Luis Alberto. *Historia comparada de las literaturas americanas*. Vol. 2: *Del naturalismo neoclásico al naturalismo romántico*. Buenos Aires: Losada, 1973.

Sánchez de Tagle, Francisco Manuel. *Arenga cívica que en el 16 de septiembre de 1830 . . . pronunció . . . en la plaza mayor de Méjico*. Mexico City, 1830.

Sánchez Facio, José. *Oración cívica pronunciada en la plaza de armas de la h[eróica] ciudad de Veracruz . . . el 16 de setiembre de 1854*. Veracruz, 1854.

Sanders, James. *Contentious Republicans: Popular Politics, Race, and Class in Nineteenth-Century Colombia*. Durham, N.C.: Duke University Press, 2004.

Sanders, Karen. *Nación y tradición: Cinco discursos en torno a la nación peruana, 1885–1930*. Lima: Instituto Riva-Agüero, 1997.

Sanfuentes, Salvador. *Leyendas nacionales*. Santiago, 1885.

Santacilia, Pedro. *Lecciones orales sobre la historia de Cuba, pronunciadas en el Ateneo Democrático Cubano de Nueva York*. New Orleans, 1859.

Santos Chocano, José. *Alma América: Poemas indo-españoles*. Paris, 1908 [1906].

———. *Obras completas*. Ed. Luis Alberto Sánchez. Mexico City: Aguilar, 1954.

Santos de Quirós, Mariano. *Colección de leyes. decretos y órdenes publicadas en el Perú, contenidas en las seis tomos de esta obra* Lima [?], c.1841.

Santos Vargas, José. *Diario de un comandante de la independencia americana, 1814–1825.* Ed. Gunnar Mendoza. Mexico City: Siglo XXI, 1982.

Sañudo, José Rafael. *Estudios sobre la vida de Bolívar.* Medellín: Bolsilibros Bedout, 1980.

Sarmiento, Domingo Faustino. *Conflicto y armonía de las razas en América.* Buenos Aires: Editorial La Cultura Argentina, 1915 [1883].

——. *Facundo, or, Civilization and Barbarism.* Trans. Mary Mann. London: Penguin, 1998 [1845].

——. *Obras.* 53 vols. Buenos Aires, 1885–1900.

S. C. *Impugnación del papel titulado "consejo prudente sobre una de las garantías."* Mexico City, 1821.

Schávelzon, Daniel, ed. *La polémica del arte nacional en México, 1850–1910.* Mexico City: Fondo de Cultura Económica, 1988.

Schell, Patience. "Capturing Chile: Santiago's *Museo Nacional* during the Nineteenth Century." *Journal of Latin American Cultural Studies* 10:1 (2001).

Schiebinger, Londa. *The Mind Has No Sex: Women and the Origins of Modern Science.* Cambridge, Mass.: Harvard University Press, 1989.

——. *Nature's Body: Sexual Politics and the Making of Modern Science.* Boston: Beacon Press, 1993.

Schmidt-Nowara, Christopher. "Conquering Categories: The Problem of Prehistory in Nineteenth-Century Puerto Rico and Cuba." *Centro Journal* 13:1 (2001).

S. D. M. M. *Discurso pronunciado el 15 de setiembre de 1847.* San Salvador, n.d.

Segura, Emilio. "Advertencia." *Ricaurte: O el Parque de San Mateo.* Bogotá, 1858.

Shumway, Nicolas. *The Invention of Argentina.* Berkeley: University of California Press, 1991.

Sierra, Justo. *Obras completas.* Ed. Manuel Mestre Ghigliazza. Vol. 5: *Discursos,* 1984. Vol. 9: *Ensayos,* 1991. Vol. 12: *Evolución política del pueblo mexicano,* 1957 [1900–2]. Mexico City: Universidad Nacional Autónoma de México.

Sierra, Justo, et al. *Mexico: Its Social Evolution.* 2 vols. Mexico City, 1900.

Silva, Osvaldo. *Atlas de historia de Chile.* Santiago: Editorial Universitaria, 1984.

Siqueiros, David Alfaro. *Art and Revolution.* Trans. Sylvia Calles. London: Lawrence and Wishart, 1975 [1973].

16 de setiembre de 1851 en la capital del Estado de México. Toluca, 1851.

Skinner-Klée, Jorge, ed. *Legislación indígenista de Guatemala.* Mexico City: Instituto Indigenista Inter-americano, 1954.

Smith, Anthony. *National Identity.* London: Penguin, 1991.

Solanos Asta-Buruaga, Francisco. *Diccionario geográfico de la República de Chile.* Santiago, 1899.

Sommer, Doris. *Foundational Fictions: The National Romances of Latin America.* Berkeley: University of California Press, 1991.

Sosa, Francisco. *Discurso pronunciado el 16 de setiembre de 1886.* Mexico City, 1886.

Spínola, Rafael. *Artículos y discursos.* Guatemala, 1896.

———. *Discurso pronunciado el 15 de septiembre de 1893.* Guatemala, 1893.

Stabb, Martin. "Indigenism and Racism in Mexican Thought: 1857–1911." *Journal of Inter-American Studies* 1:1 (1959).

Stanley Gibbons Simplified Catalogue: Stamps of the World. Vol. 3: *Countries K-R.* London: Stanley Gibbons, 2003.

Stepan, Nancy Leys. *"The Hour of Eugenics": Race, Gender, and Nation in Latin America.* Ithaca, N.Y.: Cornell University Press, 1991.

Stephens, John. *Incidents of Travel in Central America: Chiapas and Yucatan.* 2 vols. New York: Dover, 1969 [1841].

Stern, Steve, ed. *Resistance, Rebellion, and Consciousness in the Andean Peasant World, Eighteenth to Twentieth Centuries.* Madison: University of Wisconsin Press, 1987.

Stiebing, William. *Uncovering the Past: A History of Archaeology.* Oxford: Oxford University Press, 1993.

Stocking, George, ed. *Objects and Others: Essays on Museums and Material Culture.* Madison: University of Wisconsin Press, 1985.

———. *Victorian Anthropology.* New York: Free Press, 1987.

Stuven, Ana María. *La seducción de un orden: Las elites y la construcción de Chile en las polémicas culturales y políticas del siglo XIX.* Santiago: Ediciones Universidad Católica de Chile, 2000.

Suárez Cortés, Blanca Estela. "Las interpretaciones positivas del pasado y el presente 1880–1910." In *La antropología en México: Panorama histórica.* Vol. 2: *Los hechos y los dichos (1880–1986).* Mexico: Instituto Nacional de Antropología e Historia, 1987.

Sullivan-González, Douglass. *Piety, Power, and Politics: Religion and National Formation in Guatemala, 1821–1871.* Pittsburgh: University of Pittsburgh Press, 1998.

Tamayo Vargas, Augusto, and César Pacheco Vélez, eds. *CDIP*. Tomo 1: *Los ideólogos*. Vol. 9: *José Faustino Sánchez Carrión*. Lima: Comisión Nacional del Sesquicentenario de la Independencia del Perú, 1974.

Taracena, Arturo Arriola. *Invención criolla, sueño ladino, pesadilla indígena: Los Altos de Guatemala: de región a Estado, 1740–1850*. San José: Porvenir, 1997.

Tauro, Alberto, ed. *CDIP*. Tomo 23: *Periódicos*. Lima: Comisión Nacional del Sesquicentenario de la Independencia del Perú, 1973.

Tello, Julio. *Introducción a la historia antigua del Perú*. Lima: Sanmarti y cia, 1922.

Tello, Julio, and Toribio Mejía Zesspe. *Historia de los museos nacionales del Perú, 1822–1946*. Lima: Museo Nacional de Antropología y Arqueología, 1967.

Tena Ramírez, Felipe, ed. *Leyes fundamentales de México, 1808–1985*. Mexico City: Editorial Porrúa, 1985.

Tenenbaum, Barbara. *Mexico and the Royal Indian—The Porfiriato and the National Past*. College Park: University of Maryland, 1994.

Tenorio Trillo, Mauricio. *Mexico at the World's Fairs: Crafting a Modern Nation*. Berkeley: University of California Press, 1996.

———. "1910 Mexico City: Space and Nation in the City of the *Centenario*." *JLAS* 28:1 (1996).

Terán, Ramón. *Oración cívica que en la solemnidad del día 16 de setiembre pronunciada en la ciudad de Jalapa*. Jalapa, 1843.

Thibaud, Clément. *Repúblicas en armas: Los ejércitos bolivarianos en la guerra de Independencia en Colombia y Venezuela*. Bogotá: Planeta, 2003.

Thirion, Eugène. *États-Unis de Vénézuela: Notice Historique et Catalogue*. Paris, 1867.

Thomson, Guy, with David LaFrance. *Patriotism, Politics and Popular Liberalism in Nineteenth-Century Mexico: Juan Francisco Lucas and the Puebla Sierra*. Wilmington: SR Books, 1999.

Thurner, Mark. *From Two Republics to One Divided: Contradictions of Postcolonial Nationmaking in Andean Peru*. Durham, N.C.: Duke University Press, 1997.

———. "Peruvian Genealogies of History and Nation." In *After Spanish Rule*. Ed. Mark Thurner and Andrés Guerrero. Durham, N.C.: Duke University Press, 2003.

Toluca a la grata memoria de los héroes de Dolores en el glorioso día 16 de setiembre. Mexico City, 1827.

Tord, Luis Enrique. *El indio en los ensayistas peruanos, 1848–1948*. Lima: Editoriales Unidas, 1978.

Tornel, José María. *Manifiesto del orígen, causas, progreso y estado de la revolución del Imperio Mexicano con relación a la antigua España*. Mexico City, 1821.

———. *Oración pronunciada . . . el 16 de septiembre de 1827*. Mexico City, 1827.

Torre, José María de la. *Discurso pronunciado . . . la noche del 15 de setiembre*. Toluca, 1852.

Torrente, Manuel. *Historia de la Revolución de Chile: Colección de historiadores i de documentos relativos a la independencia de Chile, 1830*. Santiago de Chile, 1900.

Torres y Peña, José Antonio. *Memorias*. Bogotá: Biblioteca de Historia Nacional, 1960.

Tovar, Rafael, Gerardo Estrada, María Teresa Uriarte, Roberto Hernández Ramírez, and Graciela de la Torre, eds. *Los pinceles de la historia: De la patria criolla a la nación mexicana, 1750–1860*. Mexico City: Museo Nacional del Arte, 2000.

Trabucco, Federico, ed. *Constituciones de la República del Ecuador*. Quito: Editorial Universitaria, 1975.

Treece, David. *Exiles, Allies, Rebels: Brazil's Indianist Movement, Indigenist Politics, and the Imperial Nation-State*. Westport, Conn.: Greenwood Press, 2000.

Trigo, Ciro Félix, ed. *Las constituciones del Bolivia*. Madrid: Instituto de Estudios Políticos, 1958.

Tristan, Flora. *Les pérégrinations d'une paria, 1833–1834*. Paris: François Maspero, 1979 [1838].

Tudela, José. "Hernán Cortés en los grabados románticos franceses." *RI* 9 (1948).

Tylor, Edward Burnet. *Anahuac, or, Mexico and the Mexicans, Ancient and Modern*. London, 1861.

———. *Anthropology*. Ann Arbor: University of Michigin Press, 1960 [1881].

———. *Primitive Culture*. 2 vols. London: John Murray, 1929 [1871].

———. *Researches into the Early History of Mankind and the Development of Civilization*. London, 1865.

Ugarte Chamorro, Guillermo, ed. *CDIP*. Tomo 25: *El teatro en la independencia*. Lima: Comisión Nacional del Sesquicentenario de la Independencia del Perú, 1974.

Urban, Greg, and Joel Sherzer, eds. *Nation-States and Indians in Latin America.* Austin: University of Texas Press, 1991.

Uribe Angel, Manuel. *Geografía general y compendio histórico del Estado de Antioquia en Colombia.* Paris, 1885.

Uricoechea, Ezequiel. *Memoria sobre las antigüedades neo-granadinas.* Bogotá: Fondo de Promoción de la Cultura del Banco Popular, 1984 [1854].

Urrutia, José Antonio. *Discurso religioso pronunciado en la Santa Iglesia Catedral... el 15 de septiembre de 1868.* Guatemala, 1868.

Urrutia, Miguel. *Discurso pronunciado el 15 de setiembre de 1884... en el Teatro Nacional.* Guatemala, 1884.

Valcárcel, Luis E. *Del ayllu al imperio: La evolución-político-social en el antiguo Perú y otros estudios.* Lima: Editorial Garcilaso, 1935.

———. *Tempestad en los Andes.* Lima: Populibros Peruanos, 1963 [?] [1927].

Valenzuela, Mario. *Poesías.* Bogotá, 1859.

Valle, Manuel. *Discurso oficial pronunciado ... el 15 de setiembre de 1885.* Guatemala, 1885.

Valle, Rafael Heliodoro. "Historia intelectual de Honduras." In *Literatura hondureña: Selección de estudios críticos sobre su proceso formativo.* Ed. Rigoberto Paredes and Manuel Salinas Paguada. Tegucigalpa: Editores Unidos, 1987.

Vargas, Eugenio. *Discurso pronunciado ... en la plaza de armas de Toluca el día 27 de setiembre de 1858.* Toluca, 1858.

Vargas, Pedro. *Indicaciones económicas para la reforma del sistema tributario de Bolivia.* Potosí, 1864.

Vasconcelos, José. *The Cosmic Race: A Bilingual Edition.* Trans. Didier Jaén. Baltimore: Johns Hopkins University Press, 1979.

———. *Obras completas.* Vol. II: *Indología.* Mexico City: Libreros Mexicanos Unidos, 1958 [1927].

Vaughan, Mary Kay. *Cultural Politics in Revolution: Teachers, Peasants, and Schools in Mexico, 1930–1940.* Tucson: University of Arizona Press, 1997.

———. *The State, Education, and Social Class in Mexico, 1880–1928.* De Kalb: Northern Illinois University Press, 1982.

Vázquez de Knauth, Josefina Zoraida. *Nacionalismo y educación en México.* Mexico City: Colegio de México, 1970.

Vela, David. *Literatura guatemalteca.* 2 vols. Tegucigalpa: Tipográfica Nacional, 1985.

Velázquez, Manuel Zacarías. *Discurso político-religioso ... [pronunciado el] 15 de setiembre de 1844.* Guatemala, 1844.

Verdugo, Agustín. *Discurso pronunciado . . . en la plaza de la constitución el día 16 de septiembre de 1879*. Mexico City, 1879.

Vergara y Vergara, José María. *Historia de la literatura en Nueva Granada. Part I: Desde la conquista hasta la independencia*. Bogotá, 1867.

Vicuña Mackenna, Benjamín. *Católogo del Museo Histórico de Santa Lucia*. Santiago, 1876.

―――. *La guerra a muerte*. Buenos Aires: Editorial Francisco de Aguirre, 1972 [1868].

―――. *Lautaro y sus tres campañas contra Santiago, 1553–1557*. Santiago, 1876.

―――. *Obras completas de Vicuña Mackenna*. Vol. 12: *Discursos parlamentarios*. Santiago: Universidad de Chile, 1939.

Villanueva Urteaga, Horacio, ed. CDIP. Tomo 3: *Conspiraciones y rebeliones en el siglo XIX: La Revolución del Cuzco de 1814*. 2 vols. Lima: Comisión Nacional de Sesquicentenario de la Independencia del Perú, 1971–74.

―――. "La idea de los Incas como factor favorable a la independencia." *Revista Universitaria* (Cuzco) 115 (1958).

Villoro, Luis. *Los grandes momentos del indigenismo en México*. Mexico City: Colegio de México, 1950.

Viroli, Maurizio. *For Love of Country: An Essay on Patriotism and Nationalism*. Oxford: Oxford University Press, 1995.

Viscardo y Guzmán, Juan Pablo. *Los escritos de Juan Pablo Viscardo y Guzmán: Precursor de la independencia hispanoamericana*. Ed. Merle Simmons. Caracas: Universidad Católica Andrés Bello, 1983.

Walker, Charles. "The Patriotic Society: Discussion and Omissions about Indians in the Peruvian War of Independence." *Americas* 55:2 (1998).

―――. *Smoldering Ashes: Cuzco and the Creation of Republican Peru, 1780–1840*. Durham, N.C.: Duke University Press, 1999.

Walther, Juan Carlos. *La conquista del desierto*. Buenos Aires: Editorial Universitaria de Buenos Aires, 1970.

Watanabe, John. "Culturing Identities: The State and National Consciousness in Late Nineteenth-Century Western Guatemala." *Bulletin of Latin American Research* 19:3 (2000).

Webster, Charles K. ed. *Britain and the Independence of Latin America, 1812–1830: Select Documents from the Foreign Office Archives*. 2 vols. London: Oxford University Press, 1938.

Wertheimer, Eric. *Imagined Empires: Incas, Aztecs, and the New World of American Literature, 1771–1876.* Cambridge: Cambridge University Press, 1999.

Wheeler, Roxann. *The Complexion of Race: Categories of Difference in Eighteenth-Century British Culture.* Philadelphia: University of Pennsylvania Press, 2000.

Widdifield, Stacie. *The Embodiment of the National in Late Nineteenth-Century Mexican Painting.* Tucson: University of Arizona Press, 1996.

Williams, Derek. "Popular Liberalism and Indian Servitude: The Making and Unmaking of Ecuador's Antilandlord State, 1845–1868." *HAHR* 83:4 (2003).

Woll, Allen. *A Functional Past: The Uses of History in Nineteenth-Century Chile.* Baton Rouge: Louisiana State University Press, 1982.

———. "The Philosophy of History in Nineteenth-Century Chile: The Lastarria-Bello Controvery." *History and Theory* 13 (1974).

Woodward, Ralph Lee. *Rafael Carrera and the Emergence of the Republic of Guatemala, 1821–1871.* Athens: University of Georgia Press, 1993.

Yábar Acuña, Francisco. *El Inca de Oro: Acuñación del inca en las cecas de Lima y Ayacucho durante la Guerra del Pacífico.* Lima, 1996.

Yeager, Gertrude Matyoka. "Barros Arana, Vicuña Mackenna, Amunátegui: The Historian as National Educator." *Journal of Interamerican Studies and World Affairs* 19:2 (1977).

———. *Barros Arana's Historia General de Chile: Politics, History, and National Identity.* Fort Worth: Texas Christian University Press, 1981.

Yepes, José Ramón. *Anaida and Iguaraya.* Ed. Oscar Sambrano Urdaneta. Caracas: Ediciones del Ministerio de Cultura, 1958.

Zabala, Rómulo. *Historia de la Pirámide de Mayo.* Buenos Aires: Academia Nacional de la Historia, 1962.

Zabala, Rómulo, and Enrique de Gandía. *La enseñanza de la historia en las escuelas primarias de Hispano América.* Buenos Aires: Librerías Anaconda, 1933.

Zaldaña, José Ignacio. *Discurso pronunciado . . . el 15 de Setiembre de 1853.* San Salvador, 1853 [?].

Zárate, R. *El Cuzco y sus monumentos: Guia del viajero.* Lima: Sanmarti y cia, 1921.

Zavala, Lorenzo de. *Ensayo histórico de las revoluciones de Mégico desde 1808 hasta 1830.* 2 vols. Paris, 1831.

Zeballos, Estanislao. *La conquista de quince mil leguas: Estudios sobre la traslación de la frontera sur de la República al Río Negro.* Buenos Aires: Librería Hachette, 1958 [1878].

Zerda, Liborio. *El Dorado: Estudio histórico, etnográfico y arqueológico de los chibchas, habitantes de la antigua Cundinamarca, y de algunas otras tribus.* Bogotá, 1883.

Zulawski, Ann. "Hygiene and 'The Indian Problem': Ethnicity and Medicine in Bolivia, 1910–1920." *Latin American Research Review* 35:2 (2000).

Zúñiga, Antonio. *La Logia "Lautaro" y la independencia de América.* Buenos Aires: Est. Gráfico J. Estrach, 1922.

Index

Marmontel, Jean-François, 32, 45, 121
Martí, José, 127, 159
Martínez Izquierdo, Simón, 110
Martínez Riaza, Ascensión, 193
Marure, Alejandro, 104
Mata Linares, Benito de, 65
Maximilian I of Mexico, 70, 109
Maya: 17, 131, 133, 137, 216; alleged lack of patriotism of, 182–83; civilized, 111–12, 141, 168; savages, 167–68. *See also* Quiché
Maya nationalism, 214
Mayer, Brantz, 158
May Revolution: 37, 73; commemorated, 35–36, 47, 70, 86, 156–57
McFarlane, Anthony, 25
Medals, 51, 57, 61, 141
Medina, José Toribio, 168
Mena, Filiberto de, 135
Méndez, Cecilia, 110, 165
Mendiburu, Manuel de, 103, 257 n.3
Mendoza, Zoila, 191
Mera, Juan León, 100, 118, 121, 165
Mestizaje: in José Vasconcelos, 206–10; in Ricardo Rojas, 206, 208–10; twentieth-century ideologies of, 20, 185, 201, 204–11
Metros, 2–3, 215
Mexican Revolution, 2, 188, 205, 215
Mexico: 2, 75, 123–26, 128, 199, 206–8; centenaries of independence in, 95–96, 193, 195; conservatives in, 80, 82–84, 109, 179; constitutional status of Amerindians in, 176, 179–81; creole patriotism, 22–23, 77; cult of the *próceres* in, 69–70; elite views of nineteenth-century Amerindians in, 166–67, 169–71, 182; *historia patria* in, 105–6, 108–9, 111; independence era in, 23–24, 36, 38–39, 48–50,

53, 57, 68; *indigenismo* in, 187–90, 192–93; liberals in, 79–81, 91–92, 108–9; museums in, 139–40, 150–58; participation of, in world's fairs, 147–48, 150; place names in, 48–49, 70; preconquest ruins in, 136–41, 145; racial categories abolished in, 217–18; as reborn Aztec empire, 23–24, 33–34, 39, 81
Mexico City: 2, 15, 79–81, 136, 197, 215; civic festivals and commemorations, 35–36, 68, 75, 96, 195, 199; museums, 140, 150–58
Meyer, Jean, 131
Mier, Servando Teresa de, 23, 42, 48, 138
Milla, José, 82, 105
Milo, Daniel, 49
Miranda, Francisco de, 44, 98
Mitla, 137, 139, 141
Mitre, Bartolomé, 70, 88–89, 104, 106, 111, 113, 257 n.3
Moctezuma: 128, 214–15; in independence-era rhetoric, 24, 27–28, 33, 37–38, 49, 106; in postindependence writings, 77–78, 96, 120–22, 167
Modernismo, 117, 120–23
Modernity, 165, 210
Molina Enríquez, Andrés, 187
Molina, Víctor, 161–63
Monarchía indiana, 22
Monroy, Petronilo, 13–15
Montalvo, Juan, 121
Monteagudo, Bernardo de, 26, 32–33, 63, 217
Monte Albán, 137
Montero, Luís, 127–28
Montesquieu, Baron de, 30
Montezuma. *See* Moctezuma
Montúfar, Lorenzo, 257 n.3

REBECCA EARLE is a reader in the Department of
History at the University of Warwick. She is the author of *Spain and the
Independence of Colombia*, and the editor of *Epistolary Selves:
Letters and Letter-Writers, 1600–1945*.

Library of Congress Cataloging-in-Publication Data
Earle, Rebecca.
The return of the native : Indians and myth-making in Spanish
America, 1810–1930 / Rebecca Earle.
p. cm.
Includes bibliographical references and index.
ISBN 978-0-8223-4063-8 (cloth : alk. paper)
ISBN 978-0-8223-4084-3 (pbk. : alk. paper)
1. Indians—Politics and government. 2. Indians—Government relations.
3. Indians—Ethnic identity. 4. Ethnicity—Latin America. 5. Indian
mythology—Latin America. 6. Nationalism—Latin America. 7. Latin
America—Politics and government. 8. Latin America—Ethnic relations.
9. Spain—Colonies—America. I. Title.
E65.E49 2007
980.'00498—dc22
2007032556

1813   36